The Impact of World War II
on the Soviet Union

THE IMPACT OF WORLD WAR II
ON THE SOVIET UNION

Edited by
Susan J. Linz

University of California
Irvine

ROWMAN & ALLANHELD
PUBLISHERS

To Sarah Elisabeth and
Hilary Nicole

ROWMAN & ALLANHELD

Published in the United States of America in 1985
by Rowman & Allanheld, Publishers
(A division of Littlefield, Adams & Company)
81 Adams Drive, Totowa, New Jersey 07512

Library of Congress Cataloging in Publication Data
Main entry under title:

The Impact of World War II on the Soviet Union.

Includes index.
1. Reconstruction (1939–1951)—Soviet Union—
Addresses, essays, lectures. 2. World War, 1939–1945—
Influence—Addresses, essays, lectures. 3. Soviet Union
—History—1925–1953—Addresses, essays, lectures.
I. Linz, Susan J. II. Title: Impact of World War 2 on
the Soviet Union. III. Title: Impact of World War Two
on the Soviet Union.
D829.S65146 1985   947.084'2   84-17804
ISBN 0-8476-7378-2
ISBN 0-8476-7379-0 (pbk.)

Printed in the United States of America
84 85 86 / 10 9 8 7 6 5 4 3 2 1

Table of Contents

Tables and Figures

Tables

Figures

Acknowledgments

I am particularly indebted to James R. Millar and James Richardson for their support, encouragement, and assistance in the early stages of this project. I thank Paul Gregory, Ted Uldricks, and members of the Russian Area Studies Program at Louisiana State University for their help. My sincere appreciation also goes to each of the contributors for submitting and revising their papers in a timely manner. Working with them has been an enlightening and altogether pleasurable activity. Above all, I thank my husband and two daughters for their patience and understanding during my preoccupation with this book.

Financial assistance for this project was provided by the Research Council at Louisiana State University, the Ford Foundation, and the American Association for the Advancement of Slavic Studies.

1

Introduction:
War and Progress in the USSR

SUSAN J. LINZ

World War II represents an important watershed for the Soviet Union. Economically, it was the first real test of the Soviet system of central planning. Politically, it thrust the USSR into the world arena as a major world power. Socially, it provided a cohesive force previously lacking in Soviet society. One need only visit the Soviet Union to get a sense of the profound impact of World War II on the people. Indeed, over fifteen thousand Russian volumes have been written about the Great Patriotic War. In spite of the recognized magnitude of the impact of World War II, little research has been done in the West to understand the ways in which World War II affected Soviet economic, political, or social systems. Fortunately, this situation is reversing as more scholars are beginning serious analyses of the war period. The difficulty lies, however, in the extreme lack of statistical information pertaining to the war effort despite recent access to archival material.

A number of the essays that compose this volume were presented as original research studies to a symposium held at Louisiana State University (LSU) in April 1983. The symposium was made possible by grants from the Research Council at LSU, the Ford Foundation, and the American Association for the Advancement of Slavic Studies. The principal aim of the two-day symposium was to bring together prominent scholars from the United States and abroad in numerous disciplines including economics, political science, history, sociology, literature, and religion, to investigate the ways in which World War II affected Soviet life. In addition, several other essays were generously made available by scholars unable to attend. The essays cover the entire war and postwar period (through Stalin's death in 1953). Comprehensive coverage was not, however, a primary goal.

Emphasis was instead placed upon identifying the impact of the war in the author's area of expertise, with encouragement also given to identifying World War II's continuing impact in the USSR. As such, this volume offers a useful starting point for what promises to be a rich and extended area of study in future years. Indeed, much work still needs to be done on the impact of the war on the Soviet military. The salient and unifying theme that emerges from this collection is the overwhelming success of the Soviet system in fighting back the German onslaught in the face of almost impervious odds initially and in spite of tremendous losses of men and materiel.

This volume is divided into two parts. Part I examines the impact of World War II and its aftermath; Part II, the social and political consequences of the war. The essays are arranged in each section from general to more specific themes. In Part I, the first essay examines the impact of World War II on Soviet economic growth, using available Soviet and Western data. In addition to identifying the war's impact on aggregate economic indices, disaggregated data on the industrial sector, labor force, and household consumption are analyzed. More importantly, Chapter 2 puts the impact of World War II on the Soviet economy into perspective by developing a measure of the burden that the economic cost of the war imposed upon the postwar population. Calculations by various methods yield estimates of the postwar replacement cost of total material war losses ranging from approximately 8 to 10 years' earnings of the 1945 labor force, supporting the claim that World War II cost two Five-Year Plans. The potential for a reduction in the postwar burden of World War II, had additional aid [Lend-Lease, United Nations Relief and Rehabilitation Administration (UN-RRA) funds, the U.S. loan, Marshall Plan aid] become available, is also examined by Linz in Chapter 2. A comparison is then made between the impact of the aid actually received in the form of reparations, "pipeline" Lend-Lease, and UNRRA assistance on postwar recovery efforts and economic growth potential with that of the potential additional foreign assistance programs.

Two similar scenarios are also examined in the Appendix to Chapter 2. This essay is an edited version of a paper written in 1944 by Wassily Leontief (1973 Nobel laureate) for the Research and Analysis Division of the U.S. Office of Strategic Services. Leontief's findings were made available exclusively for inclusion in this book for comparison purposes since both the methodology and results are strikingly similar to those of Chapter 2 despite a span of nearly four decades. The primary focus of his paper was to describe capital reconstruction and postwar development of Soviet national income and consumption. The two scenarios depicted in his counterfactual analysis include one in which postwar military expenditures return to the 1938 level and reconstruction proceeds without the help of foreign credits, although domestic gold stocks are depleted for 3 years to finance reconstruction. In the second scenario, foreign credits are available to the extent of $1.5 billion per year for 3 years. Leontief calculated in 1944 that the rate of reconstruction would not be greatly increased should foreign aid become available, making only a few months' difference in terms of restoring investment levels. Both Leontief and Linz conclude, on the basis of completely separate analyses, that, although the cumulative indirect effect on Soviet national income would have been appreciable had additional foreign aid been forthcoming, reparations had a more direct and important impact on reconstruction efforts.

An important component of the successful war effort involved the massive evacuation of industry from frontline areas to locations deep in the Soviet interior. Railroads were essential during World War II both in Soviet evacuation operations and troop movement. Holland Hunter, by providing a geography of World War II in the USSR in Chapter 3, puts into relief the transport operations that were carried out to insure Soviet success in World War II. As Hunter indicates,

> World War II provided a test for the Soviet transportation and communication sector—mainly the railroads—and this sector like most others passed the test successfully. Instead of contributing to a collapse of the regime, as the Russian railroads had done in World War I, Soviet railroads in World War II provided sturdy links which held the whole country together. They weathered the massive invasion which excised their most developed portions, and through flexible adaptation and energetic responses, carried the men and materiel which enabled Soviet armed forces to eject and defeat the Nazis.

Sanford Lieberman pursues the evacuation theme in Chapter 4 by describing the special wartime system of administration and control adopted to undertake the massive effort. The primary focus of his essay involves an analysis of the operation and effectiveness of the State Defense Committee (GKO) that was superimposed upon the Soviet system during World War II in order to circumvent the traditionally rigid and time-consuming aspects of the bureaucratic procedure. The GKO provided the administrative flexibility and centralization of control that the war effort required. Special committees and commissions were set up under GKO to deal with specific aspects of the war effort: military, political, security, economic. In addition, city committees for defense and a Council for Evacuation were established during the war to deal with general crises. Yet, as Lieberman points out, in spite of the variety of extraordinary organs established, no special administrative mechanism was adopted to implement the decisions of the GKO and other extraordinary organs. Hence, GKO business was executed through regular state administration and Party channels. Lieberman contends that, given this situation, Stalin's personalized style of leadership was therefore an important factor in the successful war effort.

The impact of World War II on Soviet agriculture is analyzed by Alec Nove in Chapter 5. His essay brings to this volume both the breadth and depth of a longtime scholar of the Soviet economy. Nove's analysis of the war's impact on physical output and political controls in the agricultural sector, and on peasant incomes and welfare during the war and early postwar period, attests to his reputation in the field. Beyond simply analyzing the data, Nove brings to life the appalling situation, the desperate shortages, the errors of policy, and the hardships suffered in the rural sector during World War II. Moreover, he documents the antipeasant policies that impeded recovery after the war.

William Fletcher examines the pervasive impact of World War II on religion in the USSR in Chapter 6. He argues that World War II changed church-state relations for an entire generation after the war because it affected the nature of the church and, religiously at least, altered the nature of society in ways that were profound and probably permanent. What emerged from World War II, Fletcher contends, was a bargain between church and state. In return for political services, the state granted the church the right to exist as an institution in Soviet society. The key to understanding the effect of World War II, however, is found in the resulting religious demography. World War II created a Soviet "Bible Belt," and those areas under German occupation during the war still show the legacy of the occupation in terms of a transformation of their religious profile. More importantly, however, World War II won for the Russian church a legal, as opposed to an underground, existence in society at the cost of narrowing its mission to the purely spiritual. Fletcher concludes that World War II established a bargaining pattern of church-state relations that, modified and weakened, remains to this day.

An interesting account of the impact of World War II on Soviet policy and the division of Germany is provided by Robert Slusser in Chapter 7. He argues that

> The establishment of an East German state was not the outcome of a deliberate and conscious policy on the part of Stalin and his advisors, but rather the unforeseen and in part unwanted culmination of Soviet actions and policies toward Germany in interaction with those of the three Western Allies.

Indeed, Slusser contends that the basic lines along which Germany was dismembered were drawn up by British planners in 1943–44, with the Soviets accepting the plan because it gave them more than they could have hoped to achieve by any other means. The British plan assured the Soviets of controlling 40 percent of Germany's prewar territory, and a third of her postwar population and resources. The plan also gave them a commanding position in Berlin. According to Slusser, Soviet wartime policy toward Germany pursued a number of goals, some of them predicated on its unity, others on its dismemberment:

> In effect, Stalin wanted to have it both ways—an assured portion of German territory under Soviet control and at the same time a strong position in the postwar struggle for a united Germany. What Stalin did *not* want was a Soviet-controlled East German successor state competing with a larger, richer, more populous West German state enjoying the support of the Western Allies. Yet this is what he got.

Part II examines social and political consequences of World War II in the USSR. In spite of data difficulties, Sheila Fitzpatrick puts together a remarkably in-depth account of World War II's impact on Soviet society in Chapter 8. World War II's most devastating impact was upon the population, both in terms of actual losses and population transfers during the war and immediate postwar period. In addition to an enlightening and thorough analysis of the war's impact on urban life and labor recruitment, Fitzpatrick provides a seminal analysis of Soviet convict and conscript labor during this period. Moreover, her description of rural life and migration from the kolkhoz offers an interesting and complementary overlap with Nove's discussion of Soviet peasantry (Chapter 5). Fitzpatrick also examines the concept of a "return to normalcy" in the postwar period, which implies a release from wartime obligations and constraints, relaxation of tension, going home, and settling down. Yet, as she points out, these qualities, however desired by Soviet citizens, were not characteristic of the Soviet Union in the immediate postwar period. Instead, obligations and constraints were scarcely diminished. Many survivors uprooted by World War II could not or did not return home. In response to a query, as to why there was no return to normalcy, Fitzpatrick offers a concise analysis of the abnormal prewar period, a period of social revolution and structural transformation. She also speculates about the Soviet regime's attitude about normalcy under Stalin's reign, concluding that only after Stalin's death did things relax.

In Chapter 9, Cynthia Kaplan analyzes the impact of World War II on the Party by distinguishing between the Party as a political organization and an administrative organ responsible for the performance of other organizations in the USSR. Kaplan then compares behavioral tendencies associated with the direct effects of World War II with prewar and postwar party behavior. Having examined the war's impact in light of prewar and postwar trends, she concludes that the direct and indirect effects of World War II had long-term consequences for the Party—wartime enrollments increased the Party's size—while the prewar trend toward greater party saturation among white-collar workers continued.

The essay by Edward Bubis (formerly a Leningrad city planner) and Blair Ruble (Chapter 10) is an in-depth analysis of the impact of World War II on Leningrad, a city in which more than ten times the population died between August 1941 and January 1944 than died in Hiroshima following the atomic blast in August 1945. In addition to the loss of human life, German bombardment obliterated over 25 percent of Leningrad's capital stock (housing, streets, water and sewer lines) and caused the destruction of countless architectural and artistic treasures. Bubis and Ruble contend that more important than the physical destruction and loss of life was the war-related change in Leningrad's status in Soviet society. They perceive the war's impact as both negative and permanent, concluding that during the decade of the 1940s, the once majestic city of Leningrad became simply a second city to the larger, more dynamic, and increasingly more cosmopolitan Moscow. Their conclusions are derived from an examination of several economic and political indices that indicate a transformation of the city's work force; industrial, economic, and scientific base; and political elite:

> Despite the loss of many important functions to Moscow during the 1920s and 1930s, Leningrad had remained a direct competitor to the Soviet capital in many spheres. The War physically and psychologically destroyed much of the city. Perhaps even more important in the long run, the War's destruction provided an excuse for anti-Leningrad leaders in Moscow (who, after all, emerged as predominant in the wake of the Leningrad Affair) to justify the diminution of Leningrad economic and academic capacity. . . . By not rebuilding secondary economic sectors, . . . central economic planners insured that Leningrad would lack the kind of economic diversity so necessary for the maintenance of urban distinction. The end result has been that, to a considerable degree, Leningrad never recovered from the impact of World War II.

Barbara Anderson and Brian Silver focus their essay (Chapter 11) on the immediate impact and on the long-term, indirect consequences of World War II on a set of demographic factors involving non-Russian nationalities of the USSR. Their essay is especially topical, given the growing interest in the Soviet nationality question over the last decade. The authors review the impact of World War II on the Soviet population as a whole as background to their examination of the war's differential impact among non-Russian nationalities. The main thesis of their essay is that the differential impact of World War II on non-Russian nationalities is reflected in the differential ratios of males to females, and that these differentials contributed to varying rates of ethnic intermarriage and also to subsequent linguistic and ethnic russification of the nationalities. Anderson and Silver suggest that quite apart from the direct and immediate losses of population during the war, the normal balance between the number of males and females became so skewed for some nationalities that if unmarried women were to find spouses at all (and many would not) many had to marry men of other nationalities. Their paper clearly demonstrates the powerful effect World War II had on linguistic and ethnic russification of non-Russian nationalities. They conclude that World War II was a turning point in demographic history for most of the autonomous republic nationalities (ARN), arguing that for the ARN as a whole, the immediate losses during the war, however large they appear to be, were less significant than the ensuing accelerated russification that was induced by World War II.

The social and political consequences of World War II are evident in Soviet literature, as Deming Brown illustrates in Chapter 12. Because literature in the USSR usually represents a direct reaction to public events, the impact of World War II on Soviet literature was enormous. Indeed, between 1941 and 1945 the efforts of the Soviet writing community were almost completely devoted to the war. Writers became journalists, and poets read verses to enthusiastic audiences at the front. As Brown indicates, although wartime writing was strongly hortatory, urging Russians to endure and inciting them to smash the enemy, it was at the same time less programmed and more candid, emphasizing the strengths of simple Russians. As the war progressed and victory became more evident, however, official manipulation of literature increased. In the postwar years, the literary community was encouraged to continue to write about the war, and as Brown states, the "function of war fiction became one of demonstrating the role of the Communist Party leadership and ideology in mobilizing for victory, of showing the indispensability of Stalin's leadership, and of proving that the heroic exploits that won the war could only have been accomplished by the especially endowed New Soviet Man." Of special interest in Brown's essay is his analysis of the manner in which Stalin was portrayed in postwar war-related literature.

In the final chapter of Part II, Jerry Hough explores some of the crucial debates about the West that took place in the last years of World War II and the early postwar period. Understanding these debates is vital. In and of themselves, they remind us that much conflict was hidden behind the Soviet totalitarian facade, even in the postpurge period. More importantly, however, Hough points out that it is possible that the debates reflected divisions at the leadership level and that the origins of the Cold War are more complex than usually assumed. Moreover, even if the debates were totally irrelevant so far as policy outcome was concerned, they provide an excellent example of the types of expressions of views that were able to emerge in the press in the Stalin period and, therefore, contribute to a more sophisticated understanding of the policies of that period.

James Millar puts into perspective the combined efforts of the numerous authors who have contributed to this collection by providing an innovative overview of the war period in the concluding chapter. Like each of the authors, he brings to this volume a sense of the profound impact of World War II on the Soviet people.

Part One

World War II and
Its Aftermath

2

World War II and Soviet Economic Growth, 1940–1953

SUSAN J. LINZ

The impact of World War II on the Soviet economy has received little scholarly attention in the West, not because the economic impact was considered unimportant, but because the period from 1940 to 1953 more than any other in Soviet history is characterized by a paucity of economic data. For over a decade, Nove's *Economic History of the USSR* (1969) remained the primary Western source regarding the contours of the Soviet war effort. Beyond this, little attention has been devoted to the structural changes brought about by World War II. No one, for example, has examined in any detail the quantitative impact on planning, production, or distribution patterns that resulted from (1) the long-term increase in female labor force participation rates, (2) the movement of industry to the East, (3) technology transfer in the form of Lend-Lease aid or reparations, or (4) new territories annexed during World War II. Even less attention has been focused on the impact of World War II on Soviet national policy. Zaleski (1980) and Dunmore (1980) stand alone in their respective examinations of the impact of World War II on planning practices and regional policy. Textbooks on the Soviet economy devote at most only a paragraph or two to transition from the late 1930s to early 1950s. Fortunately, this situation is reversing as more scholars are beginning serious analyses of the war period.

This paper examines the impact of World War II on Soviet economic growth. The first section documents World War II's impact on the Soviet economy between 1940 and 1953, using available Soviet and Western statistics. In addition to identifying the war's impact on aggregate economic indices, it also analyzes disaggregated data on the industrial sector, labor force, and household consumption. The next section puts the impact of World War II into perspective by examining a measure of the burden that the economic cost of the war imposed upon the postwar population. Calculations by various methods yield estimates of the postwar replacement cost of total material (nonhuman) war losses ranging from approximately 8 to 10 years' earnings of the 1945 labor force, supporting the Soviet claim that World War II cost two Five-Year Plans (Tamarchenko 1967, 135). The war cost estimates initially presented include the reduction in the postwar burden resulting from foreign aid and reparation payments received between 1945 and 1953. As such, they do not represent the true cost of World War II to the Soviet people. It is possible, however, to estimate roughly the impact of reparations and other foreign aid ["pipeline" Lend-Lease[1] and the United Nations Relief and Rehabilitation Administration (UNRRA) funds] on postwar recovery efforts. The estimates derived in this section indicate an initial contribution of some 4 months to 1 year's earnings of the 1945 labor force. That is, had reparations and aid not been received, the immediate postwar burden on the Soviet people would have been substantially higher. This section also examines the potential for a reduction in the postwar burden had *additional* foreign assistance (the proposed U.S. loan and Marshall Plan aid) become available. The impact on postwar recovery efforts and Soviet economic growth potential of additional aid with that of reparations and aid actually received from 1945 to 1953 are compared. The results indicate that within the framework employed in this paper, Stalin was perfectly rational in declining Marshall Plan assistance. The final section offers some speculations on the cost to the Soviets of winning World War II.

The Appendix following this essay is an edited version of a paper written in 1944 for the U.S. Office of Strategic Services by Wassily Leontief (1973 Nobel laureate). The primary focus of his paper was on describing capital reconstruction and postwar development of Soviet national income and consumption. Two scenarios are depicted in his counterfactual analysis: In the first, postwar military expenditures return to the 1938 level and reconstruction proceeds without the help of foreign credits, but domestic gold stocks are depleted for 3 years to finance reconstruction. In the second scenario, foreign credits are available to the extent of $1.5 billion per year for 3 years. Leontief calculated in 1944 that the rate of reconstruction would not be greatly increased should foreign aid become available, making only a few months' difference in terms of restoring investment levels.

The Impact of World War II on the Soviet Economy

The Soviet effort in World War II began in June 1941 with the German invasion, Operation Barbarossa, and found itself at a disadvantage early on, both militarily and economically. In spite of vast natural resource reserves, the high quotas of the initial Five-Year Plans required extensive exploitation of European Russia. As a result, the resource base in eastern regions of the USSR remained largely untapped. Correspondingly, no real efforts had been made prior to 1941 to urbanize or develop transportation facilities in the East. Moreover, the purges in 1936–1937 of top political, economic, and military leaders caused a substantial prewar decline in industrial output (Katz 1975).

Within 6 months of the invasion, German forces occupied or isolated territory that prior to World War II accounted for over 60 percent of the total coal, pig iron, and aluminum production; nearly 40 percent of total grain production, and 60 percent of total livestock. Moreover, this area contained 40 percent of the prewar Soviet population, 32 percent of the state enterprise labor force, and one-third of the fixed capital assets of the state enterprise sector (Nove 1982, 271). The speed of the German advance impinged upon Soviet evacuation efforts, but official Soviet sources report that from July to November 1941, over 6 million people and 1523 industrial enterprises were removed to eastern regions (Urals, West Siberia, Central Asia, Kazakhstan), of which 1360 were large-scale enterprises (employing more than 100–500 people) (*Istoriya* 1963, 1:148; Chadayev 1965, 65; Kravchenko 1970, 123–25). An additional 150 enterprises were evacuated from behind the Leningrad and Stalingrad fronts in 1942–1943 (*Eshelony* 1960, 108, 140). Excellent analyses of the magnitude of the evacuation effort are provided by Hunter (Chapter 3), Lieberman (Chapter 4), and Nove (Chapter 5).

Evacuation, occupation, and conversion to military production caused a severe decline in aggregate output. Not until March 1942 did industrial output regain its 1940 level. Indeed, 1942 marks the turning point of the Soviet war effort. By the end of that year, the Soviets had regained occupied areas, and industrial output in eastern regions had increased over twofold its 1940 level. These gains were not sufficient, however, to offset the detrimental impact of the "scorched earth"[2] campaigns and wartime losses on aggregate output. National income at the end of the war was still some 20 percent below its prewar level. Agricultural production did not regain its prewar level until after World War II ended as Nove (Chapter 5) and Fitzpatrick (Chapter 8) indicate in their detailed analyses of World War II's impact on the agricultural sector.

Millar (1980) offers a seminal analysis of the financial aspects of the Soviet effort in World War II. Indeed, using the sources and uses of State Budget funds for the war years, he traces the impact of war costs and war-related structural changes in the Soviet economy. Because the State Budget is so comprehensive in the USSR, including all investment flows in the economy as well as military and nondefense categories of expenditure, Millar is able to provide a relatively detailed sketch of the magnitude of the Soviet war effort by analyzing budgetary data. His war budget table is reproduced in part here (see Table 2.1) to facilitate explanation of the impact of World War II on aggregate economic indices (lines A, B, J, P). Most striking is the increase in defense outlays (line A), which rose from 33 percent of all budget nonfinancial uses of funds in 1940 to nearly 60 percent in 1942, averaging over 50 percent for the war period. A comparison of the share of wartime defense outlays with the 1940 level is somewhat

Table 2.1 Soviet State Budget, 1940–1946

	1940	1941	1942	1943	1944	1945	1941-45	1946
				(billions of 1960 rubles)				
Uses of funds, non-financial								
A. Defence outlays	5.7	8.3	10.8	12.5	13.8	12.8	58.2	7.4
B. Outlays on the national economy	5.8	5.2	3.2	3.3	5.4	7.4	24.4	10.6
of which:								
C. All industry	2.9	3.0	1.8	1.8	3.1	4.4	14.0	7.0
D. Heavy and machine tool industry only	2.6	2.8	1.7	1.6	2.8	3.9	12.8	n.a.
E. Agriculture (excludes procurement)	1.3	0.9	0.5	0.5	0.7	0.9	3.6	1.3
F. MTS only	0.8	0.6	0.3	0.3	0.4	0.5	2.1	n.a.
G. Transport and communications	0.7	0.6	0.4	0.6	0.9	1.1	3.6	1.2
H. Housing and communal services	0.3	0.1	0.1	0.1	0.2	0.3	0.8	0.4
I. Trade and agricultural procurement	0.2	n.a.	n.a.	0.1	0.1	0.2	n.a.	0.3
J. Social-cultural outlays	4.1	3.1	3.0	3.8	5.1	6.3	21.3	8.0
of which:								
K. Education & enlightenment	2.2	1.5	1.0	1.3	2.1	2.6	8.5	3.8
L. Health and physical culture	0.9	0.7	0.7	0.8	1.0	1.1	4.3	1.4
M. Grants to families	0.1	0.1	0.1	0.1	0.1	0.2	0.7	0.4
N. Social insurance	0.5	0.3	0.2	0.3	0.4	0.5	1.7	n.a.
O. Social maintenance	0.4	0.6	1.1	1.3	1.7	2.0	6.6	2.1
P. Administration	0.7	0.5	0.4	0.5	0.7	0.9	3.1	1.2
Q. Total non-financial uses above	16.3	17.1	17.4	20.1	25.0	27.4	107.0	27.4
R. Other, unidentified uses of funds[a]	0.8	1.7	0.7	0.7	1.1	2.1	6.3	4.9
S. Total expenditures chargeable against ordinary receipts	17.1	18.8	18.1	20.8	26.1	29.5	113.3	32.1
of which:								
T. Republic and local budget non-financial outlays	4.2	3.1	2.2	2.6	3.8	4.8	16.5	6.6

	Sources of funds								
U.	Enterprise profit withdrawals	2.2	2.4	1.5	2.0	2.1	1.7	9.7	1.7
V.	Turnover tax receipts	10.6	9.3	6.6	7.1	9.5	12.3	44.9	19.1
W.	Total above (U + V)	12.8	11.7	8.1	9.1	11.6	14.0	54.6	20.8
X.	Income tax from cooperatives, kolkhozy, etc.	0.3	0.3	0.2	0.3	0.3	0.3	1.7	0.3
Y.	Income of the MTS	0.2	0.1	0.1	0.1	0.1	0.1	0.4	n.a.
Z.	Transfer of cash balances of socialized sector	—	2.0	—	—	—	—	2.0	—
AA.	Direct taxes and fees from population of which:	0.9	1.1	2.2	2.9	3.7	4.0	13.8	2.3
BB.	Agricultural tax	0.2	0.2	0.1	0.4	0.5	0.6	1.8	n.a.
CC.	Income tax	0.4	0.5	0.3	0.6	0.9	1.1	3.4	n.a.
DD.	Housing and cultural tax	0.4	0.4	0.2	—	—	—	0.6	n.a.
EE.	Taxes on bachelors, one-person and childless families	—	0.0	0.1	0.1	0.2	0.3	0.8	n.a.
FF.	War tax	—	—	1.4	1.7	2.1	2.0	7.2	—
GG.	War lottery receipts	—	0.1	0.2	0.3	0.5	—	1.2	—
HH.	Money gifts to Red Army & Defense Funds	—	0.2	0.5	0.5	0.5	0.1	1.8	—
JJ.	Total above (AA + GG + HH)	0.9	1.4	2.9	3.7	4.7	4.1	16.8	2.3
KK.	Local taxes and collections	0.2	0.1	0.2	0.3	0.6	0.6	2.0	n.a.
LL.	Other republic and local non-financial income	0.4	0.5	0.3	0.4	0.5	0.6	2.3	n.a.
MM.	Social insurance contributions	0.9	0.7	0.6	0.7	0.9	1.0	3.9	1.2
NN.	Total non-financial sources of funds above	15.7	16.8	12.4	14.6	18.7	20.7	83.7	24.6
OO.	Other unidentified sources of funds[b]	1.2	-0.5	2.6	3.3	4.9	6.3	16.7	5.4
PP.	Total non-financial sources of funds of which:	16.9	16.3	15.0	17.9	23.6	27.0	100.4	30.0
QQ.	Republic and local budgets	3.9	3.1	2.2	2.6	3.5	4.1	15.5	6.2

[a]Residual: (S-Q)   [b]Residual: (PP-NN)

Source: James R. Millar, "Financing the Soviet Effort in World War II," Soviet Studies, 32, no. 1 (January 1980), 109–11.

Table 2.2   Actual and Planned Soviet National Income: 1940, 1944, 1945, 1950 (billion rubles, 1940 prices)

	1940 (Actual)	%	1944 (Actual)	%	1945 (Actual)	%	1950 (Plan)	%
National Income	377.4	100.0	303.1	100.0	331.1	100.0	504.5	100.0
1. Consumption	279.3	74.0	188.3	60.5	217.7	65.8	366.0	72.5
a. Households	264.3	70.0	150.0	49.5	188.5	56.9	351.0	69.6
b. Military Personnel	15.0	4.0	33.3	11.0	29.2	8.8	15.0	3.0
2. Investment	66.1	17.5	40.6	13.4	48.8	14.7	103.5	20.5
a. Fixed Capital	40.5	10.7	22.7	7.5	27.9	8.4	56.6	11.2
b. Livestock	0.1	0.0	0.1	0.0	1.5	0.5	5.0	1.0
c. Inventories	25.5	6.8	17.8	5.9	19.4	5.8	38.0	7.5
Industrial	18.5	4.9	14.6	4.8	15.0	4.5	30.0	5.9
Agricultural	7.0	1.9	3.2	1.1	4.4	1.3	8.0	1.6
3. Defense	27.0	8.5	76.9	26.1	62.3	19.5	29.0	6.9
4. Other	5.0	1.3	2.3	0.8	2.3	0.7	6.0	1.2

Source: E. Zaleski, *Stalinist Planning for Economic Growth, 1933–1952* (Chapel Hill: University of North Carolina Press, 1980), 352.

misleading, however, because the share of defense outlays had already begun to rise sharply by 1940 in anticipation of war. Defense outlays in 1937, for example, represented only 17 percent of all budget nonfinancial uses of funds. Yet by 1940 this category had reached some 34 percent. In addition, as Millar points out, the defense category of the State Budget understates total war-related expenditures because of the exclusion of outlays connected with the conversion of plant, equipment, and manpower to war production, and the additional civilian administrative cost occasioned by World War II. These administrative costs are examined in more detail by Leiberman (Chapter 4).

Perhaps more than anything else, Table 2.1 indicates the relative and absolute decline in nondefense outlays during World War II, in addition to documenting the impact on the economy of the loss of some 20 to 50 million people[3] and 30 percent loss of the capital stock. The adverse effect upon household consumption was particularly severe, falling from 74 percent of national income in 1940 to 66 percent of a lower national income in 1945. This occurred at a time when grain stocks were reduced to augment consumption (see Table 2.2, and Nove's discussion in Chapter 5), and social security payments (which include payments to families of those killed or disabled in World War II) were rising (Table 2.1: lines M, N, O). Official Soviet sources report that capital formation also declined drastically during World War II, from 19 percent in 1940 to 4 percent in 1942. Indeed, the prewar rate of capital formation was not regained at any time during the war (Tamarchenko 1967, 50–51). Hence, expenditures on the war effort rose at the expense of consumption and investment, from 11 percent of national income in 1940 to a high of 44 percent in 1943. Yet, as Millar indicates, citing the official Soviet history of World War II, even this share understates the fraction of real national income that was absorbed by the war effort by some 15 percent in 1942.

IMPACT ON INDUSTRY

World War II caused both short- and long-term changes in Soviet industrial sectors in terms of level of production, composition of output, and regional emphasis. In total, some 31,850 large-scale industrial enterprises were "put out of production" (although not all were completely destroyed) during World War II (Voznesenskii 1948, 95), representing more than 80 percent of the prewar number of industrial enterprises located in the Ukraine, Belorussia, and occupied areas of the Russian Socialist Federated Republic (RSFSR). From 1941 to 1945, the composition of industrial output adjusted to meet the needs of the war effort. Indeed, the proportion of industrial output devoted to defense during the war exceeded that of heavy industry and light industry combined (*Narodnoe khoziaistvo* 1972, 168). Reconstruction priorities dictated the emphasis on heavy industry in the postwar period as is evident in the distribution of industrial investment (*Kapital'noe stroitel'stvo* 1961, 66–67) and the reduced share of light industry (as a percentage of gross industrial output) in the postwar period (Kravchenko 1970, 351). In spite of this, light industry experienced more rapid gains in the immediate postwar period (*Narodnoe khoziaistvo* 1972, 195).

More long-term in nature was the impact of World War II on the location of industry. New construction in eastern regions was exceedingly rapid in the first two years of World War II. Capital investment in heavy industry directed to the Urals and Western Siberia rose from 13 percent in 1940 to nearly 40 percent in 1942 (Sokolov 1946, 20). Evacuation and recruitment policies generated a 65 percent increase in the industrial work force in the Ural and Volga regions between 1940 and 1943 (Voznesenskii 1948, 65). The combined result of these policies was an expansion of industrial output in the eastern regions from 3.94 billion (new)[4] rubles in 1940, to 9.12 billion in 1944 (Voznesenskii 1948, 46).

Dunmore suggests, however, that the long-term nature of the locational shift should not be overestimated. First, growth of industrial production in the eastern regions was concentrated in the defense sector, possibly exaggerating the extent of wartime industrial growth. Second, although defense production expanded in the East, output of foodstuffs, timber, and construction materials in this region fell substantially during World War II. "To claim that the war gave the eastern areas a greatly expanded base for postwar industrial growth is to ignore the disproportionalities between sectors within that base" (Dunmore 1980, 36). Third, the quality of wartime construction in the East was significantly lower than peacetime norms because of the urgency with which these industrial enterprises were built, thereby shortening the life of both the buildings and equipment. Fourth,

Table 2.3 Soviet Employment and Wage Data, 1940–1953

	Average annual employment[a] (millions)	Average annual wage (new rubles)[b]	Average annual industrial work force (millions)
1940	31.2	397	8.3
1941	27.4	n.a.	7.8
1942	18.4	n.a.	5.5
1943	19.4	n.a.	n.a.
1944	23.6	n.a.	n.a.
1945	23.7	521	7.2
1946	30.6	570	10.2
1947	32.1	683	11.0
1948	34.3	723	12.1
1949	36.1	745	12.9
1950	38.9	767	14.1
1951	40.7	791	14.9
1952	42.2	807	15.5
1953	43.7	815	n.a.

[a]Workers and salaried officials in national economy; excludes collective farm workers and military personnel.
[b]Post-1961 rubles.

Source: *Trud v SSSR* (1968) 22; *Narodnoe khoziaistvo SSSR* (1956), 189; G. Kravchenko, *Voennaia ekonomika SSSR, 1941–1945* (1963), 98, 218; *Promyshlennost SSSR* (1964), 84.

reconstruction in western regions took priority over industrial expansion in the East. In part this was because reconstruction efforts focused on civilian (heavy) industry as opposed to armament production, which predominated in the East. "Liberated areas" received a greater share of capital investment in 1944 than in 1940 (Kravchenko 1970, 221). Lastly, reconstruction efforts in the western regions employed the latest technology, whereas "new" plants in the East utilized old technology and evacuated equipment.

IMPACT ON POPULATION AND LABOR FORCE

The most pervasive impact of World War II in the USSR is found is the devastating human loss incurred by the war. The 1939 census reports 170.6 million people living in the 1939 territory, and approximately 20 million living in newly acquired regions,[5] putting the 1939 population in present boundaries at some 190.7 million. A rough estimate, based on a 2.5 percent annual increase in population, indicates a 1959 population of 240 million; however, the 1959 census shows only 208.8 million, implying a loss of some 30 million people. The correspondingly adverse affect of World War II on the work force is shown in Table 2.3. Not shown is the increased work effort occasioned by World War II, nor the change in the composition of the work force to include more women, youths, and elderly.

A detailed analysis of the composition of wartime population loss is provided by Fitzpatrick (Chapter 8). Most striking is the war-related change in the number of women relative to men. In 1939, the number of women in the USSR exceeded that of men by some 7 million. By 1959, there were 20 million more women than men, with almost all of this surplus concentrated among women 32 years old and older. Anderson and Silver (Chapter 11) examine the demographic consequences of these wartime population losses, with particular emphasis on the impact on non-Russian nationalities.

An indirect consequence of World War II on the Soviet population and work force stems from the postwar industrialization drive, which was influenced not only by reconstruction efforts, but also by the USSR's emergence from World War II as a major world power. The impact of these conditions is evident on postwar rural-urban distribution patterns. Historically, the majority of Russians lived in rural areas: in 1913, only 18 percent of the population lived in urban centers; in 1939, less than one-third. Yet by 1959, almost half lived in urban areas. Indeed, the urban population rose from 60 to 100 million people from 1939 to 1959, while over this same 20-year span, the rural population fell from 130 to 109 million (Schwartz 1958, 109). The impact of the rapid postwar growth in urban areas is documented and analyzed by Fitzpatrick in Chapter 8. Bubis and Ruble (Chapter 10) examine postwar rural-urban distribution patterns in detail for Leningrad, and their implications for Party membership and leadership.

Another consequence of World War II is found in the shift in population to the East. Some 47 million people were located in eastern regions of the USSR in 1939. By 1959, this figure reached 63 million. During the same period, Kazakhstan experienced a 50 percent increase in population (6.1 to 9.3 million), while the population west of the Urals only rose from 144 to 146 million (Schwartz 1958, 109). Nove (Chapter 5) provides a vivid description of the movement east by the peasantry.

Mobilizing sufficient labor resources for the war effort involved strengthening labor discipline codes and imposing restrictions on labor mobility and individual employment choice. An October 1940 decree authorized compulsory transfer of engineers, technicians, and skilled workers from one enterprise to another. In July 1941, this right was granted to a number of regional and provincial committees, allowing for forced assignment of certain military personnel and workers to jobs in agriculture, industry, and construction. A decree in December 1941 forbade workers in war industries to leave jobs for the duration of the war, and in September 1942, another decree extended this to transport personnel and all workers in areas near the front. Additional restrictive decrees were issued in April and May 1943 (Shigalin 1960, 240–41). The impact of these policies on the distribution of the industrial labor force is illustrated in part by Dunmore (1980, 73, 128) and described in more detail by Fitzpatrick (Chapter 8). The most pronounced impact on labor recruitment and mobilization for the war effort resulted from the February 1942 decree that required the labor services of all men between the ages of 16 and 55 and all women 16 to 45 years old. Over 730,000 civilians were mobilized: 565,900 from urban areas, 168,000 from rural areas. Of these, 191,000 were sent to war industries (Shigalin 1960, 242).

In addition to direct controls over labor to offset manpower shortages resulting from wartime losses and increased military service, other policies adopted during World War II to combat declines in industrial production included lengthening the working day 1 to 3 hours, suspending vacations, emphasizing the replacement of male with female labor, and additional training. From June to December 1941, nearly 1 million housewives and schoolgirls (grades 8 to 10) were brought into the production process. The proportion of women in the total labor force rose from 38 percent in 1940, to 53 percent in 1942, reaching 55 percent by 1945. In industry, women represented 41 percent of the work force in 1940, 52 percent in 1942 (59 percent in the electric industry in 1942) (*Zhenshchina* 1960, 35; Kravchenko 1970, 99). Kravchenko (1970, 97–98) also reports actions taken to train skilled workers, declaring that in 1942, for example, 80 percent of all industrial workers took training courses. A parallel effort was made to train tractor drivers and agricultural mechanics.

A final consequence of World War II on the Soviet population and labor force entails the war's impact on forced labor. One U.S. estimate puts the number of persons in concentration camps in 1948 at 13 million (Schwartz 1949, 116). Other estimates range from 2–3 million to 20 million people (Jasny 1951, 405–7). Forced labor personnel included German prisoners, other enemy soldiers, and "politically dangerous" Soviet citizens (returning military personnel, former kulaks, religious officials, and political or minority group dissidents). Fitzpatrick provides an excellent discussion of conscript and convict labor in Chapter 8.

IMPACT ON HOUSEHOLD CONSUMPTION

A comparison of money incomes and expenditures of Soviet households in 1940 and 1945 yields some insight into the impact of World War II on civilian consumption patterns. Zaleski (1980, 442–47) reports that wages, salaries, and other payments (including military pay) in 1945 exceeded the 1940 level by some 2.3 billion rubles, in spite of restrictive wartime policies over wages. Income from the sale of products in collective farm markets rose fourfold (by 9.4 billion rubles) from 1940 to 1945 as a result of wartime food shortages. Similar wartime increases are found in the pensions and allowances category of household income which rose from 73 million rubles in 1940, to 2.37 billion in 1945. In spite of these increases, however, the share of total consumption in national income was much lower in 1945 than in 1940 (see Table 2.2) despite a lower level of national income in 1945 as compared to 1940.

Additional insight regarding the impact of World War II on civilian household consumption is found in war-related rationing practices adopted to mobilize resources for the war effort. The first rationing decree (July 1941) affected Moscow, Leningrad, and the surrounding provinces (21 urban areas, 17 districts) and encompassed such products as bread, macaroni, sugar, butter, fat, groats, meat and meat products, and fish. In addition, a number of manufactured products were rationed: cotton, linen, rayon fabrics, ready-made clothes, leather and rubber shoes, and soap. Rationing was extended to different products and to different cities and provinces as the war wore on.

The magnitude of war-related rationing is best illustrated by the number of individuals actually involved in the rationing process. The Commissariat of Trade (which included the Administration for Rationed Supplies) supervised the centralized allocation of consumer goods. Zaleski (1980, 351) concludes that, administratively, this occupied 14,000 persons in 3,100 offices at the end of the war, with some 13,000 persons working in 1,900 control offices to supervise the distribution of ration cards, which in turn employed 400,000 individuals (although only 20 percent were full-time employees) to distribute ration cards in industrial enterprises and apartment organizations. Nearly 61 million people in urban areas were affected by rationing in 1941. By 1944, this figure had risen to 76.8 million. In December 1945, 80.6 million Soviet people were supplied with bread under the rationing system (of which some 26.8 million lived in rural areas). Needless to say, the results of the vast apparatus of distribution and control were not always satisfactory either to the state or the Soviet people.

IMPACT ON ECONOMIC GROWTH

World War II caused a severe setback in the growth of output in the USSR. The ground lost in terms of the growth rate was not recovered by 1953, nor even by 1961. In large part this stems from the reduction in Soviet population and labor force, not only of the losses immediately attributable to World War II, but also from the reduction of the Soviet leadership's capacity to expand the labor force.

Also contributing to the detrimental impact of World War II on the aggregate growth rate of the economy was the long-term character of the 30 percent loss of capital stock. The nature of this loss includes direct destruction, curtailed investment, and hence, a reduction in productive capacity not only during World War II, but also for an indefinitely long period after the war. Available data (Moorsteen and Powell 1966, 386) suggest that had it been possible to maintain the investment growth rate indicated by prewar trends, the absolute volume of investment realized in each of the post-1950 years would have been achieved 6 to 7 years earlier, or alternatively, would have exceeded actual investment in each year by some 80 percent. From this it follows that it was *not* the case that the value of fixed capital stock, having regained its prewar level sometime in

1949 (Moorsteen and Powell 1966, 322), was thereafter unaffected by the impact of World War II.

A conventional method for analyzing the impact of World War II on Soviet economic growth examines the war's impact on the stock of capital, the quantity of labor and other inputs available for production, and changes in their productivity. Moorsteen and Powell (1966, 314–379) compiled sufficient data on Soviet employment, capital stock, capital-labor and capital-output ratios, and input productivity measures to put together a rough sketch of World War II's impact on Soviet economic growth potential in the immediate postwar period.

An important consequence of World War II on Soviet economic growth potential involved the acquisition of new territory. New territory brought under Soviet domain not only additional land and capital stock but also additional labor. The impact on employment of acquiring new territory was more pronounced in the industrial sector than in agriculture, although both sectors exhibited significant if only temporary labor force increases. A comparison of 1940 and 1945–1946 employment figures (Moorsteen and Powell 1966, 365) shows a war-related reduction in agricultural employment, caused not only by wartime losses from German occupation and destruction, but also from substantial numbers of agricultural workers who joined the Red Army and, when demobilized, found (or were assigned) employment in urban industrial centers. Included in these agricultural employment figures is the increase in the labor force that resulted from higher wartime and postwar female labor force participation. For the nonagricultural sector, World War II's impact was similar with respect to higher female labor force participation. Indeed, measured in 1937 man-years and adjusted for changes in hours, total employment in this sector in 1945 exceeded that of 1940. Tremendous war-related population losses had an adverse effect upon Soviet labor force growth potential, however. Prewar increases in total employment (approximately 3 percent from 1928 to 1940) were more than halved as a result of World War II (1 percent increase in total employment 1945–1961).

The war-related annexation of new territory also allowed for an expansion of sown area, from 137.7 million hectares in 1939 to 150.4 million in 1940 (Moorsteen and Powell 1966, 366). Yet, the devastating impact of World War II is clearly seen in the reduction of sown land by 1945, in comparison with that of 1928. As Nove (Chapter 5) points out, not until 1948 was the prewar figure of sown land attained (not until 1951, using current boundaries). This holds in spite of the expansion of agricultural production in the East. Johnson (1963) suggests that as far as grain yields were concerned, the expansion of territory did not greatly alter average quality of sown land.

The impact of World War II on Soviet capital-output and capital-labor ratios was pronounced. The average capital-output ratio (computed as the ratio of net capital stock to GNP in 1937 prices) rose irregularly in the prewar period (from 1.68 in 1928 to 1.93 in 1940). At war's end, it had reached 2.01, rising to 2.10 in 1946, before falling and remaining below 2.0 until after 1953 (Moorsteen and Powell 1966, 367–68). Wartime devastation of capital stock and slow assimilation of foreign technology would account for these changes, as would reconstruction priorities favoring heavy industry. The capital-output ratio in nonagricultural sectors behaved broadly like that of the total, although the increase over the 25-year period from 1928 to 1953 was less. The extremely high ratio for housing reflects, in addition to the usual factors making for a high capital intensity in this sector, the low level of official rents in the Soviet Union. A comparison of pre- and postwar capital-labor ratios reflects, perhaps more than anything else, the differential impact of World War II on the growth rates of capital and labor.

Productivity is cited as a major factor in explaining growth in any industrialized economy. The disruptive effects of war on productivity are no doubt pervasive. Low productivity during war and the initial postwar period is expected, perhaps unavoidable, because of the conversion to and from military production. It is not clear, however, that the overall impact of war on productivity will necessarily be unfavorable. War may impede technological developments in some areas while stimulating it in others. Moreover, even though war disrupts the functioning of existing administrative agencies, it does provide an opportunity for eliminating bureaucratic rigidities. The pervasive, yet somewhat obscure, nature of World War II's impact on several productivity measures is well-documented by Moorsteen and Powell (1966, 370, 378–79). Their productivity estimates are problematic, however, because they are sensitive to interest rate estimates, the method of aggregating inputs, and the adjustment of labor inputs for hours worked.

The delayed reaction of World War II in terms of growth rates, the "economic miracle" of the 1950s in which West Germany and Japan each recovered rapidly from a substantial degree of wartime devastation, did not occur in the Soviet Union. Extensive controls over the economy, a commitment to rapid growth, the lack of an occupying power, and a firmly established political regime with no domestic opposition would appear to be conducive conditions for economic growth. Yet, the Soviets experienced a relatively long period of remarkably low productivity growth after World War II. Certainly such factors as conversion to and from military production, the state of repair of the capital stock, bottlenecks and shortages in the supply of agricultural materials to nonagricultural areas, hours adjustments of labor inputs, unmeasured changes in the quality of labor, and the overall disorganizing effects of war, both during the hostilities and after the conflict ended, affected input productivity, and hence, Soviet economic growth, at least until 1953.

Although it is abundantly clear that World War II altered factor proportions, thereby influencing productivity, it is more difficult simply by examining the data to identify the impact of the war on the level of technology, on economies of scale, or on efficiency, all of which are determinants of productivity. These data must be examined in an analytical framework that identifies the magnitude of the war effort. The methodology employed in the next section in generating war cost estimates provides one possible analytical framework and yields additional insight into the impact of World War II on Soviet economic growth.

War Cost, Postwar Burden, and Economic Growth

Measuring the economic cost of war necessarily employs an opportunity cost approach in which the opportunity cost, by comparing potential and actual output levels, captures foregone civilian production and/or capacity expansion, or alternatively, reduced civilian consumption, or additional work effort required by the war. Calculating potential output by projecting a prewar output trend into the postwar period cannot accurately represent an estimate of what the course of output would have been in the absence of World War II, but it does make clear the nature of the loss in output which the war, in all its consequences, entailed. For example, Soviet data indicate that had it been possible to maintain the output growth rate indicated by the prewar trend (6.1 percent annually 1928–1937, or 5.9 percent 1936–1939, in 1937 prices), the absolute volume of output realized in each postwar year would have been attained 6 to 7 years earlier. Alternatively, the absolute value of output based on the prewar growth trend would have exceeded actual output from 1945 to 1950 by some 50 percent.

Analyzing the impact of World War II on the Soviet economy by using an opportunity cost approach is appropriate whether war cost is measured in terms of costs absorbed during the conflict (Millar and Linz 1978, 1980) or costs absorbed in the postwar period (Linz 1983) because these are not separate costs analytically, only temporally. Wartime costs include, for example, direct government expenditures on the war effort, wartime loss of national income because of damaged or destroyed factors of production, loss of personal consumption resulting both from lower wartime national income and the increased share of government expenditures in national income, reduced leisure time, and extra effort and resources required to convert to wartime production. War costs not absorbed during the conflict carry over into the postwar period and include such components as the cost of continued lower national income because of the net loss of factors of production, depleted capital stock, reduced birthrates and labor force growth rates, and additional medical costs for the wounded and disabled who demand special care after the war ends. Carryover war cost does not represent any *additional* war cost, however. Rather, the term is used to represent the extent to which unabsorbed war cost is allocated to the postwar period, thereby affecting economic growth potential.

Linz (1983) provides three estimates of carryover war cost for the Soviet experience in World War II. The first estimate uses Soviet claims and sources to establish a rough estimate of the war cost absorbed between 1945 and 1953. To check whether this is a reasonable interpretation of the magnitude of the postwar impact, the second estimate employs Soviet national income data, and the third, aggregate output data in a production function framework. An idea of the postwar burden imposed upon the Soviet people is obtained by calculating each estimate in terms of years' earnings, or work effort of the 1945 labor force. The estimates range from 8 to 10 years' earnings when considering only the *material* losses generated by World War II, supporting the claim that World War II cost two Five-Year Plans. If war-related population losses are taken into account, as they necessarily are in the production function analysis, carryover war cost estimates rise to 18 to 25 years' earnings.

By any measure, the postwar impact of World War II imposed a tremendous burden on the leadership's economic growth efforts and upon the postwar population as a whole. Indeed, the magnitude of these carryover war cost estimates put into perspective Soviet reparation demands after World War II and yield further insight into the economic relationships established after the war between the USSR and Eastern Europe. In the context of the debate regarding the origins of the Cold War,[6] understanding the postwar impact of World War II and the extent to which it was reduced by actual foreign assistance programs ("pipeline" Lend-Lease, UNRRA funds, and reparations) paves the way for an examination of the extent to which *additional* foreign aid (the proposed U.S. loan, and Marshall Plan aid) would have reduced the postwar burden of World War II to the Soviet people.

The following section develops several measures of the impact of actual aid and reparations on Soviet postwar recovery efforts. Similar analysis is conducted for the potential aid programs. To facilitate comparison between the various aid impact estimates derived here (and the war cost estimates described previously) each is expressed in terms of years' earnings, or work effort required by the 1945 labor force to generate an equivalent impact domestically.

IMPACT OF ACTUAL AID

The impact of actual reparation payments and other forms of economic assistance on the Soviet economy has not previously been calculated, primarily because of measurement problems. Attempts have been made, however, to estimate total economic aid and reparations received by the USSR between 1945 and 1953. The most comprehensive effort, found in Nutter (1962, 351–54), gives an estimated range of $9.1 to $21.2 billion. The smaller figure values aid and reparations in "1938 dollars," the higher estimate is in terms of "current" or 1945 dollars. This range represents a lower bound estimate of reparations and aid actually received because it does not take into account proceeds from joint stock companies established in East European countries, transit privileges, discriminatory trading prices (except for Polish coal), levies for support of occupation troops and administration, forced labor of war prisoners and interns, or the value of machinery and equipment in occupied territories dismantled and removed to Russia by Soviet occupation forces before the end of the war. Moreover, Nutter (1962, 353) concludes that these figures understate the true value of reparations received, whether valued in 1938 or 1945 prices, because prices of goods and services received as reparations were discounted substantially in favor of the USSR.

To determine the impact on Soviet postwar recovery efforts of this lower bound estimate of reparations and aid received between 1945 and 1953 requires a conversion of the estimates from dollar to ruble values. Pick (1959, 343) reports the official exchange rate during the war and immediate postwar period at 5.3 rubles to $1.00. Using the official exchange rate, however, fails to provide a meaningful measure of either the true value or significance of reparation payments or other forms of economic aid to the USSR. As Holzman (1968, 814) points out, the official exchange rate "has served as little more than an accounting device for converting foreign currency prices of Soviet exports and imports into rubles for the purposes of constructing foreign trade accounts in local currency." During the 1930s and 1940s, exchange rates between the ruble and other foreign currencies were set arbitrarily by the Soviet government. The ruble was grossly undervalued as judged by any comparison of its purchasing power with the purchasing power of nominally equal amounts of dollars, pounds, and so on. During World War II, official exchange rates remained unchanged, despite the great inflation of nonrationed consumer goods prices. Holzman (1968) therefore offers an alternative exchange rate range, based on comparisons of domestic and foreign price trends, of 2.5 to 3.5 rubles to $1 for the postwar period. Although his exchange rate range provides a more accurate picture than one based on the official rate, it is not quite appropriate for my purposes because it deals almost exclusively with export prices, without considering the differences in degrees of undervaluation of exports and imports. Moreover, because domestic prices in the immediate postwar period did not accurately reflect costs of production, the ratio between world market prices and domestic prices is understated. Holzman's exchange rates do serve as a useful basis for comparison, however.

A more meaningful method of converting dollar values into ruble values to determine the magnitudes these reparation and aid estimates represent in the postwar Soviet economy is derived using Lend-Lease information. First, Lend-Lease aid was similar to postwar aid and reparations in that it was constrained by available supplies. Second, both ruble and dollar estimates of Lend-Lease aid are readily available although both the USSR and U.S. would have a tendency to misrepresent the actual value of Lend-Lease aid. The Soviets claim that Lend-Lease aid amounted to 5 billion rubles, also stating that Lend-Lease aid came to about 4 percent of their wartime national income (Tamarchenko 1967, 57; Cherniavski 1964, 19–20). U.S. records show Lend-Lease aid ot the USSR totaled some $11 billion by the end of 1945 (Jones 1969). The first claim, 5 billion rubles to $11 billion, results in a ruble-dollar exchange rate of 0.5R to $1.

Calculating an exchange rate based on the second claim requires an estimate of Soviet national income during the war, Y_w. Available Soviet sources do not contain estimates of wartime national income but do provide

Table 2.4 Actual and Potential Aid Estimates, 1945–1953

		Dollar values (billions)	Official 5.3R to 1	Holzman 3.5R	Holzman 2.5R	Lend-Lease 0.7R	Lend-Lease 0.5R
a.	Actual Aid						
b.	1938 prices	9.1	48.2	31.8	22.8	6.4	4.6
c.	% Ypw		8.3	5.5	3.9	1.1	0.8
d.	ΔQ_1[a]			28.3	21.2	6.9	5.1
e.	ΔQ_2[b]			2.1	2.0	1.7	1.6
f.	1945 prices	21.2	111.8	73.8	52.8	14.8	10.5
g.	% Ypw		19.4	12.8	9.1	2.6	1.8
h.	ΔQ_1			59.4	48.2	14.5	10.7
i.	ΔQ_2			2.3	2.2	1.9	1.8
j.	Potential Aid						
k.	loan + ERP1	2.4	12.7	8.4	6.0	1.7	1.2
l.	% Ypw		2.1	1.4	1.0	0.3	0.2
m.	ΔQ_1				6.5		1.4
n.	ΔQ_2				1.7		1.3
o.	loan + ERP2	4.2	22.3	14.7	10.5	2.9	2.1
p.	% Ypw		3.9	2.5	1.8	0.5	0.4
q.	ΔQ_1			14.6		3.6	
r.	ΔQ_2			1.9		1.5	

[a]Change in aggregate output when all aid goes to capital formation.
[b]Change in aggregate output when all aid goes to labor or wage goods.

national income indices (1940 = 100) for the war period: 92 in 1941, 66 in 1942, 77 in 1943, 88 in 1944, and 83 in 1945 (Kravchenko 1970, 351). Bergson and Heymann (1954, 24) estimate the 1940 level of national income at 45.8 billion rubles (1940 prices). Hence, Yw equals 184 billion rubles, and Lend-Lease aid (at 4 percent of Yw) totaled some 7.4 billion rubles, yielding a second exchange-rate estimate of 0.7R to $1. For comparison purposes, results using each exchange rate described above are provided in Table 2.4.

Using Lend-Lease exchange rates, the impact of reparations and economic aid on Soviet postwar recovery is examined first by calculating the ruble value of reparations and aid as a percent of cumulative postwar national income, Ypw. Once again, available Soviet sources do not provide estimates of national income between 1945 and 1953, but do contain national income indices (1940 = 100) for this period: 85 in 1945 (Kravchenko 1970, 351); 78 in 1946 (*Narodnoe khoziaistvo* 1970, 533); 93 and 116 in 1947–48 (*Ekonomicheskaia zhizn* 1967, 1: 411); 136 and 164 in 1949–50 (Vikentev 1957, 140); 184 and 204 in 1951–52 (*Narodnoe khoziaistvo* 1956, 36); 204 in 1953.[7] Hence, Ypw totaled 577.7 billion rubles (1940 prices) between 1945 and 1953. Lend-Lease exchange rates yield reparations and aid estimates ranging from 4.6 to 14.8 billion rubles between 1945 and 1953 (Table 2.4: lines b, f), implying a 1 to 3 percent contribution to postwar national income during this period (lines c, g). Holzman's exchange rates result in an aid estimate range of 22.8 to 73.8 billion rubles, contributing some 4 to 13 percent of cumulative (1945–1953) national income.

An idea of the contribution made by reparations and aid is found in a comparison with the amount of work effort required to generate an equivalent amount of national income domestically. That is, to generate a similar total increase in national income would have taken the 1945 labor force of 27.2 million workers and salaried officials (Zaleski 1980, 607), earning an average 521 rubles per year (*Trud* 1968, 138), between four months' and 1 year's earnings using Lend-Lease exchange rates. This compares with total material war cost estimates of between 3 and 7 years' earnings of the 1940 labor force (Millar and Linz 1978, 1980; Saryadar 1980).[8] Had reparations and aid not been received, the burden of World War II upon the Soviet people would have been appreciably higher.

An alternative method of analyzing the impact of economic aid and reparation payments between 1945 and 1953 uses aggregate output data within a production function framework to relate output to available supplies of capital and labor. Actual levels of aggregate output cited in Soviet sources for 1945 to 1953 clearly include all reparation payments and economic aid received during this period. What would the level of output have been without reparation payments or economic aid? A graphical interpretation is useful for illustrating a number of feasible decision rules regarding reparations and aid that Soviet planners would necessarily have faced in 1945. Figure 2.1 identifies aggregate output levels before and after receiving reparations and economic aid. Given the Soviet system of central planning and priorities, it makes no sense to assume that capital and labor receive their marginal products; hence the price ratios have been omitted.

Prior to receiving aid, the economy operates at point A, given existing technology and actual stocks of capital and labor. When reparations and other economic assistance became available, one decision rule would have allowed for the entire amount of aid to go toward capital formation. Under this decision rule, the original capital stock would be augmented by the foreign resource inflow from K_0 to K_1, shifting the isoquant out from Q_0, the nonreparations level of output, to Q_1. Because labor has been constrained to its original level, L_0, by this decision rule, point B marks the relevant combination of capital and labor used to produce Q_1. A similar analysis follows for a decision rule that allows all aid to go toward labor or consumer goods. Alternatively, Soviet planners would necessarily have considered the impact on aggregate output of using aid to augment both capital and labor. Under this decision rule, in addition to acquiring capital goods, aid would also have been used to purchase foodstuffs or other consumer goods for payments-in-kind to attract youths, women, and demobilized soldiers to the cities or industrial centers where these goods were in short supply. As seen in Figure 2.1, this yields a greater impact on output than that resulting from using all aid in either capital or labor formation. Output reaches a maximum, Q_2, under the assumption of perfect convertibility of foreign

Figure 2.1.
Impact of Reparations and Economic Aid on Soviet Aggregate Output

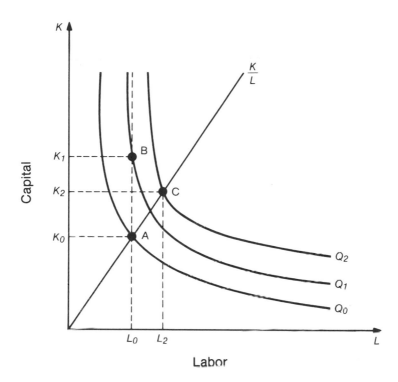

resource inflow (reparations and other economic aid) to the optimal levels of capital (K_2) and labor (L_2). The contribution of reparations and other economic aid must fall within the range defined by Q_0 and Q_2.

Translating this graphical interpretation into actual figures requires certain information regarding the structural parameters of the Soviet economy in the postwar period—elasticities of output with respect to capital and labor, and a technology measure, for example. Estimating a production function yields precisely these parameters. Results obtained by using a Cobb-Douglas specification and the ordinary least squares (OLS) estimation procedure indicate a much greater response in output levels corresponding to a change in capital than to a change in labor.[9] In large part this is explained by the changing structure of the Soviet economy, from predominantly agricultural to industrial, during the 1930s and 1940s. Correspondingly, the impact of aid on postwar growth potential differs markedly between the two decision rules.

Under the first decision rule where all aid goes to capital formation the contribution of reparations and aid to aggregate output would have fallen within the range of 5.1 to 14.5 billion rubles, using Lend-Lease exchange rates (Table 2.4: lines d, h) and estimated parameter values based on nonagricultural net national product (NNP), capital services valued at 8 percent interest rate, and employment data taken from Moorsteen and Powell (1966, 352–65). To produce an equivalent increase in aggregate output domestically would have required the 1945 labor force to work between 3 months and 1 year. This compares with a similar impact estimate of 4 months' to 1 year's earnings based on national income data. Using the aid estimate derived from Holzman's exchange rates, this decision rule implies a contribution of some 21.1 to 59.4 billion rubles (Table 2.4: lines d, h), requiring additional work effort of 1.5 to 4.2 years, which again is very similar to estimates based on national income data of 1.6 to 5 years' earnings. Had all aid gone to augment labor (Table 2.4: lines e, i), the corresponding impact on output would have been much less, between 1.7 and 2.3 billion rubles, requiring some 1.5 to 2 months' additional work effort to generate an equivalent impact domestically. These figures allude in part to the severe capital shortage created by World War II, and in part to the traditional differential emphasis on consumer goods versus producer goods in the USSR.

None of these estimates, however, represents the maximum impact reparations and aid would have had upon output for at least two important reasons. Looking only at the impact on output of augmenting either capital or labor ignores the long-run effects of net additions to capital stock or labor. This aspect might be examined within the context of a Harrod-Domar type growth model. In addition, because it makes no sense to assume perfect competition where capital and labor receive their marginal products given the Soviet system of central planning and priorities, only the boundary solutions can be determined (that is, all aid going to either capital formation or labor). Allocating reparations and other economic aid optimally between capital and labor would necessarily have had a greater impact on aggregate output than any of the estimates obtained previously. Moreover, as stated, the reparation and aid estimate itself is a lower bound estimate.

These results indicate that, whether measured with respect to national income or aggregate output, the impact of reparations and economic aid was substantial. Roughly measured, to generate an equivalent increase in income or output would have required additional work effort by the postwar labor force of some 3 months' to 1 year's earnings (1.5 to 5 years' earnings using Holzman's exchange rates). Had the Soviets not received any postwar assistance, the carryover cost of World War II to the Soviet people would have been markedly greater than current estimates indicate.

IMPACT OF POTENTIAL AID

Soviet reconstruction efforts were aided significantly by reparations, "pipeline" Lend-Lease, and UNRRA assistance. Each of these, however, represented a source of conflict between the United States, Britain, France, and the USSR. The earliest and most pervasive source of conflict arose over Soviet reparations claims, especially with respect to Germany. Discord over Poland, Romania, Hungary, and Czechoslovakia after the Potsdam Agreement further inflamed the reparations issue, and the tenuous relationship between the Allies began deteriorating rapidly. Lend-Lease posed another source of postwar confrontation specifically between the United States and USSR. The United States did not like the sporadic wartime releases of the Soviet press that never really informed the Soviet people of the importance of Lend-Lease to their war effort, nor did the Soviets like Truman's abrupt termination of Lend-Lease once Germany surrendered. Soviet-American confrontation also arose over UNRRA aid. Although UNRRA had been organized and funded (primarily by the United States) to provide food, medical care, and other assistance to war-devastated areas, protests intensified in the immediate postwar period that UNRRA funds (U.S. dollars) were being used to fund Communist expansion. As a result, UNRRA assistance was cancelled in 1946, despite existing economic conditions in the USSR and Eastern Europe.[10]

In place of the increasingly unpopular Lend-Lease and UNRRA aid, the United States proposed a loan of $1 billion in 1945 to aid Soviet reconstruction efforts. Discussions of a loan to the USSR had been initiated much earlier, however. U.S. Ambassador A. W. Harriman went to Moscow in October 1943 to meet with A. I. Mikoyan (Soviet Commissar for Foreign Trade) to talk about U.S. assistance in their reconstruction efforts. Indeed, the loan was perceived by business and government leaders alike as a way to help avoid the anticipated postwar depression in the U.S. In January 1945, V. M. Molotov (Soviet Foreign Minister) met with Harriman with the Soviet's first formal request for a postwar loan of $6 billion. By this time, conflicting interests with respect to the Soviet Union's reconstruction efforts were evident, and the loan had become more of a diplomatic tool than an economic opportunity. In spite of cooling relations between the United States and USSR, however, Harriman informed the Soviets in August 1945 that the Export-Import Bank was willing to consider Soviet proposals for postwar aid, and at Truman's request, $1 billion was earmarked by the Bank for possible loan to the USSR.

Negotiations were stalled and the loan "lost" for the first 6 months of 1946 while the U.S. State Department waited, hoping that Soviet reconstruction needs would require them to make concessions regarding reparations and other issues, and Moscow waited, believing the United States needed to finance exports to the USSR to head off a depression. By the end of 1946, the loan was no longer a current issue and the general question of U.S. assistance in Soviet reconstruction efforts was not mentioned again until June 1947 when Secretary of State Marshall gave his famous commencement speech at Harvard, offering a general plan for European recovery.

When the United States offered the Soviet Union economic assistance under the Marshall Plan in 1947, the Soviet leadership declined participation. A number of Western scholars contend that the aid was offered in such a way as to preclude any possibility of participation by the USSR.[11] Nonetheless, had they agreed to join in what became known as the European Recovery Program (ERP), what amount of aid could the Soviets have expected? Between April 1948 and June 1952, the European Recovery Program gave over $13 billion in aid (Ferrell 1978, 86). Over half of this sum was distributed among Britain, France, and Italy. Germany received approximately $1.4 billion. Assuming that another participant in the ERP would have changed the relative shares rather than the total funds appropriated by Congress, an upper bound estimate of potential aid to the USSR equaling the share actually granted to Britain of $3.2 billion can be derived. Political conditions at the time, however, suggest that this sum might be high. Alternatively, one might assume that the Soviet Union would have received only as much as Germany.

The traditional story implies that the impact of these two potential aid programs would have been substantial, allowing the Soviets to recover their prewar economic capacity much more rapidly and/or easily than they did. It is useful, therefore, to compare these potential programs with those actually received because it is quite clear that the loan and ERP aid were offered as substitutes for continued reparation payments and other existing (or terminated) aid programs. As indicated, the loan and ERP assistance at best would have amounted to some $2.4 to $4.2 billion from 1945 to 1953 (Table 2.4: lines k, o). This represents 1 to 3 billion rubles using Lend-Lease exchange rates (6 to 15 billion rubles, using Holzman's exchange rates). As such, these two potential aid programs would have amounted roughly to some 0.2 to 2.5 percent of cumulative postwar national income (lines l, p), representing approximately 1 to 3 months' earnings of the 1945 work force (5 months' to 1 year's earnings, using Holzman's exchange rates).

Employing the aggregate production function analysis described above, under the first decision rule where all aid goes to capital formation (Table 2.4: lines m, q), output would have increased by 1.4 to 3.6 billion rubles at Lend-Lease exchange rates (6.5 to 14.6 billion rubles, using Holzman's exchange rates). To generate a similar increase domestically would have required additional work effort by the 1945 work force of 1 to 4 months' earnings. Under the second decision rule, where all aid goes to augment labor (lines n, r), output would have increased by 1.3 to 1.5 billion rubles (1.7 to 1.9 billion rubles, using Holzman's exchange rates), requiring some 1 to 2 months' additional work effort to generate an equivalent increase domestically. These last figures indicate that although potential aid was absolutely smaller in value terms than actual aid received, the relative impact on output given the second decision rule would have been similar. Indeed, this again suggests a capital shortage prevalent in the postwar Soviet economy.

Calculated in this rough manner, and compared to the cost of World War II to the Soviet people, the potential impact of receiving the loan and ERP assistance was relatively modest. This is especially striking in comparison with the impact of actual reparations and aid. It does not necessarily follow, however, that the loan or ERP aid would have been insignificant. It is possible to conceive of a situation where it would have been significant at the margin. That is, the loan and ERP aid would necessarily have been used to eliminate bottlenecks in the economy (generating electricity or improving transport facilities, for example) by acquiring the most effective technology or facilities. Reparations, on the other hand, did not represent state-of-the-art technology or equipment. As such, ERP funds might have allowed for an earlier recovery of the prewar level of output, or, for example, legislation that compelled women and youths to remain in the work force after the war might not have been necessary. There is no a priori reason to think, however, that a marginal rather than an average capital-output ratio is relevant for analyzing the impact of these potential aid programs upon Soviet reconstruction efforts since a large section of European Russia was fought over with a scorched earth policy twice.

To check the reasonableness of the estimates derived above, a simple four-equation model may be employed to simulate the impact of additional aid on the size or productive capacity of the postwar economy. Assuming potential aid enters the Soviet economy as additional investment, it is possible to estimate the relationship between changes in investment, capital stock, labor, and output. The model can then be used for simulation purposes to predict output levels for various levels of additional investment. A complete specification of the model and estimation results are given in Linz (1980). The results indicate that for an exogenous change in investment of 1 billion rubles in time t, for example, aggregate output will initially rise by some 430 million rubles in the period $t + 2$. The total effect of such a change in investment on aggregate output was found to be an increase of 9.35 billion rubles.

The magnitudes of both the impact and long-run multipliers generated by the model are intuitively appealing for several reasons. The relatively small impact multiplier reflects the chronic difficulties of carrying out investment plans cited in Soviet sources. The long-run effects indicate both the fact that investment plans are used to eliminate bottlenecks in the economy, especially after World War II, and the rather low efficiency of investment resulting from the wide dispersion of investment projects and delays arising from unfinished construction (Lokshin 1937, 1952). To determine the responsiveness of aggregate output to changes in the level of investment, the investment elasticity was calculated and found to be approximately .10 for the postwar period, 1945–1953.

Calculation of these multipliers and the elasticity of investment allows for determination of the effect of potential foreign assistance on postwar aggregate output. Had the $1 billion loan been granted in 1946 and used to purchase industrial machinery and equipment, for example, aggregate investment would have been 2 to 4 percent higher in 1946–47. The impact of such an exogenous increase in investment would not be evident in the economy immediately. Given an elasticity of .10, a substantial change in aggregate output is not expected to occur in the short-run. Indeed, the model described above indicates a 2-year lag before aggregate output would rise. Hence, an additional .5 to .7 billion rubles of investment in 1946 would result in an increase in aggregate output of .21 to .30 billion rubles by 1948, generating a *total* increase of some 4.7 to 6.5 billion rubles. Similarly, had the Soviets received $1.4 to $3.2 billion of ERP funds in 1948 (the best scenario possible), aggregate investment would have increased by some .7 to 2.2 billion rubles (3.5 to 11 billion, using Holzman's exchange rates). The impact of such an exogenous increase in investment would have driven aggregate output up by some .3 to .9 billion rubles by 1950. The total increase in aggregate output of such an increase in investment is estimated at 6.5 to 20.5 billion rubles.

The combined effect of these potential aid programs is clearly much less than that of reparation payments during the same period. This is evident in a comparison not only of the absolute amounts of aid under consideration, but also of the additional work effort required to generate a similar impact domestically. Potential aid estimates represent at most only a third of the value of aid and reparations actually received, making a difference of only a few months in terms of earlier recovery. Results provided by Leontief (see Appendix) coincide very closely with those derived above using Lend-Lease aid estimates. Viewed in isolation, these figures are substantial. Relative to the magnitude of the postwar burden, or carryover cost of World War II to the Soviet people, however, these estimates appear modest.

Speculations on the Cost of Winning World War II

Although the total real cost of World War II to the Soviet Union has yet to be fully measured, there is no doubt that the economic cost of the war imposed a tremendous burden upon the Soviet people, both in absolute terms and relative to other participants. A significant portion of total material war cost carried over into the postwar period, adversely affecting economic growth efforts. In large part, certain costs were made unavoidable for the USSR by the onset of the Cold War. There is, however, no a priori reason to believe that the net effect of World War II was negative when taking into account political and social factors. Acquisition of new territory and new technology, in addition to the political and social cohesion resulting from sustaining a successful war effort, are benefits that have been omitted from the economic analysis presented here. Furthermore, little emphasis was placed on the significance of actual aid and reparation payments in Soviet postwar recovery efforts. Considering the magnitude of actual aid and reparation payments relative to potential aid programs implies that Stalin was perfectly rational in refusing to make political concessions in return for U.S. economic assistance after World War II. Moreover, considering only the absolute amount of aid in either scenario ignores the significance of the marginal contribution, which might well have been substantial for ERP assistance, as it was in Germany in the postwar period. Unfortunately, insight into this aspect benefits more from hindsight than from counterfactual analysis.

There are also other costs of winning, which have not been explicitly discussed, that quite possibly imposed an additional burden upon the Soviet population. Costs of occupation and costs of emerging from World War II as a major military power have necessitated disproportionately large annual expenditures for defense. In contrast to the U.S. economy, where continued defense spending in the postwar period created jobs, generating additional national income, the burden of a continued high level of defense expenditures in the Soviet economy (where the level of national income is fixed for a given plan period) is found in a "crowding out" of the provision of consumer goods. In this sense, the economic consequences of World War II and the relationships that arose during the postwar period stemming from the Cold War are still evident today.

Notes

1. "Pipeline" Lend-Lease involved the goods allocated but not delivered to the USSR when Lend-Lease terminated in 1945. There is no question that Lend-Lease food shipments alleviated serious Soviet shortages during the war. Shattered Red Army communication systems were rebuilt by using Lend-Lease equipment. Lend-Lease supplied specialized steels and alloys, allowing Soviet efforts to concentrate on the production of basic types of steel. Moreover, Lend-Lease aid was not entirely consumed by the war effort. Electric power machinery, a complete rubber tire factory, equipment for drilling and refining petroleum, and technical knowledge were all valuable in Soviet reconstruction efforts. It is clear, then, why the abrupt termination of Lend-Lease caused the Soviets so much concern. For an excellent discussion of Lend-Lease aid see Martel (1979).

2. Prior to, and concurrent with the German invasion in June 1941, the Soviets transferred to the East all movable capital stock, and deliberately sought to destroy everything that could not be removed. The Germans also succeeded in destroying a large portion of the remaining capital stock during their retreat in 1943. For descriptions of the military campaigns and general history of World War II see Clark (1966), Hart (1971), and Seaton (1971).

3. The population of the Soviet Union was reduced by 7 million during the course of World War II, from 198 to 191 million. Taking into account the prewar population growth rate of 2.5 percent per annum implies a total loss in population of some 20 million. A total "loss" of over 50 million people by 1959 (compared to the expected population at that time) is given in V. V. Pokshinshevskii, *Geographiia naseleniia SSSR: ekonomiko-geograficheskie orcherki* (Moscow: 1971), 34. Further discussion of population losses is found in Fitzpatrick (Chapter 8) and Anderson and Silver (Chapter 11).

4. On 1 January 1961, the Soviet government revalued the ruble, making ten rubles equal to one new ruble. Unless otherwise noted, ruble figures given in the remainder of this paper are in new rubles.

5. Lorimer (1946, 148) reports 20.1 million people in the newly acquired territory. Bergson and Heymann (1954, 6) put this figure at 23.6 million.

6. The origins of the Cold War have been the subject of controversy for over two decades. The traditional view assigns initiation of the Cold War to the Soviet Union, interpreting U.S. actions as responses to Soviet policies in Poland and Eastern Europe. The literature abounds with the traditional viewpoint. See, for example, Mosely (1949), Schlesinger (1967), Feis (1970). Revisionists do not see U.S. foreign policy after World War II as merely responding to Soviet initiatives. Rather, they see U.S. leaders using diplomatic policy and economic sanctions to try to shape the postwar world in accordance

with U.S. needs, standards, and conceptions. See especially Alperovitz (1965), Gardner (1970), Kuklick (1972). For a representative discussion of differences and attempts to classify writers into schools, see Maier (1970), Graebner (1969), and Morganthau (1967).

7. For lack of a published estimate or index, the 1953 level of national income was assumed to be at least equal to the 1952 level.

8. Calculations in terms of the 1945 work force are higher than those based on 1940 figures because of the reduced size of the postwar work force. For a complete discussion, see Linz (1983).

9. This result holds regardless of whether considering total GNP, capital services and employment; or nonagricultural, nonresidential GNP, capital services and employment. It also holds regardless of whether capital is valued at an 8 or 20 percent interest rate. For a complete discussion of specification, data, and parameter values, see Linz (1983).

10. The State Department argued that the food crisis was over (apparently disregarding the 1946 Soviet harvest) and that UNRRA aid was no longer necessary to war-ravaged countries since they were capable of importing necessary goods. In early 1947, however, the United Nations' Food and Agricultural Organization estimated a world grain shortage in that year of about 8 million tons. Furthermore, evidence indicates that Poland needed $200 million for imports for 1947 to maintain a minimum individual daily subsistence of 1800 calories, and relief deficits for Austria, Greece, Hungary, Italy, and China totaled $596 million for 1947 (Paterson 1978, 88). Perhaps a better explanation for UNRRA termination was the increasing awareness in Washington of the value of economic assistance as a diplomatic tool. The apolitical nature of UNRRA policy was not well liked—U.S. officials wanted influence over the final distribution of UNRRA funds. This position is exemplified by U.S. response to the Soviet request in 1945 for $700 million for reconstruction in the Ukraine and Belorussia, a request that required the appropriation of more funds to the UNRRA general fund. The United States, however, was unwilling to make the appropriation, supplying instead only a fraction of the amount requested. To make up the difference, the United States suggested that the Soviets apply for a loan, then failed to grant it.

11. Although Marshall invited European nations to undertake a joint economic reconstruction plan with U.S. assistance, the Marshall Plan, in a manner similar to the Truman Doctrine, equated economic recovery with political stability, anticommunism, and security against Soviet expansion. In addition, the French and British feared that the inclusion of the USSR would foreclose congressional support for a European recovery program and therefore took a decidedly cool attitude toward the Soviets at the Paris conference of the three foreign ministers. For the distribution of Marshall Plan aid and further discussion, see Patterson and Polk (1947), Paterson (1978).

References

Alperovitz, Gar. *Atomic Diplomacy.* New York: Simon & Schuster, 1965.

Bergson, Abram, and Hans Heymann. *Soviet National Income and Product 1940–1948.* New York: Macmillan, 1954.

Chadayev, Ya. *Ekonomika SSSR v period velikoi otechestvennoi voiny 1941–1945.* Moscow: 1965.

Cherniavski, Y:u. *Voina i prodovol'stvie: snabzhenie gorodskogo naseleniya v Velikuyu Otechestvennuyu voinu 1941–1945.* Moscow: 1964, 19–20.

Clark, Alan. *Barbarossa, The Russian-German Conflict 1941–1945.* London: Penguin Books, 1966.

Dunmore, Timothy. *The Stalinist Command Economy.* New York: St. Martin's, 1980.

Ekonomicheskaia zhizn Book I, Moscow: 1967, 411.

Eshelony idut na vostok: iz istorii perebazirovaniya proitvodstvennykh sil SSSR v 1941–42. Moscow: Nauka, 1968.

Feis, Harold. *From Trust to Terror: Onset of the Cold War.* New York: Norton, 1970.

Ferrell, Robert. "The Magnanimity of the Marshall Plan and the Obstructionism of Russia." In *Origins of the Cold War,* edited by T. Paterson. Lexington, Mass.: Heath, 1970.

Gardner, Lloyd. *Architects of Illusion.* Chicago: Quadrangle Books, 1970.

Graebner, Norman. "Cold War Origins and the Continuing Debate," *Journal of Conflict Resolution* 13 (March 1969):123–32.

Hart, B. H. Liddle. *A History of World War II.* New York: Macmillan, 1971.

Holzman, Franklyn. "The Ruble Exchange Rate and Soviet Foreign Trade Pricing Policies, 1929–1961," *American Economic Review* 58, no. 4 (September 1968):803–25.

Istoriiya Velikoi otechestvennoi voiny Sovetskogo Soyuza 1941–1945. Tom 2. Moscow: Voenizdat, 1963.

Jasny, Naum. "Labor and Output in Soviet Concentration Camps," *Journal of Political Economy* (October 1951):405–19.

Johnson, D. Gale. "Agricultural Production." In Bergson and Kuznets (eds) *Economic Trends in the Soviet Union,* Cambridge: Harvard University Press, 1963.

Jones, Robert. *Roads to Russia: US Lend Lease to the Soviet Union.* Norman: University of Oklahoma Press, 1969.

Kapital'noe stroitel'stvo. Moscow: 1961.

Katz, Barbara. "Purges and Production: Soviet Economic Growth 1928–1940." *Journal of Economic History* 35 no. 3 (March 1975):567–90.

Kravchenko, G. *Ekonomika SSSR v gody Velikoi Otechestvennoi voiny.* Moscow: Ekonomika, 1970.

Kuklick, Bruce. *American Policy and the Division of Germany.* Ithaca: Cornell University Press, 1972.

Linz, Susan J. "Measuring the Carryover Cost of World War II to the Soviet People: 1945–1953," *Explorations in Economic History* 20 (1983):375–86.

————. Economic Consequences of Cold War Origins? An Examination of the Carryover Cost of World War II to the Soviet People, Unpublished PhD dissertation, University of Illinois, 1980.

Lokshin, E. "Tizahelaia industriia i tekhnicheskaia rekonstrucktsia narodnogo khoziaistva," *Problemy ekonomiki,* nos 5–6 (1937), 52–7.

————. *Planirovanie materialnotekhnicheskogo snabzheniia narodnogo khoziaistva SSSR* (Moscow 1952).

————. *Promylennost' SSSR 1949–1963.* Moscow: Mysl', 1964.

Lorimer, Frank. *The Population of the Soviet Union.* Princeton: Princeton University Press, 1946.

Maier, Charles. "Revisionism and the Interpretation of Cold War Origins," *Perspectives in American History* 4 (May 1970):313–47.

Martel, Leon. *Lend-Lease, Loans, and the Coming of the Cold War.* Boulder: Westview Press, 1979.

Millar, James R. "Financing the Soviet Effort in World War II," *Soviet Studies* 32 (January 1980):106–23.

Millar, James R., and S. J. Linz. "The Cost of World War II to the Soviet People," *Journal of Economic History* 38 no. 4 (December 1978):959–62 and "Reply" 40 no. 4 (December 1980):849.

Moorsteen, Richard, and Raymond Powell. *The Soviet Capital Stock, 1928–1961.* Homewood, IL: Irwin, 1966.

Morganthau, Hans. "Arguing About the Cold War," *Encounter* 26 (May 1967):37–41.

Mosely, Philip. "Soviet-American Relations Since the War," *Annals of the American Academy of Political and Social Science* (May 1949):202–11.

Narodnoe khoziaistvo SSSR various years (Moscow).

Nove, Alec. *An Economic History of the USSR.* Rev. Middlesex: Penguin, 1982.

Nutter, G. Warren. *The Growth of Industrial Production in the Soviet Union.* Princeton: Princeton University Press, 1962.

Paterson, Thomas, ed. *Soviet American Confrontation: Postwar Reconstruction and the Origins of the Cold War.* Baltimore: Johns Hopkins University Press, 1978.

Patterson, Gardiner, and Judd Polk. "The Emerging Pattern of Bilateralism," *Quarterly Journal of Economics* 62 (1947):118–42.

Saryadar, Edward. "The Cost of World War II to the Soviet People: Two Five-Year Plans?" *Journal of Economic History* 40 no. 4, (December 1980):842–48.

Schwartz, Harry. "Soviet Labor Policy 1940–1945," *Annals of the American Academy of Political and Social Science* (May 1949).

_____. *Russia's Soviet Economy.* New York: Prentice-Hall, 1958.

Seaton, Albert. *The Russo-German War, 1941–1945.* London: Penguin, 1971.

Schlesinger, Arthur, Jr. "Origins of the Cold War," *Foreign Affairs* 46 (June 1967):22–52.

Shigalin, G. *Narodnoe khoziaistvo SSSR v period Velikoi Otechestvennoi voiny.* Moscow: Izd-vo Sotsial'no-ekonomicheskoi Literatury, 1960.

Sokolov, B. *Promyshelennoe stroitel'stvo v gody Otechestvennoi voiny.* Moscow: Gosplanizdat, 1946.

Tamarchenko, M. L. *Sovetskie finansy v period Velikoi Otechestvennoi voiny.* Moscow: 1967, 130–36.

Trud v SSSR. Moscow: 1968, 138.

Vikentev, C. *Natsdionalnyi dokhod SSSR v poslevoennoi period.* Moscow: Politizdat, 1957, 140.

Voznesenskii, N. *The Economy of the USSR During World War II.* Washington: Public Affairs Press, 1948.

Zaleski, Eugene. *Stalinist Planning for Economic Growth, 1933–1952.* Chapel Hill: University of North Carolina Press, 1980.

Zhenshchina v SSSR. Moscow: 1960.

Editor's Note

The following essay is a portion of a paper entitled "The Future Development of the National Income of the Soviet Union" written by Wassily Leontief (1973 Nobel laureate) in 1944 for the U.S. Office of Strategic Services. The most striking aspect of his paper is that, although our knowledge of Soviet national income accounting and production function analysis has broadened beyond that presented in Leontief's original paper in 1944, little additional analysis regarding the war and the immediate postwar period has been forthcoming. Leontief's essay represents an important contribution to understanding this period of Soviet economic development: first, because it was written at the time when significant policy decisions were being formulated in the United States and, second, because it was written by someone intimately familiar with the Soviet economic and political system.

Appendix to Chapter 2:
Capital Reconstruction and Postwar
Development of Income and Consumption

WASSILY LEONTIEF

Case 1: Military expenditures return to the 1938 level; reconstruction proceeds without the help of foreign credits, but gold is exported from stocks to the amount of $500 million a year for three years. (At the end of the war, Russia's total gold stocks will be in excess of $2 billion.)

THE WORKING HYPOTHESIS

Briefly, the hypothesis that is tested is that, under conditions stated above, the fixed capital in each of the various sectors of the Russian economy can be restored to the June 1941 level within 2.5 to 3.5 years after V-Day; that is, in 1947 or in 1948. In detail the hypothesis is as follows:

1. Industrial and transport capital are each restored to the June 1941 level in 1948; this requires an average annual investment at about the immediate prewar level.

2. In agriculture, the immediate policy objective is taken to be the reattainment of prewar per capita output by 1949 with a labor force somewhat below prewar; this requires the restoration of capital by the end of 1947, and some additional increase up to 1949.

3. Because of the extreme housing shortage, which already existed before the war, housing investment is taken to be at the peak prewar level in the first part of the reconstruction period and to rise gradually thereafter; the value of housing is restored to the prewar level by the end of 1948.

4. On the basis of the immediate prewar experience, annual investment in other categories of fixed capital is assumed to proceed at the same rate as investment in industry and housing.

While at first sight, it might seem implausible to assume that the volume of investment in the reconstruction period could be generally comparable to that of the immediate prewar years, it should be recalled that the burden of military expenditures will be greatly reduced as compared with prewar years.

In order to project the calculations beyond the reconstruction period, further assumptions are introduced. These assumptions are based primarily on a consideration of prewar experience and also of the trends prevailing in the reconstruction period and are of necessity somewhat arbitrary. For example, in the case of industry, the annual investment after 1948 is assumed to be a gradually increasing percentage of national income starting at the percentage reached at the end of the reconstruction period.[1]

METHOD OF CALCULATING ALLOCATION

On the basis of the above hypothesis and plausible assumptions regarding the allocation of the labor force in different sectors, it is possible to compute the new income produced year-by-year in the different sectors and hence the total corresponding annual national income produced. In the case of industry, for example, the relation between output on the one hand and capital and labor on the other, fixed by prewar trends is projected to the postwar period to determine the income produced by this sector in each postwar year.

Table 2.1A   Calculated National Income Produced, Distributed by Source, USSR, 1937–1940, 1945–1952

Case 1

Year	Total	Industry	Agriculture	Transport	Trade	Construction	Other
			Billions of 1937 dollars				
1937	23.9	11.0	3.8	1.6	3.9	3.0	0.5
1938	25.3	11.5	3.0	1.7	4.3	4.3	0.5
1939	26.9	12.0	3.4	1.7	4.7	4.4	0.7
1940	28.4	12.3	3.5	1.7	5.1	5.1	0.7
1945	20.7	10.7	2.4	1.6	3.8	1.6	0.6
1946	26.0	13.2	2.8	1.8	5.0	2.3	0.9
1947	27.1	13.7	3.2	1.9	5.3	2.2	0.8
1948	29.0	14.5	3.4	1.9	5.9	2.5	0.8
1949	31.3	15.4	3.6	2.1	6.3	3.0	0.9
1950	33.5	16.2	3.7	2.2	6.8	3.6	1.0
1951	35.9	17.1	3.8	2.3	7.4	4.2	1.1
1952	37.9	17.9	3.9	2.4	7.8	4.8	1.1
			1928 = 100 percent				
1937	307	367	138	390	429	732	172
1938	325	383	109	415	473	1,049	172
1939	345	400	123	415	516	1,073	241
1940	365	410	127	415	560	1,244	241
1945	266	357	87	390	418	390	207
1946	334	440	101	439	549	561	310
1947	348	457	116	463	582	537	276
1948	372	483	123	463	648	610	276
1949	402	513	130	512	692	732	310
1950	430	540	134	537	747	878	345
1951	461	570	138	561	813	1,024	379
1952	487	597	141	586	857	1,171	379

Source: W. Leontief, "The Future Development of the National Income of the Soviet Union," OSS Paper, (1944): Appendix C.

Total disposable national income as distinct from national income produced comprises income produced plus the value of gold exports from previously accumulated stocks. The allocation of the total disposable income is determined as follows: annual investment in fixed capital each year is established at once from the assumptions used, working capital requirements are calculated as a fixed percentage of industrial output. Under the assumption already stated as to the level of military expenditures, consumption is determined as a residual.

RESULTS

The results of the calculations are shown in Tables 2.1A and 2.2A. The 1940 national income is reattained by 1948. After that, a rapid rise occurs

Table 2.2A Calculated National Income, Distributed by Use, USSR, 1937–1940, 1945–1952 (billions of 1937 dollars)

Case 1

Year	National income produced	Disposable income[a]	Net fixed capital investment	Net increase in working capital	Military expenditures	Total non-consumption	Consumption
1937	23.9	23.9	5.2	0.8	3.6	9.6	14.3
1938	25.3	25.3	4.8	1.1	4.8	10.7	14.6
1939	26.9	26.9	4.8	1.2	8.4	14.4	12.5
1940	28.4	28.4	4.7	1.4	11.8	17.9	10.5
1945	20.7	21.2	4.4	—	4.8	9.2	12.0
1946	26.0	26.5	5.3	2.1	4.8	12.2	14.3
1947	27.1	27.6	6.0	0.4	4.8	11.1	16.4
1948	29.0	29.0	6.2	0.7	4.8	11.7	17.3
1949	31.3	31.3	6.6	0.8	4.8	12.2	19.1
1950	33.5	33.5	7.3	0.7	4.8	12.8	20.7
1951	35.9	35.9	8.1	0.9	4.8	13.8	22.1
1952	37.9	37.9	9.0	0.9	4.8	14.7	23.3

[a]This differs from national income produced by the net export of gold reserves, which is assumed to amount to $500 million a year in the years 1945–1947. No account is taken of the reverse effect of gold accumulation before the war.

Source: W. Leontief, "The Future Development of the National Income of the Soviet Union," OSS Paper (1944): Appendix C.

and by 1942 national income of $38 billion is attained which is 40 percent higher than that of 1940. A level of income corresponding to that projected for 1942 under the Third Five-Year Plan, which was interrupted by the war, is reattained in 1950–1951. Thus in terms of the expansion of total output, the war will have cost the Russians nine years.

The sharp increase in output from 1945 to 1946, it should be noted, is due to the fact that in estimating the 1946 figure a more or less arbitrary allowance was made for the initial difficulties of reconversion. At the same time, the increase from 1946 to 1947 is relatively small because of the assumption that the Russians restore their 40-hour working week after two years of reconstruction.

The dates at which the output of different sectors reaches the 1940 level are as follows: industry and transport, by the beginning of 1948; agriculture, 1948; trade, beginning of 1949. While investment in housing construction is calculated to exceed the prewar level already in 1945, the recovery of construction *income* lags behind that in other sectors.[2]

The most significant result is that the envisaged investment program could be carried out, and yet enough output would remain, after military and investment requirements are met, to enable the Russians to raise their current consumption to the immediate prewar level in the very first year after the conclusion of hostilities. However, because of the wartime destruction of consumers' stocks of clothing and household goods, the resulting living standard would still be short of the prewar. It has to be kept in mind, furthermore, that because of the high military expenditures, consumption in the immediate prewar years (1939 and 1940) was reduced to a low level. In contrast with the incomparably worst wartime living standards, however, the calculated postwar consumption would seem to be high enough to permit the Russians to carry out the envisaged investment program.

The peak consumption level of 1937–1938 is calculated to be reattained by the beginning of 1947. In the subsequent years consumption rises at the impressive rate of about 8 percent a year.

A comparison between prewar and postwar consumption, in per capita terms, substantiates these general conclusions (see Table 2.3A, Case 1).

Case 2: International political situation same as in Case 1: foreign credits are available to the extent of $1.5 billion a year for three years.

For the purposes of the present calculation it is assumed that the loans are amortized over a fifteen-year period, beginning at the time the loans are contracted; and that interest is at the rate of 2 percent per annum. The net amount of credit received in the first three years thus amounts in total to $3.8 billion, and annual service charges in the fourth year amount to $378 million.

If credits of this magnitude are available, it is improbable that Russia would be willing to export gold at a rate exceeding current output. In view of the uncertainties of world market conditions, a large gold reserve would be especially desirable if large debt commitments were contracted. Thus

Table 2.3A   Per Capita Consumption, USSR, 1937–1940, 1945–1952

| Year | Consumption in dollars | |
	Case 1	Case 2
1937	86.9	86.9
1938	88.2	88.2
1939	73.1	73.1
1940	61.0	61.0
1945	69.2	70.2
1946	81.0	85.0
1947	91.8	95.6
1948	95.0	94.1
1949	103.3	104.4
1950	110.6	111.5
1951	116.0	119.0
1952	120.5	128.0

While bringing up their capital investment to the prewar level, the Russians will obviously create a new industrial plant different in physical composition and location from that which was ravaged by the Germans. The new industrial plant will certainly be more efficient that the old. On the other hand, however, without technological progress the replacement of the destroyed *net* capital values would not necessarily mean reattainment of the prewar production capacity, particularly in the instances where the destroyed plants were old and their capital values largely written off. Since most of the Russian prewar industrial investment was quite new, the foregoing consideration is mainly relevant in the case of housing. The reconstruction of the destroyed living space will require more than a replacement of the lost *net* capital value.

disposable income in Case 2 is increased, as compared with Case 1, not by the full amount of the loan proceeds, but by the amount of these proceeds less the difference in gold exports. The total loan proceeds less the difference in gold exports amount to $2.3 billion for the three years.

Compared with the estimated total loss of fixed capital due to the war, $16 billion, this is a relatively small amount. Accordingly, it is not surprising that the calculated rate of reconstruction is not greatly increased, in comparison with Case 1 (in which foreign loans are not available). If, as is likely, the entire amount of credits is used directly to increase investment, the period of reconstruction in different sectors is reduced by only a few months, as compared with Case 1.

The corresponding development of income in the postwar years is shown in Tables 2.4A and 2.5A. While the effect of the credits in increasing the rate of reconstruction is not very marked, the cumulative indirect effect on total national income is appreciable. In 1952, national income reaches the level of $39.8 billion, as compared with $37.9 billion in the same year in Case 1. The difference, $1.9 billion, is considerably in excess of the annual service charges on the loan in that year. The investment opportunities in Russia are so great that the repayment of loans will impose no net additional burden on the economy. The magnitude of the net gains from loans realized

Table 2.4A   Calculated National Income Produced, Distributed by Source, USSR, 1937–1940, 1945–1952

Case 2

Year	Total	Industry	Agriculture	Transport	Trade	Construction	Other
			Billions of 1937 dollars				
1937	23.9	11.0	3.8	1.6	3.9	3.0	0.5
1938	25.3	11.5	3.0	1.7	4.3	4.3	0.5
1939	26.9	12.0	3.4	1.7	4.7	4.4	0.7
1940	28.4	12.3	3.5	1.7	5.1	5.1	0.7
1945	20.9	10.7	2.5	1.6	3.9	1.6	0.6
1946	26.8	13.4	2.9	1.8	5.1	2.9	0.7
1947	27.7	13.8	3.4	1.9	5.4	2.4	0.8
1948	29.5	14.6	3.6	2.0	5.8	2.4	0.9
1949	31.8	15.6	3.7	2.1	6.4	3.0	1.0
1950	34.1	16.4	3.8	2.2	7.1	3.6	1.0
1951	36.8	17.4	3.9	2.4	7.9	4.2	1.0
1952	39.8	18.5	3.9	2.6	8.6	4.8	1.4
			1928 = 100 percent				
1937	307	367	138	399	429	732	172
1938	325	383	109	415	473	1,049	172
1939	345	400	123	415	516	1,073	241
1940	365	410	127	415	560	1,244	241
1945	268	357	91	390	429	390	207
1946	344	447	105	439	560	707	241
1947	356	460	123	463	593	585	276
1948	376	487	130	488	637	585	310
1949	408	520	134	512	703	732	345
1950	438	547	138	537	780	878	345
1951	472	580	141	585	868	1,024	345
1952	511	617	141	634	945	1,171	483

Source: W. Leontief, "The Future Development of the National Income of the Soviet Union," OSS Paper, (1944): Appendix C.

by the Russians will depend, of course, on their ability to obtain on reasonable terms an export surplus necessary to meet service charges.

Consumption in the reconstruction years as well as later is somewhat greater in Case 2 than Case 1. While it is assumed in Case 2 that all the loan proceeds are used to increase investment, the indirect effect of the increased investment on income permits an increase in consumption.

The Russians have indicated that they expect reparations to make a substantial contribution to their reconstruction effort.[3] It is reported that in the case of the reparations bill included in the rejected armistice terms to Finland, the amount was fixed at one-half the material damage the Finns caused.[4] If the same principle were followed in fixing the bill to the Germans, the amount might come to $10 billion (1937 dollars). Since they are prepared to take payment-in-kind, and possibly in labor services, the Russians expect

Table 2.5A Calculated National Income, Distributed by Use, USSR, 1937–1940, 1945–1952 (billions of 1937 dollars)

Case 2

Year	National income produced	Disposable income[a]	Net fixed capital investment	Net increase in working capital	Military expenditures	Total non-consumption	Consumption
1937	23.9	23.9	5.2	0.8	3.6	9.6	14.3
1938	25.3	25.3	4.8	1.1	4.8	10.7	14.6
1939	26.9	26.9	4.8	1.2	8.4	14.4	12.5
1940	28.4	28.4	4.7	1.4	11.8	17.9	10.5
1945	20.9	22.3	5.3	—	4.8	10.1	12.2
1946	26.8	28.1	6.1	2.2	4.8	13.1	15.0
1947	27.7	28.8	6.6	0.4	4.8	11.7	17.1
1948	29.3	28.9	6.2	0.8	4.8	11.8	17.1
1949	31.8	31.4	6.6	0.7	4.8	12.1	19.3
1950	34.1	33.7	7.3	0.7	4.8	12.8	20.9
1951	36.8	36.4	8.1	0.8	4.8	13.8	22.6
1952	39.8	39.4	9.0	0.8	4.8	14.7	24.7

[a]Differs from income produced by the net proceeds from foreign credits or, alternatively, the net payments on foreign loan account.

Source: W. Leontief, "The Future Development of the National Income of the Soviet Union," OSS Paper (1944): Appendix C.

no transfer problem to thwart their efforts to obtain compensation for the damage done them.

If any such amount as that just referred to were collected from the Germans, Russian reconstruction could be greatly facilitated and the Russian interest in loans would be reduced. However, it is doubtful that the sum of $10 billion could be collected in toto within a period of three or four years. Possibly an appreciable time will elapse before any sizeable amounts can be collected, except in readily available forms such as, say, labor services and livestock.[5]

Notes

1. Assumptions and calculations are stated in detail in W. Leontief, "The Future Development of the National Income of the Soviet Union," U.S. Office of Strategic Services (OSS) paper (1944) Appendix C.

2. This lag is to be explained partly by the fact that housing investment in the reconstruction period is larger in relation to industrial investment than it was before the war, while the construction income generated by housing investment is less, per ruble of investment, than by industrial investment.

3. "Russian War Damage and Possible Reparations Claims," Research and Analysis No. 1899, U.S. OSS (26 May 1944).

4. "Finland's Capacity to Pay the Russian Reparations Demand," Research and Analysis No. 2127, 24 June 1944.

5. In view of the lengthy period required to restore depleted livestock herds, payments in this form would be of great value to the Russians.

Successful Spatial Management

HOLLAND HUNTER

A Quick Sketch of the Geography of World War II in the USSR

Much of the human drama of World War II in the USSR is associated with the sweeping movements of armies and peoples as the war drove them, first eastward and then westward, for thousands of miles across Europe and Asia. This essay on transportation aspects of the story therefore requires at least a brief sketch of its chief geographic developments.[1] It will thus put in relief the transport operations that had to be carried out to insure Soviet success in the war. It will also throw light on some postwar consequences that took several years to unfold.

The USSR was invaded by the Nazis on 22 June 1941. During the summer and fall, Nazi forces drove rapidly and deeply into the European part of the USSR, surrounding Leningrad, reaching the gates of Moscow, and crossing the Ukraine to Rostov on the Don River. In 1942, during the spring and summer, they drove southeastward into the north Caucasus and, more importantly, mounted a massive attack against Stalingrad on the lower Volga.

At Stalingrad, between November 1942 and January 1943, Soviet forces turned the tide and, after another major battle around Kursk in the spring, the USSR began a steady drive to expel the invaders. By February 1944, the siege of Leningrad had been lifted and the Soviet army was entering eastern Europe. By May 1945, the Soviet army had reached Berlin. Substantial Soviet forces were then shifted to the Far East, where they took control of Japanese forces in Manchuria in August 1945.

Large-scale transport operations were centrally involved in all these massive movements. In the summer and fall of 1941, while Nazi forces drove rapidly forward, there was hasty evacuation of people and property from the Ukraine, Belorussia, and the Baltic states. The railroads were the principal carrier, but all means of transport were utilized: trucks, carts, and tractors; ships and boats; motorcycles and bicycles. As Nove indicates (Chapter 5) hundreds of thousands of persons walked, driving their livestock before them. Equipment in hundreds of factories was dismantled for rail shipment to new locations farther east. Everything useful and movable was evacuated if possible. If the equipment escaped the invader and survived the trip, it was thrown into a great mass of supplies available for the war effort.

Even before the transport operations connected with evacuation were finished, the railroads were called on to assemble troops and materiel to defend Moscow. Special efforts were made for rapid movement of troops and supply trains from the interior to the front, burdening low-capacity interregional lines far beyond normal levels. In addition, bombing and strafing by Nazi aircraft disrupted rail operations. Nevertheless, the supplies brought to defend the capital in late 1941 enabled it to survive.

All during 1942, far larger flows of troops and materiel converged on the region around Stalingrad, where an even more decisive battle raged for seven months. Soldiers and civilians hastily completed several new rail lines to bring troops and munitions for a giant pincers movement that enveloped a large German army (600,000 survivers surrendered in January 1943). Additional flows supported the battle at Kursk.

Soviet railroad personnel played a key role in supporting the Soviet army's drive to expel the Nazis. It was necessary to restore at least single-track operation on key lines across occupied territory. The retreating Nazis were experts at demolition but Soviet railroad personnel quickly became experts at prompt restoration. This transport support continued across eastern Europe, all the way to Berlin, while the distance between front and rear steadily lengthened.

Even after VE-Day in Europe, a large-scale transport operation was required to move troops and supplies for up to eleven thousand kilometers between Germany and Manchuria. The move was accomplished in less than four months. Four decades later it may appear to have been a minor appendage of the war, but it strained a war-weary railroad system to a significant extent.

Contrasts Between World Wars I and II

The volume of railroad freight traffic is one useful indicator of an economy's overall activity, so it is instructive to compare the impact of World Wars I and II on Russia and USSR with respect to it. The two curves in Figure 3.1 trace, against a logarithmic vertical scale, the annual level of railroad freight ton-kilometers from 1913 through 1928 and from 1937 through 1952. The years 1916 and 1940 are juxtaposed as the prewar peaks; 1918 and 1942 appear as the wartime troughs. Several significant differences between

Figure 3.1.
Railroad Freight Traffic, Russia and USSR, 1913–1928, and USSR, 1937–1952, in Billions of Metric Ton-Kilometers

10^9 Ton-Kilometers

1913
1914
1915
1916
1917
1918
1920
1922
1923
1924
1925
1926
1927
1928

1937
1938
1939
1940
1941
1942
1943
1944
1945
1946
1947
1948
1949
1950
1951
1952

Source: H. Hunter, *Soviet Transportation Policy*, (1957), 112, 331.

the two periods are immediately apparent. The recovery of Soviet railroad freight traffic from 1922 to 1926 was extraordinarily rapid; the growth rates of the 1940s came nowhere near matching the earlier experience. At the same time, it is obvious that, relatively speaking, the fall in railroad freight traffic during the First World War went far deeper than during the Second. The contrast reflects not narrow aspects of railroad operations but large basic differences in the whole surrounding political and economic situation.

After the First World War, it required ten years to reach the 1916 level of railroad freight traffic in the USSR. Regaining the 1940 level after the Second World War required only six years. The horizontal lines connecting 1940 with 1948 and 1916 with 1928 enclose areas that suggest the relative differences in ground lost as a result of the two conflicts. It is clear that, through checking the initial drop in railroad freight traffic and maintaining steady growth after 1942, the Soviet government was able to avert a recurrence of the calamitous deficiencies that had to be made up during the 1920s.

This contrast in railroad performance reflects fundamental political differences between the two periods. The tsarist regime collapsed gradually over two and one-half years; in mid-1941 the Kremlin was paralyzed for only two and one-half weeks. The Nazi invasion, though not unexpected, disrupted administrative controls radiating out from Moscow, but not for long. In spite of strains and tension, effective administrative authority quickly reached out even to the territory being overrun. In particular, during the most difficult months of 1941 and 1942, the Soviet transport and communications system held together, supporting the Party and the armed forces.

The Period of Transport Compression, 1941–1942

How did the railroads do it? The answer lay partly in a long period of preparation.[2] When rapid forced industrialization began at the end of the 1920s, the railroads were asked to handle enlarged flows of heavy freight traffic without much expansion of their facilities; they quickly became a bottleneck. A transport crisis existed for three years. Its serious implications were reviewed in several major speeches at the Seventeenth Party Congress in January 1934. Urging prompt solution to the crisis, the Commissar of War, K. E. Voroshilov, referred to transport as the "twin brother of the Red Army." Soon thereafter, more resources were put into improved railroad facilities, a new set of administrators succeeded in galvanizing railroad operations, and the transport crisis was surmounted.

A key factor here was a new kind of discipline. Discipline is required in the operation of all railroad systems to ensure safety of train movement; it has been symbolized on many European railroads, including those of Russia and the USSR, by putting personnel in uniform. But an emphasis on strict observance of operating rules, on "going by the book," can lead to stodgy performance, and in the USSR from 1934 on, a new generation of railroad personnel was encouraged to be more dynamic. Both at the railroad commissariat in Moscow (NKPS) and out in the field, hard-driving youngsters replaced cautious senior officials.

The purges of 1936–1938 removed three-quarters of the officials operating Soviet railroads, thus ending the substantial progress of 1935 and 1936. Table 3.1 gives the details. The replacements for the purged officials gained useful experience as the railroads carried supplies for military clashes with the Japanese in 1939 near Vladivostok and in Manchuria, as well as in support operations when the USSR took over the Baltic nations and fought against Finland in 1939–1940.

Thus the Soviet railroad system had developed a strong and tested organizational framework by the time World War II began. In addition to the central Commissariat in Moscow, it included 26 regional railroads, each of which managed all common-carrier trackage on its territory. In July and August 1941, flexible arrangements were quickly improvised, thus facilitating the regrouping of railroad administrations in support of specific military campaigns. The organ of control was the Administration for War Communications (UPVOSO), a long-standing organization established on 5 March 1918, under the Supreme War Council, which was reorganized and restaffed to meet emergency conditions. This administration provided an effective link between the Kremlin and the railroads in dealing with ensuing emergencies.[3]

The altered balance between the demands faced by the railroads and resources available for meeting them emerged as a second factor accounting for railroad success. The western regions occupied by the Nazis had generated some 40 percent of Soviet rail freight traffic, and this demand was erased. Most of the locomotives and freight cars used to meet this demand were evacuated and were thus available for use on unoccupied territory. Difficulties arose, not because of shortages in motive power and rolling stock, but rather from a lack of trackage and space for storing or transferring cars and locomotives on the remaining parts of the railroad system.

As new demands for rail freight service arose from reestablished evacuated plants, hasty and energetic efforts began to meet them. Sidings and spur lines were added, yards were enlarged, connecting links put in, and hundreds of miles of new line were built, adding increments of rail capacity tailored to the altered demands of the wartime economy.

In a large geographic sense, it might be said that after an unintended retreat by Soviet forces, very stubborn defense of unoccupied territory ensued. The railroads illustrate this policy. During the 1920s and 1930s, no effort had been made to build lateral north-south lines near the western frontier across the radial lines leading eastward, though Russia had suffered from their absence during World War I. In the fall of 1941, however, construction work began hastily on a north-south rail line parallel to the Volga River from near Kazan through Saratov west of the river to a point above Stalingrad. This *rokadnaia* (an adjective derived from the chess term "rook") served as a "second strategic line along the Volga,"[4] which, together with two shorter lines from the south, brought huge supplies for the battle of Stalingrad.

Table 3.1 Railroad Management Personnel, by Administrative Level and Length of Time in Current Assignment, as of 13 November 1938

	Appointed before 1 November 1937		Appointed from Nov. to 1 April 1938		Appointed since 1 April 1938		Number Enumerated
	Number	%	Number	%	Number	%	
Heads of NKPS administrations	9	33.3	1	3.7	17	63.0	27
Deputy heads, NKPS administrations	16	27.0	12	20.3	31	52.7	59
NKPS section heads	42	28.5	49	33.1	57	48.4	148
Subtotal, Commissariat	67	28.5	62	26.7	105	44.8	234
Heads of individual railroads	14	35.0	9	22.5	17	42.5	40
Deputy heads, railroads	7	9.5	53	71.6	14	18.9	74
Heads of basic services	60	31.1	84	43.5	59	25.4	193
Heads of fifteen sections	170	31.2	80	14.8	293	54.0	543
Subtotal, railroad central adm.	251	29.5	226	26.8	373	43.7	850
Heads of traffic divisions	42	17.2	163	66.5	40	16.3	245
Heads of railroad stations	66	16.2	141	34.4	199	49.4	406
Heads of locomotive divisions	87	35.4	85	34.6	75	30.0	247
Heads of locomotive depots	75	20.2	93	25.0	202	54.8	370
Heads of line sections	135	21.6	205	33.5	276	44.9	616
Subtotal, railroad field adm.	405	21.5	687	36.4	792	42.1	1884
Total, all management levels	723	24.3	975	33.0	1270	42.7	2968

Source: B. P. Beshchev, chief editor, Zheleznodorozhnyi transport v gody industrializatsii SSSR (1926–1941), A. G. Naporko, chief compiler (Moscow: Izdatel'stvo Transport, 1970), 309.

In checking the Nazi attack and organizing to drive the invaders back, Soviet authorities could draw on very substantial industrial capacity, initially fully equal to Germany's. The invasion required imaginative and well-organized readjustments, however, that made use of an effective transport and communications sector. In spite of occasional setbacks and errors, this sector of the economy managed to meet the demands placed on it.

Severe winters hampered transport operations during World War II, but the USSR was better able to deal with them than were Nazi occupying forces. In the first winter of the war, Soviet troops were better clad than the invaders. A truck road across frozen Lake Ladoga provided a lifeline for Leningrad. The civilian population was resourceful in finding firewood for stoking steam locomotives when Donbas coal was not available. In front of Stalingrad, the invaders' transport difficulties in the fall and winter of 1942–1943 contributed to their defeat.

During the war and ever since, the USSR has stressed the importance of an eastern industrial base, built up before 1940 "behind the Urals,"[5] as a key factor in Soviet victory. The transport implication is that very long distances were involved between front and rear, especially as the front moved westward. Long hauls were indeed involved, and the average length of haul for railroad freight rose substantially. Another factor, however, served to hold the hauls down.

As shown in Figure 3.2, half the industrial output of the war years came from Soviet territory west of the usual boundary of the eastern regions. Even when this middle band of territory (primarily the Volga valley) was immediately behind the front and subject to Nazi bombing, it contributed half the country's output. In the later stages of the war, additional output was more readily obtained here and in temporarily occupied regions than in the east. As the need for both military and reconstruction supplies shifted steadily westward, the long distances involved in shipments from Siberia became an ever-increasing disadvantage. While the Urals, the Ural-Kuznetsk Kombinat, the Kazakh republic, and Soviet Central Asia all played vital roles in World War II, the unoccupied parts of the European USSR played an equally fundamental role.

The Emergency Restoration Period, 1943–1945

Though Nazi demolition was thorough, Soviet railroad personnel developed great skill in repairing bridges and other key installations quickly. Even during the early months of the evacuation, improvised arrangements for loading and unloading became an art. In support of massive military operations, Soviet railroad personnel invented novel ways of handling train movements, bringing supplies to a front and retrieving empty cars, using only a skeletal single-track network. In rebuilding bridges and improvising freight handling methods, the USSR demonstrated what became evident from analysis of World War II experience in Europe and later experience

Figure 3.2.
Gross Industrial Output, USSR, 1940–1944

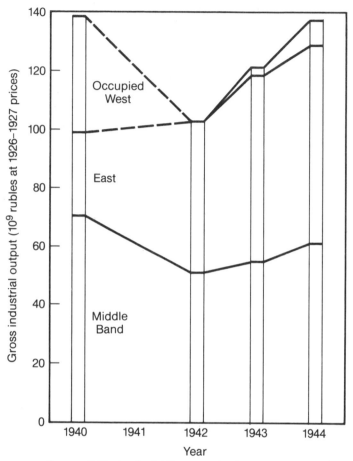

Source: H. Hunter, *Soviet Transportation Policy* (1957), 35, 315

in Korea and Vietnam: determined defenders can thwart efforts to interdict transport lines permanently.

As Soviet forces drove westward across occupied territory, service was restored initially on only a few key lines. The local economy was in ruins and supplies for the front were crucial. Then gradually the connections necessary to support the rebuilding of the general economy were restored. The rebuilding of passenger stations came some years later. Restoration of coal supplies permitted the railroads to abandon the use of wood, thus raising the efficiency of locomotives.

Among the supplies received by the USSR under Lend-Lease and Mutual Aid were almost 2000 steam locomotives and 475,000 trucks, a substantial amount of signaling and communications equipment, steel rails, and 11 million pairs of boots, all of which bolstered Soviet wartime transport performance. The supplies arrived mainly after the battle of Stalingrad, thus contributing to the westward drive during the second stage of the war.

Postwar Consequences of Wartime Transportation Developments

As already indicated, officials at the NKPS (since 1946, the MPS), along with the maritime and river administrations, had shown themselves to be seasoned, competent managers of transportation. There had been crises, controversies, and some administrative reorganization; however, the crises were surmounted and a strong group of transportation leaders emerged from the war. The two most prominent were Ivan Vladimirovich Kovalev, a key member of the War Communications Administration under the Supreme War Council from July 1941 to December 1944, who went on to be minister of railroads (from 1944 to the 1960s), and Boris Pavlovich Beshchev, the head of a major railroad (the Kuibyshev) during World War II, who served as minister for a decade thereafter.

During the Fourth Five-Year Plan (FYP) period (1946–1950), the railroads evidently held the confidence of the Party leadership. Ample resources flowed to the railroads as they helped the economy regain and surpass the prewar level. The policy of stringency toward transport investment that had prevailed in the late thirties gave way temporarily to relative generosity. However, the railroads' success in handling more traffic gave the authorities an excuse to cut back the railroads' share of investment in the Sixth FYP.

One immediate consequence of the war was an unexpected surge in railroad passenger traffic, as shown in Table 3.2 and Figure 3.3. The volume of passenger-kilometers had fallen from 98 billion in 1940 to a level of 38–39 billion in 1942 and 1943. It rose to 57 billion in 1944 and 66 billion in 1945, still far below the prewar level. But in 1946 it jumped almost 50 percent to equal the 1940 level of 98 billion passenger-kilometers, and in 1947 it reached 95 billion. In 1948, however, the total fell back to 75 billion. Both the surge from 1945 to 1946 and the fall from 1947 to 1948 were unexpected by railroad traffic planners. Clearly, the return to their homes of people dislocated by the war exceeded the expectations of railroad authorities. All these figures, incidentally, are for paying passengers; those who may have crowded into passenger cars without tickets and all who rode in freight cars are omitted.

In the early postwar years, Soviet railroads were rebuilt and expanded with unchanged technology. The Lend-Lease locomotives and a similar domestic design, the L series, were quite appropriate for poor track conditions.[6] Though L. M. Kaganovich had been displaced during the war by

Table 3.2 Annual Railroad Passenger Traffic, USSR, 1937–1951, in Millions of Passenger-Kilometers

Year	Traffic	Year	Traffic
1937	90,942	1944	58,100
1938	91,661	1945	66,200
1939	93,726	1946	97,800
1940	97,972	1947	95,100
1941	n.a.	1948	85,200
1942	38,000	1949	81,300
1943	39,300	1950	87,600
		1951	98,500

Sources: 1937–1940 and 1945–1951 from H. Hunter, *Soviet Transportation Policy* (1957), 357. 1942 from G. S. Kravchenko, *Ekonomika SSSR v gody VOV* (Velikoi Otechestvennoi voiny) (1970), 274. 1943 and 1944 from I. V. Kovalev, *Transport v VOV* (1981), 332.

Figure 3.3.
Annual Railroad Passenger Traffic, USSR, 1937–1951

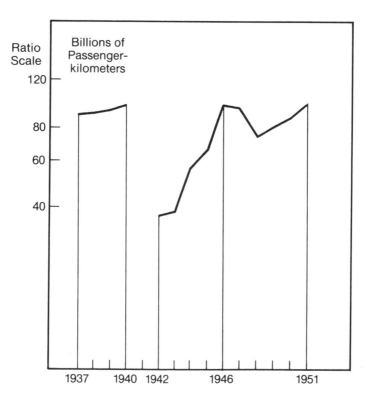

other railroad officials, he regained his influence in the early 1950s and became a focus for opposition to technological change. It was only after Stalin died and Kaganovich lost influence that the steam locomotive gave way to electrics and diesels.

The slow eastward movement of population and industry in the USSR, while temporarily spurred by World War II, was, in fact, checked as a result of postwar restoration in occupied territory. The restoration of this very large area under the Fourth FYP drained massive resources away from eastern development. Industrial centers in the Urals and west Siberia fell back from their wartime levels. Had it not been necessary to make up for Nazi destruction on occupied territory, the prewar trend toward expansion in the east would have continued, and eastern regions would have received most of the plants, equipment, and labor that went instead into rebuilding occupied territory.

Though the Fourth FYP called for a continued shift of industry toward the east, ministerial officials preferred expansion in the European part of the USSR.[7] Output increments could be obtained more quickly and cheaply by adding to existing facilities in the European part of the USSR than at new locations in the east. Labor was easier to obtain and retain. Working conditions were generally more attractive. Hence, branch level decisions thwarted policies embedded in the Fourth Five-Year Plan. Had it not been for World War II, the momentum of the eastward movement might have been better maintained.

Two Summary Judgments

In his February 1946 lecture to the Soviet people, Stalin spoke of World War II as a test of the Soviet system.[8] The Soviet transportation and communications sector—mainly the railroads—like most others, passed the test successfully. Instead of contributing to a collapse of the regime, as Russian railroads had done in World War I, Soviet railroads in World War II provided sturdy links that held the whole country together. They weathered a massive invasion that excised their most developed portions, and, through flexible adaptations and energetic responses, carried the troops and materiel responsible for the Soviet ejection and defeat of the Nazis.

More broadly, both the Party and government as a whole provided a framework of authority and power that succeeded in utilizing the transportation and communications system to maintain control on a continental scale. During World War I outlying portions of the Russian empire slipped out from under effective supervision as St. Petersburg's competence declined. In World War II, by contrast, after approximately 15 days of temporary paralysis, Stalin managed to exert effective coordination through prompt communication reaching to every part of the USSR, an example, indeed, of successful spatial management.

Notes

1. The most thorough official source is the six-volume *Istoriia Velikoi Otechestvennoi voiny Sovetskogo Soiuza, 1941–1945,* commissioned by a Central Committee decree of 12 September 1957, and published in the 1960s. For an evaluation, in English, of military developments, see John Erickson, *The Road to Stalingrad* (London: Weidenfeld & Nicolson, 1975) and *The Road to Berlin* (Boulder: Westview, 1983). The history of wartime Soviet transportation is recounted in detail by Ivan Vladimirovich Kovalev, who draws on archival sources and his own inner-circle experience, in his *Transport v Velikoi Otechestvennoi voine (1941–1945 gg.),* issued by the Institute of History of the USSR Academy of Sciences (Moscow, 1981). Another thorough study from the same institute, using archival sources, is Georgii Aleksandrovich Kumanev's *Sovetskie zhelenodorozhniki v gody Velikoi Otechestvennoi voiny 1941–1945* (Moscow: Izdatel'stvo Akedemii Nauk SSSR, 1963), which has a substantial bibliography.

2. Holland Hunter, *Soviet Transportation Policy* (Cambridge, Mass.: Harvard University Press, 1957), esp. chapters 3 and 4.

3. Kovalev, *op. cit.,* 44–79, esp. 54 and 73–75.

4. Kovalev, *loc. cit.,* 75.

5. This was the title of John Scott's influential 1942 book describing his experiences as a young welder building the steel works at Magnitogorsk.

6. J. N. Westwood, *Soviet Locomotive Technology During Industrialization, 1928–1952* (London: Macmillan, 1982), 189.

7. Timothy Dunmore, *The Stalinist Command Economy* (New York: St. Martin's Press, 1980), *passim,* esp. chaps. 4 and 6.

8. J. V. Stalin, *Speech Delivered by J. V. Stalin at a Meeting of Voters of the Stalin Electoral District, Moscow, February 9, 1946* (Moscow: Foreign Language Publishing House, 1946).

4

Crisis Management in the USSR: The Wartime System of Administration and Control

SANFORD R. LIEBERMAN

In many ways, the magnitude of many of the recurrent crises of the twentieth century has been so great as to make these events qualitatively different from almost all crises of the past.[1] Accordingly, crisis situations have compelled many contemporary regimes to respond with rapid, all-out, effective action. In administrative terms, such a response has required these regimes to circumvent the rigidities of formal bureaucratic institutions and procedures and rely to a large extent both on specially created organs and institutions and on specifically empowered individuals for the execution of particularly important assignments.[2] The use of such extraordinary forms of administration and control in the Soviet Union during World War II provides a major case in point.

Caught off guard by the German invasion of 22 June 1941, the Soviet Union was confronted with the increasingly grim prospect of defeat. Survival necessitated that the Soviet regime rapidly and fully mobilize the country's human and material resources. This, however, required the creation of a special wartime system of administration and control—one that would facilitate operative decision-making and policy implementation, while, at the same time, permitting Stalin and his top associates to retain a fair measure of centralized control over the war effort. In so doing, as would be the case in many other aspects of the war effort, the Soviet regime was to draw heavily upon its past experience in dealing with crisis situations, above all, those dating from the period of the Civil War and Intervention. That significant use was to be made of forms and techniques, especially those of an extraordinary nature that had worked successfully in earlier crises, was owing to the dictator's personal preferences and to the regime's correct perception that this was not the time for experimentation and innovation.

Of particular importance would be the establishment on 30 June 1941, of the State Defense Committee (GKO), which, in certain respects, was modeled after the Council of Workers' and Peasants' Defense that had functioned during the years of the Civil War and Intervention.[3] This extraordinary organ—a kind of inner Politburo with Stalin as chairman and Molotov, Malenkov, Beria, and Voroshilov as its other original members— was accorded "the entire plenitude of power in the country."[4] As such, the State Defense Committee

> issued resolutions which had the force of law in war time. All citizens, all Party, soviet, Komosomol and military organizations were obliged uncondi- tionally to fulfill the decisions and orders of the GKO. It exercised leadership of the national economy in the interests of war production, led the construction of the armed forces and their administration, took measures for the guaranteeing of social order and security, and created, in necessary instances, special committees and administrations on matters pertaining to military-economic and defense construction.[5]

More specifically, the GKO was concerned with

> the appointment and replacement of the higher-ranking military commanders; the preparation of reserves for the army in the field; the solution of important military-strategic questions; the adjustment of the work of industry, transport, and agriculture to the conditions of wartime; the supply of the population and the army with produce; the procurement of fuel, the preparation of labor reserves and the allocation of labor among the various industrial objects; and the battle against enemy spies.[6]

The establishment of the GKO also had an important effect on the Soviet Union's regular system of political and administrative controls. According to Leonard Schapiro, with the establishment of the State Defense Committee,

> the whole system of balance between the Party organizations on the one hand, and the soviet and economic organizations, on the other, which it had been found necessary to maintain, however imperfectly, even in the gravest emer- gencies in the past, was thus swept aside. . . .[7]

This is not to say that the GKO supplanted the regular system of controls. Rather, as indicated earlier, it was superimposed upon the entire system in order to circumvent the traditionally rigid and time-consuming aspects of bureaucratic procedure and thus to provide the Soviet regime with both the administrative flexibility and the centralization of control that the war effort required.

"The keynote of wartime administration . . . [according to Schapiro] was rationalization."[8] That this was, in fact, the case is indicated by the rather inchoate nature of the GKO's modus operandi. Of particular significance, in this respect, is the following description of the operational aspects of the State Defense Committee provided by the then head of the rear of the Red Army, General A. Khrulev:

> The *apparat* of the GKO was essentially that of the Central Committee of the Party, the Council of People's Commissars and the people's commissariats. . . . Members of the GKO making reports, prepared drafts each according to his sphere of activity, and always entered freely into the office of the Chairman of the GKO. Hither uninterruptedly came military leaders, people's commissars and other responsible individuals not only at [Stalin's] request . . . but also on their own initiative if some important, unexpected problem had come up. Meetings of the GKO in the usual sense of the term—that is, with definite agendas, secretaries and protocols—did not exist. The procedure of reaching agreement with Gosplan, the people's commissariats and departments, on questions of supply of the army, was reduced to a minimum. This enabled . . . the leaders of each sector of the economy . . . to do everything that was necessary for the front, for the defeat of the enemy more rapidly. Conscious initiative of central and local workers was the key.[9]

Sketchy though it is, Khrulev's account is the single most complete account of the GKO's modus operandi available. This description may, however, be expanded somewhat by piecing together a number of comments from various other Soviet and non-Soviet sources. First, it is evident that not all business was conducted by the full committee. Indeed, one Soviet source states that "questions frequently were examined solely by its [the committee's] chairman, assistants or individual members."[10] This same source cites such actions as an example of Stalin's failure to observe democratic procedure or free discussion.[11] While not denying this fact, it should also be pointed out that the preoccupation of committee members with a variety of important assignments—some of which took them away from Moscow—necessitated their absence from committee meetings.

As for the actual dynamics of decision-making, the following description is presented as an approximation of the committee's modus operandi. Each committee member was personally responsible for certain aspects of the war effort—political, military, security, and/or economic.[12] As such, they not only oversaw their respective areas of endeavor, but also maintained prime responsibility for solving the various problems that confronted their particular sectors. Brainstorming sessions seem to have been an extremely important problem-solving technique. Such work was done in part through a number of special committees and commissions set up under the GKO, the Council of People's Commissars, or other important central organs. For example, a transportation committee of the GKO was established in February 1942 under Stalin's chairmanship (with A. A. Andreev as assistant chairman).

> The Committee planned and regulated the freightage of railroad, sea and river transport, coordinated shipping, and worked out measures for improving the material base . . . of the country's entire transport system. . . .[13]

More frequently, however, when confronted with some problem, the individual GKO members simply called a meeting and brought people together who had the necessary degree of expertise and power to solve problems that had arisen in their particular spheres of activity. In addition to the regular participants of such meetings, individual experts and advisors were often called in on a moment's notice to help resolve a particular question.[14] Such face-to-face attempts at problem solving fit in well with the demands of wartime. Time was of the essence—writing memos or holding a series of individual meetings was too time-consuming. Emel'ianov describes a number of such sessions in his memoirs:

> I [Emel'ianov] received an invitation to the Kremlin, to a meeting called by Voznesenskii. In his reception room, I met Tevosian, Malyshev, Lomako, and several more people . . . [Voznesenskii] reported how serious the situation with respect to nickel was—"We, in essence, will allocate nickel only for the production of armor, gun steel and the aviation industry—for the production of crankshafts"—he said. "In order to fulfill the program we must have"—and he named a quantity of nickel. "We have, however, . . . and he again named a figure"—"you are specialists and Communists too. I cannot take the entire responsibility for the defense . . . [effort] . . . on myself—tell me what needs to be done? Where can we get the missing nickel? How shall we get out of this situation . . . ?"
>
> The participants of the meeting expressed their opinions on how the arsenal of science should be utilized in order to get out of the difficult situation with nickel. In the process of discussion, the idea of a steel-substitute was born and polished. A way out was found. The difficult task was decided.[15]

If the subject under consideration could not be resolved at this level or was of sufficient importance, it might be brought to the attention of several GKO members, the full committee, or perhaps Stalin himself. The same consultative process would be followed again with the responsible GKO member acting as the principal reporter. Moreover, it must be stressed that even in Stalin's presence this process frequently involved a considerable amount of genuine discussion and debate. Despite both the obvious adverse effects of one-man tyrannical rule on bureaucratic initiative[16] and statements to the effect that Stalin himself often made decisions according to his mood rather than according to his understanding of a particular question,[17] evidence exists which suggests that the Soviet leader frequently was willing to listen and accept advice from his civilian and military advisors and associates. Indeed, he seems to have done so with increasing frequency as the war progressed. In this respect, his actions were directly contrary to those of Hitler.[18]

The information and advice Stalin received came in the first instance from his immediate associates. Much of this was done in an informal setting such as late night dinners at Stalin's *dacha*. Milovan Djilas, who had occasion to attend several of these dinners, notes that at these dinners, the Soviet leaders were at their closest, most intimate with each other. Everyone would tell the news from his bailiwick, whom he met that day, and what plans he was making.[19]

And again,

Stalin was of a lively, almost restless temperament. He always questioned himself and others; and he argued with himself and others.[20]

In some instances, such questioning was an attempt on the part of the dictator to find out where other members of the State Defense Committee stood on a given issue. Such apparently was the case with the GKO meeting held on 19 October 1941, at the height of the Battle of Moscow. According to one of the participants in this meeting,

we were gathered together in the evening in Stalin's office in the Kremlin— "Will we fight for Moscow?"—asked Stalin. As usual, he paced around the room, stuffing cigarette tobacco in his pipe. All were silent, then Stalin decided to ask all those who were present personally. Going first up to Molotov, he repeated his question—"We will fight" . . . [Molotov] . . . answered. So answered, one after the other, all those who were present. Then, right there, with Stalin [himself] . . . dictating, the GKO resolution which began with those memorable words, "It hereby is declared . . ." was written.[21]

Kuznetsov also notes that Stalin relied on experts to check on the work of various people's commissars saying, "Now I will check up on you. Now we will hear what the practical workers have to say."[22] Indeed, not only does it appear that Stalin frequently sought out the opinions of his advisors and associates, but also it was sometimes possible for people who had worthwhile suggestions and the courage of their convictions to argue their points of view and eventually win the day. Marshal Bagramian, for example, notes that at a *Stavka* (General Headquarters of the Supreme Command) meeting, a report was given with which he himself did not agree. He kept silent, however, and the matter was apparently resolved to the satisfaction of everyone present, including Stalin. "Suddenly Stalin asked—'but perhaps you [Bagramian] have another opinion on this [matter]?'"[23] Thus given an opportunity to reopen the subject, Bagramian presented his views, which subsequently were approved.[24] In point of fact, it seems that Stalin placed great emphasis on achieving a clash of ideas as a way of obtaining the correct solution or best answer to a given problem. Marshals Zhukov and Konev, for example, having been recalled to Moscow from the Eastern Front in April 1945 for a top-level conference on the taking of Berlin, were asked by the Soviet dictator who should be given the task of capturing the German capital. When each man argued in favor of the use of his own forces, Stalin ordered both of them to prepare separate detailed plans and to report back within forty-eight hours. Two days later, the two marshals presented their proposals to Stalin.[25] In this instance, "having listened to the two proposals, Stalin now approved them both. But to Zhukov went the responsibility of capturing Berlin."[26]

The participants in such meetings (as well as in lower-level meetings) were expected not only to have the necessary degree of expertise in order to discuss a specific issue but also to be prepared to do so. Poor performance in such conferences was penalized rather severely.[27] Furthermore, the participants' awareness of Stalin's reputation and personality made it considerably more difficult for them to deliver a proper presentation. High-ranking officials could be reduced to stammering incoherence under the pressure of Stalin's sharp questioning.[28] Military officials, however, seem to have fared somewhat better than civilian authorities in such sessions—perhaps because, at a time when so much depended on the military, they had to be treated more circumspectly than their civilian counterparts.

In the last analysis, as was indicated by the Zhukov-Konev episode, decision-making authority rested squarely in Stalin's own hands. Once this stage had been reached, the appropriate GKO member and/or expert(s) would be given the task of drafting the actual resolution. It would then be presented to Stalin once again for final approval. Such, for example, was the case with the decision to form the rear of the Red Army. Mikoyan thus informed General Khrulev by phone that

> the Supreme Commander [entrusts] . . . you with the task of preparing a draft of a GKO resolution on the organization of the rear of the Red Army in wartime. Representatives of *Stavka* were immediately drawn into this work. . . . At the end of July, the draft of the resolution GKO was prepared. Leading workers of the GKO were gathered in Stalin's office. Having read the document, the Supreme Commander silently passed it to the head of the General Staff, G. K. Zhukov. Zhukov quickly acquainted himself with the draft and categorically declared—"I don't agree. The authors of this document want organs of the rear to replace the General Staff." Having cast an expressive glance at G. K. Zhukov, the Supreme Commander took back the draft and immediately signed it.[29]

Although other extraordinary organs, including the Council for Evacuation[30] and city committees of defense (*gorkos*) in a number of frontline areas,[31] were established during the war, no special administrative machinery existed for implementing the decisions of the GKO.[32] This meant that the greater part of the State Defense Committee's business had to be executed through the regular channels of Party and state administration. Thus, according to Sinitsyn,

> resolutions of the State Defense Committee were addressed directly to the organs of state power and administration, to Councils of People's Commissars of union and autonomous republics, executive committees of *oblast* and *krai* soviets of workers' deputies, to various governmental institutions and administrations, to people's commissariats and committees, departments and enterprises. In these resolutions, concrete assignments were given . . . [and] it was stated who and in what length of time these assignments had to be fulfilled.[33]

The superimposition of the State Defense Committee—even with the addition of other extraordinary organs—upon the regime's regular system of administration and control, however, was by itself an inadequate organizational response to the crisis of all-out war. Something more was needed, something that not only would knit the regime's regular and extraordinary organizations and institutions into one workable whole, but would also compensate for the failure of the Soviet leadership to work out a detailed set of protocols on administrative operations and jurisdictional boundaries in time of war. This something extra was provided by the personalization of power that was a hallmark of the Stalin era. Although this phenomenon did not either originate or end with Stalin, the regime's reliance on personalization of power during the Stalin era clearly owed much to the personality of the dictator. In fact, the Soviets themselves, recognizing the extent to which one man, Stalin, dominated the entire era, aptly refer to this period as "the era of the cult of the personality."

What we know about Stalin's personality, in particular his megalomania and apparent paranoia, suggests a nature that would seek to imprint itself firmly and fully upon the regime's system of administration and control—that is, to personalize (or Stalinize) it. And, indeed, during the years of his rule, Stalin proceeded to do precisely this. His nocturnal work schedule became the schedule for much of the country's bureaucracy. His ruthlessness and arbitrariness provided subordinates at all levels with a standard of behavior to emulate. His personalized style of leadership was reflected in the similar style of responsible lower-ranking officials. The system had not only its Stalin, but also its countless "little Stalins."

In addition to the considerable authority sometimes exercised informally by Soviet officials, personalization of power also existed—even before the war—in a number of institutionalized forms, the most important of which was the plenipotentiary system. Basically, what the system involved was the delegation by some governmental or Party organ (ranging in importance during the war from the GKO itself, the Central Committee of the All-Union Party, the Council of People's Commissars, and individual commissariats, to the various local organizations) of considerable and indeed, at times, almost carte blanche authority, to a particular individual, usually for the execution of a specific assignment. In the case of the State Defense Committee, the committee

> had plenipotentiaries in all military-industrial commissariats and departments, territories . . . [and regions], . . . [and] in important enterprises and construction projects. They did what had to be done to implement the decisions of the GKO . . . and to mobilize forces and resources for the war effort.[34]

In some instances, top-ranking leaders like Malenkov, Andreev, and Voznesenskii were pressed into service as plenipotentiaries. In other cases, the individual involved might, for example, be a people's commissar, a plant manager, or a local official.[35] It was hoped that, by combining powerful mandates with personal expertise (familiarity with a particular problem or geographical area) and/or personal authority, these extraordinary officials would be able to accomplish their assignments.[36]

The plenipotentiary system had something in particular to recommend its use by Stalin—it offered him a mechanism for the closest possible approximation of a one-man exercise of total power. For Stalin, the ideal system would have been one that permitted him to be everywhere at once and to do everything single-handedly. Lacking this possibility, the next best thing was to grant considerable or even near-total mandates of authority to select individuals to deal with particular problems. By doing this, Stalin was able to bring great amounts of power to bear on particular situations while still keeping responsibility focused on specific individuals. In a sense, he was not giving up any power at all because such individuals were acting as his eyes, ears, and fists in the field. This system was forceful, arbitrary, and even ruthless in its operation. This, however, was not only what Stalin desired, and in fact demanded, but was also what the Soviet Union itself would need, especially in the crisis of all-out war.

An interesting and important case study of the actual operation of this extraordinary system of administration and control is provided by the evacuation of industry during the war.[37] As noted earlier, in the summer and fall of 1941 the Soviet regime was confronted with the increasingly grim prospect of defeat. The situation in the field was critical enough. However, the ever-mounting territorial losses presented an additional deadly threat to the USSR's ability to continue to wage war. The areas already lost or in danger of being lost were rich in mineral, agricultural, and human resources and formed the heartland of the Soviet industrial complex.[38] The loss of natural and human resources, while a very serious matter, could, however, be survived since the Soviet Union had at least minimally sufficient quantities of those resources required to continue its wartime struggle. But the loss of a major portion of its industrial strength would be a different matter. Thus, for the Soviet regime to survive, it had to move quickly to evacuate as much as possible of its industrial resources from actual and potential war zones to the deep rear.

Initially, however, the evacuation project was marked by chaos, particularly in the western border regions that lay in the immediate path of the rapidly advancing enemy forces. Because the regime's evacuation machinery was not yet functioning, Party and governmental organs in these areas had to deal with the problems of evacuation themselves.[39] Indeed, at the start of hostilities, contingency plans for the evacuation of industry did not even exist! The absence of such plans, the speed of the enemy advance, the immensity of the task at hand, and the lack of power and competence on the part of the local officials in border areas to cope with the larger issues and problems of evacuation all combined, in most instances, to doom the efforts of the local organs to failure.[40]

If the evacuation was to succeed, and, indeed, if the Soviet Union was to survive the crisis of war, an all-out mobilization effort would have to be made. This, however, necessitated the creation of a special wartime system of administration and control, at the apex of which, as previously noted, would be the State Defense Committee (GKO). Accordingly, the GKO assumed overall leadership of the evacuation process. The committee itself, moreover, would issue many of the most important decrees relating to the work of evacuation.[41]

The work of the evacuation, especially overall planning and coordination, was too enormous and complex, however, to be carried out without some sort of organizational expression of its own. Accordingly, on 24 June 1941, two days after the start of the war, the regime formed a Council for Evacuation under the Council of People's Commissars of the USSR[42] and charged it with

> leading the work of re-basing enterprises, collective farms, tractor stations (MTS), population, produce . . . [and] material objects, and with placing all evacuated [objects and individuals] . . . in new locales.[43]

More specifically, the mandate given the Council for Evacuation included the following: the establishment of evacuation priorities and timetables; the determination of areas of relocation; the allocation of means of transportation; and the preservation of goods and the care of the evacuees en route to their destination in the Soviet rear.[44]

In keeping with the critical importance of the council's assignment, great emphasis was placed upon its maintaining effective, efficient leadership of the entire evacuation and relocation process. The nature of both the membership and the organizational structure of the council reflects this concern for operative leadership.

Headed at first by Lazar Kaganovich, a long-time member of the Politburo with a reputation as a tough and able economic troubleshooter,[45] the council, at one time or another, numbered among its members Mikoyan, Kosygin, Shvernik, Pervukhin, Saburov, Shaposhnikov, and a "representative from the People's Commissariat of Internal Affairs (NKVD)."[46] Being thus composed of a small number of important officials, some of whom served as representatives of organizations directly engaged in or having a significant interest in the work of evacuation,[47] and possessing a wide-sweeping and powerful mandate, the Council for Evacuation was in a position to transact much of its business quickly and with a minimum of red tape. That its *apparat* numbered only 80 to 85 people further enhanced the council's ability to maintain effective leadership of the evacuation process.[48] With a staff that small, much of the work of formulating and implementing the details of the council's evacuation-relocation plans had to be performed by the regime's regular instruments of administration and control, thereby allowing the council's staff and members to concentrate on major or particularly urgent questions and problems. At the center, such assistance was provided, in the first instance, by the commissariats, which did much of the actual planning for the evacuation of particular industrial units.[49]

In the field, the various aspects and stages of the evacuation process were controlled by a number of plenipotentiaries and other specially appointed officials. The most important of these officials were those who held mandates from the State Defense Committee. In some cases, high-ranking or technically expert officials were sent out from Moscow to oversee a particular aspect of the evacuation process. Thus, for example, A. G. Sheremet'ev, an Assistant People's Commissar for Ferrous Metallurgy, was dispatched in August 1941 to Zaporozh'e as the GKO's plenipotentiary to oversee the evacuation of the huge Zaporozhstal Metallurgical Works.[50] In other instances, the individual given such a mandate was a local Party, governmental, or economic official.[51] The utilization of such local officials in the capacity of plenipotentiaries had an obvious advantage since they had firsthand knowledge of both the enterprises and locales marked for evacuation. On the other hand, although the power attached to a GKO mandate was considerable, some aspects of the work of evacuation were considered so important that they required the leadership of very high-ranking Party and governmental officials from Moscow, officials who could add their own personal power, prestige, and influence to their already high-powered mandates. Thus, for example, on 25 October 1941,

> the . . . [Council of People's Commissars and the Central Committee of the All-Union Communist Party] instructed the vice-chairman of the Council of People's Commissars, N. A. Voznesenskii, "to represent . . . [the Council] in Kuibyshev," "to direct the work of the people's commissariats that were being evacuated to the East . . . ," and to strive to get the factories that had been evacuated to the Volga [region], the Urals, and Siberia into operation at the earliest possible date. . . ."
>
> [That same day] . . . the Politburo authorized Secretary of the Party . . . Central Committee, A. A. Andreev, who was . . . then in Kuibyshev with a part of the Central Committee's apparat . . . , to issue orders and instructions in the name of the Central Committee for the *obkoms* [regional Party committees] of the Volga region, the Urals, Central Asia and Siberia "on questions . . . concerning the organization of industry . . . [in connection with the evacuation of enterprises to these *oblasts* [regions]. . . .[52]

Although some semblance of control over the activities of these two high-ranking officials was maintained—Voznesenskii, for example, was required to send progress reports back to Moscow every five or six days[53]—the breadth and force of their mandates made it clear that the regime had, in effect, given them full discretionary power to do whatever the situation required.

In addition to the State Defense Committee plenipotentiaries, a considerable number of other special officials holding mandates from various of the regime's regular and extraordinary central organs and organizations, including the Council for Evacuation, individual commissariats, the State Planning Committee (Gosplan), the All-Union Council of Trade Unions, and the central committees of individual trade unions, also were involved in the various on-the-scene aspects of the work of evacuation, relocation, and reconstruction.

Other than the plenipotentiaries of the State Defense Committee, the most important of the extraordinary officials to participate in the evacuation process were the inspectors for the Council for Evacuation and the council's plenipotentiaries for particular commissariats. The group of inspectors, headed by the then deputy chairman of the Council of People's Commissars of the USSR, A. N. Kosygin, consisted of a relatively small number of "leading workers" who were charged with maintaining control over the evacuation process,[54] whereas the plenipotentiaries for commissariats, as their title suggests, exercised supervision over the evacuation, relocation, and reconstruction activities of particular commissariats.[55] Much of the credit for the success that the evacuation-relocation-reconstruction effort ultimately achieved must be given to them and to the other specially mandated officials who acted in the name of the regime or extraordinary organizations and instruments of control.

Just as was the case at the center, the work of evacuation and relocation required some sort of organizational expression of its own at the local level. Accordingly, a large number of local organs of the Council for Evacuation were established in areas where evacuation-relocation work was going on. Included among such organs were: city, regional, and republic commissions for evacuation; evacuation administrations for regions, territories (krais), and republics; evacuation points (evacopoints) at factories and stations; bases for transshipping (evacobases) at large railroad and port centers; and regional, city (gorod) and district (raion) commissions for the reception and placement of evacuated enterprises and their personnel.[56] Composed, as a rule, of a relatively small number of leading officials drawn from the various local organizations taking part in the work of evacuation, relocation, or reconstruction, these bodies apparently were subordinated both to the Council for Evacuation and to the regular soviet organs in the areas in question.[57]

This system of dual subordination seems to have been based, in part, on the view that the Council for Evacuation's own operative leadership of the work of evacuation could best be maintained if the council were not burdened with running a highly developed administrative system of its own. At the same time, viewed from a somewhat different perspective, the subordination of the local evacuation organs to the territorial soviet organizations undoubtedly was aimed at improving effective leadership over such work in the locales themselves. Many of the questions and problems that fell within the purview of the local evacuation organs—mobilization of manpower and evacuations into the immediate rear, to name but two—had to be dealt with on a purely local basis, and therefore, some form of local coordination and control was required. This, the regime may have felt, could best be provided by the regular soviet organs that (along with their local Party counterparts) had fulfilled such functions in the prewar period. Regular local organizations, in particular Party organizations, also played a key role in other aspects of the evacuation-relocation process such as the provision of needed information to higher bodies and plenipotentiaries[58] and the mobilization of local resources, especially manpower resources.[59] In general, however, these organizations occupied a position auxiliary to that of the higher, in particular the extraordinary, organs and their plenipotentiaries in all stages of the evacuation process.[60] Moreover, in assisting in this work, the local organs themselves made considerable use of extraordinary forms and methods of administration and control. Thus they not only appointed their own plenipotentiaries for specific geographical areas and for particular projects,[61] but also formed numerous special committees and operative groups to assist in the work of evacuation, relocation, and reconstruction.[62] As was the case at the center, such extraordinary efforts would prove to be vital to the success of the evacuation-relocation process.

In theory, at least, the on-the-scene activity of the various plenipotentiaries and special organs and commissions, especially when taken together with the work performed by both the regular local organizations and the military authorities, should have provided strong and effective leadership to the evacuation process. Given both the supposed strength of their special mandates or regular powers and their common involvement in many evacuation projects, they conceivably could have resolved many pressing issues and problems on their own. In many cases, such on-the-scene coordination was, in fact, effected and the desired results achieved. In other instances, however, the on-the-scene efforts of various plenipotentiaries, regular and special organs, and commissions clearly proved to be a source of conflict and confusion. In part, this was the result of the sheer number of officials, organs, and organizations taking part in the evacuation process.[63] In addition, many officials engaged in such work (except perhaps those charged with overall leadership) tended to view problems in terms of the interests of their own organs and organizations rather than in terms of those of the regime as a whole. For example, in Murmansk in June 1941, the representatives of several people's commissariats, not considering the interests of the oblast, attempted to take as much equipment from their factories as possible. The *obkom* and the Military Council of the Fourteenth Army, however, informed the industrial officials that

> they were categorically forbidden to take equipment and to transfer cadres beyond the boundaries of the oblast without the permission of the military council.[64]

Compounding this organizational conflict and confusion was, as noted earlier, the failure of the regime to draw up even general evacuation plans prior to the start of the war. Once the war began, such plans had to be formulated quickly and under great pressure. As a result, the Soviet leadership was in no position to pay more than cursory attention to such organizational niceties of the evacuation process as the establishment of exact jurisdictional boundaries between the various regular and extraordinary organizations and agencies involved in such work. To be sure, there was no doubting the overriding authority attached to a GKO mandate, especially in the hands of an Andreev or a Voznesenskii. But what was one to say about the relative scope (and power) of the mandate of a plenipotentiary for the Commissariat for Ferrous Metallurgy versus that of his counterpart for the Commissariat for the Chemical Industry or of their mandates vis-à-vis that of a special representative of the Commissariat for Railroads or of Gosplan?

Answers to such questions could be provided only by the central leadership of the evacuation process—the Council for Evacuation or in some instances, the GKO itself. Not surprisingly, given the importance accorded the principle of personalization of power in the Stalinist system of rule, the answer to the question of who won out in such jurisdictional disputes, as well as in competitions for scarce (and usually centrally allocated) resources seems to have depended not only on the relative importance of the various projects but also on the personal qualities and personal influence of the plenipotentiaries and other officials in charge of on-the-scene evacuation operations. At the same time, it is also quite clear that no matter what the outcome of particular incidents of interorganizational rivalry was, such demands for centralization of control as those noted previously had to place certain limits on the regime's quest for operative leadership in the field.

Despite these and many other problems and shortcomings, between July and November 1941, a total of 1523 industrial enterprises, including more than 1360 large plants were evacuated to the rear.[65] Moreover, by mid-1942, more than 1200 of these evacuated enterprises had been restored to production.[66] The struggle for survival, at least on the industrial front, had been won.

Conclusion

In viewing the first phase of the war, especially the summer and fall of 1941, historians and other students of the Soviet Union's involvement in the Second World War have tended to focus their attention on the numerous serious mistakes made and setbacks suffered by the Soviet regime. And the facts are there to justify such a focus. Yet, at the same time, all too often analysts overlook the fact that, despite the precarious position in which it found itself during this period, the Soviet regime still possessed sufficient strength, and sufficient physical, moral, and administrative resources to make the evacuation of industry the great success it was. The Stalinist system, even at the height of the crisis of war, still appears to have been viable. Indeed, despite all of the negative aspects of Stalinism, including its basic responsibility for the country's being unprepared for war in June 1941, it can be argued that, given the Soviet Union's overall position at the start of the war, it is doubtful whether the country would have been able to survive had a different system been in effect. In a way, the Stalinist system—a garrison state that made considerable use of extraordinary forms of administration and control even in the prewar period—was itself a vital factor both in the evacuation process and in the Soviet Union's ability to survive in a time of all-out war.

Notes

1. The very magnitude of twentieth-century crises has been, at least partially, the result of the revolution in technology that the century has witnessed. At the same time, rather paradoxically, this revolution, especially in the spheres of transportation and communications, has provided the technical means by which regimes have been able to make an effective administrative response to crisis situations.

2. See, for example, War Industries Board (Bernard M. Baruch, chairman), *American Industry in the War,* rev. ed. (New York: Prentice-Hall, 1941), and Merle Fainsod, Lincoln Gordon, and Joseph C. Palamountain, Jr., *Government and the American Economy,* 3rd ed. (New York, 1959), 824–869, for discussions of the use of such forms of administration and control in the economic sphere in the United States during World War I and World War II respectively.

3. For a description of both the organization and the functions of the Council of Workers' and Peasants' Defense, see *Istoriia Velikoi Otechestvennoi voiny Sovetskogo Soiuza (IVOvSS),* vol. 4:104.

4. Ibid., 6:103. Kaganovich, Mikoyan, and Voznesenskii would be added to the membership of the GKO in February 1942 and Bulganin would replace Voroshilov as a member of the State Defense Committee in 1944.

5. Ibid.

6. V. A. Tskulin, *Istoriia gosudarstvennykh uchrezhdenii SSSR 1936–1965* (Moscow, 1966), 35–36, and A. M. Sinitsyn, "Chrezvychainye organy Sovetskogo gosudarstva v gody Velikoi Otechestvennoi voiny," *Voprosy istorii,* no. 2 (February 1955):34.

7. Leonard Schapiro, *The Communist Party of the Soviet Union* (New York, 1959), 493.

8. Ibid.

9. Khrulev, A. V. "Stanovlenie strategicheskogo tyla v Velikoi Otechestvennoi voine." *Voenno-istoricheskii zhurnal,* no. 6 (June 1961), 66.

10. *IVOvSS,* 6:103.

11. Ibid.

12. For example, in addition to their other duties, Molotov exercised oversight over tank production, Malenkov over aircraft and engine production (30 September 1943), and Beria over the production of armaments and munitions. *Pravda.*

13. *IVOvSS,* 2:526.

14. The following statement is typical: "Molotov called me at the start of 1943. 'We are just beginning a meeting at my place. Can you come quickly to the Kremlin?' " [Emel'ianov, "O vremeni, o tovarishchakh, o sebe. Zapiski inzhenera." *Novy mir,* no. 2 (February 1967):132].

15. Ibid., 129.

16. That this had been the case in the prewar period was to have a serious effect both on the administrative system's ability to cope with a wartime situation and on the nature of the emergency changes that had to be introduced into the system in time of war. See, for example, N. Kuznetsov, "Before the War," *International Affairs,* no. 1 (January 1967):102–103 and no. 3 (March 1967):94, and Il'ya Ehrenburg, *The War: 1941–1945* (New York, 1964), 14.

17. N. N. Voronov, *Na sluzhbe voennoi* (Moscow, 1963), 229.

18. To be sure, Stalin's interests in and concern for certain aspects of the war effort, especially military affairs, led him on occasion to disregard the counsel of his advisors and to superimpose his own views on a given question. This was particularly true in the early stages of the war.

19. Milovan Djilas, *Conversations with Stalin* (New York, 1962), 77.

20. Ibid., 69.

21. N. G. Kuznetsov, "Gody voiny," *Oktiabr',* no. 8 (August 1968):175.

22. Ibid., 153.

23. L. Sandalov, "Put' Sovetskogo polkovodtsa," *Voenno-istoricheskii zhurnal,* no. 11 (November 1967):42.

24. Ibid.

25. Cornelius Ryan, *The Last Battle* (London, 1966), 248–256.

26. Ibid., 255.

27. Thus, for example, according to N. A. Antipenko, Mikoyan called the heads of the rears of fronts to a meeting in the Kremlin to discuss the preparation of food supplies for winter.

> The head of the rear of the Volkhov Front was the first to speak. Having gotten up, he began to leaf through his little notebook in search for information, but the temperamental Mikoyan switched from one question to another, and the reporter did not succeed in finding the required page, and had not committed anything to memory. Extremely upset by the head of the rear's lack of information, A. I. Mikoyan then and there ordered that he be dismissed from his post.

(N. A. Antipenko, *Na glavnom napravlenii* [Moscow, 1967], 88).

28. See, for example, V. Emel'ianov, *Novy mir,* no. 2 (February 1967):88–89.

29. A. Khrulev, *Voenno-istoricheskii zhurnal,* no. 6 (June 1961):68–69.

30. For a further discussion of the work of the Council for Evacuation, see 66–71.

31. Such committees of defense were formed in, among other places, Stalingrad, Sevastopol, Tula, Rostov, Murmansk, Voronezh, Kalinin, Astrakhan and Kamyshinsk. (A. M. Sinitsyn, "Chrezvychainye organy Sovetskogo gosudarstva v gody Velikoi Otechestvennoi voiny," *Voprosy istorii,* no. 2 (February 1955):35, and *IVOvSS,* vol. 6:104). The Astrakhan and Kamyshinsk committees of defense, moreover, were subordinated to the Stalingrad committee of defense (Sinitsyn, p. 36). The defense of Moscow and Leningrad, generally speaking, was handled by the State Defense Committee itself (ibid., p. 35). Furthermore, in a number of other combat areas, paramount civilian authority was vested in so-called "constricted" local *ispolkoms*. These bodies, in many respects, were quite similar to the city committees of defense.

32. However, according to Kravchenko, "the executive and control organ for the all powerful State Defense Committee . . . [was the Council of People's Commissars of the RSFSR]," Victor Kravchenko, *I Chose Freedom* (New York, 1946), 400.

33. Sinitsyn, *Voprosy istorii,* no. 2 (February 1955):34–35.

34. *IVOvSS,* 6:103–104. J. Armstrong, in *The Politics of Totalitarianism* notes that the authority of such GKO plenipotentiaries superseded that of all local officials (p. 134). That this was the case is pointed up by the following extremely interesting incident. In the fall of 1941, Voronov was sent to Leningrad as plenipotentiary of the GKO to, among other things, supervise the production of munitions in that beleaguered city. He quickly ran up against Zhdanov, the all-powerful Party boss of Leningrad. Zhdanov wished that more munitions be brought into Leningrad from the outside, while Voronov, holding his own ground, asserted that the city's industrial concerns could handle this task by themselves. Voronov won the argument—and one must surmise that at least in this instance, his having a specific mandate from the GKO outweighed Zhdanov's formal power and personal influence (N. Voronov, "V trudnye vremena," *Voenno-istoricheskii zhurnal,* no. 9 (September 1961):71–72.

35. See, for example, Emel'ianov, *Novy mir,* no. 2 (February 1967), N. V. Adfel'dt, *Istoriia Moskovskogo Avtozavoda imeni I. A. Likhacheva* (Moscow 1966), 298, and G. A. Kumanev, "Podvig zheleznodorozhnikov," Ya. A. Poliakov et al., editors, *Eshelony idut na vostok* (Moscow, 1966):130.

36. The importance of having a personal knowledge of a given area and its officialdom is pointed up by the following statement:

> The selection of I. K. Smirnov to the post of head of the rear of the Southern Front had special sense. Prior to the war . . . [he had] worked for a long time in the Ukraine. He was a member of the Military Council of the Kiev military *okrug,* and commanded the troops of the Khar'kov military *okrug*. Being a member of the Presidium of the Supreme Soviet of the Ukrainian SSR, I. K. Smirnov had great authority in republic and oblast organizations, knew all secretaries of *obkoms* and . . . leaders of soviet organs, many directors of enterprises,

secretaries of *raikoms* and *kolkhoz* chairmen. Well known to him were the material resources of the Ukraine, its rail lines, the economy of *raions.*

Khrulev, *Voenno-istoricheskii zhurnal,* no. 6 (June 1961):70. See also ibid., 72.

37. For a fuller examination of evacuation of industry, see Sanford R. Lieberman, "The Evacuation of Industry in the Soviet Union During World War II." *Soviet Studies,* 35, no. 1 (January 1983):90–102.

38. For a description of what the Soviet losses entailed, see N. Voznesenskii, *The Economy of the U.S.S.R. During World War II* (Moscow, 1948), 42 and Poliakov et al., 6.

39. See, for example, G. I. Olekhanovich, "Ot Pripiati za Volgu," in Poliakov et al., 88.

40. See, for example, I. I. Belonosov, "Evakuatsiia naseleniia iz prifrontovoi polosy v 1941–1942 gg." in Poliakov et al., 15, and A. V. Mitrofanova, 84.

41. Prior to the formation of the GKO, most important resolutions and decisions, including those pertaining to the formulation of general plans and instructions for the evacuation process were made by (or issued in the name of) the Council of People's Commissars (*Sovnarkom*) and/or the Central Committee of the All-Union Communist Party.

42. For details, see L. I. Pogrebnoi, "O deiatel'nosti Soveta po Evakuatsii," in Poliakov et al., 201–207 and M. G. Pervukhin, "Perebazirovanie promyshlennosti," in P. P. Pospelov et al., *Sovetskii tyl v Velikoi Otechestvennoi voine,* 2 (Moscow, 1974), 13–30. The Council for Evacuation actually was only one of several extraordinary organs that the regime instituted at one time or another during the war. It remained in existence until 25 December 1941, at which time it was replaced by a Committee for the Unloading of Transit Goods and Other Cargo (Iu. A. Vasil'ev, *Sibirskii arsenal 1941–1945* [Sverdlovsk, 1965], 131). Moreover, in the intervening period, the regime formed a Committee for the Evacuation of Population under the Council for Evacuation (26 September 1941–31 January 1942) and a committee for the evacuation from frontline districts of reserves of foodstuffs and industrial goods as well as plant equipment of light industries (25 October 1941–19 December 1941). Finally, in July 1942, in response to the new German offensive, the GKO placed control of the second major evacuation process in the hands of a newly created Commission for Evacuation (Poliakov et al., 10–11). Of all these extraordinary organs, only the original Council for Evacuation is considered in this essay.

43. Pogrebnoi, in Poliakov, et al., 202.

44. See ibid., 204–5, and Likhomanov, 84.

45. Poliakov et al., 10. Most earlier Soviet discussions of the evacuation process list Shvernik rather than Kaganovich as the original chairman of the Council for Evacuation. (See, for example, *IVOvSS,* 2:143). In addition, many of the same sources err in putting the creation of the Council at the start of July 1941 (Poliakov et al., 9–10).

46. Pogrebnoi, in Poliakov et al., 201–2. The role of the NKVD in the evacuation process was not limited to security matters. It was also to play a key role in the supply of manpower, especially for construction projects in the areas of relocation.

47. See ibid., and N. F. Dubrovin, "Eshelon za eshelonom," in Poliakov et al., 208.

48. Pogrebnoi, in Poliakov et al., 202. The Council's apparat was divided into three groups: one for the evacuation and relocation of industrial enterprises, institutes, organizations, and foundations and their personnel, one for the evacuation of the general population, and one for the provision of transportation.

49. The commissariats themselves frequently made use of brainstorming sessions that not only drew on the knowledge and abilities of officials in the given commissariat but also in some cases elicited assistance from leading cadres in other commissariats and organizations. For example, see Mitrofanova, 91. A fair amount of vertical consultation also seems to have taken place. An example of such consultation is provided in A. G. Sheremet'ev, "45 dnei, 45 nochei," *Gvardiia tyla,* (Moscow, 1962):19.

50. A. G. Sheremet'ev, in *Gvardiia tyla,* 19. For a good description of the dynamics of the on-the-scene work, see *ibid.,* 14–30, Mitrofanova, 90–117 and A. M. Belikov, "Tiazheluiu promyshlennost' v glubokii tyl," in Poliakov et al., 36–47.

51. The director of the Stalin Auto Works (ZIS) in Moscow, I. A. Likhachev, for example, was appointed as the GKO's plenipotentiary in charge of the evacuation of the ZIS facilities. N. V. Adfel'dt et al., *Istoriia Moskovskogo Avtozavoda imeni I. A. Likhacheva* (Moscow, 1966), 298.

52. *IVOvSS,* 2:148–149.

53. Ibid., 149.

54. Pogrebnoi, in Poliakov et al., 203.

55. Ibid. These plenipotentiaries were assisted by small groups (usually three to five individuals) specially chosen from the apparat of the particular commissariats. Moreover, the collegia of the commissariats and leaders of institutions, in order to aid the plenipotentiaries of the Council for Evacuation, "formed special commissions . . . [composed] of highly qualified specialists who worked out concrete plans for the evacuation of sectors of the economy as a whole and for individual enterprises, scientific, cultural-educational, Party, and state institution . . ." (ibid.). At the same time, the commissariats and other organizations involved in the work of evacuation frequently formed special operative groups and commissions to further their own evacuation activities. See, for example, Dubrovin, in Poliakov et al., 210.

56. Pogrebnoi, in Poliakov et al., 204.

57. The lines of authority that lead down to these organs were somewhat unclear. For example, according to L. I. Pogrebnoi, who worked in the apparat of the Council for Evacuation, the evacopoints were subordinate organs of the Council (Pogrebnoi, in Poliakov et al., 204). Another Soviet source, however, maintains that the evacopoints for the evacuation of the civilian population were organized and controlled by departments created under the Council of People's Commissars of union republics, *oblispolkoms* and *kraiispolkoms* (Belonosov, in Poliakov et al., 210). The answer to this seemingly contradictory state of affairs most likely is that while these organs were under the overall jurisdiction of the Council for Evacuation, they also were subordinate to the regular soviet organs in the areas in question.

58. See, for example, Sheremet'ev, in *Gvardiia tyla,* 21.

59. See Mitrofanova, 96–97, 99.

60. Important as the work of industrial evacuation was, it could not be allowed to interfere with the actual conduct of military operations, especially in matters of logistics. Military priorities had to be maintained. Accordingly, the work of preparing industrial plants and personnel for evacuation frequently was coordinated with, or even on occasion controlled by, the Military Councils of the particular war zones. The military's general competence to act in such matters was based, first, upon the Statute on Martial Law that had been decreed at the very start of the war. (See *IVOvSS,* 2:21). Subsequently, the military's jurisdictional authority over specific aspects of evacuation was made more explicit. By a government decision of 5 July 1941, "the evacuation of the . . . [civilian] population from [frontline areas] . . . was to be conducted by order of the local military commander." (Belonosov, in Poliakov et al., 16.). The evacuation of human and material resources into the deep rear, however, required a degree of coordination and control beyond the competence of the military commanders and councils (in terms of both their limited territorial mandates and their abilities). Their sphere of absolute authority tended, therefore, to be confined to evacuations of a more limited nature, such as the removal of the civilian population to the immediate rear. (Ibid., 16, 18). This is not to say that military commanders and councils did not play a prominent role in the larger, more important aspects of evacuation work. The planning and execution of this work was in fact frequently conducted with the participation of the appropriate military authorities. (For an example of the participation of Military Councils and military authorities in the work of evacuation, see Sheremet'ev, 19 and Khrulev, 71).

61. Mitrofanova, 109.

62. For example, the Cheliabinsk *obkom* formed a special group composed of two secretaries of the Magnitogorsk *gorkom,* the director of the Magnitogorsk Combine, the head of the department of capital construction, the director of the Magnitostroi trust and directors of seven evacuated factories and charged them with checking on the progress

of the restoration of each of the enterprises that had been evacuated to Magnitogosk (ibid., 132).

    63. Vasil'ev, 130.

    64. Mitrofanova, 118–119.

    65. *IVOvSS,* 1:148. See also Mitrofanova, 116 and Poliakov et al., 13.

    66. M. I. Likhomanov, *Organizatorskaia rabota partii v promyshlennosti v pervyi period Velikoi Otechestvennoi voiny (1941–42 gg.),* (Leningrad, 1969), 108.

References

Adfel'dt, N. V. et al., *Istoriia Moskovskogo Avtozavoda imeni. I. A. Likhacheva.* Moscow, 1966.

Antipenko, N. A., *Na glavnom napravlenii.* Moscow, 1967.

Armstrong, J., *The Politics of Totalitarianism.* New York: Random House, 1961.

Djilas, Milovan, *Conversations with Stalin.* New York: Harcourt, Brace and World, 1962.

Ehrenburg, Il'ya, *The War: 1941–1945.* New York: The World Publishing Company, 1964.

Emel'ianov, V., "O vremeni, o tovarishchakh, o sebe. Zapiski inzhenera." *Novy mir,* no. 2 (February 1967), 61–141.

Fainsod, Merle et al., *Government and the American Economy,* 3rd ed. New York: Norton, 1959.

Khrulev, A., "Stanovlenie stategicheskogo tyla v Velikoi Otechestvennoi voine." *Voenno-istoricheskii zhurnal,* no. 6 (June 1961), 64–86.

Kravchenko, Victor, *I Chose Freedom.* New York: C. Scribner's Sons, 1946.

Kuznetsov, N., "Before the War." *International Affairs,* no. 1 (January 1967), 99–104.

————, "Gody voiny." *Oktiabr',* no. 8 (August 1968), 135–182.

Lieberman, Sanford R., "The Evacuation of Industry in the Soviet Union during World War II." *Soviet Studies,* 35 (January 1983), 90–102.

Likhomanov, M. I., *Organizatorskaia rabota partii v promyshlennosti v pervyi period Velikoi Otechestvennoi voiny 1941–42 gg.* Leningrad, 1969.

Mitrofanova, A. V., *Rabochii klass Sovetskogo soiuza v pervyi period Velikoi Otechestvennoi voiny.* Moscow, 1960.

Poliakov, Ia. A. et al. editors., *Eshelony idut na vostok.* Moscow, 1966.

Pospelov, P. P. et al., *Istoriia Velikoi Otechestvennoi voiny Sovetskogo soiuza,* 6 volumes. Moscow, 1961–1965.

————. *Sovetskii tyl v Velikoi Otechestvennoi voine,* vol. 2. Moscow, 1974.

Ryan, Cornelius, *The Last Battle.* London: Collins, 1966.

Sandalov, L., "Put' sovetskogo polkovodtsa," *Voenno-istoricheskii zhurnal,* no. 11. (November 1967), 39–47.

Schapiro, Leonard, *The Communist Party of the Soviet Union.* New York: Random House, 1960.

Sheremet'ev, A. G., "45 dnei, 45 nochei," *Gvardiia tyla.* Moscow, 1962.

Sinitsyn, A. M., "Chrezhvychainye organy Sovetskogo godsudarstva v gody Velikoi Otechestvennoi voiny." *Voprosy istorii,* no. 2 (February 1955), 32–43.

Tskulin, V. A., *Istoriia gosudarstvennykh uchrezhdenii SSSR 1936–1965.* Moscow, 1966.

Vasil'ev, Iu. A., *Sibirskii arsenal 1941–1945.* Sverdlovsk, 1965.

Voronov, N., "V trudnye vremena." *Voenno-istoricheskii zhurnal,* no. 9. (September 1961), 62–76.

Voronov, N. N., *Na sluzhbe voennoi.* Moscow, 1963.

Voznesenskii, N., *The Economy of the USSR during World War II.* Moscow, 1948.

War Industry Board, *American Industry in the War,* rev. ed. New York: Prentice-Hall, 1941.

5

Soviet Peasantry in World War II

ALEC NOVE

Numerous books and articles on the peasantry during World War II have been published in the Soviet Union. Indeed, it is now possible for a Soviet author, V. T. Aniskov (1979), to publish a volume devoted to analyzing the historiography of the subject. In his book, war-related disasters and other negative aspects of World War II are played down. He regards the more critical works used extensively in this essay (e.g., Arutiunian 1969) as too critical, though he does say that some earlier publications had been insufficiently so. The very title of Aniskov's book reflects the offficial line: in the face of immense obstacles and occasional policy errors and with much self-sacrifice and hardship, the Soviet peasantry did its patriotic duty, "though only ten to twelve years previously, through collectivization, this class joined with (*priobshchilsia*) the socialist order." Indeed, this fact is said to prove the durability and sound foundation of the kolkhoz system and peasant loyalty to it (Ansikov 1979, 3–4).

In the period stretching roughly from 1961–1971, however, the view of the role of the peasantry during World War II was rather different. One sees this also in the much franker and more critical approach that has been taken in recent years toward other sensitive historical questions, including such issues as collectivization. More research on the role of the Soviet peasantry in the Second World War would clearly be both desirable and possible.

Some picture of what happened to the Soviet peasantry in the areas under German occupation would also be helpful. If any such statistics exist, neither I nor a German colleague have been able to find them. Unfortunately, the head of the German Agricultural Administration of Occupied Territories, Otto Schiller, seems to have left no account of his experiences. The only book he wrote after World War II was a short history of Soviet collective farming, published at Tubingen in 1954. In Stuttgart in the 1950s I had a long talk with Schiller, during which he related experiences of spontaneous decollectivization in areas free of Soviet *and* German control, how he welcomed this, and how his advice was overruled by the Nazi authorities who wished to preserve kolkhozy so as to maximize procurements for Germany. Beyond a brief account in Arutiunian (1969, 220–224), no Soviet published work on this aspect of the subject seems to exist. Dallin's *German Rule in Russia* (1957) naturally concentrates on other matters. For those able to use German archival material, investigating the impact of German occupation on Soviet agriculture represents a tremendous area for original research. A partial analysis may be done, using Soviet statistics on wartime agricultural production that relate only to territories under Soviet control. Indeed, for several years millions of the most fertile hectares, millions of peasants, and millions of urban consumers were behind German lines, adversely affecting wartime agricultural production.

It must be emphasized that, given such losses of vitally important agricultural areas, combined with the mobilization of manpower for the armed forces and shortages of haulage power, equipment and fuel, the performance of agriculture during World War II has to be regarded as impressive. In the first important postwar work on the economy, N. Voznesenskii (1948) contrasts this state of events with the critical food situation in 1916–1917. This is not altogether fair, however. Rural and urban shortages and hardships between 1941 and 1945 were in fact far greater than those that contributed to the collapse of the tsarist regime. This stems in part from territorial losses and the scale of defeats in 1941–1942, which far exceeded those of 1915–1917. Yet when all is said, the Soviet army and the population were fed during World War II, with only a marginal (though not insignificant) contribution from abroad through Lend-Lease. Not only ruthlessness and coercion, but also genuine patriotic commitment, are responsible for the very impressive achievements of the Soviet war ecnomy.

The Agricultural Labor Force

The village lost men not only to the armed forces—over 60 percent of armed forces were rural residents according to Ansikov (1979, 4)—but also to the industrial work force. In addition, the mobilization of many tractors and horses for the army and the virtual cessation of deliveries of new tractors placed additional burdens on the remaining agricultural labor force. As a result, women, juveniles, and old people were utilized on a large scale.[1] Table 5.1 shows, however, a decline in agricultural employment during World War II. The figures in Table 5.1 relate to *rear areas,* i.e., those behind the front. It is not clear, however, whether these vary with military retreats and advances. The implication seems to be that they refer to the *same* areas. This follows from data for the whole country cited by Arutiunian (1969, 398), which explicitly refers to unoccupied territory. The fall between the end of 1940 and the end of 1943, and the rise to 1945, are all much greater than that shown in Table 5.1. A further difficulty with any consistent

Table 5.1   Agricultural Employment, 1941–1945 (thousands, as of January 1)

	Working Age Men	Women	Total	Juveniles (12–16)	Aged and Sick	Total	Percentage of 1941
1941	8657	9532	18169	3848	2360	24368	100.0
1942	5890	9533	15423	3779	2369	21572	88.5
1943	3605	9591	13196	4035	2379	19600[a]	80.5
1944	2341	9094	11432	3821	2388	17644	72.4
1945	2770	8661	11440	3424	2390	17346	71.2

[a]The printed tables gives 12609, which is evidently an error.

Source: Arutiunian, *Sovetskoe krest'ianstvo*, p. 75, quoting *Istoricheskii arkhiv*.

interpretation of the data was that it was precisely to those areas in which industry was concentrated and food needs rose sharply that a large proportion of the peasantry migrated to work in war industry. Thus, in many areas of the Urals and West Siberia, the agricultural labor force fell by 45 percent (Arutiunian, p. 75). According to Arutiunian, in 1942 no less than 96 percent of the "aged and sick" and 95 percent of the juveniles (12–16 year olds) took part in kolkhoz production. These numbers were quite insufficient to cope with seasonal peaks, however. As a result, millions of urban citizens, students, and school children were also mobilized. In 1943 they earned 12 percent of all *trudodni* in kolkhozy as against only 4 percent in 1940.

World War II affected not only the composition and size of the agricultural labor force, but also the work effort in the agricultural sector. The compulsory minimum of *trudodni* (work days) worked by adult kolkhozniki (kolkhoz workers) was raised to 150 in 1942 in cotton-growing areas, and to 100–120 in others. Juveniles had a fifty–*trudodni* minimum (Chadayev 1963, 359). Minima within this total were established for the period of sowing, cultivation, and harvesting. These were substantially overfulfilled on average, but little doubt exists that wartime coercive measures could be taken to enforce extra work or longer hours if it was thought necessary. In some areas the minima proved too high—there was not enough *collective* work. In other areas they were easily overfulfilled—in areas where, for example, a great deal of labor-intensive tasks (livestock and vegetable production) needed to be done. Law enforcement agencies ignored this, however, taking into account neither the imposed minimum nor the objective possibilities of fulfilling it (Arutiunian 1969, 91). According to Arutiunian, the law was, not in fact, imposed with its full severity; nevertheless, the law was severe. For the first offense, "compulsory labor" in kolkhoz or Machine Tractor Station (MTS) for up to six months, with a 25 percent deduction from the value of *trudodni* earned; or, if no work was available, offenders were assigned a period of forced labor by the local NKVD.

Another indication of the severity of the law was that those failing to carry out the minimum number of *trudodni* could be deprived of their private plots (though this seems not to have been a much-used penalty).

Table 5.2   Average Annual *Trudodni*, 1940–1943

	1940	1943
Men of working age	312	338
Women of working age	193	244
Older adults	132	135
Juveniles	74	100

Source: Arutiunian, *Sovetskoe krest'ianstvo*, p. 339.

Moreover, kolkhozy chairmen and brigade leaders who failed to report breaches of the rules were themselves subject to criminal penalties. Arutiunian cites some instances where the law was not applied and others when it was applied too rigorously by kolkhoz chairmen and other officials who feared accusations of leniency. Citing archives, he states that in Kazakhstan, for example, 78,500 kolkhozniki did not work the minimum number of *trudodni* (many with extenuating circumstances) in 1943. Yet only 5180 cases were brought before the courts, with 4100 of them found guilty and condemned. During 1944, in the entire rear areas of the USSR, 11 percent of kolkhozniki did not work the prescribed minimum (Arutiunian 1969, 92). Yet, in 1944, only 3 percent of *all* those who did not work the obligatory minimum were condemned by the courts. Court cases were usually brought against only the most barefaced work avoiders. Fear of being punished was real, however, because any *repetition* of the offense was quite severely punished by a sentence of forced labor in a camp run by the NKVD (Arutiunian 1969, 90).

The actual average number of *trudodni* worked as calculated by Arutiunian, using archive materials is presented in Table 5.2. These figues represent workday units, not days worked. Scattered evidence suggests that on the average each *trudoden* represented roughly 1.5 actual days in peacetime. It seems likely that *trudodni* valuation, in terms of time and effort required, altered in wartime. In any case, one must agree with Arutiunian that the highest number of *trudodni* tended to be worked in areas where the compulsory minimum was lowest, implying that this form of compulsion was not the decisive factor in explaining additional work effort during World War II. Rather, most peasants doubtlessly felt it was their duty to work hard. Indeed, Arutiunian criticizes these regulations as "one of the stupid (*nelepyi*) products of the bureaucratic system of control over agriculture" (1969, 96).

Sovkhozy were able to maintain prewar employment levels despite the loss of men to the army by mobilizing all persons living on their territory and by hiring seasonal workers (mostly women and juveniles). According to archive data used by Zelenin (1969, 35) relating to "comparable" (i.e., nonoccupied) territory, the total sovkhoz labor force increased during World War II from 712,000 people in 1940 (falling to 639,000 in 1943) to 836,000 in 1944. Zelenin also reports war-related changes in area sown by sovkhozy.

It should be stressed that in 1940 sovkhozy were responsible for only 6.9 percent of the area sown to grain, 4.5 percent of cattle, and so forth. Hence, the main burden fell on kolkhozy throughout the war.

Bare statistics do not begin to show how hard life was for Soviet peasantry. Mechanical aids of all kinds became scarce or nonexistent. Horses were mobilized, manual labor predominated. In areas over which war had raged, many villages were destroyed. People lived in holes in the ground, used cows for ploughing, even put themselves into harness and pulled a plough or harrow. Arutiunian (1969, 156) cites memoirs: "We had to haul the plough. Eight to ten women harnessed themselves and hauled; we used a wider harness than the horses. We hauled a big stock to which the plough was attached. Behind the plough we had another woman or young lad."

Remarkable stories are told of the evacuation of people and animals as the Germans advanced. A literary description can be found in Maksimov's novel *Sem' dnei tvoreniya*, and also in contemporary publications. This, for instance, is a brief extract from *Novy mir* (1941:9–10):

> Vast flocks of sheep, cows, and goats make their way through our little town, exhausted hardly able to move their legs; some of them loaded onto carts and moved further. By the river, wherever you look it is like nomadic tribes: shepherds resting under carts, milkmaids, sick sheep, freshly-slaughtered flesh, hides. A milkmaid says: "We have been on the way for a month and four days. . . . We have to deliver the livestock to its destination, but our animals are not used to long walks, they move slowly, and then what about being machine-gunned from the air? Frightened sheep gather in a tight circle, so the bullets get them. . . . We lie in ditches, the cows scatter in the forest, almost all the sheep were killed. We had good sheep!"

Arutiunian cites harrowing stories in which many thousands of peasants, livestock, and tractors make their way to the Dnieper in July 1941. The few bridges across the Dnieper were overwhelmed. Pontoon bridges and boats partially relieved the pressure, allowing some 600,000 head of livestock and 4500 tractors to be moved to the eastern bank. "Many were killed, and much machinery and livestock were lost. . . . The Germans reached the river before the move was completed" (1969, 50). We must imagine the scenes at the bridges and ferries that were being used concurrently by retreating troops, those evacuating industrial equipment, and civilian refugees.

In the entire evacuation procedure, it was established that the extremely scarce transport was reserved for industry; peasants and animals had to walk. Citing the research work of M. Pogrebinski, Arutiunian claims that 59.3 percent of all cattle, 82 percent of all sheep, 26.7 percent of the pigs and 14 percent of the horses that were in the Ukraine at the outbreak of war in June 1941 were evacuated as were most tractors not requisitioned by the army. Many tractors were abandoned, however, for lack of fuel and spare parts. Zelenin (1969, 110) cites data on the evacuation of sovkhozy: "While the larger part of the livestock was evacuated, many never arrived.

Table 5.3 Agricultural Machinery in Sovkhozy, 1940–1944 (in thousands)

	Total USSR			Comparable territories		
	1940	1943	1944	1940	1943	1944
Tractors	74,278	37,901	40,257	42,474	26,994	23,993
Combine-harvesters	27,397	18,819	19,526	15,668	13,112	12,553

Note: These figures do not indicate that 18 percent of the tractors and 30 percent of combine-harvesters were unable to function at all, presumably because of lack of fuel and spare parts.

Source: Zelenin, *Sovkhozy SSSR*, p. 24.

[Thus] from the Ukraine, Belorussia, and the Western regions of the RSFSR, the major proportion of livestock was evacuated: 83.4 percent of cattle, 97.7 percent of sheep and goats, 66.2 percent of pigs. However, few reached their destination: about 30 percent of cattle, 20 percent of sheep. . . . Between 17 and 23 percent of evacuated livestock were delivered to units of the Red Army for meat." According to Arutiunian (1969, 53), lack of fodder and shelter led to the slaughter of the bulk of the "evacuees": by 1 January 1942, very few of them could be left alive. Many of those that *did* reach their destination (e.g., the North Caucasus) were overrun by the Germans in the 1942 summer offensive. A mass of human and animal misery is contained in such stories and statistics.

Machinery and Equipment

All sources agree that most horses and tractors were mobilized for the Red Army or destroyed by German forces and that until 1944 hardly any tractors or spare parts for other machines were supplied to agriculture. Even the favored sovkhozy got nothing prior to 1943 as Table 5.3 illustrates. The Commissar of Sovkhozy, P. Labanov, stated to his colleagues in 1941: "It is clear that we will get no new tractors this year or next." An order from the Commissariat of Sovkhozy envisaged even the use of cows (though not pedigreed cows) for ploughing (Zelenin 1969, 26–27). As a result, bottlenecks immediately arose in the supply of bridles, harnesses, and ropes, all of which were to be made on the farms. Spare parts for the remaining tractors were either improvised also or made in local industrial workshops. Only in the second half of 1943 were supplies of tractors resumed, and many were sent to the newly liberated war-devastated areas.

The Machine Tractor Stations (MTS) were in worse shape than the sovkhozy. As a result, in 1942 as much as 79 percent of all kolkhoz grain had to be harvested by horse or by hand (Arutiunian 1969, 164). Much of the sowing was also done by hand. Given the lack of machines, it was not surprising that harvest yields fell. The average harvest of grain in kolkhozy was 7–8 centners per hectare in 1938–1942 but only 4.6 centners in 1942 despite favorable weather. As a result, there was not enough left for seed, which further complicated the food supply situation in 1943.

Wartime grain procurements further compounded the grave situation in rural areas. Payment-in-kind by kolkhozy for the work done by the MTS remained a major source of state grain procurements and a major burden for kolkhozy, especially as these payments were based on the greatly exaggerated "biological" yield, and not the much lower real harvest.

The biological [*vidovoi*] harvest was roughly estimated. . . . Some directors of MTS and regional officials increased it without even bothering to visit the fields. . . . At the end of 1942, when food shortages were particularly grave, the collection of any information about the harvest other than the biological yield was altogether forbidden. Even the drafting of a food and fodder balance using data of the actual threshed harvest was seen as a breach of this rule.

Kolkhoz chairmen tried to avoid excessive procurements by fair means or foul. Some were sentenced to long prison terms for "sabotaging grain procurements." Party officials were threatened with punishment too and then had to be warned: "do not overdo things, do not remove seed grain and beat up (kolkhoz) officials." There were "arrests and searches by NKVD" in the course of grain procurements, with all sorts of excesses, so that "many kolkhozy in almost every area were left without enough seed" (Arutiunian 1969, 200–204).

Political Control

In the early stages of World War II (November 1941), "political departments" in the MTS were reconstituted, acting as a species of Party watchdog over kolkhoz agriculture. Their task included both encouragement and, where necessary, coercion. Thus, it was their task to oversee the enforcement of the minimum number of *trudodni* and of agricultural delivery plans. Only harsh controls could extract so great an output from the village. Voznesenskii (1948, 90) contrasts the total procurements of grain in 1918–1921 (920 million poods) with the 1941–1944 figure (4264 million poods) "despite the German occupation of the richest farming areas of the USSR." He could as well have added, "despite the food shortages this created in the villages."

Reoccupied areas posed great difficulties in terms of enforcement. In Belorussia and the Ukraine, for example, "there were anti-kolkhoz, private property, and anti-state attitudes," and some peasants joined the Ukrainian nationalist armed bands. In the Kursk oblast it was alleged that former kulacks had returned to their villages. Some (formerly) collective horses had been taken away and hidden by peasants, and altogether there was much to do "to restore collective land utilization" (Arutiunian 1969, 250–252). In fact, we must suppose that in many places it was necessary to re-collectivize.

Arutiunian (1969, 399) cites statistical data about the political officers of the MTS and sovkhozy. It is noteworthy that 96.2 percent of them were male, nearly all of military age. The political departments were abolished in May 1943 as unnecessary, but inasmuch as 1943 was a particularly unsuccessful year, Aniskov (1969, 107) wonders if this abolition was not premature.

Peasant Incomes and Welfare

Official Soviet sources agree that peasant life was exceedingly hard both in terms of physical conditions of work and in levels of consumption. Sovkhoz workers and permanent staff of the MTS, as well as rural officials, were paid predominantly in money, and fairly well paid by Soviet standards of the time. Engineer-technicians in sovkhozy received 700 (old) rubles per month, tractor drivers 200–700, truck drivers 320–330, and "MTS pay was similar" (Arutiunian 1969, 83). Kolkhoz members were paid very little in comparison. In spite of these adequate salaries, however, manufactured goods were practically unobtainable, and free-market food prices were astronomical. Thus, in the RSFSR in 1942, the *average* price of a kilogram of grain was 53.80 rubles (compared to 1.88 rubles in 1940). A liter of milk was priced at 38 rubles, and a kilogram of pork fetched 261 rubles (Arutiunian 1969, 352). Many peasants refused to sell for money, preferring barter. Payments-in-kind were therefore widespread, including bonuses-in-kind. In one region, for example, a tractor driver who overfulfilled his ploughing norm received a piglet or a beehive. Regular issues of grain and potatoes as partial payment and/or the right to purchase at the official (ration) price became the rule.

Payment-in-kind was always the rule for kolkhoz members. Along with the produce of their private plots, these payments were decisive in their survival. But low wartime production and high state procurements left them very little. The price paid by the state for compulsory deliveries during World War II was quite negligible. Indeed, Arutiunian calls it "symbolic," for example, three kopeks for a kilogram of potatoes. "In 1942–1943 the amounts issued per *trudoden* were only about 800 grams of grain and 200–400 grams of potatoes, or about half of the amount issued in 1940" (Arutiunian 1969, 79). Given the acute shortage and the huge free-market prices, however, these smaller amounts were greatly valued. According to a speech by party leader A. S. Shcherbakov, some "sold" *trudodni* they earned for large sums. The amounts paid to *kolkhoz* members, even on the average, represented starvation rations. Table 5.4 illustrates the nominal "value" of the average *trudoden*.

The figures given in Table 5.4 actually overstate the amount of produce available because (according to Arutiunian) they represent only the quantities "allocated." In fact, however, part of the amount formally "allocated" as payment to the peasants was taken away as compulsory deliveries. Thus,

Table 5.4   Nominal Value of Average *Trudoden*, 1940–1945

	1940	1941	1942	1943	1944	1945
Grain (kg)	1.60	1.40	0.80	0.65	n.a.	0.70
Potatoes (kg)	0.98	0.33	0.22	0.40	n.a.	0.26
Money (old rubles)	0.98	1.07	1.03	1.24	1.12	0.85

Source: Arutiunian, *Sovetskoe krest'ianstvo,* p. 339.

4.4 million tons were supposed to be allocated in 1942, but only 2.9 million were issued. Arutiunian estimates that on a per capita basis this was less than 200 grams of grain and one potato per day. Yet, this had to feed a family whose head was probably away in the army. Survival thus depended on the private plot. But private plot production was also subject to compulsory state deliveries, for example, 456 liters of milk per cow. As if this were not enough, there was a fivefold increase in the agricultural tax on notional income from private plots and livestock. Other burdens on private animals included mobilization of surviving private cows to haul carts filled with grain to the procurement centers. In 1944, for example, there were 60,000 cows engaged in such work in Kuban' alone! (Arutiunian 1969, 263). Taxes, delivery quotas, and shortage of fodder led to a steep decline in the number of private livestock in the rear areas.

It might be thought that the peasant household could make a great deal of money given the very high free-market prices. Only a few could benefit from this, however, because of transport problems and lack of time. In any case, there was little that could be bought for money. Some peasants were able to engage in barter trade with urban residents who came to nearby villages. Near Barnaul (Altai), for example, a metal bucket was exchanged for six kilograms of flour. Kolkhoz markets, even in such towns as Moscow, sold little in 1942–1943 despite huge prices (the prices were huge because so few peasants were selling). True, some made a small fortune in paper rubles, but most peasants lived in dire poverty.

It must be stressed that there were great variations. In one Uzbek region, 30 percent of kolkhozy issued no money or grain whatever in payment for *trudodni* (Arutiunian 1969, 29). In the USSR as a whole, 5.4 percent of kolkhozy paid no grain, 37.5 percent paid less than 300 grams per *trudoden,* and 75 percent issued no potatoes in 1945 (Arutiunian 1969, 351).

Output

During the war and first postwar years, false "biological" harvest statistics were the basis of claims that, despite all the difficulties, wartime harvests compared well with those of the prewar period. Such a bright picture is

Table 5.5   Real and Biological Yields, Kazakhstan, 1940–1943

	1940	1941	1942	1943
Biological yield	6.4	10.9	9.1	5.6
Real yield	4.8	7.2	3.9	2.6

Source: Arutiunian, *Sovetskoe krest'ianstvo*, p. 200, citing archives.

found, for instance, in the third volume of Lyashchenko's economic history, published as late as 1956. Yet harvest losses were immense during World War II (about a third), owing to orders to increase sown area under conditions in which labor and equipment were desperately lacking, both for sowing and harvesting. These conditions were compounded by all the other problems referred to previously. The difference between real and official biological yields are illustrated for Kazakhstan in Table 5.5. Note the increase in official overestimates, on which payments for MTS services were based.

The areas under Soviet control in 1942 produced 24.9 million tons of grain on 58 million hectares of sown area, resulting in the low yield of only 5 centners per hectare. By all accounts, 1943 was climatically a much less favorable year, and it was also one in which all the disasters of the war bore particularly heavily. Thus, although several major liberated areas (for example, Karsnodar, Rostov, Stavropo) were in the 1943 area but not in the 1942 area, only 56.6 million hectares could be sown with 52.5 million hectares harvested. Total grain harvested in 1943 was only 20.6 million tons. No wonder both Zelenin and Arutiunian conclude that 1943 was an appalling agricultural year, representing the lowest point of all the wartime miseries. Data found in Zelenin provides ample evidence of this fact (see Table 5.6). By 1944, it was possible to deliver more equipment, tractors, and fuel to the agricultural sector. As a result, recovery commenced in reconquered regions, generating a notable improvement over the dreadful year of 1943.

In his survey of Soviet historiography of the period, Aniskov takes Arutiunian to task for being overcritical with regard to the policy of increasing sowings in rear areas. He insists that it was a necessary consequence of the heavy losses of territory to the invaders. But the point of the criticism

Table 5.6   Grain Yields in Sovkhozy and Kolkhozy, 1940, 1943–1945 (centners per hectare)

	1940	1943	1944	1945
Sovkhozy	8.9	3.8	7.0	6.7
Kolkhozy	8.5	3.9	5.7	2.1

Source: Zelenin, *Sovkhozy SSSR*, p. 83.

Table 5.7 Kolkhozy Livestock in Rear Areas, 1940–1943 (year end, millions)

	1940	1941	1942	1943
Cattle	22.7	21.6	22.5	22.9
Sheep & Goats	56.4	59.7	61.2	63.7
Pigs	6.1	6.5	5.6	3.6
Horses	14.8	12.2	10.7	9.8

Source: Arutiunian, *Sovetskoe krest'ianstvo*, p. 188.

is that the extra areas could not be properly sown, cultivated, or harvested, and as such, were thus wasteful.

As might be expected, data on livestock show very heavy losses of horses and pigs; however, a surprisingly high proportion of cattle and sheep in the rear areas survived. Meat and milk production fell steeply (after an initial upsurge in slaughtering) because of critical shortages of fodder. Table 5.7 tells the basic tale.

By 1 January 1945, when almost the whole prewar territory was back under Soviet rule, Chadayev (1963, 359) reports total livestock numbers, as a percentage of 1941 levels, as: cattle 81 percent (cows 77 percent), pigs 32 percent, sheep and goats 47 percent (all categories of owners). Extremely heavy losses occurred in occupied areas due to attempted evacuation during the Soviet retreat, the German practice of requisitioning, and destruction during their retreat. It took many years to repair the damage and to rebuild villages, cowsheds, etc. In kolkhozy, yields per cow fell from 949 kilograms in 1940 to 751 in 1943, the worst year (Chadayev 1965, 443). In sovkhozy, the fall was from 1803 to 1138 kilograms in the same period (Zelenin 1969, 96).

The First Postwar Years

The Soviet peasantry had borne immense burdens during World War II. On top of all the hardships they experienced during the war, there were appalling problems after it: a shortage of haulage power, a heavy loss of manpower (millions of peasants had been killed in the war), and the destruction of thousands of villages in the fighting. At first survivors had to live in improvised holes in the ground. On top of all this, 1946 was a year of drought. The harvest was very poor. Only 39.6 million tons of grain were harvested in 1946, even less than in 1945. As a result, many went hungry, some actually starving. According to Khrushchev, Stalin nonetheless ordered that some food be exported (*Pravda* 10 December 1963).

At first there was hope of reform of the kolkhoz system. Many peasants must have felt that their wartime efforts deserved this. Some evidence exists to the effect that such optimism was actually encouraged by the political officers. Be this as it may, the same bitter year saw these hopes dashed by a decree "on measures to liquidate breaches of the kolkhoz statute" (19 September 1946). Breaches in policy had been allowed in wartime. For example, management permitted some collective land to be cultivated by peasant families, and state plans were perforce modified on the spot to fit in with what was possible in the extremely harsh wartime circumstances. In the postwar period, the previous tight controls over production and procurements were reasserted and the size of private plots restricted. In many instances, land that was being cultivated by peasant families had to be abandoned even if the kolkhoz had no possibility of growing any crops on it. A Council for Kolkhoz Affairs was set up under Andreyev to exercise general supervision and to combat breaches of the kolkhoz statute. Moreover, the Ministry of Agriculture was divided into three parts (food crops, industrial crops, and livestock). Evidently, this was not a success, and in 1947, it was reunited, while the Council for Kolkhoz Affairs was quietly wound up.

Tighter control over farms was reasserted in the resolution of the February 1947 Plenum of the Central Committee of the Party. Sowing plans were imposed on farms in great detail and delivery obligations were made more specific and onerous and could be arbitrarily varied by local officials (who notoriously abused their power to squeeze ever more out of agriculture), while procurement prices remained at the low, prewar levels. Political supervision over kolkhozy was to be based on the MTS, and these were each to have a political deputy-director for this purpose. This was the period during which Lysenko was achieving supremacy in the "biological sciences," and his charlatan-nostrums were imposed by order on the farms through the party-state machine, regardless of local circumstances.[2]

As if this was not bad enough, financial burdens were increased on kolkhozy and on peasant households. The later were dealt with particularly harshly. Cash payments per workday unit remained low. In today's rubles, it was 14 kopeks even as late as 1952, probably only about 10 kopeks in 1947–1948, or the same tiny sum as before the war, though retail prices had risen sharply in the interval. To buy one bottle of vodka required 20 days' work at least; a pair of trousers was hardly thought of. Payments-in-kind, mainly grain, were more important than money, and of course, the private plot and private livestock continued to be the primary source of the family's food (other than bread) and cash income (via free-market sales).

Free-market prices fell as the acute wartime shortages were overcome, and the unfortunate kolkhoz households found themselves paying two kinds of tax: one was a high-rates tax on the notional income received from specific crops or animals[3] and the other took the form of high compulsory-procurement quotas on the output of the private plot, paid for at nominal, extremely low prices. The peasants were caught either way. If they had a cow, then they had to pay tax in cash on the income that was deemed to have derived from it, *and* to deliver milk to the state. If there was no cow, then they avoided the tax *but* still had to deliver milk to the state, since the delivery obligation was independent of the possession of a cow. If necessary, the peasant had to buy milk (at a free and therefore high price) to deliver to the state (at a very low price).

Kolkhozy were poor, could invest little, and were starved of materials because priority in material allocation went to urban industry. One example of the low priority of agriculture was that for several postwar years, kolkhozy were not even allowed to obtain electricity from the national electricity network, in other words, they had to generate their own or go without. This did not prevent socialist-realist painters from producing many oil paintings showing Stalin against a background of electric tractors that seemed to be getting their own current from wires attached to long-distance transmission lines (I saw such paintings as late as 1955. Needless to say, there were and are no electric tractors in real life!). When kolkhozy were able to purchase industial inputs, they had to pay high retail prices, thus still further reducing their ability to pay their members. The year 1947 also marked the beginning of the painful process of imposing collectivization on the peasants of the areas annexed in 1939–1940, notably the three Baltic republics. As a result, output showed a sharp, though temporary, decline, particularly in Lithuania. The one relatively bright spot was the revival of tractor production, which eased the haulage problem.

In all these circumstances, agricultural recovery was slow. Grain harvests, according to official statistics, surpassed the 1940 level by 1949, but these statistics were in terms of the grossly inflated biological yield. Revised figures show that the 1940 levels were not reached when Stalin died in 1953, while livestock numbers stagnated and remained below the levels of 1940, 1928, and even 1916, as Khrushchev pointed out in his speech to the September 1953 Plenum, which ushered in the first of a large number of measures designed to restore health to Soviet agriculture.

Conclusion

One must agree with Arutiunian's judgment, a realistic picture of the appalling situation, that the desperate shortages, the errors of policy (on sown areas), and the hardships suffered, do not detract from, but on the contrary, magnify the achievement of the Soviet peasantry during World War II. He rightly points out that the *prodrazverstka* (requisitionings) of War Communism took a far smaller share of the harvest than did the procurement agencies in 1941–1945. The peasants in 1918–1920 rebelled, those in the "Great Patriotic War" did not. He asserts that this shows their commitment to the system and their sense of patriotism. We may reasonably point out that their patriotism overrode their hatred of the system, and that the organs of Soviet power were much more strong in the villages in 1941–1945 than in 1918–1920. Yet we should, in my view, accept the fact that there was much that was genuinely heroic in the conduct of the millions of overworked and underfed peasants, mostly women, who somehow kept the towns and the soldiers fed under conditions that we have difficulty even imagining. Recovery after the war was impeded by anti-peasant policies (as evidenced in the decrees of 1946), the continuation of heavy taxes on private plots, the ever-increasing compulsory delivery quotas, and the extremely low procurement prices. Khrushchev had much to say about this after Stalin's death.

I will end by drawing attention again to the very extensive Soviet literature on the war years, much of which is conveniently listed in Aniskov's book on historiography. Only a few sources have been utilized in this paper, and even these could have provided data for a paper three times the present length. Anyone looking for a research topic need look no further.

Notes

1. Many women not only drove tractors and combine-harvesters during World War II, but also tried to repair them in cold, ill-equipped workshops, or out in the fields. Soviet tractors were (and indeed many still are) very difficult for women to handle.

2. For an excellent discussion of Lysenko's impact on the biological sciences, see R. Medvedev, *The Rise and Fall of T. D. Lysenko.*

3. For details of this iniquitous tax, which discouraged production and caused some peasants to cut down fruit trees to save tax, see A. Nove, "Rural taxation in the USSR," *Soviet Studies,* (October 1953).

References

Aniskov, V. T., *Podvig sovetskogo krest'ianstvo v Velikoi Otechestvennoi voine.* Moscow, 1979.

Arutiunian, Yu. V., *Sovetskoe krest'ianstvo v gody Velikoi Otechestvennoi voiny.* Moscow, 1969.

Ya. Chadayev, *Ekonomika SSSR v period Velikoi Otechestvennoi voiny 1941–1945.* Moscow, 1965.

Voznesenskii, N. A., *Voyenneya ekonomika SSSR* (Moscow, 1948).

Zelenin, T. E., *Sovkhozy SSSR, 1941–1945* (Moscow, 1969).

6

The Soviet Bible Belt: World War II's Effects on Religion

WILLIAM C. FLETCHER

World War II was the most important event in the modern history of religion in the USSR. In the magnitude of the changes it wrought, the War eclipsed even the cataclysm of the Russian Revolution. This essay contends that the war changed church-state relations for the next generation, determined the form of the church, altered its function and, religiously at least, altered the nature of society profoundly and probably permanently.

There really is no way to describe how the German invasion shocked the Soviet regime. Even the unrestrained hyperbole of the Moscow Patriarchate's wartime propaganda does not, for a change, overstate the case.

> Like thunder on the Russian land was the horrifying news of Hitler's hordes falling upon us. His Holiness learned of it on Sunday, 22 June 1941, when after service he returned from the Cathedral. This news disturbed him so deeply that after some meditation, assured by prayer and confident of heavenly help, he [made his first wartime proclamation]. . . .[1]

Official Moscow, however, panicked. For a fortnight Stalin uttered not a word. He was nowhere to be seen. Only a single voice—and not an official one at that—made any public response to the Nazi invasion. Immediately after the invasion began, on June 22, Metropolitan Sergii, the Moscow Patriarchate's leader, made a ringing proclamation:

> Fascism, knowing no law but naked force and accustomed to ridiculing the highest postulates of honour and morality, has once more shown itself true to its nature. The Fascist brigands have fallen upon our native land. . . .
>
> Our Orthodox Church has always shared the destiny of the people, bearing their trials, rejoicing in their successes, and this time too it is not going to

forsake its people, bestowing, as it does, the blessing of Heaven upon the forthcoming heroic exploit of the whole people.

For us, above all, it is right to recall Christ's commandment, 'Greater love hath no man than this, that a man lay down his life for his friends.'[2]

The die was cast. The battle commenced, and religion in the USSR began its profound, irreversible change.

Church-State Relations

World War II marked the close of the prewar chapter in the relations between church and state in the USSR. A new pattern emerged. It was not permanent, for what prevails today, forty years later, is only a part of the relationship established during the war. However, the informal concordat of 1943 would remain in place, unchanged for a decade and a half, and even though much of it eroded away thereafter, it has not yet disappeared entirely.[3]

What emerged from World War II was a bargain between church and state. In return for political services, the state granted the church the right to exist as an institution in Soviet society.

This was no new position for the Moscow Patriarchate. As early as in 1927, with his church organization at the point of collapse, Metropolitan Sergii had no alternative but to seek an accommodation with the regime. In place of the earlier hostility, or even the neutral position which had followed it, he declared that in political matters, at least, the church is completely subservient to the government:

> We must show, not in words but in deeds, that not only people indifferent to Orthodoxy, or those who reject it, can be faithful citizens of the Soviet Union, loyal to the Soviet government, but also the most fervent adherents of Orthodoxy, to whom it is as dear with all its canonical and liturgical treasures as truth and life. We wish to be Orthodox and at the same time to claim the Soviet Union as our civil motherland, the joys and successes of which are our joys and successes, the misfortunes of which are our misfortunes. . . . Remaining Orthodox, we remember our duty to be citizens of the Union "not from fear, but from conscience," as the Apostle has taught us (Rom. 13:5).[4]

It was the church's only hope: perhaps the government, in return for political services, would withdraw its attack.

It did not work. A year later the regime descended upon what remained of the Russian Orthodox church, along with all other religions in the country, with unrestrained ferocity. The church was decimated. Within ten years it was brought to the brink of extinction.

It was only the advent of World War II that reversed this dismal situation for the church. The invasion of eastern Poland, and then the occupation, created a situation in which, for the first time, the regime needed all the help it could get. Sergii seized every opportunity to render service to the state. Along with others who had done likewise, he condemned his namesake and subordinate, Metropolitan Sergii (Voskresenskii), for defecting. Without waiting for the government's permission he began the distribution of highly effective, mimeographed encyclicals against the Germans. By the first anniversary of the invasion, Russian Orthodox propaganda leaflets were being flown behind German lines. Appeals were made to Romanian, Yugoslav, Czech, and Greek soldiers in the German forces. Despite the fact that it was illegal to do so, the church began organizing collections for the war effort, and late in 1942 Sergii asked for and then received permission from Stalin himself to collect contributions for a column of tanks. The church formed a special organization to care for war orphans. In addition, it added its voice to agitation among the Western Allies for the opening of a second front and supported the state's ongoing propaganda against the Vatican.[5]

Sergii's strategy succeeded. The state could ill afford to refuse his offered services. Instantly it began to change its policies toward religion. The antireligious campaign was cancelled forthwith. Restrictions against church activity, if not rescinded, were forgotten. By 1943, when the tide of battle began to turn, an informal concordat between church and state had been worked out, which continued in effect unchanged for the rest of Stalin's rule and on into the future. The state accepted the bargaining situation proposed by Sergii in 1927.

The state conceded to the church the right to exist as an institution in society. Its freedom of operation was severely limited, but it was given sufficient concessions to permit its continued survival. The central administration was allowed to rebuild, and Metropolitan Sergii, after sixteen years, was finally allowed to be elected Patriarch. The number of bishops was allowed to increase to a spare and thinly staffed corps, marginally sufficient for administering the church, and finally stabilizing at sixty-nine or seventy bishops. A tightly limited educational network was established to supply at least some part of the church's critical need for priests. Closed churches were reopened; by the end of the war some 15,000 Orthodox churches were operating, and that number was allowed to continue unchanged.[6]

For its part, the church was diligent in continuing to serve the state in political matters. As the war moved westward the pattern of services changed, with the direct war effort and propaganda activities giving way to assisting the state in establishing political control. After the war the church continued to serve the state: in the peace campaign in the fifties, in the ecumenical movement under Khrushchev, and once again in the anti-Western propaganda, as the sterner foreign policy of Brezhnev was continued by his successors.[7] But the state remained faithful to its part of the bargain only as long as Stalin lived. Under Khrushchev the church was reduced to perhaps half of its former strength, and this situation has continued unchanged.

In summary then, the war's effect on church-state relations was profound. It inaugurated a new chapter in the history of religion in the USSR, a bargaining situation in which each side made concessions. The church rendered to the state unquestioning, obedient service in political matters. In return, the state permitted the church to survive as an institution in society. This approach to church-state relations remains in force, but it has been much changed, much modified, and not at all to the church's advantage.

The Form of the Church

As far as the Russian Orthodox church is concerned, the most important effect of World War II is to be found in the nature of the church. Church-state relations were affected by the war, and the new pattern resisted erosion for decades; indeed, it is still visible in some of its aspects. The change in the nature of the church, however, was much more profound and promised to be permanent. That the Russian Orthodox church exists today in the USSR as a recognizable Orthodox, patriarchal institution, able to worship openly in society, is the direct result of the war.

In 1939, with Sergii's church organization on the point of collapse, there was a mighty rival for the affections of the Russian Orthodox believers: underground Orthodoxy.

It is curious that the existence and importance of underground Orthodoxy seldom appears in Western scholarship. I have reviewed elsewhere in some detail its history and development, the evidence for which (increasingly, from Soviet sources) is massive and convincing.[8] Here I shall outline merely the history of this phenomenon in order to indicate how decisive was the war's preservation of the official church, the Moscow Patriarchate.

Sergii's change of policy in 1927 resulted in a storm of protest. It was completely unacceptable to large sectors of the church. For example, the Moscow Patriarchate sent five thousand copies of the proclamation to the various dioceses and parishes; over 90 percent of the recipients refused to disseminate the proclamation, returning it to the sender, and the state had to intervene by publishing it shortly thereafter in *Izvestiia* in order to ensure that the change in policy became known.[9] Great numbers of Orthodox clerics and believers broke relations with the Moscow Patriarchate over this issue. At least in terms of the number of bishops who went into schism rather than accepting the new policy, Sergii's 1927 proclamation resulted in the greatest schism in all of Russian history. (In the Great Schism, or *Raskol,* of the seventeenth century, not a single bishop joined the dissenters.)

The schismatics quickly became known as Tikhonites (from Patriarch Tikhon, whose policy towards the Soviet government was opposition at first, and then neutrality, but never unconditional political loyalty). This was a generic term, however, and was used to describe a large number of local, regional, and national organizations which were formed in opposition to Sergii's new policy.

The largest and most important of these was the Josephite schism, under the nominal leadership of Metropolitan Iosif. Shortly after making his proclamation, Metropolitan Sergii ordered Iosif transferred from Rostov

(Iaroslavl province) to Leningrad. The state, however, refused him a residence permit for Leningrad, and so Sergii subsequently ordered him transferred to Odessa. Iosif broke relations with Sergii rather than accept this second transfer.

The protest spread like wildfire. Beginning in Leningrad, it quickly reached neighboring dioceses and then expanded all over the country, and a large number of bishops, priests, and parishes proclaimed Iosif as their ecclesiastical leader rather than submit to the Moscow Patriarchate.

Nor was this the only schism. Numerous others sprang up independently around the country. Perhaps the most notable was the Iaroslav Church Oblast, led by the most senior prelate in the church, Metropolitan Agafangel. At least twenty bishops supported this movement, which was sympathetic to but not affiliated with the Josephites. A host of other regional and local schisms sprang up: the Viktorianskii schism, the Varlaamovtsy, the Buevtsy, the Danilovskii movement, the Mechevtsy—more than forty names of such groups appear in the data, which are far from complete. Many of these groups affiliated with the Josephites, and most of them looked to Metropolitan Petr, whom Sergii succeeded when Petr was exiled by the regime, for canonical validity.

Such matters as loyalties and affiliations, however, soon became academic. As has been noted, the state embarked on an unrestrained antireligious campaign in 1929, and its wrath fell especially heavily on these schismatic groups. Most of the known leaders were rounded up during the winter of 1929, and the movement was forced to go underground completely. The churches that had remained loyal to the Moscow Patriarchate, however, were not spared, and very quickly the vast majority of the Orthodox believers were forced to illegal, clandestine practices to continue any semblance of their religious life. The difference between loyalty and schism became moot, and confusion swept over the Russian Orthodox church throughout the country.

Regular, strict adherence to Orthodox practice soon became impossible. There was no way of ensuring that clergy were properly ordained, that they carried out their services in strict accordance with the canons of the church, or that heresies did not creep in. Believers were forced to accept a broad range of expedients: existence of wandering priests who avoided the authorities and went from group to group; services conducted by minor clergy, or even laymen; ad hoc celebrations at a local shrine (a spring, a holy apple tree); prayer meetings conducted from memory when nothing else was available; sacraments distributed and divine rites administered by correspondence; and a host of other innovations.

New organizations sprang up, some of them Orthodox but many of them with more and more tenuous claims to that title: the Imiaslavtsy, who struggled against collectivization and all other contact with the sinful Soviet order; the Ioannity (followers of St. John of Kronstadt) who advocated celibacy in expectation of the end of the world; the Apokalypsisty, who preached what their name suggests; the Fedorovtsy, a widespread movement expecting the imminent Second Coming of Christ; and in the background were stranger movements such as the Cherdashniki, the Shashkovtsy, and the other Sects of the Red Dragon (an allusion to the biblical prophecy in Revelation 13) melting into the wilder extremes of Pentecostalism and the ancient Russian madness of the *Khlysty.*

It was inevitable. Once the lines of ecclesiology, church discipline, and church doctrine were broken, even the best ordered of parishes, when it was forced underground, risked a cascading process of detachment from Orthodoxy. After a few years, what survived might have been called Orthodoxy, but it was a long way from anything recognizable in terms of the thousand-year tradition of the Russian Orthodox church. Nevertheless, these movements were congenial to the Russian people, and in the absence of openly functioning Orthodox churches, they were mightily attractive. Had the official Russian Orthodox church been forced to that last, small step over the brink of complete collapse, these underground Orthodox movements would have taken its place.

They very nearly did so anyhow. During World War II, as will become apparent later, the underground Orthodox surfaced immediately in the occupied areas, created their local and even district church organizations, and began vigorous activity. In the areas which were not occupied a similar phenomenon took place.

Even after the war was over, underground Orthodoxy was able to offer serious competition to the Patriarchal churches for some years. The war years and the preceeding decade of pressure had effected the amalgamation of underground Orthodoxy. What had been a congeries of local and regional groupings, more or less (or not at all) affiliated nominally to some prelate, now coalesced into two identifiable movements: the True Orthodox Church and the True Orthodox Christians.

The former was the more highly organized. It attempted to reproduce in clandestine circumstances as much of traditional Orthodoxy as possible. Its worship and activities were premised on the services of a functioning priesthood. At least for the decade of the 1940s the True Orthodox Church was able to provide itself with priests. To be sure, given the necessities of the illegal, underground position, the True Orthodox Church was not able to ensure that all priests had received a canonical ordination. Probably they had, for the secret ordaining of young men into the priesthood has been a tradition in all branches of Orthodoxy, legal as well as illegal, throughout the Soviet period. Nor could the canonical services of the episcopacy often be provided. Although from time to time there were administrative leaders on a district or regional basis, there is no evidence that the True Orthodox Church possessed (or even pretended to possess) any substantial corps of secret bishops.

Despite these limitations, the True Orthodox Church was able to provide a structured approach to Orthodoxy which, on the local level, differed little from the traditional services the Russian people had enjoyed from their church in happier times. Certainly the differences between such services and those of the legalized, patriarchal church were negligible to most of the people, and great numbers of the Orthodox Russians actually preferred the True Orthodox Church services when they had the choice.

While there were real advantages to the highly structured approach of this clandestine movement, there also were disadvantages which led to the movement's disappearance. Given the necessity of the services of a priest, all the state needed to do was discover and remove the priests, and the movement could no longer function. This the state did in the early fifties, and the True Orthodox Church ceased to exist except in remote, scattered groups here and there across the vast country.

The other postwar movement, the True Orthodox Christians, was much less highly organized. Indeed, no structure at all was required, merely the desire to give expression together to the Orthodox faith. If a priest was available (a wandering priest dropping by, for example, or someone who claimed to be a priest [even if not very credibly], or even someone who remembered the liturgy) his services were gratefully accepted. If not, then True Orthodox Christians would perform whatever worship services were possible: observing the vesper service, or parts of it, under the leadership of a layman or (more often) an old woman; singing the *akafisti* from memory; listening to an extemporaneous exhortation or sermon; or merely reciting from memory the Orthodox prayers learned at the grandmother's knee.

Most of the time, and in most places, the True Orthodox Christians could provide only the palest shadow of the rich liturgical life of Orthodoxy. Where a patriarchal church was open, however tainted its leaders may have seemed, the True Orthodox Christians generally did not exist or, if they did, were confined to the most adamant of the Moscow Patriarchate's foes. The problem, however, was that there were so few open churches in the postwar period. As will become apparent below, the geographic distribution of the limited number of churches that the regime permitted to function was far from uniform, and vast reaches of the Russian land had no church whatsoever available. Here the True Orthodox Christians sprang up in village after village, town after town, and even in the cities. They constituted a formidable competitor to the Moscow Patriarchate for the affections of the Russian believers simply because they could function in places where the state would not permit patriarchal churches to exist.

Their informal structure made them almost impervious to state pressure. Time and again the authorities would attempt to disrupt a functioning unit of the True Orthodox Christians by arresting all its known adherents, but they would miss one or two, and within weeks the group would be functioning as vigorously as before. The True Orthodox Christians handily survived the concerted attempt in the early fifties to suppress underground Orthodoxy; indeed, they grew significantly, for the campaign against the more highly structured True Orthodox Church, once it had succeeded in removing a group's priest, inevitably caused that group to evolve into yet another parish of the True Orthodox Christians.

The state made a much more serious attempt to eradicate this group in the antireligious campaign of the sixties. The severity of that campaign certainly reduced the numbers of the True Orthodox Christians. But strangely enough, it also had the effect of giving birth to more highly structured forms of the movement. When the increasing pressure forced the True Orthodox Christians to go deep, deep into the underground, then it became more feasible for them to organize on a regional and even on a national basis. Leaders of the movement could no longer appear openly in society; thus they went completely underground and were able to organize their life into networks which reached from Siberia to the western borderlands.

Over the years, however, the Moscow Patriarchate was generally able to win out over the underground movements. The True Orthodox Christians still exist, but they are not, numerically, a very important challenge to the legalized churches. The advantages of being able to work openly in society are overwhelming; the concessions gained during World War II were sufficient to allow the Russian Orthodox church to revive and to continue to the present as a Patriarchal church. Had the war not effected this change, Orthodoxy in the USSR would not today be a Patriarchal church functioning openly in society.

The Function of the Church

But World War II had an even more profound effect than this. It determined the structure of the modern Russian Orthodox church, to be sure, but it also ratified profound changes in the mission and, indeed, the very nature of the church itself.

The concessions that the state gave to the church from the war onwards were very tightly proscribed and limited. In particular, both the constitution of the USSR and the legislation on religion limited the church's function to worship services only. All other forms of religious activity are prohibited. It was implicit, of course, in the church's offer of political support and in its endeavor to gain permission to function as an institution in society that the church would agree to abide by the laws of that society. Perforce, then, the church had to accept the limitations inherent in the society's laws.

This meant that the church's mission was purely spiritual. The church "considers politics from the point of view of their contribution to her cause—the cause of the spiritual salvation of man."[10] The new situation meant "a return to [the church's] own sphere of activity—that of concern for the salvation of the souls entrusted to its leadership."[11] Or, as a Western observer, for example, reported on a conversation with an archbishop: "In answer to my question, 'What is the main task of the church?' his answer was immediate, 'It prepares people for the next life.'"[12] All social activities were prohibited—Sunday schools, young people's associations, charitable activities, anything at all other than worship services. The church had to accept the bitter realization that in exchange for the right to exist legally, its mission was reduced exclusively to the spiritual. All social concern, any mission to society, all responsibility for moral improvement in the public realm were prohibited. The church's mission was vertical only, and there was no horizontal dimension to it at all.

This was a profound, wrenching change for the Russian Orthodox church to absorb. For Russian Orthodoxy traditionally was deeply involved in the social concerns of Christianity as well as the spiritual. That facile Western misunderstanding that presumes Orthodoxy to be an otherworldly, purely mystical, ethereal approach to the faith is, quite simply, wrong. Orthodoxy, especially Russian Orthodoxy, has traditionally been deeply rooted in the soil of the land, and its prime concern—often to the despair of its mystics— has been with *this* world, with *today's* society, with Christianizing the culture in this world too.

The prerevolutionary church is a case in point. In the Russian Empire, Russian Orthodoxy was profoundly involved in the social affairs of what would now be called the secular society. It spent a great deal—most?—of its efforts in providing for the civil ceremonies of society: birth registration (baptisms), marriage (weddings), and death (funerals). It ran the school system for the entire country. It was vigorously involved in missions, both within the Empire as the borders were pushed eastward, and abroad in Alaska, North America, and elsewhere. And these missions, while they may well have had a spiritual dimension, certainly had a full measure of social concern: spreading the Russian culture. The Russian people were much involved in ceremonies, in the polysyllabic titles deriving from religious precedents, and in the quasi-superstitious reverences of Orthodoxy, but not many of them seemed profoundly spiritual. The church was a part of their society, a part of their humdrum lives.

Not so today. Today the church has a purely religious, purely supernatural function in society. It can have no interest in, and it can make no efforts for, the improvement of society in any way. Although it is deeply concerned with ethics (all Christianity is), it can only deal with the personal ethics of individual believers; the ethics of society at large is legally beyond its purview.

This acceptance of a purely spiritual role in society, this renunciation of any social mission, is really what is at the heart of the controversy with the schismatics. It is a peculiarity of our times that both the Soviet sources and militantly anticommunist observers in the West claim that underground Orthodoxy is a purely political phenomenon, that these people refuse the Moscow Patriarchate because of their political hostility to the atheistic, communist regime.[13] This is not the case. The point at issue was, in fact, the interference of the state in the internal life of the church, its mission, and its procedures for carrying out that mission.

Metropolitan Sergii's acceptance of the Soviet regime in 1927 was distasteful to a large sector of the church, probably the majority. The Leningrad diocese, for example, had acquiesced to the declaration, but when the fruits that it bore proved to be Soviet interference in the internal life of the church—in the critical matter of deployment of bishops—then the diocese went into schism. The initial announcement of the formation of the independent Iaroslav Church Oblast led by Metropolitan Agafangel makes this point explicitly.

> We welcome this [1927] requirement and testify that we have always been, are, and will be loyal and obedient to the civil government; always have been, are, and will be honorable and conscientious citizens of our mother country; but this, we consider, has nothing in common with the policy called for by you and does not invite and require the children of the church to voluntary renunciation of those rights of freely organizing the inner religious life of the society of the church which that policy itself grants to the civil government (allowing congregations of believers to elect their own clerical leaders).[14]

This was the critical issue: interference in the life and mission of the church, not politics. To be sure, it is difficult to separate the one from the other, and when the pressure of the antireligious campaign became severe, then quite naturally a great many of those who had been forced underground reacted with hostility toward the state, and apocalyptic denunciations proliferated. But most of those who went underground were willing to accept the Soviet regime, grudgingly, perhaps, but in good conscience. What they could not accept was the regime's insistence that the only function of the church was worship services while every other facet of life must be under the regime's exclusive control.

This attitude persisted. Under the German occupation, for example, when Orthodox believers came out into the open from the underground, the massive religious resurgence was by no means confined to worship services. Nikita Struve, in his description of the Pskov mission of the Orthodox church under the occupation, points this out vividly.

> Particular attention was paid to the young who had been affected by Marxism. Priests were authorized to teach the catechism in the primary schools; special courses on religion were organized for adolescents, and requests for admission exceeded the limits of space and staff available. In Pskov, study circles met five times a week. Neither were social activities neglected by the mission, so far as the occupying power allowed them. In 1943 each parish adopted a prison camp and entrusted the young with the task of collecting food, and clothing, etc., for it.[15]

In the sixties one underground Orthodox movement, the True Orthodox Christians Wanderers, was discovered to maintain a system of theological schools on the elementary, secondary, and advanced levels; facilities for production and distribution of literature; a network of "safe houses" and supply personnel; a nationwide postal service; and the like.[16]

Indeed, it may be a general rule of our times: people who reject the legalized churches in the USSR do so not primarily because of political hostility to the Soviet regime; rather, they choose an underground existence, with all its dangers and discomforts, because they do not agree that the faith can be restricted to the purely spiritual, purely worship functions as the Soviet laws demand.

The Russian Orthodox church has accepted these laws. Thanks to the intervention of World War II it was able to preserve its traditional, patriarchal structure in the Moscow Patriarchate. The price it paid was acceptance of a mission confined exclusively to the spiritual, with no social dimension at all. This is a new phenomenon in Orthodoxy, and is certainly the most profound change that the war brought to the Russian church.

The Nature of Society

Perhaps the most important, and certainly the most widespread effect of World War II on religion is to be found in the religious character of the society which has emerged. Disappointing the fond hopes of the professional atheists, religion has not disappeared from Soviet society, but the profile of religion was profoundly altered by the war.

The key to understanding this effect of World War II is to be found in the country's resulting religious demography. The war created a sort of Soviet "Bible Belt." All of those areas which were under German occupation during the war, in more or less of a crescent from Volgograd to the gates of Leningrad, still show the legacy of the occupation. Perhaps they always will.

During the occupation, the German authorities either ignored religion entirely or, in some cases, actually encouraged and facilitated its revival.[17] This religious revival gave a marked character to the entire belt of lands under German occupation. The character persists to this day.

The evidence is unanimous that all of the various indices of religiousness increase as one goes westward into these formerly occupied areas of the Soviet Bible Belt.[18] The number of believers rises from a minority in parts of European Russia toward a majority of the population in these regions, and sometimes an overwhelming majority. This high incidence of religious belief is both the cause and the consequence of the distribution of churches in the USSR. In most denominations half of the legally operating churches are to be found in the Bible Belt.[19] All of the other identifiable indices of religiousness in society repeat this pattern of increase in the Bible Belt as compared to the Russian areas which were not under occupation.

Nor is this all: there are profound changes in the religious composition within the Bible Belt, many of which are the direct result of World War II.

Perhaps the most important of these is an increase in the non-Orthodox sector of the population.[20] Even in Slavic populations, which traditionally have been Orthodox—e.g., parts of the Ukraine—the growth of sectarian movements such as Baptist, Pentecostal, Jehovah's Witness, and the various indigenous sects, has been one of the most remarkable features of the society's postwar development. When the flourishing underground Orthodox and especially (in the formerly Uniate areas) the underground Catholic movements are added to the Protestant sects, the religious profile of the society is profoundly different from that of other parts of European Russia.

Although this phenomenon has yet to be studied extensively, several possible reasons for this transformation of the religious profile of Bible Belt areas can be suggested. First, during World War II, and especially in the early months of the war, these areas were bitterly anti-Soviet, and the population went over to the Germans en masse. The Wehrmacht was welcomed as a liberating army, and the awful history of the preceding two decades of Soviet rule was repudiated with all that went with it. The Moscow Patriarchate, of course, which had steadfastly proclaimed its loyalty to the Soviet government despite the worst of the regime's atrocities against the people, could scarcely hope to escape at least some of the taint. And especially when the Patriarchate entered into the war effort with enthusiasm and outspoken support of the Soviet forces (along with condemnation of all who forsook the regime), alienation from the Moscow Patriarchate became more and more pronounced in the occupied areas. Not only did the believers there shun the Patriarchate by conviction, they also found it expedient to do so to avoid giving occasion to the growing wrath of the Nazi rulers against the populations of the occupied areas.

When the Red Army returned to these areas, these anti-Soviet sentiments continued and, indeed, grew.

Much of the region was embroiled in a virtual civil war with the returning Soviet authorities. This sorry chapter in the history of these regions is virtually ignored in the West, but the resistance to the reimposition of Soviet control was widespread and, in a great many times and places, bloody. Bandera's army ranged through the western Ukraine and was not overcome for a decade. The resistance in Lithuania was widespread and vicious, and there is some evidence that churchmen were not entirely uninvolved.[21] This bitter struggle which raged through these lands in the months and years following World War II only intensified the endemic hatred of Soviet rule throughout the Bible Belt.

And the corollary of this dissatisfaction with the social controls which had been imposed from the east was a rise of nationalism. Throughout the Bible Belt, the nationalistic sentiments of the population were intensified and grew as a result of the wartime events. More and more the people began to insist on their own identity as contrasted with the Russians who came, first to reoccupy their lands and then in a continuing and increasing stream of immigration. Not surprisingly, religious elements were enlisted in the burgeoning nationalism of the population. Not to be Orthodox, or in some regions to be Orthodox but to reject the Moscow Patriarchate, became one of the touchstones of nationalism. The increased incidence of religion throughout the Bible Belt went hand in hand with the increase of nationalism.

There is a further difference in the religious composition of the Bible Belt societies. The ultimate effects of these religious differences are difficult to foresee; however, they may be profound. In most of Russia, overt religiousness seems to be concentrated in a certain sector of the population. In far greater proportions than their incidence in the general population would suggest, the elderly and women predominate among those who admit to being religious. Not so in the Bible Belt. Here a significantly higher percentage of the religious believers are middle aged and younger, and the number of men and women tend to be represented more equally. Indeed, in much of the region the age distribution and the proportion of men to women replicate the patterns of the general population.[22]

To date no observer has been able to suggest reasons for this pattern. Is it because there are fewer social sanctions against religiousness in these regions, and that it is less risky to declare one's beliefs openly? Is it because the religious organizations are less compromised in the eyes of the citizenry than the Moscow Patriarchate with its close association with the authorities? Is it because religion is identified with nationality?

The result of these changes is that by and large the non-Russian nationalities of the Soviet Union have become markedly more religious than the Russians. In the western borderlands much of this change can be directly linked to the war. In the Ukraine, studies of the number of people who believe in God consistently yield aggregate totals of 45 percent of the population or even more, as compared with 25–35 percent, and sometimes less, in the Russian areas. The same pattern persists in Belorussia. In the Baltic states neither Latvia nor Estonia, with their European cultures, display the rampant secularization of Western Europe, but instead, half or more of the population remains religious. And in Lithuania, with the exception of 20 percent of the population who are Russian immigrants, the pattern of religiousness much more closely emulates postwar Poland than Russia, with the vast majority of the population overtly religious.[23]

These western borderlands, then, have come to display the same high incidence of religion that has long been the case among other minority nationalities. Religion is much more pervasive—far more common than among the Russians—in the minority nationalities of Muslim extraction in central Asia.[24] Similarly, the Armenians and the Georgians tend to embrace religion as a natural part of their culture. None of these, of course, nor any of the dozens of other nationalities like them, can trace their religiousness even in part to the wartime experience; that is a peculiarity of the Bible Belt nationalities.

The Bible Belt has thus joined the other minority nationalities in the USSR in the virtual identity of religion with nationality. To be a member of one of these nationalities almost automatically means also to be religious. Conversely, to be Russian in these areas not only means to be a foreigner but also, by and large, to be irreligious. And it is a very short step from viewing outsiders as atheists to viewing them as uncivilized barbarians.

The strange result, then, is that at least insofar as religion is concerned, the Russians have become barbarians within their own domain. In earlier times the Russians could claim—indeed, they took great pride in doing so—that their expansion was a divine mission bringing the blessings of Christian civilization to the heathen, irreligious barbarians. This is no longer so.

One illustration may bear this out: morality. The connection between religion and ethics is universally perceived in the USSR. Religious people are expected to behave more ethically than others to such an extent that when they do not, even atheistic researchers express indignation.[25]

With the spread of atheism, or, more properly, irreligion (for committed atheists are as rare as Christians in the Russian lands—rarer, in fact) this connection with ethics has been broken, and the leaders of atheism in the USSR have enjoyed scant success in attempting to provide a foundation for ethics in the absence of religion.[26] When upwardly mobile Russians, then, move in to live among or dominate minority nationalities, they are viewed (and generally correctly) as irreligious; the corollary would be that they are not expected to abide by Christian ethics.

The problem is vastly compounded, of course, by the economic and political system that the Russians represent. This is largely because the Soviet Union insists upon a peculiar approach to industrialized life that, to date at least, has proven unworkable without increasing reliance on theft, fraud, bribery, and all manner of extralegal expedients. Especially in the countryside, life in the USSR is virtually impossible without recourse to influence, cheating, and illegality in providing for one's needs.

At least in the eyes of the minority nationalities, then, the Russians have become the religious barbarians of the twentieth century. According to some reports, at least, the "Russian soul," the fascination with metaphysics, the search for meaning has by and large succumbed to a crass, opportunistic pursuit of material gain.[27]

This is especially visible among the educated elite, large sectors of which seem obsessed with the pursuit of a better apartment, a choice work assignment or, above all, the right to live in Moscow or Leningrad. The high commitment of the nineteenth-century *Narodniki,* who idealistically abandoned all to "go to the people" in service, the soul-searching agonies of the "useless sons" questing for some high calling in life, and even the salon posturing searchers for high metaphysical truth are not very visible today, apparently, having been swallowed in the endless gray of materialism among the elite.

Among the rank and file, the common citizens, matters are doubtless worse in the Russian hinterlands. The data are sparse, for we really know surprisingly little of life outside the urbanized centers. But certainly it is apparent that there is little or nothing left of at least the outward paraphernalia of religion that used to be so visible among the Russian peasants—the daily ritual, the incessant crossing of oneself, the appeals to the saints, the reliance on imprecations (which today exists only in the remarkably inventive cadences of Russian profanity).

The net result, then, is a reversal of what was at least claimed under the old empire. Within the Soviet domain, the Russians are no longer bringing Christianity and civilization to the benighted peoples of the non-Orthodox world. At least from the point of view of the minority nationalities and the Bible Belt, the Russians represent the new invasion of irreligion, immorality, and barbarianism.

This is the enduring legacy of World War II. It transformed the religious profile of the societies of the occupied areas, forming them into a new Bible Belt. It narrowed the church's mission to the purely spiritual, with no social dimension at all. It won for the Russian church a legal, as opposed to an underground, existence in society. And it established a bargaining pattern of church-state relations which, modified and weakened, remains to this day. In all these respects, World War II was the single most important event in the twentieth century for the history of religion in the USSR.

Notes

1. Russian Orthodox Eastern Church, *Patriarkh Sergii i ego dukhovnoe nasledstvo* (Moscow: Moscow Patriarchate, 1947), 234.

2. Russian Orthodox Eastern Church, *The Truth about Religion in Russia* (Moscow: Moscow Patriarchate, 1942), 8–9.

3. For a more detailed examination of the evolution of this approach to church-state relations, see William C. Fletcher, *A Study in Survival: The Church in Russia, 1927–1943* (New York: Macmillan, and London: SPCK, 1965), and also Richard H. Marshall, Jr., "Fifteen Years of Change: A Review of the Post-Stalin Era," in Max Hayward and William C. Fletcher, eds., *Religion and the Soviet State: A Dilemma of Power* (New York: Praeger, 1969): 1–18.

4. *Izvestiia,* 18 August 1927.

5. Russian Orthodox Church, *The Truth about Religion.*

6. William C. Fletcher, "USSR," in *Western Religion: A Country by Country Sociological Inquiry,* ed. Hans [J. J.] Mol (The Hague and Paris: Mouton, 1972): 565–86.

7. William C. Fletcher, *Religion and Soviet Foreign Policy* (London: The Royal Institute of International Affairs [Oxford University Press], 1973).

8. William C. Fletcher, *The Russian Orthodox Church Underground, 1917–1970* (London: Oxford University Press, 1971).

9. Archimandrite Ioann (Snychev), "Tserkovnye raskoly v russkoi tserkvi 20-kh i 30-kh godov XX stoletiia—grigorianskii, iaroslavskii, iosiflianskii, viktorianskii i drugie. Ikh osobennost' i istoriia" (Magister's diss.: Moscow Theological Academy, 1965), 189, 196.

10. Russian Orthodox Eastern Church, *The Russian Orthodox Church, Organization, Situation, Activity* (Moscow: Moscow Patriarchate, 1959), 230.

11. Ibid., 7.

12. Marcus Bach, *God and the Soviets* (New York: Crowell, 1958), 158.

13. Fletcher, *The Russian . . . Church Underground,* 13.

14. *Delo Mitropolita Sergiia* (unpublished typescript, n.p. [1930?]), 66: 170. Cf. Ioann (Snychev), *Tserkovnye raskoly,* 165.

15. Nikita Struve, *Christians in Contemporary Russia* (London: Harvill Press, 1967), 71–72.

16. Fletcher, *The Russian . . . Church Underground,* 235–49.

17. Wassilij Alexeev, "The Drama of Exarch Sergii Voskresenskii," *Irenikon,* no. 2 (1957): 189–201.

18. William C. Fletcher, *Soviet Believers: The Religious Sector of the Population* (Lawrence, Kans.: Regents Press of Kansas, 1981), 68, 70–71.

19. Ibid., 178.

20. Iibd., 71–72.
21. V. Stanley Vardys, *The Catholic Church, Dissent and Nationality in Soviet Lithuania* (New York: East European Quarterly [Columbia University Press], 1978), 69–72.
22. Fletcher, *Soviet Believers*, 81–82.
23. Iu. B. Pishchik, "Sovremennyi protestantizm: problemy teorii i praktiki," in A. F. Okulov, ed., *Voprosy nauchnogo ateizma* 13 (1972): 410.
24. Fletcher, *Soviet Believers*, 70.
25. Ibid., 165–167.
26. Ibid., 167.
27. For example, see Andrea Lee, *Russian Journal* (New York: Random House, 1982).

References

Alexeev, Wallilij. "The Drama of Exarch Sergii Voskresenskii." *Irenikon,* no. 2 (1957): 189–201.

Bach, Marcus. *God and the Soviets.* New York: Crowell, 1958.

Delo Metropolita Sergiia. Unpublished typescript, n.p. (1930?).

Fletcher, William C. *Religion and Soviet Foreign Policy.* London: The Royal Institute of International Affairs (Oxford University Press), 1973.

_____. *The Russian Orthodox Church Underground, 1917–1970.* London: Oxford University Press, 1971.

_____. *Soviet Believers: The Religious Sector of the Population.* Lawrence, Kansas: Regents Press of Kansas, 1981.

_____. *A Study in Survival: The Church in Russia, 1927–1943.* New York: Macmillan, and London: SPCK, 1965.

_____. "USSR," in *Western Religion: A Country by Country Sociological Inquiry,* ed. Hans [J. J.] Mol. The Hague and Paris: Mouton, 1972.

Hayward, Max and William C. Fletcher, eds. *Religion and the Soviet State: A Dilemma of Power.* New York: Praeger, 1969.

Ioann (Snychev), Archimandrite. "Tserkovnye raskoly v russkoi tserkve 20-kh i 30-kh godov XX stoletiia—grigorianskii, iaroslavskii, iosiflianskii, viktorianskii i drugie. Ikh osobennost' i istoriia." Magister's diss., Moscow Theological Academy, 1965.

Lee, Andrea. *Russian Journal.* New York: Random House, 1982.

Marshall, Richard H., Jr. "Fifteen Years of Change: A Review of the Post-Stalin Era," in Hayward & Fletcher, *Religion,* 1–18.

Okulov, A. F., ed. *Voprosy nauchnogo ateizma.* Moscow: "Mysl'," biennially.

Pishchik, Iu. B. "Sovremennyi protestantizm: problemy teorii i praktiki," in Okulov, *Voprosy,* 13 (1972): 410.

Russian Orthodox Eastern Church, *Patriarkh Sergii i ego dukhovnoe nasledstvo.* Moscow: Moscow Patriarchate, 1947.

_____. *The Russian Orthodox Church, Organization, Situation, Activity.* Moscow: Moscow Patriarchate, 1959.

_____. *The Truth about Religion in Russia.* Moscow: Moscow Patriarchate, 1942.

Struve, Nikita. *Christians in Contemporary Russia.* London: Harvill Press, 1967.

Vardys, V. Stanley. *The Catholic Church, Dissent and Nationality in Soviet Lithuania.* New York: East European Quarterly (Columbia University Press), 1978.

7

Soviet Policy and the Division of Germany, 1941–1945

ROBERT M. SLUSSER

In October 1949 the Soviets sponsored the establishment, in their zone of occupation in Germany, of the communist-controlled German Democratic Republic. Approximately one month earlier a West German state, the Federal Republic of Germany, had been formed in the three Western zones of occupation—British, U.S., and French.

The establishment of an East German state was not the outcome of a deliberate and conscious policy on the part of Stalin and his advisers, but rather the unforeseen and, in part, unwanted culmination of Soviet actions and policies toward Germany in interaction with those of the three Western Allies. Each of the four occupying powers contributed to the final outcome, but only two, Great Britain and France, deliberately framed their policies with that goal in view.

Initial Soviet War Aims: The Eden-Stalin Talks

For Stalin during the first six months of the war, the single overriding war aim was survival. It was only when the minimum conditions for achieving that goal had been ensured by the Soviet victory in the Battle of Moscow that Stalin was able to formulate other, broader, war aims looking to the eventual defeat of Nazi Germany and her allies.

The occasion for Stalin's initial formulation of long-range Soviet war aims was the visit to Moscow of British Foreign Secretary Anthony Eden

The research on which this chapter is based was made possible in part by a grant from the American Council of Learned Societies.

on 16–20 December 1941. In the course of their conversations, Eden and Stalin ranged widely over the problems facing the Soviet Union and Britain as wartime allies, among them the future of Germany. As reported by Eden, Stalin put forward a number of specific proposals for weakening Germany, both by transferring portions of her territory to other states, including the USSR, and by splitting Germany itself into a number of independent states. The Rhineland, and possibly Bavaria, were to become autonomous; Austria was to regain her independence; Poland would receive East Prussia; the Sudetenland would be restored to Czechoslovakia; and for the USSR Stalin demanded a strip of territory north of the Nemen River, including the Baltic port of Königsberg.[1]

Strictly limited in his negotiating powers by his directives from the War Cabinet, Eden was unable to make any formal commitments on behalf of Britain, but he received a vivid perception that Stalin was determined to see Germany dismembered after the war, and this impression, conveyed to Churchill and the War Cabinet, played a major role in shaping British concepts of the probable direction of Soviet policy toward Germany and thereby, indirectly, in shaping British policy itself.

Among the topics discussed during the Eden-Stalin talks was that of the postwar occupation of Germany. Eden told Stalin:

> There was no doubt that some kind of military control over Germany would be necessary and . . . Great Britain, the Soviet Union and the United States, if they would help, would have to undertake it.[2]

There is no indication, however, that Stalin responded to this suggestion or recognized in it the germ of an idea which would eventually determine the future of Germany. Stalin's overriding concern, according to Eden, was for Soviet security. It was this concern that underlay his insistence on British recognition of the Soviet frontiers with Poland of September 1939, a recognition that Eden refused to give.

Sharply contrasting with the plans for Germany's dismemberment, which Stalin outlined in his talks with Eden, were his public utterances. In an order of the day to the Red Army on 23 February 1942, Stalin said, "The experience of history teaches us that Hitlers come and go but the German people, the German state remain."[3] Stalin elaborated the idea in a speech on Red Square on 6 November 1942:

> Such a goal as the destruction of Germany we do not have, since it is impossible to destroy Germany, just as it is impossible to destroy Russia. But we can and must destroy the Hitler state. Our task is to destroy the Hitler state and those who have inspired it.

But even here Stalin sounded a moderate note:

> It is not our aim to destroy all military force in Germany, for every literate person will understand that it is not only impossible in regard to Germany

as it is in regard to Russia, but it is also inexpedient from the point of view of the future. But Hitler's army can and should be destroyed.[4]

The British, meanwhile, were contemplating the bleak prospect of a weakened postwar Britain unable to secure the cooperation of her wartime allies, Russia and the United States. In that unpromising eventuality, Eden reported to the cabinet on 5 October 1942,

we should eventually have to accept the collaboration of Germany, with the feeble hope that the Germans would undergo a change of heart and turn away from aggression.[5]

It was early in 1943 that the British began seriously to formulate plans for the zonal occupation of Germany. In a paper submitted to the cabinet on 16 January 1943, Eden advocated not only "the joint occupation of Germany by the three major Allies" after the war but also the exercise by the occupying powers of "a very close control over its economic life."[6]

The greatest danger, as Eden reported on March 8, 1943, was that of . . . an orientation of German policy toward the USSR and the conclusion of a Russian-German alliance directed against the West.

"The ultimate aim of the communists," Eden warned,

. . . would be not regional autonomy but the seizure of power in a united Germany.[7]

It was with these thoughts in mind that Eden traveled to Washington in March 1943 for talks with President Roosevelt and his advisers. Aware that the future of Germany was likely to take a prominent place in these Anglo-American talks, the Soviets called into play their diplomatic representatives to register Soviet views on this vital topic. In London Soviet Ambassador Ivan Maisky told Eden that

the Soviet Government, which wishes to see Germany broken up, would countenance some kind of federal union between the parts.[8]

At approximately the same time the same point was being made by the Soviet ambassador to the United States, Maxim Litvinov, in a conversation with Roosevelt's close associate, Harry Hopkins.[9]

With his memories of the December 1941 talks with Stalin thus refreshed, Eden told Roosevelt that "Stalin was likely to insist on breaking up Germany into a number of states." As to Stalin's views on the future of Germany, Eden expressed his "private opinion," that, far from wishing to dominate a defeated postwar Germany, Stalin was anxious to have U.S. and British forces fully committed in Europe at the time of Germany's collapse, in order that Russia would not have to "take full responsibility for what would happen in Germany or the rest of Europe."[10]

During the Eden-Roosevelt talks Harry Hopkins suggested that the British and Americans should jointly work out plans for the future of Germany and then present them to the Russians.[11] Roosevelt approved the suggestion and the Americans assumed it had British acceptance as well. Instead, the British, shortly after Eden's return to London, began formulating their own plans for Germany's postwar treatment. It was these plans, discussed neither with the Americans nor the Russians, which determined Germany's fate.

The process began with a memorandum to the cabinet by Eden on 25 May 1943, in which he outlined the division of Germany after her defeat into three zones of occupation.[12] Unable to reach a conclusion on the matter because of disagreement over the question of total military occupation, the cabinet referred the problem to the Armistice and Postwar Committee (APW), one of a number of agencies established within the British government to work out policy on questions concerning the conduct of the war and planning for the postwar period. Among these the APW was one of the most important, by reason of the urgency of the tasks with which it was charged, an importance recognized by the designation of Deputy Premier Clement Attlee as its chairman, whence its common designation as the Attlee Committee.[13] On 31 July, the APW was reorganized and renamed the Committee on Armistice Terms and Civil Administration (ACA), with Attlee continuing as chairman.[14]

It was in the Attlee Committee that detailed plans for the occupation of Germany were drawn up. By the late summer of 1943 the committee had prepared its final report, including a plan for the division of Germany into three zones of occupation, with the Soviets in the east, the British in the northwest and the Americans in the southwest. Berlin would be deep inside the Soviet zone but not part of it; instead, Berlin would be subject to three-power occupation. The plan made no provision for access to Berlin by the Western powers.[15]

Meanwhile, Soviet planning was proceeding on the assumption that Germany would retain her unity after defeat. The problem, therefore, as the Soviets saw it, was how to obtain a dominant position in postwar Germany. In a step toward this goal the Soviets on 12 July 1943, announced the formation of a National Committee for a Free Germany, headed by the veteran German Communist leader Walter Ulbricht. A week later the first issue of the committee's newspaper, *Freies Deutschland,* appeared, and on the following day the committee began radio broadcasts to Germany from a transmitter in the Soviet Union.[16]

The Soviets were aware, however, that Communist appeals would need reinforcement from other opinion-making circles in Germany if their objectives were to be reached. They were also aware of the potential leverage their control over vast numbers of German prisoners of war gave them. It was in response to considerations of this kind that the Soviets in September 1943 announced the formation of a League of German Officers.[17]

The Americans, meanwhile, were also drawing up plans for Germany's postwar future. A Department of State report entitled "The Political Reorganization of Germany," issued on 23 September 1943, took a forthright stand against the forcible dismemberment of Germany, seeing it as "a grave danger to future world order." Instead, the paper favored a unified but decentralized Germany, organized on the federal principle, within which a democratic nation could emerge. Failure to pursue wise and enlightened policies in Germany, the paper warned, entailed the risk that Russia might achieve dominance of postwar Germany.[18] This paper formed part of the preparatory material which U.S. Secretary of State Cordell Hull took with him to the Conference of Foreign Ministers (CFM) which met in Moscow from 18 October to 1 November 1943. Hull himself remained undecided on the subject of Germany's future, but his chief had no such hesitations. In a meeting with Hull on October 5 the president "stated 'categorically' that he was in favor of the partition of Germany into three or more sovereign states. These states must be held together only in a customs union."[19]

Neither the Americans nor the Russians, however, came to the Moscow CFM with a fully worked-out plan for Germany's future. Hull, despite Roosevelt's urging, stuck by his experts' preference for a united but decentralized Germany. As to the Russians, Molotov, in response to a query from Eden, said the Soviet government was "somewhat backward" in its study of the question of dismembering Germany, because of its leaders' preoccupation with the military aspects of the war. Molotov added that, "He was sure, however, that [the Soviet leaders] would give weight to any opinion in favor of dismemberment [of Germany] by force."[20]

Two measures to weaken Germany were agreed on by the conference: the transfer of East Prussia to Poland and the reestablishment of Austrian independence. For the rest, the conference decided to set up a three-power European Advisory Commission (EAC), based in London with a mandate which included preparing recommendations to the three governments on problems concerned with the end of the war. The EAC's first task, it was agreed, was to prepare detailed recommendations on the terms of surrender by Germany and her allies and the methods of controlling them after the war.[21]

Despite its origins as a three-power body, the EAC did not enjoy equal support from each of the Allies. Both the Russians and the Americans feared it might take on attributes of policy making rather than restricting itself to recommending policies on which the heads of state could then say the final word. The British, however, quickly recognized in the EAC an instrumentality which could be used to translate into three-power decisions plans which had been thus far British alone.

British officials operating within a combined Anglo-American staff had meanwhile drawn up plans for the military occupation of Germany immediately after her defeat. Like the Attlee Committee's plan for zonal occupation, the military plan (designated by the cover name RANKIN) called for Soviet occupation in the east, Britain in the northwest, and U.S.

in the southwest. Shown a draft of RANKIN en route to the Teheran Conference, Roosevelt expressed strong objections to it, not with regard to the proposed Soviet zone but with regard to the two western zones. The United States, he felt, should have the northwest zone, leaving the southwest to the British.[22]

Roosevelt's objections to RANKIN marked the start of a protracted and acrimonious dispute between the British and Americans that was finally resolved by a compromise at the Second Quebec Conference in September 1944, under which the two western zones remained as designated in the original RANKIN plan, but with the United States receiving special rights in port enclaves at Bremen and Bremerhaven in the British zone.[23]

The squabble over zones served to deflect the Americans' attention from the long-range implications of the British plan for postwar Germany, including its anomalous provisions for Berlin. It was not the military planners, however, who determined Germany's future; RANKIN, for all the controversy it generated, was merely a temporary plan for the short-term military occupation of Germany. The crucial planning for Germany's future was that pioneered by the Attlee Committee in the summer of 1943 and carried through, on British initiative, in the European Advisory Commission in 1944.

Germany's Future at the Teheran Conference

The question of Germany's future occupied a prominent place among the topics discussed at the Big Three conference in Teheran (28 November–1 December 1943). By this time the outcome of the war in Europe could be regarded as decided—Germany's ultimate defeat was inevitable, given the forces arrayed against her, and the Allies, for the first time, were in a position to draw up meaningful strategic plans for the coming year.

It was Churchill who introduced the subject of Germany's future, on the first day of the conference. Germany, he said, should be subjected to "far-reaching territorial changes"; its place in the center of Europe might be taken by a federation of Austria, Bavaria, and Hungary.[24] Stalin rejected this proposal as "insufficient," but avoided committing himself to anything more definite.

At dinner on November 29 Stalin spoke of the need for "really effective means to control Germany . . . otherwise Germany would rise again within 15 to 20 years to plunge the world into another war." As to the measures he had in mind, they included the liquidation of "at least 50,000 and perhaps 100,000 of the German commanding staff" and the retention by the Allies of

the important strategic positions in the world so that if Germany moved a muscle she could be rapidly stopped.

As to the territorial settlement, Stalin's ideas had changed little since his talks with Eden in December 1941. All German territory east of the

Oder-Neisse line should go to Poland; Russia would demand Königsberg, but Poland should have the rest of East Prussia. Russia, said Stalin, wanted terms which "will leave Russia on the neck of Germany." The possibility that these might turn out to be Stalin's minimum demands was raised when he told Churchill, "There is no need to speak at the present time about any Soviet desires [with regard to Germany], but when the time comes, we will speak."[25]

The problem of Germany's future was taken up again at the last plenary session of the conference, on the evening of December 1. Stalin introduced the subject and indicated briefly his preference for dismemberment but then sat back and let the Western leaders set forth their views. Churchill limited himself to advocating the separation of Prussia, "the evil core of German militarism," from the rest of Germany. Roosevelt set forth a plan for the division of Germany into five self-governing states, together with United Nations "or some form of international control" over the Kiel Canal and the Ruhr and Saar industrial areas.[26]

It was Roosevelt's improvised plan that earned Stalin's approval; he preferred it, he said, to that of Churchill. If Germany was to be dismembered, "it should really be dismembered." But there would always be the danger of German reunification, ". . . no matter what measures were taken, there would always be a strong urge on the part of the Germans to reunite."[27]

No final decision was taken on dismemberment; instead the three heads of state agreed to refer the question to the European Advisory Commission. Stalin closed the discussion by restating Soviet desire for the acquisition of Königsberg.

> He said that the acquisition of that part of Eastern Prussia would not only afford the Soviet Union an ice-free port but would also give to Russia a small piece of German territory which he felt was deserved.[28]

The Western leaders made no commitment on this demand, but the Soviets construed their silence as assent, claiming at the Potsdam Conference that they had agreed to Stalin's request.

Strang Presents the British Plan

The discussions at the Teheran Conference left the future of Germany unsettled. It was not the Big Three's ideas on dismemberment which determined Germany's fate but their decision to turn the problem over to the European Advisory Commission, for it was in that body that the decisive steps were taken.

The first meeting of the EAC, which took place in London on 15 December 1943, saw the establishment of a secretariat, the adoption of working procedures, and the designation of a date in mid-January for the commission's first substantive meeting. In preparation for that event the British military and civil bureaucracy swung into action. On December 12 the British Chiefs of Staff Committee (COS) sent the Committee on Armistice Terms and Civil Administration (ACA) a report entitled The Military Occupation of Germany in which the latter's division of Germany into three zones of occupation was adopted, placing Berlin inside the Soviet zone but under three-power administration. Approval by the ACA was prompt, but on December 30 Sir William Strang, a senior foreign service officer who had been designated British representative on the EAC, wrote to Eden, requesting permission to delay presentation of the British plan. Strang's argument was that he needed more time to discuss the plan with the Russians and Americans.[29] Instead Strang was instructed to present the plan at the first suitable opportunity.

The reason for haste appeared to be twofold: first, the Red Army, in its drive westward, was rapidly approaching the eastern boundary of Germany, and Eden was anxious to get Allied agreement on occupation zones before the Soviets entered Germany; second, General Eisenhower, who was known to favor the intermingling of Allied occupation troops throughout Germany, was scheduled to arrive in London on January 14 to take up his duties as Commander in Chief of the Supreme Headquarters, Allied Expeditionary Forces (SHAEF).

British initiative was facilitated by the fact that neither the Russians nor the Americans came to the EAC with definite proposals for Germany's future. Thus the British plan had no competitors when Strang laid it on the table at the EAC's meeting on 15 January 1944. Strang's presentation comprised three drafts: "Terms of Surrender for Germany"; "Military Occupation of Germany," including a map showing the three zones of occupation and Greater Berlin; and "Allied Control Machinery in Germany during the Period of Occupation."[30]

The Soviets at this point were still thinking in terms of a unified Germany after defeat, to judge by an event which took place a few days before Strang's presentation. The head of the German Communist Party (KPD) in Russia, Wilhelm Pieck, acting in response to a briefing by ex-Comintern leader Georgi Dimitrov, appointed a team of twenty KPD members to work out a comprehensive program for "The Solution of Political Tasks in Germany After the War."[31]

It took the Soviets exactly one month to decide on their response to the British proposal. At a meeting of the EAC on 15 February 1944, Fedor Gusev, Soviet ambassador to Great Britain and Soviet representative on the EAC, submitted a draft for surrender terms by Germany including a map showing occupation zones to be allocated to each of the three allies. The zonal boundaries in the Soviet draft were virtually identical with those in the documents laid before the EAC by Strang on January 15.[32]

The Americans, meanwhile, locked in interagency disputes and hampered by high-level distrust of the EAC, had nothing concrete to propose. Thus the tacit agreement between the Soviets and the British effectively settled the question of Germany's occupation.

Why had the Soviets accepted the British plan? Essentially because it gave them more than they could have hoped to achieve by any other means.

It not only assured them of controlling 40 percent of Germany's territory and a third of her population and resources, but it also gave them a commanding position in Berlin, from which Soviet influence over all of Germany could be extended. Until the British plan was presented, Stalin had no idea of the concrete terms which the Western Allies might offer the Soviets for postwar controls in Germany. Soviet acceptance of the British plan indicates that the British had done their work well: the prize offered the Soviets was glittering enough to ensure their acceptance of an arrangement which allocated to the British control of Germany's industrial heartland, the Rhine-Ruhr region.

The Soviets, meanwhile, were still uncertain as to the best course to follow in regard to Germany's dismemberment. At a meeting of the EAC on 25 January 1944, Strang, acting in response to a directive of the Teheran Conference, proposed the setting up of a Committee on Dismemberment. Gusev said that the Soviet delegation "has not had sufficient material or experts" to study the question.[33] It was not until March 1945, in fact, that the Soviets were ready to state their official position on dismemberment.

British Rationale for
the Planned Occupation of Germany

The prolonged wrangling between the British and Americans over their zones in western Germany preoccupied both sides throughout much of 1944 and was not resolved until the Second Quebec Conference in September 1944 by a compromise that in effect gave the British what they wanted, control of northwest Germany. On that basis the EAC was able to sign the three-power protocol which put the stamp of Allied approval on what had originally been a purely British plan. During the months which intervened between Strang's initial presentation of the plan and its final validation, the British conducted a vigorous internal debate over the merits and drawbacks of the plan, a debate which casts a revealing light on the real British motives.

The debate got under way early in June 1944 when a Foreign Office spokesman sent letters to the Economic and Industrial Planning Staff (EIPS) and the Chiefs of Staff (COS) requesting them to consider the question of dismemberment in its economic and military aspects respectively.[34] Also active in the debate were the Armistice and Postwar Planning Committee (APW) and its successor, the Post-Hostilities Planning Committee (PHP). During the second half of 1944 these agencies produced a steady stream of reports and comments in which they took sharply divergent views on the value to Britain of a policy aimed at the dismemberment of Germany.

It was the strongly held view of the Chiefs of Staff, for example, that

a Germany with single centralized control as regards politics, industry, and science will be potentially a greater threat to the peace of Europe than she will be if she is dismembered. This argument is all the stronger if there is taken into account the possibility of Germany falling under the domination of a hostile power.[35]

Military advocacy of dismemberment was given powerful civilian backing by the Attlee Committee. At a session of the committee on 20 July 1944, Attlee spoke in favor of destroying the "central machine" of government in Germany and condemned as an illusion the idea that there was a "normal Germany" which could be revived, as distinct from the "centralized and militaristic machine" that, in his view, had ruled Germany for the past fifty years.[36]

In a PHP report dated 10 August 1944, the conclusion was reached that "the dismemberment of Germany would, on balance, be to our [i.e., British] strategic advantage." Rejecting a Foreign Office spokesman's characterization of the report as "hopelessly unsound,"[37] the PHP in a report dated 25 August 1944, spelled out the rationale behind its conclusions.

(a) The dismemberment of Germany into three or more independent States, without any central government or federal organization, would be to our strategic advantage, both in relation to an aggressive Germany and a hostile USSR.

In the existing though not yet formally adopted EAC draft protocol for the zonal occupation of Germany, the PHP found a convenient basis for dismemberment:

If dismemberment took the form of a devolution into three States, the areas of those States would correspond broadly, though not necessarily exactly, with the zones of occupation at present contemplated.

Among the advantages of dismemberment, in PHP's view, was that of "Insurance Against a Potentially Hostile USSR":

If the USSR were eventually to develop hostile intentions toward us, a situation would arise, not only in Europe but in the Middle Eastern and Far Eastern areas, which would require a complete reorientation of our present policy. In that event, we should require all the help we can get from any source open to us, including Germany. We must above all prevent Germany combining with the Soviet Union against us.

It is open to argument whether a united Germany would be more likely to side with the USSR than with ourselves. In any event it is most unlikely that the USSR would ever permit the rearmament of a united Germany unless she were satisfied that she could dominate a Germany so rearmed. Thus, we are unlikely to secure help from the whole of Germany against the USSR.

Our interests are therefore likely to be better served in this event by the acceptance of dismemberment, for we might hope eventually to bring north-western, and possibly southern Germany also, within the orbit of a Western European Group. This would give increased depth to the defenses of the United Kingdom and increase the war potential of that group.

We conclude that dismemberment would at least reduce the likelihood of the whole of Germany combining with the USSR against us, and that as an insurance against a hostile USSR, it would be to our long-term strategic advantage.

With a frankness that was often lacking in more widely distributed state papers, the PHP report asserted that, "If we are to secure the positive benefits of dismemberment it is vital that the northwestern area of Germany should be a British zone of occupation."[38]

The U.S.-British conflict over the western zones, as we have seen, was finally resolved by a compromise at the Second Quebec Conference. With the question of the western zones settled, the way was open for three-power agreement, and on 12 September 1944, the EAC adopted a draft "Protocol on Zones of Occupation in Germany and Administration of the 'Greater Berlin' Area" which, with minor adjustments on November 14, was forwarded to the heads of state for their approval. Thus the plan originally mapped out by the Attlee Committee in 1943 was acquiring the binding force of an Allied agreement on Germany's future.

In October 1944 Churchill and Eden met with Stalin in Moscow. Stalin once again championed the idea of dismembering Germany. As reported to Roosevelt by Churchill, Stalin advocated that the Ruhr and the Saar be

detached and put out of action and probably under international control and a separate state formed in the Rhineland. He would also like the internationalization of the Kiel Canal.[39]

Eden, though it was he who had initiated the process of planning for Germany's dismemberment, still hesitated formally to endorse it. In a memorandum written toward the end of 1944 he said that dismemberment would raise "grave political as well as practical issues to which an answer would have to be found before we could support such a policy."[40]

In a deeply troubled mood as the war's end approached, Churchill wrote a long memorandum to Eden summing up his views on the position of Germany in a restructured Europe. "It is much too soon," Churchill said,

for us to decide these enormous questions. . . .

We have yet to settle the practical questions of the partition of Germany, the treatment of the Ruhr and Saar industries, etc. These may be touched upon at our forthcoming conference, but I doubt whether any final decision will be reached then. . . .[41]

What both Churchill and Roosevelt lost sight of was the fact that, in the absence of enlightened, consistent, and forceful leadership, policy formulation on major issues would not simply mark time, but would be shaped at the level of working committees, expert consultation, and the like. This was what happened to U.S. and British policy with regard to the dismemberment of Germany. While Roosevelt was drawing up or endorsing plans for postwar Germany, which a State Department historian later castigated as "technically amateurish and morally indefensible,"[42] and while Churchill and Eden were agonizing over the moral and material problems raised by dismemberment, British officials at a lower level were making detailed plans on the assumption that postwar Germany would be split into three parts, with the clear recognition that this division would very likely lead to the absorption of eastern and western zones into rival spheres of influence.

Dismemberment at the Yalta Conference

At the Yalta Conference (4–11 February 1945) it was the Soviets who appeared to be keenest for the dismemberment of Germany. Molotov, on February 5, urged the Western Allies to commit themselves in favor of dismemberment, and later on the same day, Stalin insisted on inclusion of the word "dismemberment" in the surrender instrument for Germany, without, however, specifying its exact implications.[43] Vojtech Mastny's suggestion that Stalin wanted inclusion of the word to discourage any German thought of trying to negotiate a separate surrender to the Western Allies has merit.[44] Whatever Stalin's motives, this was the last discussion of the topic by the Big Three; by mutual agreement the subject was referred to the foreign ministers, and they in turn passed it on to the Committee on Dismemberment which had been stalled for most of the past year.

On February 6 Stalin gave formal approval to the EAC protocol (already ratified by the British and Americans) on occupation zones in Germany and administration of the Greater Berlin area.[45] On the same day he ordered Zhukov to halt the Red Army's drive toward Berlin and shift the weight of his offensive to the north, in Pomerania.[46] The two decisions were logically connected: by accepting the EAC protocol Stalin ensured the approval by his allies for Soviet control of 40 percent of Germany's territory without the need to push the Red Army to the limit. A slowdown in the Soviet westward advance would permit a more orderly, less hectic pace and would give Stalin the opportunity to gauge Soviet actions in response to his perception of Western plans.

While the discussion of the surrender instrument and approval of the EAC protocol appeared to be the most salient aspects of the Yalta discussions bearing on the future of Germany, two other agreements reached at the conference played an important role in shaping that future. The first concerned reparations, with the Soviets calling for a total of $20 billion, half to go to the Soviet Union. Churchill refused to accept the Soviet figures, but the Americans, in the interests of compromise, agreed to do so, "as the basis for discussion."[47] This gesture gave the Soviets the opening they needed to present the $20 billion figure later, at the Potsdam Conference, as the one on which they and the Americans had "agreed." The compromise on reparations worked out at Potsdam in turn helped lay the foundation for actions in the postwar years which contributed directly to the splitting of Germany.

Of equal significance was the decision to include France as an occupying power in postwar Germany, with a seat on the Allied Control Council for Germany. Stalin agreed to these proposals only on the final day of the conference, and only on condition that the territories to be assigned to France should be drawn from the British and American zones. He may have felt that he was thereby protecting Soviet interests, but the consequences of his action were far from favorable for Soviet goals in Germany. As a member of the Control Council for Germany after the war, France systematically blocked any action directed toward the maintenance of German unity.

Later, when the economic policies imposed in the Soviet zone deepened the split between East and West Germany, the French supported the Anglo-American policy of strengthening the West German economy, with the result that in the postwar struggle for Germany the Soviets found themselves confronting not just a weakened Britain and a reluctant America but a firmly united Western alliance enjoying the support of a revived and vigorous West German population.

Soviet Policy in the Final Stages of the War

The Soviet decision to champion German unity can be dated to shortly after the Yalta Conference. The first concrete evidence the Western Allies obtained of this decision was Gusev's announcement at the second meeting of the Committee on Dismemberment on 26 March 1945.[48] Gusev's statement came just twelve days after the Soviets initiated their own plan for the dismemberment of Germany by turning over to the Polish Provisional Government German territories lying east of the Oder-Neisse line.[49] Transfer to Poland of the East German territories, which included the rich Silesian coal fields and industrial complex, provides indirect but cogent evidence that at this stage Stalin was thinking in terms of a united (though truncated) Germany, in which the Soviets could work toward an eventual Communist takeover, rather than the establishment of a Communist-dominated state in the reduced Soviet zone. The Polish transfer significantly weakened the prospects for a viable Soviet-zone state. When the Soviets, after Germany's defeat, carried out a massive program of stripping industrial equipment from their zone under the guise of reparations, they further weakened the economic base of a potential successor state in East Germany. Thus by pursuing incompatible goals in Germany, Stalin was planting the seeds for the postwar setbacks and reversals which Soviet policy encountered in Germany.

Although the EAC agreements provided for four-power administration of Berlin, the Soviets were determined to establish their control over the German capital well before the Western Allies could reach the city. On April 21 Eisenhower informed Stalin of his plan to halt the Western Allies' drive at the Elbe River, information which evidently convinced the suspicious Stalin that their *real* goal must be Berlin. Recognizing that the war was now entering its final phase, and determined to acquire the most favorable strategic position in a collapsing Germany, Stalin ordered Zhukov from the north and Konev from the south to capture Berlin at the earliest possible moment.[50] Even before the Soviets entered the city, their planes flew two teams of Soviet-trained German Communists into Soviet-held territory near the German capital, and on May 1 the group led by Walter Ulbricht began its operations.[51]

It was the Soviets who first disclosed the plans for zonal occupation of Germany, in a press report on 7 June 1945.[52] With a speed that took the Western Allies completely by surprise, the Soviet military administration in East Germany then adopted a number of measures aimed at seizing the initiative in the new Germany that could be expected to emerge from defeat. On June 10 Zhukov authorized the formation of political parties in the Soviet Zone, an action which Mastny describes as "an incipient Soviet bid for a dominant role in the whole of Germany."[53] In order to give the revived German Communist Party (KPD) a commanding lead in the political race, the Soviets on June 12 sponsored a conference in their zone to mark the reorganization of the party.[54]

Pleading the need to reestablish order after the German surrender, the Soviets imposed a month's delay before the Western armies were authorized to enter Berlin. By this time the EAC was approaching the end of its official activities, with only a few last-minute details to iron out, among them the exact delineation of the French sector of occupied Berlin. A protocol of July 12 took care of that problem, and the occupying forces of the Western Allies were at last able to settle into their new quarters.

Soviet Policy at the Potsdam Conference

The final Big Three conference of the war was held at Potsdam, just outside Berlin, in the Soviet zone, from 17 July to 2 August 1945. In regard to the treatment of Germany the conference produced few surprises but rather marked the formal adoption of decisions reached earlier. Thus, the Western Allies in effect sanctioned the transfer to Poland of the German territories east of the Oder-Neisse line, retaining only the legal fiction that the transfer was provisional pending the conclusion of a peace treaty with Germany. Transfer of Königsberg to the USSR also received approval in principle pending a peace settlement.

The problem that caused the greatest conflict at the conference was that of reparations. The Soviets now strongly put their case for a total of $20 billion, half to go to the USSR. Without formally endorsing these figures, the Western Allies agreed that the Soviets should be free to take reparations in kind from their own zone of occupation, as well as from "appropriate German external assets."[55] This elastic formula gave the Soviets extensive leverage in formerly German-occupied Eastern Europe, and helped them lay the foundations for economic domination of that region.

Since even these measures failed to satisfy the Soviet demand for reparations, U.S. Secretary of State, Jimmy Byrnes, offered a formula under which the Soviets, in addition to taking reparations from their own zone, were to receive 25 percent of such industrial capital equipment from the Western zones as was unnecessary for the German peacetime economy, 15 percent to be compensated by shipments of foodstuffs and industrial goods, 10 percent without compensation. Within less than a year this complicated arrangement had broken down, and General Lucius D. Clay, commandant in the U.S. zone, halted shipments to the Soviets.

France, which was not represented at the conference and thus not bound by its decisions, was given a seat on the Allied Control Council for Germany, an illogical arrangement which contained the germs of future dissension.

The Balance Sheet

Stalin's high regard for the work of the EAC was shown indirectly by his request to Truman, on 15 August 1945, for a zone of occupation in Japan.[56] Evidently Stalin hoped to repeat in the Far East the dual policy which he found so congenial in Europe: control of an occupation zone in the defeated nation as a springboard to influencing and eventually controlling the ex-enemy state as a whole. Truman's sobering experience with the zonal division of Germany, however, led him to reject Stalin's request. The absence of a Far Eastern counterpart to the EAC—the result of America's priority in determining Allied strategy in that theater—was an essential prerequisite to Truman's decision, which spared Japan the trauma of dismemberment to which Germany was subjected. (The division of Korea into Soviet and U.S. zones of occupation resulted from entirely different processes, however similar the results may appear.)[57]

Soviet wartime policy toward Germany pursued a number of goals, some of them predicated on its unity, others on its dismemberment. In effect, Stalin wanted to have it both ways—an assured portion of German territory under Soviet control and at the same time a strong position in the postwar struggle for a united Germany. What Stalin did *not* want was a Soviet-controlled East German successor state competing with a larger, richer, more populous West German state enjoying the support of the Western Allies. Yet that is what he got.

The basic lines along which Germany was dismembered were drawn up by British planners in 1943–1944. By accepting their blueprint and attempting to combine it with other Soviet goals in Germany, Stalin helped make dismemberment a reality.

Notes

1. Sir Llewellyn Woodward, *British Foreign Policy in the Second World War,* (London: Her Majesty's Stationery Office, 1971), 2:551. (Hereafter cited as Woodward 2.) For a

Soviet view of the Eden-Stalin talks, see V. G. Trukhanovsky, *British Foreign Policy During World War II 1939-1945* (Moscow: Progress Publishers, 1970), 213–23. In Trukhanovsky's presentation Stalin's paramount concern is with Soviet security. Trukhanovsky omits any reference to Stalin's proposals for the dismemberment of Germany. (Hereafter cited as Trukhanovsky, *British Foreign Policy.*)

2. Sir Anthony Eden, *The Reckoning: The Memoirs of Anthony Eden, Earl of Avon* (Boston: Houghton Mifflin, 1965), 335. (Hereafter cited as Eden, *Reckoning.*)

3. Joseph Stalin, *The Great Patriotic War of the Soviet Union* (New York: International Publishers, 1945), 44.

4. Ibid., 69.

5. Sir Llewellyn Woodward, *British Foreign Policy in the Second World War* (London: Her Majesty's Stationery Office, 1962), 435. (Hereafter cited as Woodward 1962.)

6. Sir Llewellyn Woodward, *British Foreign Policy in the Second World War,* Vol. 5 (London: Her Majesty's Stationery Office, 1976), 16. (Hereafter cited as Woodward 5.)

7. Ibid., 25, 29.

8. Eden, *Reckoning,* 429.

9. John L. Snell, *Wartime Origins of the East-West Dilemma over Germany* (New Orleans: Hauser Press, 1959), 38. (Hereafter cited as Snell, *Wartime Origins.*)

10. Robert E. Sherwood, *Roosevelt and Hopkins: An Intimate History,* rev. ed. (New York: Harper & Brothers, 1950), 711–12.

11. Ibid.

12. Woodward 1962, 443–45; Woodward 5, 46–48.

13. Tony Sharp, *The Wartime Alliance and the Zonal Division of Germany* (New York: Oxford University Press, 1975), 35, note 4. (Hereafter cited as Sharp, *Wartime Alliance.*) Woodward 1962, 445.

14. Sharp, *Wartime Alliance,* 35.

15. Woodward 1962, 445–48, 465–70. Winston S. Churchill, *The Second World War* (Boston: Houghton Mifflin, 1953) Vol. 6, *Triumph and Tragedy,* 507–8.

16. Vojtech Mastny, *Russia's Road to the Cold War. Diplomacy, Warfare, and the Politics of Communism, 1941-1945* (New York: Columbia University Press, 1979), 80. (Hereafter cited as Mastny, *Russia's Road.*) Snell, *Wartime Origins,* 36.

17. Ibid., 36. For the view that these moves were related to Moscow's disappointment with the Western Allies' failure to open a Second Front and its consideration of a possible separate peace with Germany, see William O. McCagg, Jr., *Stalin Embattled 1943-1948* (Detroit: Wayne State University Press, 1978), 38.

18. H. A. Notter, *Postwar Foreign Policy Preparation, 1939-1945* (Washington, D.C.: Department of State, 1949), 558–60.

19. Cordell Hull, *The Memoirs of Cordell Hull* (New York: Macmillan, 1948), 2:1265–66.

20. Woodward 5:77.

21. Woodward 2:588–89. Philip E. Mosely, "The Occupation of Germany: New Light on How the Zones were Drawn," in *The Kremlin and World Politics* (New York: Vintage Books, 1960):158. (Hereafter cited as Mosely, "Occupation.") In the Soviet view the establishment of the EAC was the result of a Soviet initiative. Trukhanovsky, *British Foreign Policy,* 373. For a West German analysis of the work of the EAC see Hans-Gunter Kowalski, "Die 'European Advisory Commission' als Instrument alliierten Deutschlandplanung 1943-1945," *Vierteljahrshefte für Zeitgeschichte* 19 (July 1971) 3:261–93.

22. U.S. Department of State. *Foreign Relations of the United States. The Conferences at Cairo and Tehran, 1943* (Washington, D.C.: Government Printing Office, 1961), 254–56. (Hereafter cited as *FRUS, Cairo and Tehran.*) Sharp, *Wartime Alliance,* 42. Donald J. Nelson, *Wartime Origins of the Berlin Dilemma* (University, Alabama: University of Alabama, 1978), 30–32. William M. Franklin, "Zonal Boundaries and Access to Berlin," *World Politics* 6 (October 1963):10–11. (Hereafter cited as Franklin, "Zonal Boundaries.")

23. Mosely, "Occupation," 178–79. Franklin, "Zonal Boundaries," 21.

24. Woodward 5:78.

25. Ibid., 553–54. Snell, *Wartime Origins,* 46–47.

26. *FRUS, Cairo and Tehran,* 600. In the Soviet-bloc version it was only the Western Allies who favored the dismemberment of Germany at Teheran. See for example the

Polish historian Stefan Boratyski (S. Boratynskii), *Diplomatiia perioda Vtoroi Mirovoi voiny. Mezhdunarodnye konferentsii 1941–1945 godov* (Moscow: Izd-vo inostrannoi literatury, 1959), 222. This has become the standard Soviet treatment of the subject. For a recent example, see V. Nekrasov, "Istoricheskie uroki Tegerana," *Kommunist* 17 (November 1983):110–21, 119. In Soviet documentary publications this interpretation is supported by the deletion of statements by Stalin favoring the dismemberment of Germany. See for example *Sovetskii Soiuz na mezhdunarodnykh konferentsiiakh perioda Velikoi Otechestvennoi voiny 1941–1945 gg.* Vol. 2. *Tegeranskaia konferenstsiia rukovoditelei trekh soiuznykh derzhav—SSSR, SShA, Velikobritanii (28 noiabria–1 dekabria 1943 g.) Sbornik dokumentov* (Moscow: Izd-vo politicheskoi literatury, 1975), 165. For commentary, see Robert Beitzell, ed., *Teheran Yalta Potsdam: The Soviet Protocols* (Hattiesburg, Miss.: Academic International, 1970), 4. Beitzell lists Stalin's statements on Germany as one of four deletions "[which are] of such importance as to seriously distort the record of the proceedings at Teheran."

27. *FRUS, Cairo and Tehran,* 602.

28. Ibid., 604.

29. (a) "The Military Ocupation of Germany. Report by Chiefs of Staff Committee." London: Public Record Office (PRO), PREM 3.1014/11, 21–37. (b) Strang to Secretary of State on Procedure in the European Advisory Commission, PRO. F.O. 371.40580, 22.

30. U.S. Department of State. *Foreign Relations of the United States. 1944* (Washington, D.C.: Government Printing Office, 1966), 1:112–59. (Hereafter cited as *FRUS 1944*-I.) Nelson, *Wartime Origins,* 38. Sir William Strang, *Home and Abroad* (London: Andre Deutsch, 1956), 213–14. (Hereafter cited as Strang, *Home.*) Sharp, *Wartime Alliance,* 56. Woodward 5, 198–200.

31. Mastny, *Russia's Road,* 146.

32. "Iz materialov Evropeiskoi Konsul'tativnoi Komissii," *Mezhdunarodnaia zhizn',* 5 (1968):158–60. Nelson, *Wartime Origins,* 40. Sharp, *Wartime Alliance,* 57. *FRUS 1944*-I, 177–78. Franklin, "Boundaries," 13. In the view of a Soviet historian, the Soviet Union accepted a zone of occupation smaller than its contribution to Allied victory would have entitled it to in order "to give further proof of its desire and readiness to co-operate with its Western Allies in peace as in war." Trukhanovsky, *British Foreign Policy,* 431. See also Alexander Fischer, *Sowjetische Deutschlandpolitik im Zweiten Weltkrieg 1941–1945* (Stuttgart: Deutsche Verlagsanstalt, 1975), 79–80.

33. Minutes of the Third Meeting of the EAC. PRO. F.O. 371.40580, 186. *Pravda o politike zapadnykh derzhav v germanskom voprose* (Moscow: Gosudarstvennoe izdatel'stvo politicheskoi literatury 1959), p. 12. (Hereafter cited as *Pravda o politike.*)

34. Letter from Oliver Harvey, 7 June 1944, Foreign Office. PRO. F.O. 371.39079, 233–36, 237–39.

35. PRO. F.O. 371.39080, 170.

36. Woodward 5, 214–15.

37. PRO. F.O. 371.39080, 393–401.

38. Ibid., 15–17.

39. Churchill, *Triumph and Tragedy,* 240–41. Snell, *Wartime Origins,* 102–3.

40. Woodward 5, 243.

41. Churchill, *Triumph and Tragedy,* 350–51.

42. Ernest F. Penrose, *Economic Planning for the Peace* (Princeton: Princeton University Press, 1953), 258.

43. Woodward 1962, 488. Woodward 5, 272–74. Trukhanovsky omits any reference to Soviet insistence on the dismemberment of Germany at Yalta and asserts that it was the British and Americans who favored that policy. Trukhanovsky, *British Foreign Policy,* 432. This has become the standard Soviet interpretation. See, for example, A. Iu. Borisov, "Sovetskaia diplomatiia na mezhsoiuznicheskikh konferentsiiakh v gody Velikoi Otechestvennoi voiny," *Voprosy istorii,* 6 (1980):21–38, 32.

44. Mastny, *Russia's Road,* 242.

45. Nelson, *Wartime Origins,* 73.

46. Sharp, *Wartime Alliance,* 26.

47. Snell, *Wartime Origins,* 150. U.S. Department of State. *Foreign Relations of the United States. The Conferences at Malta and Yalta* (Washington, D.C.: Government Printing Office, 1955), 921–22, 937, 978–79.

48. According to the statement by Gusev, the Soviet government understood the decision of the Yalta conference regarding the dismemberment of Germany "not as an obligatory plan, but as a possibility for exerting pressure on Germany with the object of rendering her harmless in the event of other means proving inadequate." Mosely, "Dismemberment," 144. *Pravda o politike zapadnykh derzhav,* 13, citing *Mezhdunarodnaia zhizn'* 5 (1955):44. Woodward 1962, 527. In the Soviet view it was thanks to Soviet policy, as enunciated in part by Gusev, that Germany escaped dismemberment at the end of the war. Trukhanovsky, *British Foreign Policy,* 432.

49. Hans W. Schoenberg, "The Partition of Germany and the Neutralization of Austria" in Thomas T. Hammond, ed., *The Anatomy of Communist Take-overs* (New Haven: Yale University Press, 1975), 373. (Hereafter cited as Schoenberg, "Partition.")

50. Peter Calvocoressi and Guy Wint, *Total War. Causes and Course of the Second World War* (London: Allen Lane, the Penguin Press, 1972), 536.

51. Schoenberg, "Partition," 375.

52. Sharp, *Wartime Alliance,* 157.

53. Mastny, *Russia's Road,* 290.

54. Schoenberg, "Partition," 376.

55. Herbert Feis, *Between War and Peace: The Potsdam Conference* (Princeton: Princeton University Press, 1960), 253–58.

56. Herbert Feis, *The Atomic Bomb and the End of World War II* (Princeton: Princeton University Press, 1966), 152–53.

57. The origins of the United States-Soviet agreement which led to the division of Korea are analyzed in my article, "Soviet Far Eastern Policy, 1945–50: Stalin's goals in Korea" in Yonosuke Nagai and Akira Iriye, eds., *The Origins of the Cold War in Asia* (Tokyo: University of Tokyo Press, 1977), 123–46.

References

Beitzell, Robert, ed. *Teheran Yalta Potsdam: The Soviet Protocols.* Hattiesburg, Miss.: Academic International, 1970.

Boratynskii, S. *Diplomatiia perioda Vtoroi Mirovoi voiny. Mezhdunarodnye konferentsii 1941–1945 godov.* Moscow: Izd-vo inostrannoi literatury, 1959.

Borisov, A. Iu. "Sovetskaia diplomatiia na mezhsoiuznicheskikh konferentsiiakh v gody Velikoi Otechestvennoi voiny." *Voprosy istorii* 6. 1980:21–38.

Calvocoressi, Peter, and Wint, Guy. *Total War. Causes and Course of the Second World War* London: Allen Lane (the Penguin Press) 1972.

Churchill, Winston S. *The Second World War.* Vol. 6. *Triumph and Tragedy.* Boston: Houghton Mifflin, 1953.

Eden, Anthony. *The Reckoning: The Memoirs of Anthony Eden, Earl of Avon.* Boston: Houghton Mifflin, 1965.

Feis, Herbert. *The Atomic Bomb and the End of World War II.* Princeton: Princeton University Press, 1966.

———. *Between War and Peace: The Potsdam Conference.* Princeton: Princeton University Press, 1960.

Fischer, Alexander. *Sowjetische Deutschlandpolitik im Zweiten Weltkrieg 1941–1945.* Stuttgart: Deutsche Verlagsanstalt, 1975.

Franklin, William M. "Zonal Boundaries and Access to Berlin." *World Politics* 16. October 1963:1–31.

Hull, Cordell. *The Memoirs of Cordell Hull.* New York: Macmillan, 1948.

"Iz materialov Evropeiskoi Konsul'tativnoi Komissii" *Mezhdunarodnaia zhizn'.* 5. 1968, 158–60.

Kowalski, Hans-Gunter. "Die 'European Advisory Commission' als Instrument alliierten Deutschlandplanung 1943–1945," *Vierteljahrshefte für Zeitgeschichte* 19. 1971, 3:261–93.

London. Public Record Office. Files PREM 3.1014/11; F.O. 371.39079, 39080, 40580.

McCagg, William O., Jr. *Stalin Embattled 1943–1948*. Detroit: Wayne State University Press, 1978.

Mastny, Vojtech. *Russia's Road to the Cold War: Diplomacy, Warfare, and the Politics of Communism. 1941–1945*. New York: Columbia University Press, 1979.

Mosely, Philip E. "The Occupation of Germany: New Light on How the Zones Were Drawn." In *The Kremlin and World Politics*. New York: Vintage Books, 1960, 155–88.

Nekrasov, V. "Istoricheskie uroki Tegerana." *Kommunist* 17, November 1983, 110–21.

Nelson, Donald J. *Wartime Origins of the Berlin Dilemma*. University, Alabama: University of Alabama Press, 1978.

Notter, H. A. *Postwar Foreign Policy Preparation, 1939–1945*. Washington, D.C.: Department of State, 1949.

Penrose, Ernest F. *Economic Planning for the Peace*. Princeton: Princeton University Press, 1953.

Pravda o politike zapadnykh derzhav v germanskom voprose. Moscow: Gosudarstvennoe izdatel'stvo politicheskoi literatury, 1959.

Schoenberg, Hans W. "The Partition of Germany and the Neutralization of Austria." In Thomas T. Hammond, ed., *The Anatomy of Communist Take-overs*. New Haven: Yale University Press, 1975, 366–84.

Sharp, Tony. *The Wartime Alliance and the Zonal Division of Germany*. New York: Oxford University Press, 1975.

Sherwood, Robert, E. *Roosevelt and Hopkins: An Intimate History*, rev. ed. New York: Harper & Brothers, 1950.

Slusser, Robert M. "Soviet Far Eastern Policy, 1945–50: Stalin's Goals in Korea." In Yonosuke Nagai and Akira Iriye, eds., *The Origins of the Cold War in Asia*. Tokyo: University of Tokyo Press, 1977, 123–46.

————, ed. *Soviet Economic Policy in Postwar Germany: A Collection of Papers by Former Soviet Officials*. New York: Research Program on the USSR, 1953.

Snell, John L. *Wartime Origins of the East-West Dilemma over Germany*. New Orleans: Hauser Press, 1959.

Sovetskii Soiuz na mezhdunarodnykh konferentsiiakh perioda Velikoi Otechestvennoi voiny 1941–1945 gg. Vol. 2. *Tegeranskaia konferentsiia rukovoditelei trekh soiuznykh derzhav—SSSR, SShA, Velikobritanii* (28 noiabria–1 dekabria 1943 g.) *Sbornik dokumentov* Moscow: Izd-vo politicheskoi literatury, 1975.

Stalin, Joseph. *The Great Patriotic War of the Soviet Union*. New York: International Publishers, 1945.

Strang, Sir William. *Home and Abroad*. London: Andre Deutsch, 1956.

Trukhanovsky, V. G. *British Foreign Policy During World War II 1939–1945*. Moscow: Progress Publishers, 1970.

U.S. Department of State. *Foreign Relations of the United States: The Conferences at Cairo and Tehran, 1943*. Washington, D.C.: Government Printing Office, 1961.

————. *The Conferences at Malta and Yalta*. Washington, D.C.: Government Printing Office, 1955.

————. *1944*, 1. Washington, D.C.: Government Printing Office, 1966.

Woodward, Sir Llewellyn. *British Foreign Policy in the Second World War*. London: Her Majesty's Stationery Office, 1962.

————. *British Foreign Policy in the Second World War*, 2. London: Her Majesty's Stationery Office, 1971.

————. *British Foreign Policy in the Second World War*, 5. London: Her Majesty's Stationery Office, 1976.

Part Two

Social and Political Consequences of World War II

8

Postwar Soviet Society: The "Return to Normalcy", 1945–1953

SHEILA FITZPATRICK

The two great wars of the twentieth century were fought by societies, not simply by their armies. In the belligerent countries, civilians as well as military conscripts found their way of life, occupation, and often place of residence changed for the duration of the war. The disruption was greatest when there was enemy occupation of territory (as in much of the Soviet Union in World War II), mass evacuation, and flight of population. But even in the direst wartime circumstances, as long as hope of victory remained, civilians and soldiers thought of this disruption as temporary. They expected that when the war ended normal life would be resumed.

For the Soviet population, however, normalcy and stability remained elusive goals in the postwar years from 1945 until Stalin's death in 1953. In the first place, the process of ending the war produced social dislocations almost comparable with those associated with fighting it since tens of millions of people had to be demobilized, repatriated, returned from evacuation, and released from wartime jobs that their holders regarded as temporary or to which they had been drafted. Many chose not to return to their prewar homes and occupations. Many others found themselves unable to do so.

In the second place, the regime's coercive policies precluded the kind of relaxation and peacetime readjustment that the Soviet population hoped for after the war. Some types of postwar Soviet repression had prewar analogues, others were modeled on wartime experience. Some coercive policies were particularly associated with the incorporation of new territories into the Soviet Union and others with the perceived imperatives of postwar economic reconstruction, but it would be difficult to find a sphere of postwar Soviet life in which coercive policies were entirely absent. In the aftermath of war, the regime wanted to tighten controls on the society, not loosen them.

After the Second World War, as after the First World War and Civil War in Russia, millions of people were in movement from one geographical or social location to another, and a substantial part of the movement was spontaneous and uncontrolled. But in the second half of the 1940s, unlike the early twenties, there existed a strongly entrenched regime with coercive capacities and intentions; and the regime's own policies (resettlement, deportation, and labor conscription) added significantly to the demographic and social upheaval. The regime quickly demobilized much of the Red Army after the Second World War, but it was not ready to demobilize society in 1945. For the long-suffering Soviet population, more years of privation, storm, and stress lay ahead.

The War and Its Immediate Impact on the Soviet Population

During the Second World War, German and Axis troops occupied the Ukraine, Belorussia, the Baltic Republics, the Crimea, the Northern Caucasus and large areas of European Russia—in all, territory with a prewar population of 85 million, or 45 percent of the total Soviet population.[1] Some 12 to 15 million Soviet citizens were evacuated or fled eastward away from the Germans.[2] Moscow almost fell in October 1941, Leningrad was under siege from September 1941 to January 1944, and German troops penetrated as far east as the Volga before being turned back at the Battle of Stalingrad. According to official Soviet claims, the occupying forces destroyed and plundered 1710 towns and more than 70,000 villages. In addition 32,000 industrial enterprises and 65,000 kilometres of railroad track were completely or partially destroyed.[3] As they retreated, the Germans drove off livestock, seized or destroyed agricultural machinery, set fire to buildings, and blew up bridges. In addition to this devastation, banditry and anti-Soviet resistance movements were rife at the end of the war in reclaimed areas like the Ukraine and the newly acquired Western territories.

In the course of the war, over 5 million Soviet soldiers and officers were captured by the Germans, although only one million of these were alive in prisoner-of-war (POW) camps at the end of the war.[4] To provide labor for the Reich, several million Soviet citizens were transported to Germany and, like the surviving prisoners of war, required repatriation at the end of the war.[5] Out of 3 million Jews in the Soviet population of 1939, it is estimated that 800,000 were captured in German-occupied territories and perished in Nazi concentration camps, and an additional 909,000 Jews were captured in eastern Poland—the area occupied by the Soviet Union in 1939, taken by the Germans in 1941, and reoccupied and incorporated into the

Soviet Union in 1944–1945—and met the same fate.[6] For the Soviet population as a whole, the official Soviet estimate of wartime population losses—usually expressed as casualties, but probably also covering Soviet citizens who remained in or fled to the West at the end of the war—is a staggering 20 million,[7] out of a total population of something over 190 million at the outbreak of war.[8] Of the 20 million, about half are attributed to military casualites and half to civilian losses. The male population suffered much heavier losses, particularly in the fighting age-groups, than the female.

On the home front, war brought drastic changes in the composition of the work force. Perhaps 20 million men were conscripted into the armed forces during the war, and this meant that agriculture and industry—particularly agriculture—were drained of male workers.[9] On the collective farms, the number of working-age men (16–59 years old) dropped by 12.4 million between 1940 and 1944, leaving a sexual imbalance of four women of working age for every man.[10] In Belorussian kolkhozy in 1945, there were almost six women of working age for every man.[11] Among civilian wage earners in industry, agriculture, and other sectors of the national economy, the number of men dropped by 8 million between 1940 and 1945, and the proportional share from 61 to 44 percent.[12] Previously unemployed women, adolescents, invalids, and the elderly were drawn into employment to replace the men.

Strict labor discipline was characteristic of the wartime period, as was labor conscription (*trudovaia mobilizatsiia*). By a law of 26 June 1940, all workers were prohibited from leaving their jobs without the permission of their employers, violations being punishable by imprisonment of two to four months. After the outbreak of war, the defense industry and transport workers were put under military discipline, with punishment of five to eight *years* imprisonment for unauthorized departure from the job.[13] Boys and girls in the 14–17 age group were liable to compulsory draft into labor reserve schools, after which they were supposed to work at assigned jobs for a period of four years.[14] Urban adults became liable for labor conscription to industry and construction projects in 1942, and a decree of the same year authorized temporary conscription of urban adults and schoolchildren to help with agricultural work.[15] But the rural population was also subject to labor conscription: in the years 1942–1944, 1.4 million rural dwellers were drafted, mainly for industrial work in the same region.[16] Altogether, 7.6 million persons were conscripted for work in industry, construction, forestry, and agriculture in 1943.[17]

Just before the war, as a result of the Nazi-Soviet pact of 1939, the Soviet Union acquired new territory in the west by occupying and incorporating eastern Poland (divided between the Ukrainian and Belorussian Republics); part of Romania (Moldavia); and the three Baltic states, Lithuania, Latvia and Estonia. About 20 million people were thereby added to the Soviet population;[18] and in the short period before German occupation of the whole area in 1941, the Soviet authorities took the first steps towards

Sovietization—land reform, nationalization of industry and trade, and the arrest and deportation to distant parts of the Soviet Union of many local bourgeois nationalists. Poland suffered most from the repression: an estimated 880,000 of its former citizens were deported to special settlements and labor camps in 1940–1941 (though it was also more fortunate than the other countries in that, by special agreement with the Polish government in exile, half the Poles were released before the end of the war).[19]

Population Transfers, Resettlement and Sovietization Policies

Transfers of large ethnic populations, by decision of the Soviet government or as a result of agreements between the Soviet Union and foreign states, were characteristic of the 1940s (before, during and after the war). They deserve particular attention in any study of the impact of the Second World War on Soviet society and the Soviet regime because this was a form of social engineering that the regime had not practised on any significant scale before 1939. Its introduction was associated with broader changes in Soviet policy towards the non-Russian Soviet population in the late Stalin period the significance of which has yet to be adequately assessed by historians. This was a period of unprecedented suspicion, repression, and arbitrary handling of non-Russian nationalities by the Soviet regime.

The first ethnic population transfers took place in the period from 1939 to 1941, probably not on Soviet initiative. By the terms of the Nazi-Soviet pact, tens of thousands of Baltic Germans were repatriated to Germany, and more than 100,000 Germans living in Soviet-controlled Polish territory were moved into the areas of Poland occupied by the Germans. In return, the Soviet Union acquired about 50,000 Ukrainians, Russians, Belorussians, and Lithuanians who were transferred from German-controlled territory in 1940–1941.[20] By a similar population exchange with Finland in 1940, after the Winter War, 415,000 inhabitants of the Karelian provinces captured by the Soviet Union were transferred to Finnish territory.[21]

Although these transactions were not Soviet-inspired, and in the case of the German exchange were clearly related to the Nazi drive to reunite the German *Volk*, they provided the Soviet regime with a precedent for uprooting whole ethnic groups. The idea evidently took hold since after the outbreak of war the Soviet regime carried out operations of a similar kind involving Soviet ethnic minorities. The first such operation, formally prophylactic but actually punitive in nature, was the removal of the entire German population of the Volga region (about 400,000 people, according to the 1939 census) and its resettlement in Siberia and Central Asia in the fall of 1941.[22] This was followed in 1943–1944 by the forcible deportation of the Crimean Tatars and five small nationalities from the Northern Caucasus (Chechens, Ingushi, Karachai, Balkars and Kalmyks), a total of about a million people who were resettled in Kazakhstan and Central Asia.[23] These peoples had lived in areas that came under German occupation, and the stated reason for their deportation was that they were collectively guilty of collaboration with the Germans.

The postwar settlement in Europe involved large-scale population transfers in which the Soviet Union participated. These were necessitated by the existence of millions of displaced persons and by the reconstitution of nations with new borders. In this settlement, the Allies were guided by the principle that ethnic homogeneity within a given area was desirable, because heterogeneity had been the cause of so much recent conflict. As in the immediate prewar period, the Soviet Union was a participant rather than an initiator of the postwar policies of population transfer. But its participation cannot be dissociated from the emergence of coercive russification tendencies, especially in the western territories of the Soviet Union in the late Stalin period.

The major postwar population exchange involving the Soviet Union was with Poland, a country that was newly reconstituted under Soviet auspices, with the loss of its former eastern provinces to the Soviet Union and compensatory gains in the west at the expense of Germany. By Soviet-Polish agreements of 1944 and 1945, ethnic Poles and Jews (but not other nationalities) who had been Polish citizens before 17 September 1939 and who resided in the eastern provinces that were now incorporated into the Soviet Union, had the option of moving from the Soviet Union to Poland. Conversely, Ukrainians, Russians, Belorussians and Lithuanians (but not Jews) living in Poland had the option of moving to the Soviet Union.[24] More than half a million Ukrainians, Russians, Belorussians, and Lithuanians actually moved from Poland to the Soviet Union under this agreement— probably involuntarily in many cases, since they evidently constituted the great majority of the population eligible for transfer. Two million Poles, or about half those eligible for transfer, made the journey in the opposite direction.[25] In addition, a substantial group of Jews got out of the Soviet Union via the Polish-Soviet exchange though a high proportion of them subsequently left Poland for Palestine and other destinations.[26]

In resettling the transferees, Soviet authorities showed more anxiety about the security of border areas than about ethnic homogeneity. The incoming Ukrainians and Belorussians were not settled in the border districts of the western Ukraine and western Belorussia from which the Poles had been repatriated. Instead, most of them were settled in the southern Ukraine, while Russians and Ukrainians who had formerly resided in Siberia and Kazakhstan were brought in to rebuild the population of the border districts.[27] Western Ukrainian towns like Borisov, denuded of skilled workers and specialists by war and population exchanges, were sent cadres from Russia and Azerbaidzhan, and this kind of organized mixing and reshuffling of nationalities seemed to be typical of postwar policy.[28] Despite Belorussia's heavy wartime population losses and labor shortage, many Belorussian peasants were sent to work in industry and construction in Karelia, Altai, Siberia, and the Far East.[29] According to Harrison Salisbury, Jews deported from central and western regions of the Soviet Union during the "anticosmopolitan" campaign of the late 1940s were not sent to Birobidzhan, the Jewish autonomous region in the Far East, but to Yakutia. But when Salisbury visited Birobidzhan in 1954, he found a large contingent of Crimean Tatars who had been resettled there after their wartime deportation and who were still not permitted to return to their homeland.[30]

The Baltic states and other newly acquired territories were subjected to heavy Russification in the postwar period. Estonia, with a prewar population of not much over a million, lost many of her own nationals through deportation and received in return an influx of 180,000 non-Estonians, mainly Russians, in the years from 1945 to 1949.[31] The same happened in Latvia, where Russians rose from 12 percent of the population in 1935 to 27 percent in 1959.[32] In an allegedly voluntary program of "organized resettlement", half a million peasants from overcrowded regions of European Russia were moved to the border areas of Kaliningrad (formerly Königsberg and recently acquired from Germany), Sakhalin (the southern half of which had just been acquired from Japan), Eastern Siberia, the Far East, and elsewhere.[33] The russification element in the program was sometimes overt: "Slavs are again settling on this ancestral Slavic soil," wrote *Izvestiia* in December 1946, describing the trek of Russian and Belorussian kolkhozniks with "their livestock, poultry, farm implements, and seeds" to Kaliningrad.[34]

The newly acquired territories—the Baltic states, western Ukraine, western Belorussia, and part of Moldavia—had to be "Sovietized" as well as "Russified" after the war, continuing the process begun in 1940–1941 and interrupted by German occupation. "Sovietization" meant nationalizing industry and trade, expropriating the old bourgeoisie, intimidating the local intelligentsia, creating new administrative cadres and, finally, collectivizing peasant agriculture. Reaching back to the experience of the Soviet Russian past, the authorities deported large numbers of "class enemies" and created temporary "Sovietizing" institutions like *rabfaks,* whose purpose was to bring workers and peasants into higher education and thus transform the old elites[35] who were no longer to be found in the old territories of the Soviet Union. In the spring of 1949, an all-out collectivization drive was launched in the newly acquired territories.[36] This closely followed the model of its Russian precursor (the collectivization drive of the winter of 1929–1930) and included expropriation of kulaks and their deportation to Siberia and other distant parts. As in the earlier Russian case, collectivization was a major social upheaval, accompanied by large-scale migration of peasants from countryside to town. In Estonia, the rural share of total population dropped from 53 percent at the beginning of 1950 to 46 percent only four years later, representing an out-migration from the countryside of over 50,000 peasants.[37]

Repatriation and Demobilization

By January 1953, 5.5 million Soviet citizens were repatriated to the Soviet Union, the majority of them returning within a year of the end of the war.[38] Most of the repatriates were former Soviet POWs[39] and civilians from occupied Soviet territories who had been transported to the Reich as foreign laborers during the war[40] although some had probably left the Soviet Union voluntarily during the German army's retreat.

Repatriation was a tricky question from everybody's point of view. As far as the Soviet authorities were concerned, Soviet soldiers and officers who had allowed themselves to be captured were a suspect group: on the one hand, they should have preferred death to the dishonor of falling into enemy hands;[41] on the other hand, there was the possibility that they had been collaborators (like the million or more Soviet POWs who had served with the Wehrmacht's *Osttruppen* or joined the Vlasov Army)[42] or been recruited as spies during their period of internment. The same suspicion attached to the *Ostarbeiter* group (some of whom had volunteered to go and work in Germany), and indeed to all Soviet citizens other than those on active service with the Red Army who found themselves in Europe at the end of the war.

At Yalta the Allies had obliged themselves to repatriate all Soviet soldiers and civilians from Europe, and between May and September 1945 they did so conscientiously, despite growing uneasiness as it became clear to the Allied personnel directly involved that many of their charges did not want to be repatriated. The effort slackened after September, and, in the end, an estimated half million Soviet displaced persons remained in the West.[43] However, over 2 million Soviet citizens were repatriated from Western occupation zones to the Soviet Union in 1945.[44]

There were many accounts of the strange reception the repatriates received as they crossed the border into the Soviet Union—"first welcomed at the dock with a brass band," as an American diplomat reported in Murmansk, "and then marched off under heavy armed guard to an unknown destination."[45] The repatriates were interrogated on arrival by the NKGB's Vetting and Screening Commissions, which sought to establish who were the collaborators and who might have been recruited for espionage. Part of the group—how large a proportion is not clear[46]—received labor camp sentences, thus passing from one form of confinement to another; and the rest either returned home, were drafted back into the Army, or drafted for civilian labor.[47]

Demobilization of Red Army servicemen was a similarly massive operation, though less fraught with political and internal security tensions. There were 11.4 million men in the army in May 1945.[48] Large-scale demobilization began in July of that year, and by September almost 3.5 million soldiers and officers were returning to civilian life.[49] By 1948, the total number of demobilized Soviet soldiers had reached 8.5 million[50]—an enormous influx for the civilian economy to absorb. In contrast to the repatriation operation, demobilization was a fairly loosely organized process. Initially, those discharged were given their papers on the spot and allowed to go where they pleased. The practice was reportedly changed later so that soldiers had to pick up their papers—necessary documents for reentry into civilian life—at the place where they had been inducted into the service.[51]

The purpose of this policy was to ensure that peasant soldiers returned to the kolkhoz after demobilization.

But there were still many ways of evading this requirement. Since labor shortages were endemic immediately after the war, local authorities and enterprises did everything possible to encourage soldiers stationed in the area to remain after demobilization, regardless of their place of induction. In Azerbaidzhan, for example, soldiers stationed there at the end of the war were wooed with concerts, movies, and meetings with workers from local plants and oilfields, and lectures "on the economy of the republic and its prospects for development"; and as a result, 50,000 settled in Baku after demobilization.[52] Soviet historians estimate—there are not exact statistics, underlining the spontaneous aspect of the process—that about half of all demobilized soldiers found work in the towns after the war, while half went to the countryside.[53] But this indicates a significant demographic shift: before the war, not half but two-thirds of the Soviet population was rural, and presumably the same applied to the cohort conscripted for military service. Clearly, large numbers of peasant soldiers chose not to return to their former homes and occupations after the war, and the controls were not strict enough to force them back.

While it is clear that veterans had many informal privileges in the poverty-stricken society of the immediate postwar period, their treatment in the Soviet Union was not generous by comparison with other Allied countries. On demobilization, veterans were entitled to the cost of their transport home; food for the journey; a set of clothes; a pair of shoes; and a lump sum calculated on the basis of army pay and length of service (not, however, a significant amount except for officers).[54] There was no Soviet equivalent of the G.I. Bill in the United States, encouraging ex-soldiers to continue their education.[55] Soviet admissions boards did favor veterans in practice, but those who went to college after the war had to live on the same low stipends as other students. Employment was supposed to be arranged by the veterans' local soviets, "taking into consideration their experience and specialties acquired in the Red Army, but not in positions lower than those they held before they joined the Army".[56]

For many soldiers, however, army service in World War II turned out to be a channel of upward mobility. This was true of peasants who entered the urban labor force after demobilization. It was also true of soldiers who rose to be noncommissioned officers (NCOs) and officers during the war, joined the Communist party, and moved into administrative and managerial positions after the war. It should be remembered that at the end of the war half the Communist party was in the armed forces. A quarter of all soldiers (more than 3 million) belonged to the Party,[57] most having joined during the war. The dominant prewar pattern of elite recruitment—large-scale admission of workers into the Party and systematic promotion of lower-class Communists into administrative jobs—had begun to lose favor with the political leadership before the war and was dropped altogether in the 1940s.[58] What took its place in the immediate postwar period was the appointment of veterans who had joined the Party during the war to positions of civilian leadership.[59]

Aggregate figures on this process are not available, but a good deal of fragmentary data is provided by Soviet historians. By the end of 1946, almost 30,000 demobilized Communists had been appointed to leading work in the Ukrainian oblasts of Kharkov, Odessa, Stalino, and Poltava.[60] Of 22,000 demobilized soldiers starting work in enterprises of the Ministry of Ferrous Metallurgy in 1946, almost 7,000 went into managerial-technical jobs, where they constituted 15 percent of the whole managerial-technical cohort.[61] Very large numbers of veterans from peasant backgrounds became kolkhoz chairmen after the war. In the Krasnodar oblast alone, 1720 demobilized soldiers were elected chairpersons of kolkhozy in 1946.[62]

Urban Life and Labor Recruitment after the War

Life in the towns was even harder in the postwar years than it had been in the 1930s. The overwhelming problem was the shortage and low quality of housing. Overcrowding, including multiple-family occupancy of communal apartments not designed for the purpose, had been characteristic of Russian urban housing since the great peasant migration to the towns in the First Five-Year Plan. But during the war, more than 50 percent of urban living space in the territory occupied by the Germans was damaged or destroyed;[63] and housing in other parts of the Soviet Union deteriorated because of lack of upkeep and the pressures of accommodating large numbers of evacuees. In Moscow at the end of the war, for example, 90 percent of central heating and 48 percent of water and sewage systems were out of commission, and urgent repairs were needed on 80 percent of roofs, 60 percent of electrical equipment, and 54 percent of gas equipment.[64]

Urban population grew rapidly after the war (by 1950 the number of urban dwellers was more than 6 million above the 1940 level),[65] and housing construction and repair did not keep pace with it. Per capita urban living space dropped from 4.09 square meters in 1940—already below any acceptable minimum—to 3.98 square meters in 1950.[66] In Kemerovo (Siberia), the *obkom* reported in 1946 that a substantial proportion of workers "still lived in hostels with two tiers of bunks, and the real average norm of living space for one inhabitant does not exceed two square meters".[67] In Moscow, too, hundreds of thousands of workers lived in hostels, the great majority of which were actually barracks or improvised accommodations in basements, factory premises, and unfinished buildings.[68] Ministries and enterprises in Belorussia, where wartime damage to towns had been particularly severe, built barrack-type housing for their workers in the first postwar years, and it was not until 1949 that this form of housing construction became less common.[69]

Rationing of food and manufactured goods was introduced in the summer of 1941 and remained in force until 1947. Of course it was no novelty for the Soviet urban population since the rationing imposed during the First

Five-Year Plan had been lifted only in 1935. In 1942–1943, bread was often the only rationed commodity distributed, and the bread ration in Moscow at the end of 1943 was 300–650 grams per day according to the rationing category.[70] However, as in earlier periods of stringency, most wage earners could get a hot meal, albeit of low quality, at their place of work. In 1944, "commercial stores," selling food and other goods at very high prices, were revived, but those were far beyond the means of the average wage earner.

Real wages were at a very low level in the first postwar years. Because of the drought and harvest failure of 1946, rationing was not lifted on schedule and food shortages became more severe. Prices on rationed goods were approximately tripled in September 1946.[71] Consequently, the fact that commercial prices were simultaneously lowered did not benefit the average wage earner. The lifting of rationing in 1947 was accompanied by a currency reform designed to take excess cash out of circulation.[72] This was primarily aimed at urban speculators and peasants who had amassed savings during the war by selling produce at high prices on the free market, but it was also intended to encourage the largest possible number of urban dwellers to remain or become wage earners. Only in 1949, with the first of three successive rounds of price cuts, did the economic situation of the urban population begin to improve.

During the war, the work force was boosted by the presence of "temporary" workers—women who had not previously worked, pensioners, invalids, and adolescents. It was feared that when the war ended, large numbers of these workers would withdraw from the labor force despite the continued critical need for labor. Although adolescents did, in fact, withdraw,[73] primarily to continue their education, it seems that many of the other temporary workers remained in the work force after the war. This was probably because food prices were so high that families could not afford nonworking members. There may have been some withdrawal from the work force by urban women in 1945–1946, but as Table 8.1 suggests, this was not significant over the longer term (even allowing for the increase associated with peasant women coming into the labor force). In Moscow, for example, the proportion of women among blue- and white-collar workers dropped between January 1945 and March 1947, but the actual number increased slightly.[74] The number of pensioners employed in the national economy also increased—from 400,000 in 1945 to 484,000 in 1946[75]—reflecting not only the high price of food but also the inadequacy of pensions.

The twelve-million person increase in the size of the employed labor force between 1945 and 1950 (Table 8.1) was unmatched in Soviet history except in the First Five-Year Plan period. Demobilized veterans must have provided the largest single recruitment source, but the contingent of new workers included repatriates, peasants coming from the kolkhozy, graduates of the labor reserve schools, young urban dwellers entering employment, and labor conscripts. (Conscript and convict labor will be dealt with separately in the next section.) Quite a large proportion of the new workers, including all the veterans and most of the urban entrants to the labor force, were

Table 8.1   Wage and Salary Earners in the Soviet National Economy in Millions, with Breakdown by Sex

	Average No. for Year	No. of Men	as percent	No. of Women	as percent
1940	33.9	20.7	61	13.2	39
1945	28.6	12.7	44	15.9	56
1950	40.4	21.2	53	19.2	47

Source: *Narodnoe khoziaistvo SSSR 1922–1972 g. Iubileinyi statisticheskii ezhegodnik,* 345, 348.

hired individually by the given enterprises from the labor market. But there were also mechanisms of organized recruitment—*orgnabor,* the labor reserve system, and labor conscription—all of which took recruits from the kolkhozy (for the most part) and transported them to assigned employment, often in distant regions of the country.

Orgnabor (organized recruitment) was a term from the 1930s that was usually (that is, in the usage that was prevalent during the 1930s and the postwar Stalin period) applied to recruitment of labor from the kolkhozy for work under contract with specific enterprises. The organizing agent in the postwar period was the Ministry of Labor Reserves (created in 1947); and *orgnabor* was used mainly to provide unskilled labor for high priority sectors of heavy industry in areas of the country where labor was scarce. Thus, as Tables 8.2 and 8.3 suggest, *orgnabor* recruits were much more likely to be sent to Siberian coal mines than to the more sophisticated and accessibly located enterprises of the heavy machine-building industry. In 1948, 73.6 percent of *orgnabor* recruits went to the north, the Urals, and Siberia.[76] Kolkhozniki signed 71 percent of *orgnabor* contracts in 1950.[77]

The *orgnabor* share in total labor recruitment during the Fourth Five-Year Plan (1946–1950) cannot be determined with precision. One set of figures puts the number of *orgnabor* recruits for this period at 3.8 million,[78] another at 2.4 million.[79] This would mean that *orgnabor* provided a fifth to a third of all labor recruited during the Fourth Five-Year plan (a total of 11.6 million[80]), but the upper estimate—and perhaps even the lower one—is too high, judging from the breakdowns for particular industries and regions of which Tables 8.2 and 8.3 provide a sample. If in the late 1940s, as in the 1950s,[81] it was not uncommon for one individual to sign a succession of *orgnabor* contracts, this would explain why the figures are exaggerated.

The system of labor reserve schools, created in 1940 (see p. 131) and generally regarded as a wartime expedient, remained in active operation after the war. 1948 was the peak year;[82] but while the schools' output dropped rapidly in the early 1950s, it was not until 1959 that the system was abolished and the schools became ordinary technical schools.[83] In the postwar period students were still being drafted into labor reserve schools

Table 8.2   Labor Recruitment Sources for Heavy Machine-Building Enterprises of the USSR, 1946–1949

	1946	1947	1949
Number of new workers	22,344	26,631	27,803
Percentage recruited from			
Individual hiring	66.1	49.5	55.5
Labor Reserve Schools	3.5	27.4	23.3
Orgnabor	—	0.6	1.6
Transfer from other enterprises	1.8	1.2	7.8
Other sources	28.4	21.3	7.8

Source: A. V. Smirnov, "Changes in the Number and Composition of Workers of the Heavy Machine-Building Industry in the USSR in the Years of the Fourth Five-Year Plan (1946–1950)," in *Izmeneniia v chislennosti i sostave sovetskogo rabochego klassa. Sbornik statei,* 235.

rather than volunteering. In contrast to the *orgnabor* draft, which one memoir of the period describes as often welcomed by the kolkhozniki (though not by the kolkhoz administration), the labor reserve draft was evidently unpopular: "The boys disliked the schools because living conditions there were bad and because they had to do very hard work; to avoid being drafted into the schools, boys would run away from the villages to hide in the cities, where they frequently became delinquents."[84] But the labor reserve schools were conduits to more skilled employment than *orgnabor,* as well as supplying different branches of industry (see Table 8.2 and 8.3). During the Fourth Five-Year Plan period, 3.6 million students are said to have passed through the schools,[85] thereby amounting to over 30 percent of all labor recruitment.

The share of free hiring in labor recruitment obviously varied enormously according to circumstances. Looking at Table 8.2, for example, we can see that the heavy machine-building industry was doing a lot of individual hiring in 1946 as the veterans returned from the war, but less in 1947 and 1949 when there were fewer veterans and more labor reserve graduates. However, Kuzbass Coal, with its remote location and heavy dependence on conscript and other involuntary labor, did relatively little individual hiring. All in all, assuming that 5 or 6 million new workers came into the work force via *orgnabor* and the labor reserve schools during the Fourth Five-Year Plan and that there was not a high rate of renewal within the conscript labor contingent, it seems likely that a bit less than half of the total labor recruitment in this period was done by individual hiring on the labor market. The "other" category in Table 8.2 is likely to cover the labor of convicts or deportees.

However, a much higher figure, 79 percent, is quoted for the proportion of all job openings in 1950 that were filled by individual hiring.[86] This reflected an increase in individual hiring at the end of the Fourth Five-Year Plan period. But it was also a product of that old Soviet *bête noire,*

Table 8.3   Composition of Labor Force of Kuzbass Coal Combine (Siberia), with Breakdown by Sources of Recruitment (percentage)

	1 Dec. 1945	1 May 1946	1 Oct. 1947
Cadre (prewar) workers	21.4	19.0	17.2
Hired by enterprises	6.1	9.0	23.1
Labor reserve schools	5.3	5.5	7.8
Orgnabor	—	9.7	11.9
Evacuees	2.8	2.3	1.1
Conscripts (*mobilizovannye*)	23.2	18.3	7.8
Other	41.2	36.2	31.1

Source: G. A. Dokuchaev, *Rabochii klass Sibiri i Dal'nego Vostoka v poslevoennye gody (1946–1950)*, 66.

high labor turnover, for we must assume that among the almost 3 million people who found themselves new jobs in 1950, a proportion had earlier been assigned other jobs (that they had subsequently quit) as labor reserve school graduates or *orgnabor* recruits. Despite the law of 26 June 1940, binding workers to their jobs—which stayed on the books, along with other disciplinary measures of the immediate prewar and early wartime period, until 1956 (although the penal stipulations were quietly dropped in 1951[87])—people who took new jobs were not necessarily new workers. In 1951, it was estimated that more than 40 percent of newly recruited workers were either transferring from other jobs or returning to their original work place after an absence.[88]

The main causes of labor turnover in the postwar period were poor living and housing conditions. From January to May 1946, according to data of the Ministry of Ferrous Metallurgy, 32,000–33,000 workers were taken on and 62,700 left, 10,000 of them without permission from the authorities. In the year from September 1947 to September 1948, 289,300 workers left the mines of the Donetsk and Moscow basins, a quarter of them without permission.[89] At the Glukhovo Cotton Combine in Noginsk almost half the workers hired in 1946 left in the same year.[90] Out of 13,650 graduates of labor reserve schools sent to Belorussian industrial enterprises in 1947 only 7459 were still at their jobs on 1 January 1948, and 6191 had departed for unknown destinations because of bad housing and problems of food supply.[91]

Convict and Conscript Labor

At the end of the war the Soviet Union had two different types of convict labor at its disposal: its own indigenous convicts (together with foreigners arrested in the Soviet Union and sent to labor camps) and German, Japanese, and other prisoners of war captured during World War II. In both cases the question of numbers seems intractable. Estimates of the population of

Soviet labor camps in the postwar period range from 3–5 million to 12–15 million[92] (the higher estimates evidently including Axis POWs, the lower ones not), but they are all quite speculative. The estimates depend heavily on extrapolations from data on the immediate prewar period, almost ignoring the specific postwar situation.

Information on the number of enemy POWs in Soviet hands after the war is also highly unsatisfactory. Soviet wartime communiqués claimed that 3.7 million German military prisoners had been taken,[93] but Molotov stated in 1947 that after the return of a million German POWs only 890,532 remained in Soviet hands.[94] The first figure is probably exaggerated, whereas the second is likely to be an underestimate since Molotov was responding to criticism of the Soviet Union for not releasing its prisoners of war. In addition to the Germans, some hundreds of thousands of Japanese, Hungarian, Romanian, and other POWs were in Soviet hands after the war.

Although the order of magnitude may be disputed, some statements about the convict population in the postwar Soviet Union can be made with reasonable confidence. First, the number of Soviet convicts (excluding enemy POWs) must surely have been greater in 1945–1946 than it had been in 1939. It had been swollen by waves of arrests associated particularly with territorial changes and war: the occupation and initial Sovietization of eastern Poland and the Baltic states in 1939–1941, the liberation of Soviet territories from German occupation and the punishment of collaborators, anti-Soviet partisans, and bandits in the Ukraine, Belorussia, and elsewhere; renewed Sovietization in the Baltic states, Moldavia, western Belorussia and the western Ukraine; and the return of millions of Soviet POWs and repatriates whose loyalty was regarded as suspect.

Second, convict and POW labor in the immediate postwar period was useful to the Soviet Union—much more useful and central to the economy than it had been in the prewar period. It was the most extreme form of drafting labor to areas of acute need as for example, in the rebuilding of cities and the repair of roads, bridges, and railroads in territories heavily damaged under the German occupation, not to mention the "traditional" forced-labor sphere of mining and lumbering in remote parts of the Soviet Union. The political leaders may have perceived forced labor as essential to postwar economic reconstruction—whatever the merits of this judgment—in view of wartime population losses and the difficulties of mobilizing free labor and keeping it on the job when living conditions were bad.

By the beginning of the 1950s, however, the economic argument in favor of maintaining such a large convict population had become much less plausible. The daunting economic situation of the early postwar years had improved, and the most urgent and basic tasks of postwar economic reconstruction were done. In the sphere of nonconvict labor, conscription of various kinds was giving way to unorganized recruitment. Nevertheless, the prisoners and POWs were not released, and some of the projects on which they were used in the early 1950s—the Volga-Don Canal and the construction of the new Moscow University building on Lenin Hills[95]—had a grandiose rather than strictly practical quality.

From the swift dismantling of the convict labor empire following Stalin's death, it must be surmised that Stalin himself was the roadblock, either because he was generally blocking policy change or because he had developed an attachment to the idea of forced labor. Release of political prisoners— those arrested in the prewar purges, as well as wartime and postwar internees—began on a small scale in 1953. Soviet citizens accused of collaboration with German occupation forces were amnestied in 1955, and the Soviet POWs and repatriates who had been arrested on their return to the Soviet Union were released not long afterwards. An unofficial Soviet estimate, which unfortunately cannot be confirmed or documented in any way, puts the number of prisoners released in 1956–1957 at 7–8 million, out of an estimated total labor-camp population of 12–13 million.[96]

German POWs, whom the Soviet authorities had refused to repatriate earlier on the grounds they were war criminals, were also released after Stalin's death: about 10,000 returned to West and East Germany in 1953–1954, and another 10,000 were repatriated following the Bulganin-Adenauer talks in 1955.[97] This, of course, was only a small fraction of the number of German soldiers believed to have been taken prisoner by the Soviet Union. If, as seems to be generally thought, the Soviets really did return almost all of the surviving German POWs in 1955, the implied mortality rate is staggering.

Conscript labor in the postwar period is a less familiar and less dramatic topic than convict labor. But the two are linked—functionally, if not institutionally—and the more accessible data on conscript labor should throw light on the broader phenomenon. Labor conscription (*trudovaia mobilizatsiia*) of the civilian population was introduced during the war (see above, p. 131), and in 1943–1944, 2.4 million labor conscripts were working in industry and construction.[98] Labor conscription was not a punishment but an obligation comparable to military service, and historians have generally treated it as purely a wartime expedient. It continued into the postwar period, however; and, although many conscripts were probably just serving out terms begun during the war, others must actually have been conscripted for labor after the war ended.[99] Conscript labor was used all over the Soviet Union in the period between 1945 and 1948, but its share *vis-à-vis* nondrafted labor was highest in eastern Siberia and the Far East, remote but developing areas; in the Northern Caucasus and Crimea, presumably because of the deportations of nationalities (see above, p. 134); and also in Moldavia (much of which was newly acquired territory) where over half of all workers in 1945 were labor conscripts. Between 1945 and 1948 quite large numbers of labor conscripts were sent to the Western borderland regions: Belorussia, the Ukraine, the Karelo-Finnish Republic, Latvia, and Estonia.[100]

According to the Soviet historian B. I. Gvozdev, postwar labor shortages made it necessary to use conscript labor on a surprisingly large scale throughout the Soviet Union.[101] In his breakdown of the industrial work force (see Table 8.4), conscript labor evidently accounts for most of the category "others",[102] which is notable not only for its size but also for the fact that it actually grows in absolute terms between 1945 and 1948. (Other fragmentary data, such as those cited in Table 8.3, do not confirm this, but Gvozdev's figures are certainly the most comprehensive available.) It may be inferred from Gvozdev's data that labor conscription had been completely phased out by the spring of 1950.[103] But this is only an inference, and the actual terminal date of labor conscription (not counting short-term drafting of kolkhozniki for lumbering, road building, etc.) has still to be established.

Rural Life and Migration from the Kolkhoz

The war greatly weakened the material base of the kolkhozy (see Table 8.5). Horses and manpower were taken for military purposes, and the sown area contracted. As they retreated from the occupied territories, the Germans plundered the kolkhozy of animals and machinery and destroyed buildings. Moreover, a good deal of kolkhoz property found its way into private hands during the war as external supervision slackened. In occupied Belorussia and the Ukraine, expropriated kulaks came back and repossessed their old houses, blacksmith shops, and mills.[104] Elsewhere, peasants expanded their private plots at the expense of the kolkhoz, and there were concealed sales and leasing of land.[105]

Procurement levels were high throughout the war, and the average daily payment to the individual kolkhoznik for his workdays dropped from 350 grams of cereal and 330 grams of potatoes in 1940 to 190 grams of cereal and 70 grams of potatoes in 1945.[106] On the other hand, prices on the kolkhoz market were very high, and many peasants acquired large savings in cash by selling produce from their private plots. The most vexing problem for the kolkhozy was the shortage of manpower resulting from wartime military conscription. The working-age men were gone, and even some of the working-age women had been conscripted to work in industry (see Table 8.6). The old and the young had to become full-time workers on the kolkhoz, and women who had normally spent most of their time on the private plots had to take the men's place cultivating the kolkhoz fields.

The war's end brought men back to the countryside, but in far smaller numbers than had departed. This was not only because of casualties but also because many of the surviving peasant soldiers chose not to go home after demobilization, or at least chose not to stay. Of those that did return, many were invalids and unable to work. A year after the war ended, the ratio of working-age women to men in all Soviet kolkhozy was two to one (Table 8.6) whereas on Russian kolkhozy it was three to one.[107] This must surely have been the cause of much bitterness and disappointment. In territory that had been occupied by the Germans, war damage was still visible on every side, and agriculture was often reduced to a primitive level. Many kolkhozy in Russia, the Ukraine, and Belorussia were still using cows as draft animals in 1946, and others were digging with spades instead

Table 8.4 Breakdown of the Industrial Work Force of the USSR, 1945 and 1948

	1 April 1945		1 April 1948	
	Number	Percentage	Number	Percentage
Total	9,505,300	100	11,607,600	100
Workers	6,525,900	69	8,251,200	71
Employees	487,500	5	559,800	5
ITR[a]	746,200	8	926,700	8
Others	1,745,700	18	1,869,900	16

[a]Engineers and technical personnel

Source: B. I. Gvozdev, "Size of the Working Class," 114–16.

Table 8.5 Livestock and Sown Area of Kolkhozy, 1941–1950

	Cattle (millions)	Horses (millions)	Sown area (million hectares)
1941	20.1	14.5	117.7[a]
1945	15.4	6.2	83.9
1946	15.9	6.5	84.0
1947	15.8	6.6	89.2
1948	17.0	6.9	101.8
1949	20.9	7.9	111.1
1950	25.4	9.7	121.0

[a]1940 figure.

Source: *Sovetskaia derevnia v pervye poslevoennye gody 1946–1950,* 212, 255.

Table 8.6 Size and Breakdown of the Kolkhoz Population of the USSR (boundaries of 1939), in Millions

	1940	1944	1945	1946
Working-age[a]	35.4	22.0	23.9	25.0
Men	16.9	4.5	6.5	8.2
Women	18.6	17.6	17.4	16.8
Adolescents	7.1	6.4	6.1	5.4
Outside working-age not fit to work, etc.	33.3	34.0	34.5	33.1
Total number	75.8	62.4	64.5	63.5

[a]Excluding invalids

Source: Iu. V. Arutiunian, *Sovetskoe krest'ianstvo,* 318.

of ploughing and sowing by hand. There were no horses at all in 120 kolkhozy in the Novgorod oblast.[108]

But 1946 was also a year of natural disaster. A severe drought hit large parts of the Soviet Union—Moldavia, most of the Ukraine, parts of the central black-earth region, the lower Volga, and the Maritime Province in the Far East—causing harvest failures in these regions. Despite this, procurements quotas remained high; and by dint of enormous pressure on the peasants, grain deliveries were actually not much lower in 1946 than they had been in 1945 (17.5 million tons as against 20 million).[109] But this reduced much of the rural population to a desperate condition because so little was left for the peasants' own consumption. As Table 8.6 shows, departures of working-age peasant women and adolescents went up—probably a combined result of drafting for industry and hunger—and the total number of very old and very young persons in the kolkhoz population fell, suggesting increased mortality associated with famine.

In the postwar years, Alec Nove has written, it was "as if Stalin was determined to make the peasants pay for the necessary postwar reconstruction".[110] Compulsory state deliveries and payments to the Machine-Tractor Stations (MTS) amounted to half of all kolkhoz grain production in 1947 and 1948 and to more than half the kolkhoz production of milk and meat.[111] Moreover, prices paid by the state for deliveries were not only far below market prices, they were also way below production costs, leading some Soviet scholars to refer to postwar procurements as a tax-in-kind rather than an equivalent exchange.[112] Prices for grain had scarcely been raised since the beginning of the 1930s; in 1950 they covered about one-seventh of production costs. Moreover, prices varied by region, to the disadvantage of some of the regions most severely affected by the war. In Belorussia, for example, the state bought pigs at one-twentieth the cost of raising them.[113]

However, there were exceptions to the general pattern of low procurements prices. Cotton, citrus products, and tea were the main items for which the state was paying high prices after the war, and the result was a great disparity of income between kolkhozy in favored areas like Uzbekistan and the Caucasus on the one hand, and Belorussia on the other (see Table 8.7).

Payment for work on the kolkhoz was in kind (mainly grain and potatoes) as well as in money, but the payments were well below the prewar level, and kolkhozniki were very much dependent on their private plots for subsistence and money income. However, the private plots were a source of revenue to the state as well as the individual households in the postwar years. First, individual households had to make compulsory deliveries of vegetables, eggs, milk, and so on at below-market prices. If a household could not make deliveries out of its private plot—for example, if it had no cow to produce milk—the specified amount of milk had to be borrowed or bought on the market and delivered to the state regardless. Second, individual households had to pay the agricultural tax in addition to taxes levied on the kolkhoz as a whole. The agricultural tax was calculated by assigning a ruble value for each private-plot asset—animals, vegetable garden, fruit trees—and taking a percentage.

Table 8.7 Money Income of Kolkhoz Households by Region, 1945–1950 (in rubles of the given year)

	1945	1946	1947	1948	1949	1950
USSR	1,144	1,112	1,319	1,196	1,387	1,684
Uzbekistan	4,627	4,260	4,405	4,345	7,165	11,861
Caucasus	2,308	2,2⁻2	2,584	2,264	2,777	3,323
Central black earth region	1,237	1,056	1,267	1,000	1,070	986
Ukraine	619	618	830	834	925	1,103
Belorussia	236	335	503	458	485	463

Source: *Sovetskaia derevnia*, 288.

Table 8.8a   Kolkhoz Population of the USSR (excluding newly acquired territories), in Millions, 1945–1950

	1945	1948	1949	1950
Total	64.4	65.4[a]	63.8	62.3
Working-age	23.9	no data	26.7	25.9

[a]I. M. Volkov, "The Kolkhoz Peasantry in the First Postwar Years (1946–1950)," *Voprosy istorii*, 1970, no. 6: 7.

Source: *Sovetskaia derevnia*, 109.

Add to this the fact that the December 1947 currency reform wiped out peasant savings and that *corvée* obligations laid on the kolkhoz were a constant source of resentment, and it is not hard to find explanations for peasant dissatisfaction, expressed in the high rate of out-migration from the kolkhozy (only temporarily balanced in 1945–1947 by the return of the demobilized soldiers) in the postwar years. Kolkhoz population in Russia had far from reached the prewar level when the tide turned in 1947–1948 and numbers started to drop again (see Table 8.8b). In 1948 and 1949, more than a million working-age peasants left Russian kolkhozy. Many of those departing, though by no means all, were *orgnabor* recruits.[114] But the migration cannot be satisfactorily explained as a government-sponsored effort to attract peasant workers to industry. There was actually an excess of workers in industry after the 1947 currency reform encouraged nonworking urban residents to find jobs: in 1948, industry had 147,000 workers more than its planned contingent, and the situation had not changed by 1951.[115] From the government point of view, the utility of peasants staying in the countryside was greater than the utility of their migrating to towns and becoming urban wage earners at this time.

Yet the agricultural policies of the latter part of the Stalin period were not calculated to enhance the quality of rural peasant life. In many parts of the Soviet Union, notably in Russia, the old Ukraine, and Belorussia, fiscal and economic pressure on the kolkhozy became almost intolerably severe at the end of the 1940s. The tax on kolkhoz income was raised in

Table 8.8b   Kolkhoz Population of the RSFSR in Millions, 1940–1950

	1940	1944	1945	1946	1947	1948	1949	1950
Total	44.8	35.7	36.6	36.1	37.6	37.1	35.7	34.5
Working-age	20.8	12.5	13.5	14.2	15.7	15.9	15.4	14.7

Source: Verbitskaia, "Changes in the Size and Composition of the Kolkhoz Peasantry," 126, 131.

Table 8.8c   Population of the USSR, Rural and Urban, 1940–1954 (in millions, data for the beginning of each year)

	Population Total	Of Which		As Percentage of Total Population	
		Urban	Rural	Urban	Rural
1940	194.1	63.1	131.0	33	67
1950	178.5	69.4	109.1	39	61
1954	191.0	83.6	107.4	44	56

Source: *Narodnoe khoziaistvo SSSR 1922–1972,* 9.

August 1948, and the burden of this was felt most in areas like the Central black-earth region and Belorussia[116] where kolkhoz incomes were low and falling (see Table 8.7). Quotas for kolkhoz delivery of meat and milk also went up at the end of the 1940s,[117] meaning that less was available for consumption and sale on the market.

As for the individual households and their private plots, an average of 16.6 percent of eggs, 12.9 percent of grain and 5–6 percent of potatoes and milk products produced on private plots went to the state in the form of compulsory deliveries in 1950.[118] The agricultural tax became a very heavy burden since the value assigned to peasant assets did not reflect falling free-market prices and since the percentage taken for tax was increased: according to a Soviet calculation, the average agricultural tax on a kolkhoz household in 1950 was 93.6 rubles, as against 59.5 rubles in 1945.[119] In fact, the burden was so great that in 1949–1950 peasants started to dispose of their assets—chopping down orchards (in the example made famous by Khrushchev),[120] selling off animals, and reducing the acreage under cultivation in their private plots. The percentage of peasant households owning a cow, which in the first postwar years had held fairly steady at a level comparable with that of 1940, fell from 74 in 1948 to 64 in 1950.[121] In the period from 1950 to 1953, the area under cultivation in private plots declined from 7.5 million hectares to 6.9 million.[122]

It was in these years, 1950–1953, that migration from countryside to town became a flood. In the period 1950–1954, 9 million persons are said to have migrated permanently to the towns, out of a total rural-urban migration of 24.6 million over the twenty-year period 1939–1959,[123] and the rural share of total population dropped from 61 percent to 56 percent (see Table 8.8c). The rate of departure was greatest in areas where the economic plight of the kolkhozy was most acute, which in Russia meant the Moscow, Smolensk, Ryazan, Kaluga, Penza, Tambov, and Orlov oblasts, where in 1950 from 60 to 90 percent of kolkhozy were paying out no more than one kologram of grain per workday.[124] In a raion of Moscow oblast said to be fairly typical, the number of working-age kolkhozniki, expressed as a percentage of the number in 1946, went up to 108.5 percent in 1949 only to drop to 80 percent in 1952.[125]

In response to this crisis, the basis of *orgnabor* recruitment was changed to draw proportionately more heavily on the urban population than on the rural,[126] and one would suppose that rural soviets were instructed to place strict limitations on the number of passports issued to kolkhozniki. But these measures were obviously not effective in stemming the flow. After Stalin's death, the leadership decided that "mistakes" in policy towards the kolkhoz peasantry were to blame, and later Soviet historians have held to this opinion. The outflow from the countryside slowed down in the mid-1950s only after a series of policy changes had made the economic situation of the peasantry more viable.

The concept of a "return to normalcy" is often applied to postwar societies. It implies release from wartime obligations and constraints, relaxation of tension, going home, and settling down. But these qualities, however desired by Soviet citizens, were not characteristic of the Soviet Union in the immediate postwar period. Obligations and constraints were scarcely diminished. Many survivors uprooted by the war could not or did not return home. The kolkhoz had to cope with abnormally great government demands despite its depleted population and predominance of women. Peace brought *un*settlement to all those who were involved in population exchanges and resettlement programs, as well as the population of the newly acquired territories subject to Sovietization measures.

If the anticipated return to normalcy did not occur in the immediate postwar years, how is this to be explained? The first point to bear in mind is that the prewar Soviet Union did not provide a very satisfactory or complete model of normalcy to which the society could return after the war. Though the turmoil of social revolution had subsided by the mid-1930s, the spirit of struggle and conflict—kept alive by the growing threat of war in the latter part of the decade—was deeply rooted in the Party's political culture. The kolkhoz still seemed an alien institution to most peasants, whose idea of a return to normalcy was a return to the old precollectivization village. The New Economic Policy of the twenties, with its private businesses, small traders, and generally more relaxed and *gemütlich* atmosphere, was probably still the model of normal life for most town dwellers. Within the elite, the purges of the late 1930s had left a traumatic legacy of fear and insecurity. As a result of collectivization, the liquidation of NEP, and the purges, the Soviet Union had acquired a large convict population in prisons and labor camps. Although forced labor was to some extent integrated into the national economy, the camps were treated as a shameful secret, and it is very doubtful that the Soviet leadership—let alone the population—saw them as normal or systemic in the prewar decade.

After the war, the perpetuation of an essentially wartime atmosphere can partially be explained in terms of the urgent problems of economic reconstruction and manpower shortages. However, this rationale faded as the economy became stronger at the end of the 1940s. A contrast must surely be drawn, for example, between the pressures on the kolkhoz in the first postwar years, and the even greater pressures imposed at the beginning of the 1950s. The former were harsh, but acceptable within a context of war-associated sacrifice. The latter seemed almost gratuitous, reviving old suspicions that the regime was basically antagonistic to the peasantry, and leading millions of peasants to abandon the kolkhoz and seek a new life in the towns.

The regime itself was a major barrier to a return to normalcy in the immediate postwar years. In the first place, it was taking a stance of repressive vigilance in all areas, indicating to the population that the time of crisis, emergency, extraordinary measures, and sacrifice was not yet past. Soviet leaders were undoubtedly aware of differences between their own definition of normalcy and that of the population, or large segments of it: they knew that during the war peasants had talked of a postwar abolition of the kolkhoz, intellectuals of a postwar easing of cultural controls, and so on. Before any return to normalcy occurred, from the regime's standpoint, it was necessary to establish that the relevant norms were "Soviet", not "counterrevolutionary".

In the second place, the regime's policies towards non-Russians were an impediment to normalization. It was trying to Sovietize the newly acquired territories in the west with extremely disruptive social consequences, while at the same time promoting Russification of the population of these and other border regions. The antisemitic aspects of the "anticosmopolitan" campaign reinforced the impression that non-Russians were in deep disfavor as a group and further destabilizing innovations in official nationalities policy might be expected. If the regime had not quite replaced the old "class enemies" with ethnic enemies in Stalin's last years, it certainly seemed to be moving in that direction.

However, in talking of regime attitudes in Stalin's last years, we should possibly make a distinction between the attitudes of Stalin himself, and those of his colleagues and potential successors. To judge by the speed and thoroughness of change after Stalin's death, there must have been something like a silent consensus of dissatisfaction, or at least uneasiness, with Stalin's position on many questions emerging within the Party leadership at the end of his life. Part of the consensus might be expressed as a desire to lift wartime obligations and constraints that had survived into the postwar period, lower the level of repression and social tension, and put the society on a more normal peacetime footing.

Within a few years of Stalin's death, there were to be basic changes of policy towards the kolkhoz peasantry, relaxation of labor discipline measures, abandonment of the labor reserves system, and a partial dismantling of the whole empire of convict labor. Overt russification policies were dropped, and some ethnic groups deported during the war (though not the Crimean Tatars or Volga Germans) were allowed to return to their homelands. Soviet "collaborators", together with the Soviet POWs and *Ostarbeiteren* imprisoned on their return from Europe after the war were released. German POWs were finally—ten years after the war's end—repatriated.

This was essentially the long-awaited postwar relaxation, the return to normalcy that had never really occurred in the years 1945 to 1953. That harsh and stringent period, seen by many contemporary Western observers as the quintessence of Stalinism, perhaps deserves a less grandiose label like Jerry Hough's "petrification".[127] The system, clumsily attempting a transition from war to peace, seemed to have stuck halfway and be floundering. It was only when Stalin died that the balance eventually tipped, allowing Soviet society to lurch foward into the postwar era.

Notes

1. Michael K. Roof and Frederick A. Leedy, "Population Redistribution in the Soviet Union, 1939—1956," *Geographical Review* (April 1979):210.

2. Ibid.

3. *Istoriia Kommunisticheskoi Partii Sovetskogo Soiuza* 2d ed. (Moscow: Politizdat, 1962), 605.

4. Alexander Dallin, *German Rule in Russia 1941-1945* (London: Macmillan, 1957), 427.

5. 1.7 million Soviet citizens were working in Germany in 1943, according to data cited in Edward L. Homze, *Foreign Labor in Nazi Germany* (Princeton: Princeton University Press, 1967), 195. Malcolm J. Proudfoot, a repatriation official in Europe in the immediate postwar years, puts the numbers at something over two million, citing ILO and OSS estimates of 1944, in his *European Refugees: 1939-52. A Study in Forced Population Movement* (Evanston, Ill.: Northwestern University Press, 1956), 80. However, a recent Soviet estimate is much higher, almost six million—see G. A. Kumanev's article in P. A. Zhilin, ed., *Vtoraia mirovaia voina i sovremennost'* (Moscow, 1972), 262, cited in Mark R. Elliott, *Pawns of Yalta, Soviet Refugees and America's Role in their Repatriation* (Urbana, Ill.; University of Illinois Press, 1982), 23, 29 (note 3).

6. Proudfoot, *European Refugees,* 322-23.

7. *Istoriia Velikoi Otechestvennoi voiny Sovetskogo Soiuza 1941-1945,* vol. 6 (Moscow; Viennoe izdatel'stvo, 1965), 30.

8. The estimate of Soviet population is 190.7 million, including newly acquired territories (W. Ukraine, W. Belorussia, Moldavia, Latvia, Lithuania, Estonia) at the end of 1939. *Narodnoe khoziaistvo SSSR v 1960 g. Statisticheskii ezhegodnik* (Moscow; Statistika, 1961), 7.

9. This estimate is obtained by adding the alleged 10 million military casualties to the 11.4 million in the Soviet armed forces in May 1945 (*Istoriia Velikoi Otechestvennoi voiny,* 6: 123). Obviously this is only a rough approximation.

10. Iu. V. Arutiunian, *Sovetskoe krest'ianstvo v gody velikoi otechestvennoi voiny* (Moscow; Izdatel'stvo Akademii Nauk SSSR, 1963), 318.

11. A. A. Levskii, "Restoration of the villages of Belorussia in the postwar period," *Voprosy istorii,* no. 4 (1975):50.

12. *Narodnoe khoziaistvo SSSR 1922-1972 gg. Iubileinyi statisticheskii ezhegodnik* (Moscow: Statistika, 1972), 345, 348.

13. Harry Schwartz, *Russia's Soviet Economy,* 2nd ed. (Englewood Cliffs, N.J., Prentice-Hall, 1958), 525, 528.

14. The Labor Reserves system was created shortly before the war by a decree of 2 October 1940. Although the 1940 quota was essentially filled by volunteers, real conscription was practised from the summer of 1941. E. S. Kotliar, *Gosudarstvennye trudovye rezervy SSSR v gody Velikoi Otechestvennoi voiny* (Moscow, 1975), 14, 27.

15. Harry Schwartz, *op. cit.,* 528.

16. Arutiunian, *Sovetskoe krest'ianstvo,* 322.

17. Harry Schwartz, *op. cit.,* 528.

18. *Narodnoe khoziaistvo SSSR v 1960 g.,* 7.

19. S. Swianiewicz, *Forced Labour and Economic Development, An Enquiry into the Experience of Soviet Industrialization* (London: Oxford University Press, 1965), 41–42.

20. Joseph B. Schechtman, *European Population Transfers 1939–1945* (New York, 1946), 135, 150.

21. Ibid., 389.

22. Ibid., 383–84.

23. Aleksandr M. Nekrich, *The Punished Peoples* (New York: Norton, 1978), 115; Robert Conquest, *The Nation Killers: The Soviet Deportation of Nationalities* (New York: Macmillan 1970), 64–65.

24. Joseph B. Schechtman, *Postwar Population Transfers in Europe 1945–1955* (Philadelphia: University of Pennsylvania Press, 1962), 157–65.

25. Ibid., 161–162, 167, 172.

26. Most of the Jewish transferees on this exchange had been among the estimated 600,000 Jews who were either deported from Soviet-occupied Poland just before the war or fled from that area and other parts of the western Soviet Union as the Germans advanced in 1941. The total number of Jewish transferees is unknown, but 140,000 moved from the Soviet Union to Poland in 1946. Proudfoot, *European Refugees,* pp. 322–23 and 340–59.

27. Schechtman, *Postwar Population Transfers,* p. 168; V. I. Naulko, "Contemporary ethnic composition of the population of the Ukrainian SSR", *Sovetskaia etnografiia,* no. 5 (1962); 50.

28. Naulko, *op. cit.,* 50.

29. I. E. Marchenko, *Rabochii klass BSSR v poslevoennye gody (1945–1950)* (Minsk, 1962), 128.

30. Harrison E. Salisbury, *American in Russia* (New York; Harper, 1955), 284.

31. Tonu Parming, "Population Changes in Estonia, 1935–1970," *Population Studies* 36 (March 1972):58; R. N. Pullat, ed., *Problemy sotsial'noi struktury respublik Sovetskoi Pribaltiki* (Tallin: Eesti raanat 1978), 96.

32. Janis Sapiets, "The Baltic Republics," in *The Soviet Union and Eastern Europe. A Handbook,* edited by George Schoplin, (New York; Praeger, 1970), 222.

33. O. M. Verbitskaia, "Changes in the Size and Composition of the Kolkhoz Peasantry of RSFSR in the First Postwar Years (1946–1950)," *Istoriia SSSR,* no. 5 (1980):127.

34. Quoted in Eugene M. Kulischer, *Europe on the Move. War and Population Changes 1917–1947* (New York: Columbia University Press, 1948), 300.

35. Pullat, ed., *Problemy,* 80–82

36. *Sovetskaia derevnia v pervye poslevoennye gody* (Moscow: Nauka 1978), 383–84.

37. Pullat, ed., *Problemy,* 94.

38. *Istoriia Velikoi Otechestvennoi voiny,* 6: 107; Verbitskaia, *op. cit.,* 125.

39. Over five million Soviet soldiers were taken prisoner by the Germans, and almost two million had died in POW camps by 1944. On the status of the rest at the end of the war, see Proudfoot, *European Refugees,* 80.

40. As of May 1944, over two million Soviet citizens were in Germany as foreign laborers. Dallin, *German Rule,* 427.

41. See Dallin, *op. cit.,* 142 (note); Alexander Werth, *Russia at War 1941–1945* (New York: Dutton, 1964), 380–89.

42. Elliott, *Pawns of Yalta,* 19 and 27–28 (note 55).

43. Ibid., 122. The estimate must be only approximate, given the incentive for would-be nonreturners to conceal their Soviet citizenship: see Alexandra Tolstoy, "The Russian DPs," *Russian Review* 9 (January 1950):54.

44. Elliott, *op. cit.,* 82.

45. Quoted ibid., 194.

46. Swianiewicz (*Forced Labour,* 44) suggests that about half—2.5 million—were sent to labor camps. Alexander Werth, *Russia: The Post-War Years* (New York: Taplinger, 1971), 28, suggests the much lower figure of 500,000 for POWs, without mentioning other categories of repatriates. Both estimates are guesses, based on rumors circulating after the war in Munich and Moscow respectively.

47. Just over a million were drafted into the Red Army, according to a Soviet source (M. I. Semiriaga, *Sovetskie liudi v evropeiskom soprotivlenii* [Moscow, 1970], 327; quoted in Elliott, *Pawns of Yalta,* 202). At the end of 1945, half a million repatriates were

working, probably as labor conscripts, in territories liberated from German occupation (Iu. A. Prikhodko, "Steps in the Restoration of Industry in the Regions of the USSR Liberated from German-Fascist Occupation," *Voprosy istorii*, no. 5 [1969]:29).

48. *Istoriia Velikoi Otechestvennoi voiny*, 6:123.

49. V. N. Donchenko, "Demobilization of the Soviet Army and Resolution of the Problem of Cadres in the First Postwar Years," *Istoriia SSSR*, no. 3 (1970):98.

50. M. I. Khlusov, *Razvitie sovetskoi industrii 1946-1958* (Moscow; Nauka, 1977), 90.

51. Peter Pirogov, *Why I Escaped* (New York, 1950), 233.

52. A. M. Eldarov, *Rost rabochego klassa Azerbaidzhana v gody poslevoennogo sotsialisticheskogo stroitel'stva* (Baku; Maarif, 1971), 29.

53. Verbitskaia, "Changes," 125.

54. Carol Jacobson, "The Soviet G. I.'s Bill of Rights," *American Review on the Soviet Union* 7 (November 1945):57-8.

55. This question is discussed in Sheila Fitzpatrick, "Social Mobility in the Late Stalin Period: Recruitment into the Intelligentsia and Access to Higher Education, 1945-1953" (unpublished paper).

56. Jacobson, *op. cit.*, 57.

57. A. V. Krasnov, ed., *Bor'ba partii i rabochego klassa za vosstanovlenie i razvitie narodnogo khoziaistva SSSR (1943-1950 gg.)* (Moscow; Mysl', 1978), 53.

58. For an indignant and detailed account of postwar party recruitment in Moscow, stressing failure to recruit workers, see V. E. Poletaev, *Rabochie Moskvy na zavershaiushchem etape stroitel'stva sotsializma 1945-1958 gg.* (Moscow: Nauka, 1967), 188-90. After Stalin's death, recruitment of workers into the party increased, but this was not so closely linked with promotion to administrative jobs as it had been in the 1920s and 1930s.

59. Donchenko, "Demobilization," 102.

60. Krasnov, ed., *Bor'ba partii*, 56.

61. B. I. Gvozdev, "Size of the working class of the USSR in the first postwar years (1945-1948)," *Istoriia SSSR*, no. 4 (1971):113.

62. Krasnov, ed., *Bor'ba partii*, 56.

63. Harry Schwartz, *Russia's Soviet Economy*, 456.

64. Poletaev, *Rabochie Moskvy*, 252.

65. See Table 8.8c, p. 149.

66. Timothy Sosnovy, *The Housing Problem in the Soviet Union* (New York: Research Program on the U.S.S.R., 1954), 106.

67. A. F. Khavin, "A new might upsurge of heavy industry of the USSR in 1946-50," *Istoriia SSSR*, no. 1 (1963):28.

68. Poletaev, *Rabochie Moskvy*, 256.

69. Marchenko, *Rabochii klass BSSR*, 201.

70. Solomon Schwarz, *Labor in the Soviet Union* (New York: Praeger, 1951), 215-6 (note 38).

71. Ibid., 220.

72. Harry Schwartz, *op. cit.*, 478-80.

73. In 1945, 10.5 percent of those working in industry were adolescents (16 years and under), but this dropped to 4.9 percent by mid-1948 (Khlusov, *Razvitie sovetskoi industrii*, 147).

74. Poletaev, *Rabochie Moskvy*, 71.

75. Khlusov, *op. cit.*, 149.

76. M. Ia. Sonin, *Vosproizvodstvo rabochei sily v SSSR i balans truda* (Moscow; Gosplanizdat, 1959), 196.

77. Ibid., 207.

78. Ibid., 186.

79. Krasnov, ed., *Bor'ba partii*, 121.

80. Khavin, "A New Mighty Upsurve," 27.

81. Sonin's Table 62 (*op. cit.*, 215), "Composition of *orgnabor* recruits in terms of previous occupation" (RSFSR, July–August 1953) has 17.7 percent in the category "Released from enterprises and construction sites at the end of a labor contract".

82. Harry Schwartz, *op. cit.*, 527.

83. Kotliar, *Gosudarstvennye trudovye rezervy*, 236.

84. Fedor Belov, *The History of a Soviet Collective Farm* (New York: Praeger, 1955), 55–56, 104 and 108.

85. Khlusov, *op. cit.*, 95.

86. Krasnov, ed., *op. cit.*, 127.

87. R. Fakiolas, "Problems of Labour Mobility in the USSR," *Soviet Studies* 14 (July 1962):17.

88. Khlusov, *op. cit.*, 103.

89. Khavin, *op. cit.*, 27–28.

90. M. I. Khlusov, "Worker cadres of the Glukhovo 'V. I. Lenin' Cotton Combine in 1946–1950," *Istoriia SSSR*, no. 4 (1958):94.

91. Marchenko, *Rabochii klass BSSR*, 141.

92. For a survey of the estimates, see S. G. Wheatcroft, "On Assessing the Size of Forced Concentration Camp Labour in the Soviet Union 1929–1956," *Soviet Studies* 33 (April 1981):267–8. The lower estimates come from Timasheff (1948) and Bergson (1961), the higher from Dallin and Nicolaevsky (1947) and Rosefielde (1981).

93. Swianiewicz, *Forced Labor*, 42.

94. Cited in David J. Dallin and Boris Nicolaevsky, *Forced Labor in the Soviet Union* (New Haven: Yale University Press, 1947), 277.

95. For a list of construction projects using convict labor, see Aleksandr I. Solzhenitsyn, *The Gulag Archipelago 1918–1956*, 3–4 (New York: Harper & Row, 1975), 591–3.

96. Roy A. Medvedev and Zhores A. Medvedev, *Khrushchev: The Years in Power* (New York: Columbia University Press, 1978), 19–20.

97. Keesing's Research Report, *Germany and Eastern Europe since 1945* (New York: Scribner, 1973), 127–8.

98. Krasnov, ed., *Bor'ba partii*, 118.

99. See Table 8.4, p. 145.

100. Gvozdev, "Size of the Working Class," 114–7.

101. Ibid., 120.

102. In one of Gvozdev's tables (*op. cit.*, 119), the "others" category is broken down into "junior service personnel and guards" (5.5 percent of industrial personnel in 1940, 5.6 percent in 1945) and "not distributed by category" (zero in 1940, 12.8 percent in 1945). The latter is evidently the main conscript labor group, but Gvozdev states that the former also included conscript labor (*op. cit.*, 118–9).

103. See ibid., 119 (Table 5).

104. Arutiunian, *Sovetskoe krest'ianstvo*, 243–4; Belov, *History*, 20.

105. Arutiunian, *op. cit.*, 329–30.

106. Iu. V. Arutiunian, *Sovetskoe krest'ianstvo v gody velikoi otechestvennoi voiny*, 2nd ed., (Moscow: Nauka, 1970), 340.

107. Verbitskaia, "Changes," 130.

108. *Sovetskaia derevnia*, 204–5.

109. Ibid., 276.

110. Alec Nove, *An Economic History of the U.S.S.R.* (London; Penguin, 1972), 298.

111. I. M. Volkov, "The Kolkhoz Peasantry in the First Postwar Years (1946–1950)," *Voprosy istorii*, no. 6 (1970):13.

112. G. Ia. Kuznetsov, *Tovarnye otnosheniia i ekonomicheskie stimuly v kolkhoznom proizvodstve* (Moscow, 1971), 136, quoted in *Sovetskaia derevnia*, 269.

113. *Sovetskaia derevnia*, 272.

114. In 1949, 768,600 Russian kolkhozniki departed for permanent work in industry: of these, 621,900 were sent on *orgnabor* and 146,700 left "in a nonorganized manner" (Verbitskaia, *op. cit.*, 128).

115. Khlusov, *Razvitie sovetskoi industrii*, 104.

116. *Sovetskaia derevnia*, 294–5.

117. Ibid., 280.

118. Ibid., 462.

119. Ibid., 464.

120. Quoted from *Kommunist,* no. 12 (1957), in Robert Conquest, *Power and Policy in the USSR* (New York; St. Martin's Press, 1961), 122.

121. *Sovetskaia derevnia,* 461.

122. Sonin, *Vosproizvodstvo,* 92.

123. Ibid., 144 and 148.

124. Verbitskaia, *op. cit.,* 128.

125. Iu. V. Arutiunian, "Formation of Mechanizer Cadres of Kolkhoz Production in the Postwar Period (1946–1957)," *Istoriia SSSR,* no. 5 (1958):6.

126. Sonin, *op. cit.,* 206–7.

127. Jerry F. Hough and Merle Fainsod, *How the Soviet Union is Governed* (Cambridge, Mass.: Harvard University Press, 1979), 178–84.

9

The Impact of World War II on the Party

CYNTHIA S. KAPLAN

The Second World War found the Soviet Union and the Party on the verge of transition. The Stalinist revolution and the purges had transformed the Soviet society, economy, and political institutions. By the late 1930s, the policies which produced this new reality were replaced by policies seeking to administer it. As new economic and social conditions began to influence informal Party behavior, official policies sought to transform the role of the Party apparatus in Soviet society.[1] For the most part, these policies had yet to be realized when war engulfed the USSR. From this perspective, the war intervened in an ongoing process of political change. Thus, in addition to the immediate impact of the war, two central questions must be examined in order to assess the war's consequences for the Party. First, how did the war affect tendencies present in prewar Party behavior and the formal policies which sought to reshape the Party's role? Second, to what extent did the war's consequences for behavior correspond to prewar trends?

In analyzing the war's impact on the Party, I will distinguish between the Party as a political organization and as an administrative organ responsible for the performance of other organizations. As a political organization, the war's direct impact on the Party was immense; as a bureaucracy, its influence was more complex. The war's impact on Party composition, the professional experiences of the apparatus, and the formal policies redefining the Party's role all contributed to party behavior, as did a wide range of other factors that affect organizational behavior. These include the economic and political environment, the difficulty of the tasks set by postwar recovery plans, and the relative experience and expertise of economic leaders. While I consider these factors crucial to party behavior and worthy of detailed study, the present article's focus remains more limited. The prewar and postwar Party behavior will be compared with the behavioral tendencies associated with the direct effects of the war on the Party's composition, organizational penetration of society, and wartime experiences. If it is assumed that the war maintained or intensified the factors affecting organizational behavior, while retaining their relative relationship to each other, then it becomes possible to assess the war's influence on Party behavior.[2]

The Prewar Context

The Soviet regime began to shift its focus from structural change to a more conservative perspective in the 1930s. The Party's instrumental role in the socioeconomic revolution had waned by the mid-1930s. During the immediate prewar period (1938–1941), the Party began to reestablish itself as an organization, while simultaneously redefining its administrative role. These efforts were reflected in the Party's recruitment of increasing numbers of the new Soviet intelligentsia (as opposed to workers) and in the reshaping of its role in economic administration.[3] Such policies were consistent with the growth of the new Soviet technical elite, who enjoyed an increasing degree of professional autonomy.[4]

Although the Party sought to centralize its authority over cadre questions and to become more involved in local matters, this was not inconsistent with the aforementioned trends. The Party was not to replicate the functions of Soviet and economic organizations. Indeed, the latter organizations were also to be strengthened.[5] The central policy of the prewar period evidenced a growing desire to remove the Party from direct, daily involvement in local economic activities. These efforts, although not without some countervailing tendencies, foreshadowed the postwar period's emphasis on the Party's supervisory activities and the principle of *edinonachalie* (one man management), among industrial managers.[6]

The agrarian sphere remained distinct from the prewar trends found in the urban industrial context. Soviet policy's strong urban, industrial preference contributed to the Party's distinctive role in agriculture. The maximization of overt political authority over expertise or remunerative inducement was further enhanced by the weakness of local rural Party organizations, the Party's reliance on machine tractor station personnel, the heavy reliance on plenipotentiaries, agricultural policies that sought to complete the structural change begun during collectivization, rather than simply adjust administrative patterns to the presence of established institutions, and the absence of a specialized and politically reliable agricultural elite.[7] These factors contributed to formal policies that encouraged local Party organizations to become more directly involved in agricultural production.[8] Due to the rural sector's low level of political reliability, the Party's own organizational weakness in the countryside, interventionist policies, and the absence of alternative leaders, the Party confronted a different set of conditions and problems in agriculture than in industry.

Although many prewar conditions and policies were suggestive of future trends, formal policies aimed at transforming the Party's role remained substantially unrealized before prewar mobilization modified them.[9] Among the most important prewar tendencies affecting the Party were the increase in Party membership among the new intelligentsia, formal policies that sought to remove the Party from direct involvement in economic matters, especially in industry, and to promote its supervisory role, and attempts to strengthen the local Party's role in agriculture.

The Effects of the War

PARTY COMPOSITION

The Party's composition reflects its relation to society. As Soviet social and economic policies have changed, so has Party recruitment. Such trends, of course, are influenced by the reigning political preferences of the era in which they occur. Thus, industrialization witnessed an influx of workers into the Party, whereas collectivization did not produce an analogous phenomenon among peasants. As economic and social policies began to change in the 1930s, the Party chose to incorporate greater numbers of the Soviet technical elite. Party recruitment during the period between 1937 and 1941 clearly concentrated on the white-collar stratum.[10] Enrollments increased rapidly due to their long abeyance during the purges. This was facilitated by the new Party program presented at the Eighteenth Party Congress in 1939, which eased admission requirements.[11] Thus, the war intervened as the Party pursued a recruitment policy aimed at transforming it from a worker-dominated organization to one composed increasingly of white-collar employees.

To what extent did the war affect the Party's composition? Specifically, how did wartime recruitment change the distribution of political generations, social origins, and education levels found among Party members? What regional variations existed among local Party organizations? Did the war affect urban and rural Pary organizations differently? How extensive were changes within the Party apparatus? The answers to these questions provide at least a partial quantitative basis for understanding the war's impact on the Party.

THE MASS PARTY

The war affected Party organizations throughout the Soviet Union. Provincial and Republican parties sent from 36 to 74 percent of their entire memberships to the army during the course of the war.[12] Wartime mobilization was rapid. In 1941, only 16.5 percent of the Party were in the armed services, while 83.5 percent were members of territorial Party organizations. By 1942, the respective figures were 42.4 and 57.6 percent.[13] Smaller Party organizations sent a high percentage of their memberships to the front.[14]

High losses necessitated a massive Party-recruitment campaign among the armed forces and the civilian population. Indeed, from 1941 to 1945 the party recruited 8,400,000 members and candidates, of these 6,381,000 or 79.6 percent were from the armed forces.[15] The extraordinary nature of the wartime recruitment is clear when it is compared to recruitment during the period from 1936 to 1940, when 3,276,318 members and candidates were admitted, and to the 1946–1951 period when 3,237,012 were admitted.[16] The war's immense impact on Party membership is shown not only by the magnitude of newly recruited members but also by wartime losses. Prewar Party membership stood at 3,872,456 in 1941, while the postwar membership was 5,760,360 in 1945.[17] Clearly, wartime enrollment and losses deeply affected the Party membership.

Two-thirds of all postwar Party members had joined during the war.[18] Although the Nazi occupation, the effect of evacuees, and the prewar size of Party organizations all helped to determine the extent to which wartime losses and new inductees changed local Parties, almost all organizations were deeply affected (see Table 9.1). Occupied areas were most significantly affected, those far from the front to a lesser degree.[19] Thus, a substantial proportion of local Party members were new to their organizations, many recently recruited. Table 9.1 shows the percentage of new Party members and those who were demobilized in local Party organizations. Given the high mortality rate among those Party members serving in the armed forces, there is a substantial overlap between the two categories.

The distribution of political generations also reflects the influx of new Party members.[20] Data presented in Table 9.2 show the magnitude of the political generation recruited during the war and how it compares to the postpurge inductees. Taken together, these two political generations clearly dominated the postwar Party.

How did the massive influx of new party members affect the social composition of the Party? Prewar Party recruitment focused on the new Soviet intelligentsia. Although the percentage of workers and peasants during wartime recruitment increased in comparison with the 1939–1941 period (when they represented 20 and 10 percent respectively), the trend towards an increasingly white-collar Party membership continued during the war. Wartime enrollments among civilians and members of the armed forces included 32.1 percent with working class backgrounds, 25.3 percent peasants, and 42.6 percent white-collar employees. White-collar representation is even greater when measured by occupation, rather than by social origin.[21]

Wartime recruitment and losses produced a shift in the distribution of social origins found within the Party. National data on Party members show an increase from 34.1 percent with white-collar backgrounds in 1941 to 48.3 percent in 1947. (These data include the effect of demobilized Party members.) The percentage of workers dropped from 43.7 percent in 1941 to 33.7 percent in 1947, whereas peasants declined from 22.2 to 18 percent.[22] Although only partial data on the social composition of local Party membership are available, with the exception of Siberia, Central Asia, and the newly incorporated areas, provincial Parties appear to have increased representation of those with white-collar backgrounds. The distribution of Party members with peasant and worker origins reflects the predominant economic activities of the regions in which the local Parties are located. These effects are evident in Table 9.3.

Economic changes induced by the war also affected the distribution of social origins among Party members. The wartime industrialization of the Urals, the evacuation of Party members from western regions, and the transfer of urban cadre to the countryside in Western Siberia changed the social composition of many local Party organizations. Party organizations in Western Siberia and Central Asia clearly show the effect of the evacuees.[23] The relative democratization of Party enrollments during the war did not alter the trend towards increasing white-collar representation.[24] The sexual composition of Party membership also changed because of the war. The number of women in the Party increased due to their wartime recruitment and male losses. The percentage of female Party members rose from 14.5 percent before the war to 18.3 percent at its conclusion.[25]

Wartime recruitment led to a younger, better educated Party membership. Those under twenty-five years old constituted only 8.9 percent of total Party membership before the war, whereas after it they composed 18.3 percent of the Party. Indeed, two-thirds of the entire Party was younger than thirty-five years old in 1946.[26] Thus, as a result of wartime losses and the Party's recruitment practices, the "number of Communists with higher, secondary, and incomplete secondary education grew from 39.8 percent to 57.4 percent."[27] "Not less than one-third of all persons who had completed institutions of higher education were Party members."[28]

Available data from local Party organizations show the increase in educational levels to be a universal trend.[29] Those organizations whose members with higher and incomplete higher education surpassed the national average for the USSR in 1947 were located in areas whose population was generally better educated or that received large numbers of Communists from other regions.[30] Thus, Party members in previously occupied areas and in newly industrialized regions had educational backgrounds surpassing national averages.

While Party membership clearly grew during the war, what effect did the war have on the Party's organizational presence in society? How did the war affect the distribution of Communists in Soviet society? Was there a difference between urban industrial organizations and rural Party organizations?

Among the war's most immediate consequences was a dramatic decline in the number of Primary Party Organizations (PPOs). During the first six months of the war, PPOs declined by 987,000 organizations (more than 50 percent). Economic PPOs declined from 98,000 to 63,000.[31] Although the dissolution of PPOs located in occupied areas accounts for most of this decline, the number of kolkhoz PPOs also fell in areas behind the lines. Due to the low level of Party membership in rural areas, some PPOs

Table 9.1 Local Party Membership

	New Members (Percentage)	Demobilized Members (Percentage)
Bashkir[a]		60 (1948)
Belorussia[b]	72 (1946)	
Eastern	55.3	
Western	158	
Briansk[c]	68.7 (1946)	
Cheliabinsk[d]	41.8 (1946)	
Chernigov[a]		41 (1947)
Chkalov[a]		36.6 (1947)
Gorki[e]		28.7 (1946)
Kalinin[f]	50 (1947)	
Kaluga[g]	75 (1946)	
Khabarovsk[h]	75 (1946)	
Kherson[a]		54 (1947)
Kiev[e]		64.2 (1946)
Kirgiz[a]		34 (1947)
Kirov[a]		67 (1948)
Kostroma[a]		46.6 (1947)
Krasnodar[i]	63 (1950)	
Kuibyshev[i]	75 (1946)	
Kursk[a]		38.7 (1948)
Leningrad[k]	70 (1946)	52.9 (1947)
Moldavia[l]	40 (1946)	
Moscow[m]	34.4 (1946)	
Odessa[a]		50.3 (1947)
Orlovsk[a]		63.6 (1947)
Perm (Molotov)[a]		39 (1947)
Rostov[n]	55.2 (1946)	39.6 (1947)
Saratov[o]	92.8 (1946)	
Smolensk[a]		37.6 (1947)
Stanislav[a]		25.8 (1947)
Stavropol[a]		45.3 (1947)
Tadzhikistan[a]		51 (1948)
Tiumen[p]	82 (1946)	
Tula[q]	75.9 (1950)	
Udmurt[a]	60 (1946)	
Ukraine[r]	62.8 (1946)	
Vladimir[s]		22.4 (1947)
Voronezh[a]		41.8 (1947)
Voroshilovgrad[t]	74 (1947)	

aV. N. Donchenko, "Perestroika riadov VKP(b) v period perekhoda SSSR ot voiny k miru (1945–1948 gody)" (Candidate Dissertation, Moscow State University, 1972), 276.
bN. N. Akimov et al., eds., Ocherki istorii kommunisticheskoi partii Belorussii. Chast' II (1921–1966) (Minsk: Izdatel'stvo Belarus', 1967), 408–9.

[c]V. A. Smirnov, ed., *Ocherki istorii Brianskoi organizatsii KPSS* (Tula: Priokskoe knizhnoe izdatel'stvo, 1968), 335.

[d]Z. V. Shestakov et al., eds., *V boevykh riadakh leninskoi partii: Chliabinskaia oblastnaia organizatsiia KPSS v tsifrakh 1917–1977* (Cheliabinsk: Iuzhno-ural'skoe knizhnoe izdatel'stvo, 1978), 33, 44.

[e]V. N. Donchenko, "Demobilizatsiia sovetskoi armii i reshenie problemy kadrov v pervye poslevoennye gody," *Istoriia SSSR*, no. 3 (May 1970):102.

[f]V. I. Smirnov, ed., *Ocherki istorii Kalininskoi organizatsii KPSS* (Moscow: Moskovskoi rabochii, 1971), 545.

[g]A. F. Sladkov, ed., *Ocherki istorii Kaluzhskoi organizatsii KPSS* (Tula: Priokskoe knizhnoe izdatel'stvo, 1967), 306.

[h]A. K. Chernyi, ed., *Ocherki istorii Khabarovskoi kraevoi organizatsii KPSS 1900–1978 gody* (Khabarovsk: Khabarovskoe knizhnoe izdatel'stvo, 1979):263.

[i]I. I. Alekseenko et al., eds., *Ocherki istorii Krasnodarskoi organizatsii KPSS*, 2nd ed. (Krasnodar: Krasnodarskoe knizhnoe izdatel'stvo, 1976), 409.

[f]F. P. Zakharov et al., eds., *Kuibyshevskaia oblastnaia partiinaia organizatsiia v dokumentakh i tsifrakh (1902–1977 gg.)* (Kuibyshev: Kuibyshevskoe knizhnoe izdatel'stvo, 1978), 111.

[k]S. S. Dmitriev et al., eds., *Leningradskaia organizatsiia KPSS v tsifrakh 1917–1973* (Leningrad: Lenizdat, 1974), 46 and V. A. Kutuzov, "Nekotorye voprosy partiinogo stroitel'stv v leningradskoi organizatsii v pervye poslevoennye gody (1946–1948 gg.)," *Uchenye zapiski Institut istorii partii leningradskogo obkom KPSS I* (1970):221.

[l]E. S. Postovoi, ed., *Ocherki istorii kommunisticheskoi partii Moldavii* (Kishinev: Partiinoe izdatel'stvo TsK KP Moldavii, 1964), 309.

[m]G. I. Shitarev et al., eds., *Moskovskaia gorodskaia i moskovskaia oblastnaia organizatsii KPSS v tsifrakh* (Moscow: Moskovskii rabochii, 1972), 27, 47.

[n]Calculations by the author. V. N. Donchenko, "Perestroika," 252 and P. V. Barchugov, ed., *Ocherki istorii partiinykh organizatsii Dona (1921–1971) Chast' II* (Rostov-on-the-Don: Rostovskoe knizhnoe izdatel'stvo, 1973), 426.

[o]V. A. Rodionov et al., eds., *Saratovskaia oblastnaia organizatsiia KPSS v tsifrakh 1917–1975* (Saratov: Privolzhskoe knizhnoe izdatel'stvo, 1977), 25, 42.

[p]D. A. Smorodinskov, ed., *Ocherki istorii partiinoi organizatsii Tiumenskoi oblasti* (Sverdlovsk: Sredne-Ural'skoe knizhnoe izdatel'stvo, 1965), 254.

[q]N. I. Shmarakov, ed., *Ocherki istorii Tul'skoi organizatsii KPSS* (Tula: Priokskoe knizhnoe izdatel'stvo Tula, 1967), 504.

[r]V. I. Iurchuk, ed., *Ocherki istorii kommunisticheskoi partii Ukrainy*, 4th ed. (Kiev: Izdatel'stvo politicheskoi literatury ukrainy, 1977), 370.

[s]S. I. Surnichenko, ed., *Ocherki istorii Vladimirskoi organizatsii KPSS* (Yaroslavl': Verkhne-Volzhskoe knizhnoe izdatel'stvo, 1972), 370.

[t]L. G. Sharaev, ed., *Ocherki Voroshilovgradskoi oblastnoi partiinoi organizatsii* (Kiev: Izdatel'stvo politicheskoi literatury ukrainy, 1979), 33.

Table 9.2 Distribution of Political Generations in Party Organizations (percentage of Party membership)

Party Organization	1937–1940 (Percentage)	1941–1946* (Percentage)
Belorussia		
(1946)	28.2[a]	35.8[b]
Cheliabinsk Oblast		
(1946)	11.7[c]	67[c]
Kalinin Oblast		
(1945)	25.6[d]	47.2[d]
(1950)	12[d]	61.3[d]
Leningrad Oblast		
(1945)	12.4[e]	50.2[e]
(1946)	10.6[e]	58[e]
(1947)	9.4[e]	58.2[e]
Moscow Oblast		
(1947)	13.2[f]	56.4[f]
Perm Oblast (Molotov)		
(1946)	16[g]	58.5[g]
(1951)	9.7[g]	60.1[g]
Saratov Oblast		
(1947)	15.2[h]	65.8[h]
Ukraine		
(1946)		60[b]
Uzbekistan		
(1948)	17.6[i]	65.2[i]
(1950)	13.6[i]	49.2[i]
Volgograd Oblast		
(1945)	27.9[j]	35.1[j]
(1947)	16.6[j]	62.8[j]

[a]I. M. Ignatenko and S. S. Mokhovikov, eds., *Kommunisticheskaia partiia Belorussii v tsifrakh 1918–1978* (Minsk: Belarus', 1978), 115.

[b]T. I. Baradulina, "Povyshenie ideino teoreticheskogo urovnia kommunistov v raionakh osvobozhdennykh ot fashistskoi okkupatsii," in L. V. Shivikov, ed., *Deiatel'nost' KPSS v pervye gody posle Velikoi Otechestvennoi voiny* (Moscow: Akademiia obshchestvennykh nauk pri TsK KPSS, 1978), 2.

[c]Z. V. Shestakov et al., eds., *V boevykh raidakh leninskoi partii: Cheliabinskaia oblastnaia organizatsiia KPSS v tsifrakh 1917–1977* (Cheliabinsk: Iuzhno-ural'skoe knizhnoe izdatel'stvo, 1978), 114.

[d]A. V. Egorov, ed., *Kalininskaia oblastnaia organizatsiia KPSS v tsifrakh 1917–1977 gg.* (Moscow: Moskovskii rabochii, 1979), 63.

[e]S. S. Dmitriev et al., eds., *Leningradskaia organizatsia KPSS v tsifrakh 1917–1973* (Leningrad: Lenizdat, 1974), 89–90.

[f]G. I. Shitarev et al., eds., *Moskovskaia gorodskaia i moskovskaia oblastnaia organizatsii KPSS v tsifrakh* (Moscow: Moskovskii rabochii, 1972), 110.

[g]G. G. Chazov et al., eds., *Permskaia oblastnaia organizatsiia KPSS v tsifrakh 1917–1973* (Perm: Permskoe knizhnoe izdatel'stvo, 1974), 92.

[h]V. A. Rodionov et al., eds., *Saratovskaia oblastnaia organizatsiia KPSS v tsifrakh 1917–1975* (Saratov: Privolzhskoe knizhnoe izdatel'stvo, 1977), 95.

[i]N. T. Bezrukov, ed., *Kommunisticheskaia partiia Uzbekistana v tsifrakh* (Tashkent: Uzbekistan, 1979), 141, 159.

[j]A. P. Nevstuev et al., eds., *Volgogradskaia oblastnaia organizatsiia KPSS v tsifrakh 1917–1978* (Volgograd: Nizhne-Volzhskoe knizhnoe izdatel'stvo, 1978), 38–39.

*Unless noted otherwise, data are for the 1941–1946 generation. Kalininskaia Oblast and Volgogradskaia Oblast Party data in 1945 are for the 1941–1944 generation. Data for the Leningradskaia Oblast Party in 1945 are for the 1941–1945 generation. Uzbek Party data in 1950 are for the 1941–1945 generation.

Table 9.3 Social Composition of Local Party Membership (by percentage)

	Worker				Feasant				White Collar			
	1941	1945	1946	1947	1941	1945	1946	1947	1941	1945	1946	1947
Northwest												
Leningrad[a]	61.7	51.1	49.2	48.1	9.3	3.6	4.1	4.5	29.0	45.3	46.7	47.5
Central Chernozem												
Kuibyshev[b]	39.4	44.0	40.7	39.6	28.7	12.7	16.2	16.4	31.9	43.4	43.1	44.0
Saratov[c]	42.7*	37.2	35.2	34.7	25.7*	19.0	20.8	21.0	31.6*	43.8	44.0	44.3
Central												
Kalinin[d]	37.6	30.1	28.6	31.2	23.3	19.2	26.5	22.5	39.1	50.7	44.9	46.3
Urals												
Chelyabinsk[e]	47.4	47.8	47.1	47.1	13.3	8.7	9.9	10.3	39.1	43.5	43.0	42.6
Molotov[f]	45.3	39.9	36.9	36.4	17.0	11.1	14.3	15.4	37.7	49.0	48.8	48.2
Western Siberia												
Altai[g]	30.9	30.6	N.A.	N.A.	3.5	27.3	N.A.	N.A.	30.5	42.0	N.A.	N.A.
Kazakhstan[h]	28.0	26.5	25.0	26.2	36.4	30.7	31.3	29.5	35.6	42.8	43.7	44.3
Uzbekistan[i]	28.2	25.1	23.7	23.6	32.1	31.7	32.3	30.7	39.7	43.2	44.0	45.7
VKP(b)[j]	43.7	N.A.	N.A.	33.7	22.2	N.A.	N.A.	18	34.1	N.A.	N.A.	48.3

[a]S. S. Dmitriev et al., eds., *Leningradskaia organizatsiia KPSS v tsifrakh 1917–1973* (Leningrad: Lenizdat, 1974), 72–74.

[b]F. P. Zakharov et al., eds., *Kuibyshevskaia oblastnaia partiinaia organizatsiia v dokumentakh i tsifrakh (1902–1977 gg.)* (Kuibyshev: Kuibyshevskoe knizhnoe izdatel'stvo, 1978), 142.

[c]V. A. Rodionov et al., eds., *Saratovskaia oblastnaia organizatsiia KPSS v tsifrakh 1917–1975* (Saratov: Privolzhskoe knizhnoe izdatel'stvo, 1977), 64.

[d]A. V. Egorov, ed., *Kalininskaia oblastnaia organizatsiia KPSS v tsifrakh 1917–1977 gg.* (Moscow: Moskovskii rabochii, 1979), 39.

[e]Z. V. Shestakov et al., eds., *V boevykh riadakh leninskoi partii: Cheliabinskaia oblastnaia organizatsiia KPSS v tsifrakh 1917–1977* (Cheliabinsk: Iuzhno-ural'skoe knizhnoe izdatel'stvo, 1978), 76.

[f]G. G. Chazov et al., eds., *Permskaia oblastnaia organizatsiia KPSS v tsifrakh 1917–1973* (Perm: Permskoe knizhnoe izdatel'stvo, 1974), 64.

[g]N. Ia. Grishchin et al., *Obshchestvenno-politicheskaia zhizn' sovetskoi sibirskoi derevni* (Novosibirsk: Nauka, 1974), 111.

[h]S. B. Beisembaev and P. M. Pakhmurnyi, eds., *Kommunisticheskaia partiia Kazakhstana v dokumentakh i tsifrakh* (Alma Ata: Kazakhskoe gosudarstvennoe izdatel'stvo, 1960), 250, 281, 303.

[i]N. T. Bezrukov, ed., *Kommunisticheskaia partiia Uzbekistana v tsifrakh 1924–1977 gg.* (Tashkent: Uzbekistan, 1979), 123, 129, 140.

[j]Data for 1941 are from, V. Beliakov and N. Zolotarev, *Partiia ukrepliaet svoi riady* (Moscow: Izdatel'stvo politicheskoi literatury, 1970), 143. Data for 1947 are from "KPSS v tsifrakh," *Partiinaia zhizn'*, no. 21 (November 1977):28.

*Data are for 1940.

Table 9.4   Kolkhozy with Primary Party Organizations by Oblast and Republic

	Percentage	
	1946	1947
Chernigov	2.0	21.0
Chkalov	37.0	60.0
Chuvash	15.1	41.7
Gorki	11.8	23.6
Kaluga	1.0	4.4
Kherson	4.3	22.1
Kirgiz	57.1	67.4
Kirov	1.8	5.2
Kostroma	8.0	12.4
Krim	8.0	20.2
Kurgan	3.0	22.0
Odessa	1.2	9.6
Perm (Molotov)	3.0	8.1
Tadzhikistan	20.6	26.1
Turkmen	41.5	54.3
Tiumen	5.5	14.6
Udmurt	3.6	8.0
Uzbekistan	46.2	56.0

Source: V. N. Donchenko, "Perestroika riadov VKP(b)," 158.

collapsed as a result of military mobilization of Communists, while other organizations were transformed into candidate and komsomol groups.[32] In 1940, 12.6 percent of kolkhozy had PPOs; in 1945, 15.5 percent.[33] These figures, however, are somewhat misleading. From the beginning of the war until 1943, the number of kolkhoz Primary Party Organizations declined, with the exception of those in Western Siberia and Central Asia as seen in Table 9.4.[34] The disproportionately high percentage of kolkhozy with PPOs in Central Asia stems from the larger size of kolkhozy there. In Siberia, the expansion of the Party network reflects the influx of evacuees and urban cadres as well as agriculture's heightened priority due to the Nazi occupation of the country's most fertile land.

Primary Party Organizations located at kolkhozy tended to be smaller than those at industrial enterprises.[35] During the war, many kolkhoz PPOs had only three to five Communists.[36] This can be attributed to the low levels of rural Party membership before the war as well as the direct effect of military mobilization. During the first year and a half of the war, the number of rural Communists declined by 56 percent. By 1945, the number of Communists working in agriculture reached 67.6 percent of their January 1941 complement.[37] With postwar demobilization, rural communists exceeded their prewar numbers by 11.6 percent (1946) *na sele* and their primary party membership by 22.8 percent.[38]

Rural Party personnel policies from 1946 until the amalgamation of kolkhozy in 1950 transferred Communists from Territorial Party Organizations to small kolkhoz Party organizations. These policies also focused recruitment efforts on members of the rural intelligentsia.[39] Thus, the war increased the number of rural Communists, strengthened prewar trends that sought to establish kolkhoz PPOs, and decreased the scope of Territorial Party Organizations. Nevertheless, the degree of the Party's penetration and saturation in the countryside remained low.

Overall, the war transformed the nature of the Party through a massive influx of new members. Local Party organizations in occupied areas and those with small prewar memberships were most extensively affected by the war, those in Central Asia the least. The war's direct effects on local Party membership were modified by the evacuation of Party members from occupied regions, civilian recruitment, and the transfer of experienced Party members to newly incorporated areas.[40] The immensity of wartime Party enrollments resulted in the domination of Party organizations throughout the country by the 1941–1946 political generation. As a whole, postwar Party members were better educated and younger than their predecessors, but they lacked political education and professional experience. This was due to an easing of admission requirements during the war.[41]

The massive wartime recruitment broadened but did not reverse the prewar trend toward enrolling increasing numbers of white-collar employees. The number of Party members with white-collar social origins rose in Party organizations throughout the Soviet Union. The distribution of workers and peasants in local Parties reflected regional economic characteristics. Often, however, data on social composition hid the actual occupational distribution of Party membership since white-collar employees with worker and peasant backgrounds were classified in the latter categories rather than the former.

Despite wartime changes, the major prewar characteristics of rural Party organizations remained—the small number and size of kolkhoz PPOs, the transfer of territorial Party members to new kolkhoz PPOs, and the recruitment of the rural intelligentsia. The impact of peasant recruitment during the war was moderated by urban migration and frequent appointments of rural Party members to positions of authority (usually white-collar) in the countryside.[42]

War-induced changes in the mass Party contributed to the development of a number of postwar policies. The massive influx of young Party members with little political education contributed to the intensification of political indoctrination during the 1940s. Political education was expanded by establishing local, regional, and national Party schools as well as by heightening emphasis on propaganda and agitation.[43] Concern over the political reliability of new Party members, and in particular, the lower levels of the apparatus, led to a period of Party consolidation during the late 1940s. Recruitment during the postwar period became increasingly selective, emphasizing individual qualifications.[44]

Wartime Party recruits were frequently chosen for important local economic and political positions. The appointees' lack of political experience and specialized training contributed to the high turnover rates found among local Party secretaries (*raikom* and PPO secretaries) and agricultural leaders, particularly kolkhoz chairmen.[45] Industrial managers were to some extent exempted from these trends due to selection criteria requiring greater technical educational qualifications. Most of all, the war delayed postpurge cadres from gaining professional experience. After the war, these inexperienced leaders were joined by the Party's raw recruits from the wartime generation.

THE PARTY APPARATUS

The Second World War's primary impact on the Soviet political elite rests in the nature of the elite's experience rather than changes in its composition. Although Party leaders made frequent shifts among positions, the war did not produce a change in the political generation at the upper and intermediate levels of the Party apparatus.[46] Thus, the impact of the wartime experience was determined at least in part by the characteristics of wartime Party leaders. These leaders were to dominate Soviet politics for decades to come.[47]

Most postwar Party leaders assumed their first leadership roles during the years from 1939 to 1941 as a result of the purges. The absence of older political generations allowed postpurge leaders to establish their own patterns of informal behavior.[48] Such behavior was subject to formal policies, personnel characteristics, and conditions affecting informal activities. Prewar mobilization prevented the evolution of postpurge Party behavior from developing into stable administrative patterns. The war not only destroyed this process but itself proved a source of professional socialization. Thus, the question is not so much one of how the war affected the composition of the Party apparatus, but rather how sensitive and open the postpurge generation was to the wartime experience.

Although Stalin and his direct subordinates dominated the political process in the USSR, an exclusive focus upon them misses the informal aspects of political life. The Party apparatus, viewed as an organization, was capable of affecting policy through implementation. Party behavior evolved as a product not only of formal directives but also of those factors that affect local Party *apparatchiki* in carrying out their functions. Among the most important participants in this process are members of the *oblast* (provincial), *gorod* (city), and *raion* (district) Party committees, their bureaus and secretaries. Who were these members of the postwar Party apparatus?

First *obkom* secretaries in 1941 had entered the Party during the 1920s, often completing their education after some work experience. They were educated during a period when academic standards were lax and political subjects constituted a large percentage of the curriculum. Often such leaders served in political capacities while they pursued their educations.[49] *Obkom* secretaries serving in agricultural oblasts tended to be somewhat older and more poorly educated than those in industrial oblasts.[50]

During the postwar period, the immediate beneficiaries of the purges began to give way to a slightly younger and better educated cohort who

Table 9.5   Education of Obkom, Raikom, and Republic Central Committee Secretaries (percentages)

	Higher and Incomplete Higher	Secondary	Incomplete Secondary	Primary
1946	50.2	27.9	11.1	10.8
1952	77.8	17.8	3.7	.7

Source: Data for 1946 are from V. N. Donchenko, "Perestroika riadov VKP(b)," 213. Data for 1952 are from "KPSS v tsifrakh," Partiinaia zhizn' 14 (July 1973), 25.

entered the Party during industrialization and collectivization. This was particularly true in industrial oblasts. The political tenure of *obkom* first secretaries in 1955 reflects these postwar elite personnel changes. Approximately one-fifth of the *obkom* first secretaries in industrial oblasts and RSFSR oblasts had pre-1950 tenure.[51] Such changes resulted in an increase in the educational levels found among *obkom, kraikom,* and republican central-committee Party secretaries as shown in Table 9.5.

Although Party leaders' educations remained primarily political, industrial specializations did increase. A relatively small percentage of first *obkom* secretaries prior to 1953 pursued agricultural specializations.[52] Thus, the trend toward increased expertise was much stronger among secretaries in industrial areas than among those in agricultural regions.[53]

These educational differences contributed to different styles of Party leadership. Better educated Party leaders in industrial regions were more likely to comprehend the complex problems confronted by industrial managers and less likely to attempt to impose political solutions. *Obkom* secretaries increasingly shared a common background with industrial managers. This fostered a cooperative relationship between political and industrial leaders. Party secretaries relied upon industrial managers' greater expertise and experience, whereas the managers looked to the secretaries for assistance in circumventing production problems.[54]

Party secretaries' relations with agricultural leaders differed significantly from those of their counterparts in the urban industrial sphere. Rural political leaders during the 1940s and 1950s functioned within a relatively unsophisticated, politicized environment. *Obkom* secretaries had to depend upon lower-level political leaders to insure agricultural policy implementation because of the nature of agricultural production. *Obkom* Party members increasingly became monitors of results and issuers of directives, the latter subject to further specification by *raikom* secretaries. The central economic figure in policy implementation in agriculture was the kolkhoz chairman. The potential for Party leaders to develop an interdependent relationship with kolkhoz chairmen was low, since the majority of kolkhoz chairmen were inexperienced, lacked specialized education and training, and frequently, were not even Party members.[55] Political solutions and the supplanting of kolkhoz chairmen by raion-level cadres or their representatives was a frequent response to *obkom* pressure, especially when plan targets failed to be met.[56]

From an agricultural perspective, political leaders from *gorkoms,* urban *raikoms,* and especially rural *raikoms* influenced Party behavior through their roles in policy implementation. Their qualifications reflected the preferences of central policy makers and the unintended consequences of the war. To what extent was this intermediate level of the Party apparatus affected by the war? How do the background characteristics of this group compare to those at the oblast level?

Like their *obkom* counterparts, many of the prewar *apparatchiki* at city and district levels assumed their positions in the immediate postpurge period.[57] This group was subject to wide-scale mobilization at the beginning of the war.[58] Many of those mobilized or who joined partisan movements did not survive.[59]

Local Party apparatus included large numbers of new, inexperienced cadres after the war. In Rostov Oblast, for example, only 17 out of 155 oblast committee workers had prewar Party experience.[60] In Leningrad, 88.5 percent of the *gorkom* and *raikom* members had departed during the first months of the war.[61] At the end of the war, 82.6 percent of the Leningrad Party apparatus was new.[62] In Belorussia in 1946, 28 percent of the *raikom* and *gorkom* secretaries were elected for the first time, 45 percent of the *raikom* and *gorkom* bureau members, and 64 percent of the total *raikom* and *gorkom* membership.[63] In Smolensk, out of 1037 members of *raikoms* and *gorkoms* before the war, only 178 remained at its conclusion.[64] Party organizations located away from the front were also affected. In Saratov, *gorkom* and *raikom* membership sharply declined during the war.[65] Even in Siberia, *gorkom* and *raikom* secretaries underwent a substantial renewal.[66]

Data from Kalinin Oblast provide a somewhat more detailed picture of cadre changes caused by the war. According to the First Secretary of the Kalinin Obkom, I. Boitsov, Kalinin's experience was typical. Of the *raikom* and *gorkom* members as of 1 January 1945, a total of 28.9 percent had less than one year of job tenure, 57.6 percent had one to three years, while only 13.5 percent had three or more years. Among the total membership of 396 individuals in the Kalinin Party apparatus, 86 percent (319) had embarked upon leading Party work during the war. According to Boitsov, there was a tendency to retain first *raikom* secretaries more frequently than other members of the apparatus, but nonetheless, "the majority of cadres were young and their leadership experience—was the experience of the wartime period."[67]

The Kalinin findings are supported by data from other Party organizations. The number of *apparatchiki* without full-time Party work experience grew even after the initial military mobilization. Cadre turnover rates reflect this. For example, Moscow urban *raikoms* and *gorkoms* had a turnover rate of 32.5 percent in 1943; from 1944 to the beginning of 1945, one-half of the urban *raikom* and *gorkom* members were replaced, as were 68 percent of those in the oblast.[68] In Kuibyshev during the period from 1945 to 1946, more than 75 percent of *gorkom* and *raikom* secretaries were replaced.[69] In Western Siberia after the postwar elections, one-fourth to one-third of all Party secretaries were new to their positions.[70] In Belorussia, 494 *raikom* secretaries were removed (1945–1946), in Kaluga Oblast, 36.2 percent of Party workers were replaced, including 23 *raikom* secretaries (1946), in Vologodskaga Oblast 40 percent of *raikom* secretaries (1946), in Kirov Oblast 46 percent of *raikom* secretaries (1947) were replaced.[71] Thus, by the conclusion of the postwar Party electoral meetings, local Party apparatus had undergone a substantial renewal throughout the country. Among *raikom* secretaries, 39.9 percent were newly elected, including 27.5 percent for the first time. Similarly, 52.2 percent of raion bureau members were newly elected, 35.3 percent for the first time.[72]

As a result of wartime and immediate postwar cadre changes, the 1931 to 1940 political generation dominated the apparatus. Some *apparatchiki* at the intermediate level were even wartime recruits. Thus, political leaders at the district and city level came from a more recent political generation than their superiors at the oblast level. Thus, middle-level Party leaders had less practical political experience and education than those oblast Party cadres who had assumed their first full-time Party positions at the end of the purges (Table 9.6).

Intermediate level *apparatchiki* after the war had relatively low levels of education. Their education levels rose during recovery as a result of both personnel changes and the further education of incumbents. This trend is reflected in data dealing with areas throughout the USSR (Table 9.7).[73]

National data conceal important educational disparities among Party organizations that correspond to an urban-rural cleavage.

In some oblasts, the percentage of leading Party workers with only primary education was much higher, especially among secretaries of rural *raikoms*, significantly higher than the average. Thus, in the Gor'kovskoi oblast Party organization the percentage of *raikom* secretaries with only primary education was 27.5 percent, in Nizhnego Povolzh'ia—38 percent, in Kurganskoi—40 percent, in Kaluzhskoi—43.2 percent, and in Stalingradskoi—61 percent.[74]

The Leningrad Party organization exemplifies these differences. In 1946, 58 percent of city *raikom* secretaries had higher educations, while only 8.5 percent of the *raikom* and *gorkom* secretaries in the oblast organization had attained a comparable level of education. During 1947, the Party made a concerted effort to increase educational levels within the apparatus. By 1948, 77.4 percent of Leningrad's urban *raikom* and *gorkom* secretaries had a comparable level.[75] In Moscow Oblast, 45 percent of *raikom* secretaries had at least an incomplete higher education as compared to 70 percent of those in the capital.[76] Although rural *raikom* secretaries' educations improved, this increase did not alleviate sectoral differences.

The distribution of specialized education within the apparatus also conformed to sectoral differences. In 1947, 9.8 percent of the total Party had higher and incomplete higher educations, and 47.1 percent secondary

Table 9.6   The Political Generation of Raion Party Committee and Revkom Members (1948)

	Secretaries (Percentage)	Bureau Members (Percentage)	Committee Members (Percentage)
Pre-1930	31	28.3	20.2
1931–1940	54	49.4	39.2
1941–1948	15	22.3	59.4

Source: "Povyshat' rol' raikomov kak organov," 27.

and incomplete secondary. Of those with higher education 40.1 percent were in the field of engineering and 6.3 percent agronomy, veterinary science, and other agricultural specialities. The strong preference for industrial fields was also found among those with secondary level education—25.8 percent had technical training and 5.1 percent training in agronomy, veterinary science, and other agricultural fields.[77] The disparity in educational levels and fields of specialization suggests a more technically competent urban Party leadership, particularly at the district level, than in the rural Party. However, the influence of education on behavior should be evaluated in light of the relative qualifications of state and economic cadres as it affected their informal authority relations and their ability to perform their jobs.

The postwar local Party apparatus was composed of politically inexperienced leaders drawn primarily from the postpurge and wartime generations. While their educational levels rose during the postwar period, urban-rural differences remained. Overall, the inexperience of local Party leaders in full-time Party positions suggests that the wartime experience was likely to strongly influence their future behavior.[78]

The Wartime Experience and Party Behavior

The war represented a crucial experience in the professional socialization of postwar Party *apparatchiki*. Its impact was heightened by the inexperience of postwar Party leaders and by the fact that the Party's prewar role was in transition. While wartime experiences undoubtedly influenced individual Party members, how did the war affect the Party's organizational behavior?

The war encouraged the centralization of power and authority throughout the Soviet system.[79] This centralization had different consequences for the Party in the military and civilian sectors. In the army, Party professionals were removed from direct military command. Political workers in the armed forces could not officially intervene in military decision making.[80] This strengthened the principle of *edinonachalie* (one man management), among military leaders. In addition to its agitational activities, the Party recruited large numbers not only of enlisted personnel but also of military commanders. While three-fourths of those recruited were from the ranks of the armed

Table 9.7   The Education of Okruzhkom, Gorkom, and Raikom Party Secretaries

	Higher and Incomplete Higher (Percentage)	Secondary (Percentage)	Incomplete Secondary (Percentage)	Primary (Percentage)
1946	18.7	3.2	23.9	25.4
1952	62.3	25.5	9.2	3.0

Source: Data for 1946 are from V. N. Donchenko, "Perestroika riadov VKP(b)," 213. Data for 1952 are from "KPSS v tsifrakh," *Partiinaia zhizn'* no. 14 (July 1973):25.

forces, Party saturation among commanders was high. Eighty percent of commanding officers were either Party or *komsomol* members.[81] During the postwar period, demobilized Party members with some command experience were frequently chosen for positions of authority. This fostered a direct style of Party leadership.

The question of centralization within the civilian sector was more complex than in the military. Indeed, centralization when applied to the civilian sector is somewhat of a misnomer. Authority was concentrated in the hands of the party, but central control by Moscow of local party organs varied. This concentration of authority also called into question party economic and political duties. Were party members to become involved in directing the economy, or were they to limit their activities to the supervision and verification of economic activities in order to concentrate on political matters?

During the prewar mobilization, the party became increasingly involved in economic matters, especially in industry. The Eighteenth Party Conference held in 1941 established enlarged local departments within party committees based on industrial branches, thus reversing the functional organization established in 1939.[82] Defense and heavy-industry departments sought to redirect production to wartime needs. At the same time, party bureaus and cells in industry were granted the rights of PPOs.[83] All of this led to the party's direct participation in local decision making during the war.[84]

Many of the party's activities, however, involved regional coordination in the industrial sector.[85] Although "a countrywide production network was established by central planning organizations, in practice, a system existed based upon local party organizations."[86] What did this mean for the role of Party members vis-à-vis industrial managers?

Party members' industrial activities increased. As a report by the Kirov Factory Party committee noted, economic and political leadership was united. Yet, at the factory level this frequently meant that the Party enforced the directives of the factory director.[87] At the *obkom* level, the Party assumed coordination of responsibilities associated with areal administration. Thus, Party leaders became economic administrators without displacing industrial managers. N. S. Patolichev's account of his wartime experience in Cheliabinsk as first *obkom* secretary provides a description of the Party leader's relationship with industrial leaders. Patolichev states that in spite of close, direct relations with the Ministry of Ferrous Metallurgy, he nonetheless relied upon experienced factory directors in decisions affecting their enterprises. Indeed, the absence of specific directives from Moscow forced Patolichev and local industrial managers to act as a decision-making team.[88] Thus, an interdependent relationship appears to have arisen between Patolichev as first *obkom* Party secretary and the directors of major industrial enterprises. Patolichev recognized and relied upon directors' expertise, while they turned to him for expediting and coordinating functions.

During the war, *obkoms, gorkoms,* and *raikoms* were involved in coordinating economic activities throughout the Soviet Union. This type of behavior occurred in areas which redirected existing industrial production to wartime needs as well as in those which received evacuated enterprises.[89] At times, the Party's increased wartime involvement did lead to direct intervention, especially in areas located closest to the front.[90] Yet, coordination remained the dominant pattern. Many local Party organizations, particularly urban *raikoms,* expanded their coordinating role at the expense of raion soviets. In part, this resulted from the formation of *troikas,* which united Party, soviet, and economic leaders, but which were inevitably headed by the raion Party secretaries.[91] Overall, the Party's responsibility for and involvement in industry and economic administration increased, but at least in the case of heavy industry, this did not include the Party's displacement of industrial managers.

The Party confronted a different set of problems in agriculture than in industry. Although the Party had yet to develop an extensive involvement in this sector before the war, the Central Committee's decision to make *raikom* members and *politotdel* workers at Machine Tractor Stations and sovkhozy personally responsible for agricultural production, forced local Parties to respond to the wartime crisis.[92] The Party's direct intervention was encouraged by its low penetration of the countryside, the absence of Party members in positions of authority in agriculture, and the generally low level of qualifications and lack of experience found among agricultural leaders—all factors intensified by the war.[93]

The weakened state of agricultural production along with the Party's low rural profile fostered its reliance on extraordinary measures. Although *raikoms* and *raiispolkoms* (executive committees of district soviets) decided the major economic and political questions of the countryside during the war, crisis management fell to the purview of special Party representatives such as the heads of political sections at Machine Tractor Stations and sovkhozy and *raikom* plenipotentiaries.[94] These leaders frequently supplanted local economic cadres, especially kolkhoz chairmen.[95] According to published reports of the period, they showed minimal interest in political activities.[96] The *raikom* itself often functioned as a district agricultural administration with relatively little direct involvement in production activities.[97] With the abolition of *politotdely* in 1943, the major responsibility for agricultural performance fell to the *raikom*. Rural *raikoms* continued to rely on plenipotentiaries who, in fact, constituted the major link between kolkhozy and the district center. Thus, the rural Party developed a style of crisis management that depended on special representatives who ultimately undermined the authority of agricultural leaders.

In general, the war increased the economic activities of local Party cadres, while downgrading their political role. Their expanded economic role varied between industry and agriculture. In industry, the Party's wartime role emphasized coordinating activities and, less frequently, economic administration. A cooperative relationship between *obkoms* and the leaders of heavy industry developed during the war, a relationship that reinforced the growing autonomy found among industrial managers during the 1930s. To the extent that *raikom* and *obkom* Party *apparatchiki* assumed economic tasks during the war, the postwar regime's desire to focus Party efforts on propaganda and agitation activities and supervision and verification in industry was inhibited.

Efforts begun at the end of the 1930s to strengthen rural *raikoms* were thwarted by the war, particularly through the reestablishment of political sections at Machine Tractor Stations and sovkhozy.[98] The increased formal responsibility of rural *raikoms* fostered their further reliance on plenipotentiaries, who often supplanted agricultural leaders. This response, reinforced by the wartime crisis atmosphere, became a common modus operandi during the postwar years. Overall, the war reinforced rural Party leaders' tendency to resort to extraordinary means, usually political, in order to insure agricultural production. The displacement of agricultural leaders by Party representatives limited their professional autonomy. This pattern of behavior hindered postwar efforts that sought to encourage a less direct style of leadership.

The Consequences of the War

The war intervened as the Party was relinquishing its instrumental role in economic and social development and assuming a more conservative administrative role over Soviet institutions. Postwar Party policy sought to create a Party that would realign its political and economic functions. Rather than acting as state administrators or line personnel, the postwar Party was to develop an indirect style of leadership, emphasizing the supervision and verification of policy implementation. These changes were consistent with those begun during the late 1930s. They should not, however, be confused with the increased centralization of internal Party control that arose in response to the postwar apparatus' lack of political experience and training. The Party's increased participation in economic decision making and the close relationship that arose between some Party leaders and industrial managers complicated the realization of its new, officially prescribed role.[99]

The postwar model of Party behavior included tasks that were in some tension with each other. As Lazar Slepov, a leading Party theoretician, noted, Party committees are organs of political leadership. Their tasks are to unite and direct the activities of all state and public organizations. Party committees are responsible for the economy. The Party judges the work of one or another Party organization according to tangible results in the field of economy and culture, the standard of living, and the serving of workers' needs. However, Party organizations have the possibility of rendering necessary leadership in the course of economic construction on the activities of economic organizations: not supplanting economic enterprises and administrations, and not taking upon themselves the direct decision of all economic questions.[100]

Thus, Party leadership involved not only the indirect influence of other organizations through personnel decisions, but the "supervision (*kontrol'*) of cadre work and the rendering of assistance in the actual implementation of party and government decisions. An important aspect of political leadership rests in the Party organizations' supervision of the work of economic organs."[101] The desire to have Party organs follow the details of policy implementation and assume responsibility for economic results, although restrained from economic decisionmaking, made the realization of the Party's new role difficult. Slepov was clearly aware of this tension when he wrote that "Party organs are called upon to unite, direct, and supervise, but not to supplant nor to eliminate the personal responsibility of soviet and economic organs."[102]

This style of postwar Party leadership required economic leaders whose expertise could help insure satisfactory plan fulfillment and necessitated the existence of PPOs that could monitor work-place activities and carry out propaganda and agitation. These prerequisites were better met in industry than in agriculture. The economic and human consequences of the war— the decline in the labor force, wide-scale economic destruction, and investment preferences—also favored industry. Party recruitment among white-collar employees who often held industrial positions further assisted the party's transition to an indirect role in industry. Indeed, even economic targets were more reasonable in industry than in agriculture.[103] All this meant that the better educated industrial managers were more likely to succeed within a sector that relied increasingly on expertise. Thus, both industrial managers and Party leaders benefited from an interdependent relationship in which the former enjoyed increasing autonomy and the latter assisted through obtaining and coordinating support for industrial production. The wartime experience of Party leaders encouraged this evolving relationship.

Of course, not all factors favored the Party's adoption of a new role in industry that focused on "principled questions," policy issues, and critical supervision. For example, *obkom* secretaries were accused of developing a narrow approach to industrial questions.[104] Indeed, they may have favored the interests of industrial leaders on whom they depended to fulfill the plan, rather than those of Moscow. Another potential problem was the transformation of urban *raikom* activity from an economic focus to a political one. *Raikoms* often limited their activities to collecting data for reports to the *obkom*, virtually ignoring their duty to lead plant-level Party organizations. While the less direct, more explicitly political postwar Party role in industry was not fully realized during recovery, the increasing qualifications of *obkom* secretaries and the inexperience and youth of the Party cadres, nonetheless, facilitated behavorial change.

The wartime experience and poor qualifications of rural Party leaders, the difficult conditions of agricultural production, the superficial nature of Party penetration in the countryside, Lysenkoism, and the poor qualifications of agricultural leaders all made the abandonment of direct political intervention in agricultural production unlikely. Postwar policies, such as the reestablishment of *politotdely* at Machine Tractor Stations in 1947, the transfer of Party members from rural Territorial Party Organizations to kolkhoz PPOs, and the appointment of Party members with organizational skills as kolkhoz chairmen, sought to modify the factors which hindered the realization of the postwar Party model. In spite of the efforts inherent in central policies to redirect *raikom* activities towards personnel issues and political indoctrination, *raikom* plenipotentiaries continued to supplant kolkhoz chairmen, especially in poorer agricultural areas. This behavior resulted in the *raikom*'s condemnation and removal of kolkhoz chairmen. Such practices were officially condemned.[105] Nonetheless, the persistence of high turnover rates among agricultural personnel suggests that poor agricultural results normally led to political intervention.

Both the direct and indirect effects of the war had long-term consequences for the Party. Wartime enrollments increased the Party's size, while at the same time, they continued the prewar trend toward greater Party saturation among white-collar workers. This was almost a precondition for a less interventionist Party role in industry and the increased professional autonomy of economic managers. At the elite level, the break with the prepurge political apparatus was deepened through the appointment of young, inexperienced cadres to their first positions either during the war or the immediate postwar years. These new cadres' postwar behavior was influenced by their wartime experience. This behavior was reinforced by the economic and social effects of the war. The distinctive patterns of Party behavior evident in industrial and agricultural activities continued to exist decades later.[106] Thus, the war's political, economic, and social effects helped to shape a generation of Soviet Party leaders whose domination is only now drawing to a close.

Notes

1. This is my own interpretation. See *XVIII s''ezd vsesoiuznyi kommunisticheskoi partii (b) 10–12 marta 1939 g. Stenograficheskii otchet* (Moscow: Gosudarstvennoe izdatel'stvo politicheskoi literatury, 1939) and *Resheniia partii i pravitel'stva po khoziaistvennym voprosam,* vol. 2: *1929–1940 gody* (Moscow: Izdatel'stvo politicheskoi literatury, 1967).

2. See Cynthia S. Kaplan, "The Role of the Communist Party of the Soviet Union in the Implementation of Industrial and Agrarian Policy: Leningrad, 1946–53" (Ph.D. diss., Columbia University, 1981).

3. T. H. Rigby, *Communist Party Membership in the U.S.S.R. 1917–1967* (Princeton: Princeton University Press, 1968), 221–31. The VKP (b) during 1939–1941 recruited less than 20 percent workers, 10 percent peasants, and over 70 percent intellectuals and white-collar employees based on social origin. *Ibid.,* 225. "Izmeneniia v ustave VKP (b) dokladchik T. Zhdanov," *XVIII s″ezd,* 516.

4. Kendall E. Bailes, *Technology and Society under Lenin and Stalin* (Princeton: Princeton University Press, 1978), 297–336.

5. "Rech't. Andreeva," *XVIII s″ezd,* 104–21.

6. "Otchetnyi doklad t. Stalinana XVIII s″ezde partii o rabote TsK VKP(b)," *XVIII s″ezd,* 37.

7. See M. A. Vyltsan, *Sovetskaia derevnia nakanune Velikoi Otechestvennoi voiny* (Moscow: Politizdat, 1970), idem., *Zavershaiushchii etap sozdaniia kolkhoznogo stroia (1936–37 gg.)* (Moscow: Izdatel'stvo Nauka, 1978), idem., *Ukreplenie material'no-tekhnicheskoi bazy kolkhoznogo stroia vo vtoroi piatiletke (1933–1937):* (Moscow: Izdatel'stvo Akademii Nauk SSSR, 1959), Iu. S. Borisov, *Podgotovka proizvodstvennykh kadrov sel'skogo khoziastva SSSR v rekonstruktivnyi period* (Moscow: Izdatel'stvo Akademii Nauk SSSR, 1960), N. A. Lysenko, *Podgotovka kadrov dlia sotsialisticheskogo sel'skogo khoziaistva 1929–1958 gg.* (Moscow: Vysshaia shkola, 1975), Robert Miller, *One Hundred Thousand Tractors* (Cambridge: Harvard University Press, 1970), Roberta T. Manning, "The Collective Farm Peasantry and the Local Administration: Peasant Letters of Complaint in Belyi *Raion* in 1937," paper presented at the National Seminar for the Study of Russian Society in the Twentieth Century, 1983, Merle Fainsod, *Smolensk Under Soviet Rule* (New York: Vintage Books, 1958), and Rigby, *Membership,* 231–35.

8. "Andreeva," *XVIII s″ezd,* pp. 109, 120. *Resheniia,* vol. 2, 646–49, 661–62, 707–13, 719–59.

9. An example of this was the party's abolition of special departments in the Secretariat as a means of increasing the authority of industrial managers. (Agriculture was exempted from this policy.) This policy was reversed at the Eighteenth Party Conference in February 1941. Leonard Schapiro, *Communist Party of the Soviet Union* (New York: Random House, 1959), 450–51 and Rezoliutsiia XVIII Konferentsii VKP (b) 18 February 1941, "O zadachakh partiinykh organizatsii v oblasti promyshlennosti i transporta," *Resheniia,* vol. 3: 1941–1952 gody (Moscow: Izdatel'stvo politicheskoi literatury, 1968): 14–24.

10. I. N. Iudin, *Sotsial'naia baza rosta KPSS* (Moskow: Izdatel'stvo politicheskoi literatury, 1973), 186–87 and Rigby, *Membership,* 221–31.

11. "Zhdanov," *XVIII s″ezd,* 516.

12. Iu. P. Petrov, *Partiinoe stroitel'stvo v sovetskoi armii i flote (1918–1961 gg.)* (Moscow: Voennoe izdatel'stvo Ministerstva oborony SSSR, 1964), 351.

13. Ibid., 352.

14. L. N. Ul'ianov, *Trudovoi podvig rabochego klassa i krest'ianstva Sibiri 1945–1953 gg.* (Tomsk: Izdatel'stvo Tomskogo Universiteta, 1979), 34.

15. "KPSS v tsifrakh," *Kommunist,* no. 15 (October 1967): 93, and Petrov, *Partiinoe stroitel'stvo v armii,* 397.

16. "KPSS," *Kommunist* (1967), 91.

17. "KPSS v tsifrakh," *Partiinaia zhizn'* (21 November 1977): 24.

18. *Partiinaia zhizn',* no. 1 (1956), 24 cited by V. Beliakov and N. Zolotarev, *Partiia ukrepliaet svoi riady* (Moscow: Izdatel'stvo politicheskoi literatury, 1970), 162.

19. Rigby, *Membership,* 261–67.

20. Ibid., 200–35, 259–72. Only about 500,000 of the demobilized soldiers had been party members before the war. Ibid., 272.

21. Rigby, *Membership,* 224, 225, 239, and 268. In addition to party recruitment data for Kirov Oblast cited by Rigby (*Membership,* 269–71), data for Leningrad and Rostov-on-the-Don are available. Leningrad party recruits classified according to occupation during 1941–45 included 48.8 percent white collar, 31.2 percent industrial and transport, and 4.27 peasant. The comparable data for Rostov-on-the-Don were 55.4 percent, 19.7 percent, and 20.4 percent. S. S. Dmitriev et al., eds., *Leningradskaia organizatsiia KPSS v tsifrakh 1917–1973* (Leningrad: Lenizdat, 1974), 114–5 and I. M. Kriulenko et al., eds., *Rostovskaia*

oblastnaia organizatsiia KPSS v tsifrakh 1917–1975 (Rostov-on-the-Don: Rostovskoe knizhnoe izdatel'stvo, 1976), 94.

22. Beliakov and Zolotarev, *Partiia ukrepliaet,* 143 and "KPSS", *PZh* (1977), 28.

23. On Siberia, see Iu. A. Vasil'ev, *Sibirskii arsenal 1941–1945* (Sverdlovsk: Sredne-Ural'skoe knizhnoe izdatel'stvo, 1965), 75, M. R. Akulov, et al., *Podvig zemli bogatyrskoi* (Moscow: Izdatel'stvo Mysl', 1970), 115, and Ul'ianov, *Trudovoi podvig,* 34.

24. For example, 65.9 percent of the new party members in Omsk had white-collar social origins during 1941–1943. N. Ia. Grishchin et al., *Obshchestvenno-politicheskaia zhizn' sovetskoi sibirskoi derevni* (Novosibirsk: Nauka, 1974), 110.

25. Beliakov and Zolotarev, *Partiia ukrepliaet,* 158.

26. Ibid.

27. V. A. Vasilenko et al., *Istoriia Velikoi Otechestvennoi voiny Sovetskogo Soiuza 1941–1945,* vol. 6: *Itogi Velikoi Otechestvennoi voiny* (Moscow: Voennoe izdatel'stvo Ministerstva oborony soiuza SSR, 1965), 367.

28. Beliakov and Zolotarev, *Partiia ukrepliaet,* 158.

29. Data showing an increase in Party members' educational levels according to local Party organizations between 1941 and 1946 were found for Volgograd, Leningrad, Kuibyshev, Cheliabinsk, Perm, Rostov-on-the-Don, Georgia, Kalinin (1945), Saratov, Moscow, Belorussia, Kazakhstan, and Moldavia. The data are available in the party statistical handbooks published for the respective organizations. Exact citations and a table summarizing the information are available from the author.

30. For example, Leningrad, Georgia, Belorussia, and Moldavia.

31. *Lektsii po istorii KPSS,* vyp. 3, 2d ed. (Moscow: Mysl', 1974), 59 cited by V. K. Beliakov and N. A. Zolotarev, *Organizatsiia udesiateriaet sily* (Moscow: Izdatel'stvo politicheskoi literatury, 1975), 98.

32. I. E. Zelenin, *Obshchestvenno-politicheskaia zhizn' 1946–1958 gg. sovetskoi derevni* (Moscow: Izdatel'stvo nauka, 1978), 12 and Iu. V. Arutiunian, *Sovetskoe krest'ianstvo v gody Velikoi Otechestvennoi voiny,* 2d ed. (Moscow: Izdatel'stvo Nauka, 1970), 67, 68. Although the Eighteenth Party Congress had encouraged the establishment of kolkhoz PPOs, most rural communists remained in territorial party organizations. In 1939, only 4.9 percent of all kolkhozy had PPOs. N. N. Shushkin, *Vo imia pobedy* (Petrozavodsk: Izdatel' Karelia, 1970), 87. In 1941, there were 623,400 rural communists among whom only 62,300 were in PPOs. V. N. Donchenko, "Perestroika riadov VKP(b) v period perekhoda SSSR ot voiny k miru (1945–1948 gody)," (Candidate dissertation, Moscow State University, 1972), 170.

33. Zelenin, *Obshchestvenno-politicheskaia zhizn',* 36.

34. See "O partiinykh organizatsiiakh v derevne," *Partiinoe stroitel'stvo,* no. 12 (June 1942): 44–45, Beliakov and Zolotarev, *Partiia ukrepliaet,* 155, and Grishchin et al., *Obshchestvenno-politicheskaia zhizn',* 110. Complete data necessary to document the exact nature of the decline in kolkhoz PPOs are unavailable.

35. For example, Dmitriev, *Leningradskaia organizatsiia KPSS,* 134–35.

36. "O partiinykh," *PS,* 45.

37. Zelenin, *Obshchestvennoe-politicheskaia zhizn',* 11.

38. Donchenko, "Perestroika riadov," 170.

39. Rigby, *Membership,* 292–93.

40. Ibid., 266–67.

41. Postanovlenie TsK VKP(b), 19 August 1941, "O poriadke priema v partiiu osovo otlichivshikhsia v boiakh krasnoarmeitsev i nachal'stvuiushchego sostova krasnoi armii," in V. S. Vasilenko and E. P. Orekhov, eds., *Kommunisticheskaia partiia v period Velikoi Otechestvennoi voinu (iiun' 1941 goda–1945 god)* (Moscow: Gospolitizdat, 1961), 95, 96, and Postanovlenie TsK VKP(b), "O prieme v chleny VKP(b) kandidatov, otlichivshikhsia v boiakh s nemetskimi zakhvatchikami," in V. B. Kalinin, V. I. Nechipurenko, and V. M. Savel'ev, eds., *Kommunisticheskaia partiia v Velikoi Otechestvennoi voine (iiun' 1941 g.–1945 g.)* (Moscow: Izdatel'stvo politicheskoi literatury, 1970), 61, 62.

42. Rigby, *Membership,* 266–67 and Cynthia S. Kaplan, "The CPSU and Agriculture: The Emergence of Postwar Party Behavior," Chapter 3, "Postwar Agricultural Policies," 19. (Typewritten manuscript.)

43. Postanovlenie TsK VKP(b), "O podgotovke i perepodgotovke rukovodiashchikh partiinykh i sovetskikh rabotnikov," 2 August 1946, *KPSS v rezoliutsiiakh i resheniiakh s"ezdov, konferentsii i plenumov TsK,* vol. 6: *1941–1954* (Moscow: Izdatel'stvo politicheskoi literatury, 1971), 162–72, G. D. Komkov, *Ideino-politicheskaia rabota KPSS v 1941–1945 gg.* (Moscow: Izdatel'stvo Nauka, 1965), 370–83, and A. V. Krasnov, *Bor'ba partii i rabochego klassa za vosstanovlenie i razvitie narodnogo khoziaistva SSSR (1943–1950 gg.)* (Moscow: Mysl', 1978), 56–57.

44. Rigby, *Membership,* 278–79. Jerry Hough notes that given the small size of the potential candidate pool, it is surprising that the party recruited so many new members, rather than so few. Jerry F. Hough and Merle Fainsod, *How the Soviet Union Is Governed,* rev. and enl. ed. (Cambridge: Harvard University Press, 1979), 331–34.

45. Krasnov, *Bor'ba partii,* 56, 67, Shushkin, *Vo imia,* 277, Arutiunian, *Sovetskoe krest'ianstvo,* 401–3, and 170–71.

46. This observation is based on an analysis of *obkom* and republican party secretaries who attended the Eighteenth Party Congress in 1939 and the Nineteenth Party Congress in 1952.

47. See Jerry Hough, "The Soviet Elite II: In Whose Hands the Future?," *Problems of Communism* 16 (March–April 1967): 18–25 and Robert E. Blackwell, Jr., "Elite Recruitment and Functional Change: An Analysis of the Soviet Obkom Elite 1950–1968," *Journal of Politics* 37, no. 1 (February 1972): 124–52.

48. Seweryn Bialer, *Stalin's Successors* (New York: Cambridge University Press, 1980), 101 and Arthur L. Stinchcombe, *Constructing Social Theories* (New York: Harcourt, Brace and World, 1968), 107–17.

49. Bialer, *Stalin's Successors,* 114, Jerry F. Hough, *The Soviet Prefects* (Cambridge: Harvard University Press, 1969), 40–44, and Borys Lewytzkyj, "Generations in Conflict," *Problems of Communism* 16 (January 1967): 39.

50. The average birth date for RSFSR obkom secretaries in agriculture in 1941 was 1900, age at party entry—twenty-two, and one out of the eight were engineers. The comparable data for those in industry are: birth date 1904, age at party entry twenty-one, and eight out of fourteen were engineers. Hough, *Prefects,* 39.

51. Ibid., 50, 52, 65, and 71.

52. Blackwell, "Elite Recruitment," 136.

53. Educational differences associated with service in industrial and agricultural oblasts have persisted. Hough, *Prefects,* 37.

54. For example, for behavior during the late 1930's see Bailes, *Technology and Society,* 326–28, and Hough, *Prefects,* 80–100.

55. In 1946, 90.7 percent of kolkhoz chairmen had primary education and 5.5 percent were illiterate. I. M. Volkov, ed., *Sovetskaia derevniia v pervye poslelvoennye gody 1946–1950* (Moscow: Izdatel'stvo Nauka, 1978), 132. Forty-one percent of kolkhoz chairmen in the USSR had held their jobs for less than one year. Idem., "Kolkhoznaia derevniia v pervyi poslevoennyi god," *Voprosy istorii,* no. 1 (1966): 19. In 1948, only 40 percent of kolkhoz chairmen were party members. Rigby, *Membership,* 434. Also see, Iu. P. Denisov, "Kadry predsedatelei kolkhozov v 1950–1968 gg.," *Istoriia SSSR,* no. 1 (1971): 38–57 and Jerry F. Hough, "The Changing Nature of the Kolkhoz Chairmen," in James Millar, ed., *The Soviet Rural Community* (Urbana: University of Illinois Press, 1971), 110.

56. See Kaplan, "CPSU," Chapter 6, "The Party in Action: Agriculture," and Cynthia S. Kaplan, "The Communist Party of the Soviet Union and Local Policy Implementation," *Journal of Politics* 45 (February 1983), 14–16.

57. Beliakov and Zolotarev, *Organizatsiia udesiateriaet sily,* 85.

58. Within the first two years of the war, Leningrad sent 1786 of its leading party members, Belorussia 19 out of 69 obkom secretaries and 285 out of 600 gorkom and raikom secretaries, Ivanov 600 responsible workers and 2400 PPO secretaries, Kirov 32.5 percent (first 2.5 months) of the heads of raikom otdels, Volgograd 519 out of 1509 of the obkom nomenklatura, Uzbekistan 25 percent of obkom, gorkom, and raikom secretaries, Kirgiz 1300 of its central committee nomenklatura and Tadzhik 1079. N. A. Krasnov, *Partiinye mobilizatsii na front v gody Velikoi Otechestvennoi voinu* (Moscow: Izdatel'stvo Moskovskogo Universiteta, 1978), 17–25. In Kazakhstan by the end of 1942, 15.7 percent

of gorkom and raikom secretaries, 65.4 percent of heads of sections, and 42.2 percent of PPO secretaries had left for the front. S. B. Beisembaev and P. M. Pakhmurnyi, *Kommunisticheskaia partiia Kazakhstana v dokumentakh i tsifrakh* (Alma Ata: Kazakhskoe gosudarstvennoe izdatel'stvo, 1960), 256. In Siberia, the Irkutsk party had 71.7 percent of its secretaries mobilized. Vasil'ev, *Sibirskii arsenal,* 233.

59. Rigby, *Membership,* 272.

60. P. I. Dubonosov, "Organizatorskaia i politicheskaia rabota kommunisticheskoi partii po vosstanovlenniiu i razvitiiu narodnogo khoziaistva v poslevoennyi period (1946–1950 gg.)" (Doctoral dissertation, Rostov State Pedagogical Institute, 1972), 133.

61. N. M. Kiryaev and I. V. Stavitskii, "Rost i ukreplenie riadov KPSS v period Velikoi Otechestvennoi voiny," *Voprosy istorii,* no. 9 (September 1959): 11 cited by Sanford R. Liberman, "The Party Under Stress: The Experience of World War II," in Karl W. Ryavec, ed., *Soviet Society and the Communist Party* (Amherst: The University of Massachusetts Press, 1978), 120.

62. P. P. Danilov, "Bor'ba kommunisticheskoi partii sovetskogo soiuza za vypolnenie chetvertogo piatiletnego plana v oblasti tiazheloi promyshlennosti" (Candidate dissertation, Leningrad State University, 1964), 53.

63. T. I. Baradulina, "Povyshenie ideino teoreticheskogo urovnia kommunistov v raionakh o svobozhdennykh ot fashistskoi okkupatsii," in L. V. Shivikov, ed., *Deiatel'nost' KPSS v pervye gody posle Velikoi Otechestvennoi voiny* (Moscow: Akademiia obshchestvennykh nauk pri TsK KPSS, 1978), 2.

64. P. I. Kurbatova, *Smolenskaia partiinaia organizatsiia v gody Velikoi Otechestvennoi voiny* (Smolensk: Smolenskoe knizhnoe izdatel'stvo, 1958), 113.

65. D. F. Frolov, *Edinstvo tyla i fronta* (Saratov: Saratovskoe knizhnoe izdatel'stvo, 1961), 114.

66. Vasil'ev, *Sibirskii arsenal,* 75, 233, 234. For example, 48 percent of the raikom and aikom secretaries in the Buriat party organization were new during the war, as were 80 percent of sections heads.

67. I. Boitsov, "Vydvizhenie i rost kadrov v gody voiny," *Partiinoe stroitel'stvo,* no. 11 (June 1945): 36.

68. Γ. L. Aleksandrov et al., eds., *Ocherki istorii Moskovskoi organizatsii KPSS (1883–1965 gg.)* (Moscow: Moskovskii rabochii, 1966), 601, 603.

69. N. S. Chernykh, I. B. Kogan, and V. P. Chistiakov, eds., *Ocherki istorii Kuibyshevskoi organizatsii KPSS* (Kuibyshev: Kuibyshevskoe knizhnoe izdatel'stvo, 1967), 492.

70. Ul'ianov, *Trudovoi podvig,* 28.

71. Donchenko, "Perestroika riadov," 214–15.

72. "Povyshat' rol' raikomov kak organov politicheskogo rukovodstva (S raionnykh partiinykh konferentsii)," *Partiinaia zhizn',* no. 5 (March 1948): 27.

73. Information on the educational backgrounds of gorkom and raikom secretaries for the late 1940s and early 1950s is selective. In Yaroslav Oblast 34.5 percent of gorkom and raikom secretaries had higher to incomplete secondary education in 1947, 67 percent in 1949; Cheliabinsk Oblast 32.8 percent had higher and incomplete higher in 1946, 53.8 percent in 1949; Kalinin Oblast 13.5 percent higher and incomplete higher in 1945, 51.3 percent secondary and incomplete secondary and 36.2 percent primary, in 1950 the respective figures were 42.6 percent, 51.5 percent, and 6.8 percent; Kostromsk Oblast 51 percent in 1947 (1st gorkom and raikom secretaries), 86 percent for second secretaries; Krasnodar Krai 21 percent higher and incomplete higher in 1948, 54 percent in 1950. P. M. Volkov, ed., *Ocherki istorii Iaroslavskoi organizatsii KPSS* (Yaroslavl': Verkhne-Volzhskoe knizhnoe izdatel'stvo, 1967), 442, E. M. Tiazhel'nikov, ed., *Ocherki istorii Cheliabinskoi oblastnoi partiinoi organizatsii* (Cheliabinsk: Iuzhno-ural'skoe knizhnoe izdatel'stvo, 1967), 369, A. V. Egrov, ed., *Kalininskaia oblastnaia organizatsiia KPSS v tsifrakh 1917–1977 gg.* (Moscow: Moskovskii rabochii, 1979), 112, M. L. Siniazhnikov, ed., *Ocherki istorii Kostromskoi organizatsii KPSS* (Yaroslavl': Verkhne-Volzhskoe knizhnoe izdatel'stvo, 1967), 305, and I. I. Alekseenko, ed., *Ocherki istorii Krasnodarskoi organizatsii KPSS* 2d engl. ed. (Krasnodar: Krasnodarskoe knizhnoe izdatel'stvo, 1976), 407.

74. Donchenko, "Perestroika riadov," 214.

75. *Leningradskaia pravda,* 23 December 1948, and V. A. Kutuzov, "Nekotorye voprosy partiinogo stroitel'stva v Leningradskoi organizatsii v pervye poslevoennye gody (1946–1948 gg.)" *Uchenye zapiski* Institut istorii partii Leningradskogo Obkoma KPSS, 1 (Leningrad: Lenizdat, 1970), 231.

76. A. Ia. Utenkov, *Bor'ba KPSS za vosstanovlenie narodnogo khoziaistva i dal'neishee razvitie sotsialisticheskogo obshchestva 1946–1955 gg.* (Moscow: Izdatel'stvo vysshaia shkola, 1974), 58.

77. "KPSS," *PZh* (1977), 29, 30.

78. Primary party secretaries have not been included due to their high turnover rates, lack of experience, and the fact that most only joined the party during the war. Their behavior was more clearly a product of the postwar period. Krasnov, *Bor'ba partii,* 67.

79. Beliakov and Zolotarev, *Organizatsiia udesiateriaet sily,* 93–98.

80. Ukaz presidiuma Verkhovnogo Soveta SSSR 9 October 1942, "Ob ustanovlenii polnogo edinonachaliia i uprazdnenii instituta voennykh komissarov v krasnoi armii," Vasilenko and Orekhov, eds., *Kommunisticheskaia partiia,* 127–28.

81. A. G. Ershov, "Partiinye i komsomol'skie organizatsii armii i flota v gody Velikoi Otechestvennoi voiny (1941–1945)," *Voprosy istorii KPSS,* no. 6 (1975): 64.

82. Rezoliutsiia XVIII konferentsii VKP(b), 18 February 1941, "O zadachakh partiinykh organizatsii v oblasti promyshlennosti i transporta," in *Resheniia,* vol. 3: 14–24.

83. Beliakov and Zolotarev, *Organizatsiia udesiateriaet sily,* 96, 99.

84. M. L. Gutin, "Sozdanie otraslevykh promyshlennykh otdelov partiinykh organov i ikh deiatel'nost' v gody Velikoi Otechestvenoi voiny," *Voprosy istorii KPSS,* no. 9 (1978): 103–4.

85. Ibid.

86. P. R. Sheverdalkin, I. Z. Zakharov, and M. I. Likhomanov, *KPSS—vdokhnovitel' i organizator pobedy sovetskogo naroda v Velikoi Otechestvennoi voine* (Moscow: Izdatel'stvo politicheskoi literatury, 1973), 182.

87. "Vse dlia fronta! Vse sily na razgrom vraga!" *Voprosy istorii KPSS,* no. 12 (1975): 89.

88. N. S. Patolichev, *Ispytanie na zrelost'* (Moscow: Politizdat, 1977), especially 200, 281–2.

89. For example, see the Leningrad and Tomsk party organizations. V. S. Flerov et al., eds., *Tomskaia gorodskaia partiinaia organizatsiia v gody Velikoi Otechestvennoi voiny* (Tomsk: Tomskoe knizhnoe izdatel'stvo, 1962), 250–51 and S. P. Kniazev et al., eds., *Ocherki istorii Leningradskoi organizatsii KPSS,* chast' 2: *noiabr' 1917–1945* (Leningrad: Lenizdat, 1968), 587.

90. Kniazev et al., eds., *Ocherki istorii Leningradskoi organizatsii,* 586, 626 and Gutin, "Sozdanie otraslevykh," 104 (Iaroslavl').

91. This practice was noted in Leningrad, Perm, the Northwest Region, Rostov-on-the-Don, and Penzensk. V. V. Stemilov, "Leningradskaia partiinaia organizatsiia v period blokady goroda (1941–1943 gg.)," *Voprosy istorii KPSS,* no. 5 (1959): 118; A. G. Naumova, *Permskaia partiinaia organizatsiia v gody Velikoi Otechestvennoi voiny (1941–1945 gg.)* (Perm: Permskoe knizhnoe izdatel'stvo, 1960), 20; V. V. Iarobkov, "Partiino-politicheskaia rabota v zheleznodorozhnykh voiskakh v iiune-avguste 1944 g." in N. N. Shushkin et al., eds., *Iz istorii partiinykh organizatsii severo-zapada RSFSR (1941–1945 gg.)* (Petrozavodsk: Petrozavodskii Gos. Universitet, 1976), 83; D. I. Dubonosov, "Osveshchenie v istoriko-partiinoi literature deiatel'nosti KPSS po vosstanovleniiu i razvitiiu narodnogo khoziaistva (1945–1950 gg.) in V. I. Ivanov et al., eds., *Nekotorye voprosy partiinogo i sovetskogo stroitel'stva* (Rostov-on-the-Don: Rostovskii na Donu Gos. Ped. Institut, 1969), 200; and N. V. Khristoforov, ed., *Penzenskaia partiinaia organizatsiia v gody Velikoi Otechestvennoi voiny (1941–1945 gg.)* (Saratov: Privolzhskoe knizhnoe izdatel'stvo, 1964), 153–54.

92. Shushkin, *Vo imia,* 237 and "O merkakh uvelicheniia podgolov'ia skota v kolkhozakh i sovkhozakh i povysheniia ego produktivnosti," 13 April 1943, *Resheniia,* vol. 3: 121–30.

93. The number of communists in the countryside declined from 623,400 in 1941 to 277,700 in 1943. Zelenin, *Obshchestvenno-politicheskaia zhizn',* 11. During the first years

of the war up to 70 percent of leading kolkhoz cadres left for the front. Shushkin, *Vo imia,* 267. The leaders replacing them were "young, inexperienced, needing study and practical help." Ibid., 277. In 1943, 44 percent of all kolkhoz chairmen held their positions less than one year; in 1945 37.8 percent. Arutiunian, *Sovetskoe krest'ianstvo,* 401–3.

94. Political sections were reestablished at machine tractor stations and sovkhozy during the war. Arutiunian, *Sovetskoe krest'ianstvo,* 63. Postanovlenie politbiuro TsK VKP(b) "Ob organizatsii politotdelov v MTS i sovkhozakh," 17 November 1941, *KPSS v rezoliutsiiakh:* 36–38.

95. A. Grigor'ev, "Neskol'ko vyvodov iz opyta raboty politotdelov MTS," *Partiinoe stroitel'stvo,* no. 17–18 (September 1942): 21, S. Tarasov, "Umelo podkhodit' k liudiam," *Partiinoe stroitel'stvo,* no. 22 (November 1942): 29, and A. Larionov, "Sekretar' sel'skogo raikoma," *Partiinoe stroitel'stvo,* no. 8 (April 1943): 27.

96. "Sel'skii raikom partii," *Partiinoe stroitel'stvo,* no. 5–6 (March 1943): 7.

97. See F. A. Karevskii, *Kolkhoznoe krest'ianstvo Kuibyshevskoi oblasti v otechestvennuiu voinu* (Kuibyshev: Kuibyshevskoe knizhnoe izdatel'stvo, 1970), 37.

98. See Miller, *Tractors,* especially, 249–89.

99. L. Slepov, *Mestnye partiinye organy* (Moscow: VPSh pri TsK KPSS, 1954), 8, 25.

100. L. Slepov, "Stalinskaia programma pod'ema partiino-politicheskoi raboty," *Bol'shevik,* no. 3 (February 1952): 26. For a discussion of these issues, see Jerry F. Hough, "The Soviet Concept of the Relationship Between the Lower Party Organs and the State Administration," *Slavic Review,* no. 2 (June 1965): 215–40.

101. Slepov, "Stalinskaia programma," 27.

102. L. Slepov, "Zadachi i soderzhanie kursa 'Partiinoe stroitel'stvo'," *Lektsiia Vysshaia partiinaia shkola pri TsK KPSS* (Moscow: n.p., 1953): 22.

103. Eugene Zaleski, *Stalinist Planning for Economic Growth, 1933–1952,* trans. and ed. Marie-Christine MacAndrew and John H. Moore (Chapel Hill: The University of North Carolina Press, 1980).

104. Slepov, *Mestnye,* 25.

105. A. Kolosev and U. Zhukovin, eds., *Opyt Tselinskogo raikoma partii (Pis'ma o sel'skom raikome)* (Astrakhan': Izdatel'stvo gazeta Volga, 1948). This book reprints the major articles on rural raikoms which appeared in *Pravda.* N. Sudarikov, "Berezhno otnosit'sia i kadram presedatelei," *Sotsialisticheskaia zakonnost',* no. 12 (December 1947): 6.

106. See Kaplan, "The CPSU and Local Policy Implementation," 16–23.

References

Akimov, N. N. et al., eds. *Ocherki istorii kommunisticheskoi partii Belorussii.* Chast' 2 *(1921-1966).* Minsk: Izdatel'stvo Belarus', 1967.

Akulov, M. R. et al. *Podvig zemli bogatyrskoi.* Moscow: Izdatel'stvo Mysl', 1970.

Aleksandrov, F. L. et al., eds. *Ocherki istorii Moskovskoi organizatsii KPSS (1893-1965 gg.).* Moscow: Moskovskii rabochii, 1966.

Alekseenko, I. I. et al., eds. *Ocherki istorii Krasnodarskoi organizatsii KPSS.* 2d ed. Krasnodar: Krasnodarskoe knizhnoe izdatel'stvo, 1976.

Arutiunian, Iu. V. *Sovetskoe krest'ianstvo v gody Velikoi Otechestvennoi voiny.* 2d ed. Moscow: Izdatel'stvo Nauka, 1970.

Bailes, Kendall E. *Technology and Society under Lenin and Stalin.* Princeton: Princeton University Press, 1978.

Barchugov, P. V., ed. *Ocherki istorii partiinykh organizatsii Dona (1921-1971).* Chast' 2 Rostov-on-the-Don: Rostovskoe knizhnoe izdatel'stvo, 1973.

Beisembaev, S. B. and Pakhmurnyi, P. M., eds. *Kommunisticheskaia partiia Kazakhstana v dokumentakh i tsifrakh.* Alma Ata: Kazakhskoe gosudarstvennoe izdatel'stvo, 1960.

Beliakov, V. and Zolotarev, N. *Partiia ukrepliaet svoi riady.* Moscow: Izdatel'stvo politicheskoi literatury, 1970.

Bezrukov, N. T., eds. *Kommunisticheskaia partiia Uzbekistana v tsifrakh.* Tashkent: Uzbekistan, 1979.

Bialer, Seweryn. *Stalin's Successors.* New York: Cambridge University Press, 1980.

Blackwell, Robert E., Jr. "Elite Recruitment and Functional Change: An Analysis of the Soviet Obkom Elite 1950–1968." *Journal of Politics,* 37 (February 1972): 124–53. *Bol'shevik.*

Borisov, Iu. S. *Podgotovka proizvodstvennykh sel'skogo khoziaistva SSSR v rekonstruktivnyi period.* Moscow: Izdatel'stvo Akademii Nauk SSSR, 1960.

Chazovet, G. G. et al., eds. *Permskaia oblastnaia organizatsiia KPSS v tsifrakh 1917–1973.* Perm: Permskoe khnizhnoe izdatel'stvo, 1974.

Chernyi, A. K., ed. *Ocherki istorii Khabrovskoi kraevoi organizatsii KPSS 1900–1978 gody.* Khabarovsk: Khabarovskoe knizhnoe izdatel'stvo, 1979.

Chernykh, N. S., Kogan, I. B., and Chistiakov, V. P., eds. *Ocherki istorii Kiubyshevskoi organizatsii KPSS.* Kuibyshev: Kuibyshevskoe knizhnoe izdatel'stvo, 1967.

Danilov, P. P. "Bor'ba kommunisticheskoi partii sovetskogo soiuza za vypolnenie chetvertogo piatiletnego plana v oblasti tiazheloi promyshlennosti." Candidate dissertation, Leningrad State University, 1964.

Denisov, Iu. P. "Kadry predsedateli kolkhozov v 1950–1968 gg." *Istorii SSSR,* no. 1 (1971): 38–57.

Dmitriev, S. S. et al., eds. *Leningradskaia organizatsiia KPSS v tsifrakh 1917–1973.* Leningrad: Lenizdat, 1974.

Donchenko, V. N. "Demobilizatsiia sovetskoi armii i reshenie problemy kadrov v pervye poslevoennye gody." *Istoriia SSSR,* no. 3 (May 1970): 96–102.

——— . "Perestroika riadov VKP(b) v period perekhoda SSSR ot voiny k miru (1945–1948 gody)." Candidate dissertation, Moscow State University, 1972.

Dubonosov, P. I. "Organizatorskaia i politicheskaia rabota kommunisticheskoi partii po vosstanovleniiu i razvitiiu narodnogo khoziaistva v poslevoennyi period (1946–1950 gg.)." Doctoral dissertation, Rostov State Pedagogical Institute, 1972.

Egorov, A. B., ed. *Kalininskaia oblastnaia organizatsiia KPSS v tsifrakh 1917–1977 gg.* Moscow: Moskovskii rabochii, 1979.

XVIII s"ezd vsesoiuznyi kommunisticheskoi partii (b) 10–12 marta 1939 g. Stenograficheskii otchet. Moscow: Gosudarstvennoe izdatel'stvo politicheskoi literatury, 1939.

Ershov, A. G. "Partiinye i komsomol'skie organizatsii armii i flota v gody Velikoi Otechestvennoi voiny (1941–1945)." *Voprosy istorii KPSS,* no. 6 (1975): 57–67.

Fainsod, Merle, *Smolensk Under Soviet Rule.* New York: Vintage Books, 1958.

Flerov, V. S. et al., eds. *Tomskaia gorodskaia partiinaia organizatsiia v gody Velikoi Otechestvenno voiny.* Tomsk: Tomskoe knizhnoe izdatel'stvo, 1962.

Frolov, D. F. *Edinstvo tyla i fronta.* Saratov: Saratovskoe knizhnoe izdatel'stvo, 1961.

Grishchin, N. Ia. et al. *Obshchestvenno-politicheskaia zhizn' sovetskoi sibirskoi derevni.* Novosibirsk: Nauka, 1974.

Gutin, M. L. "Sozdanie otraslevykh promyshlennykh otdelov partiinykh organov i ikh deiatel'nost' v gody Velikoi Otechestvennoi voiny." *Voprosy istorii KPSS,* no. 9 (1978): 98–106.

Hough, Jerry F. "The Soviet Concept of the Relationship Between the Lower Party Organs and the State Administration." *Slavic Review,* no. 2 (June 1965): 215–40.

——— . "The Soviet Elite II: In Whose Hands the Future?" *Problems of Communism,* 16 (March–April 1967): 18–25.

——— . *The Soviet Prefects.* Cambridge: Harvard University Press, 1969.

——— . "The Changing Nature of the Kolkhoz Chairman." *The Soviet Rural Community.* Edited by James Millar. Urbana: The University of Illinois Press, 1971.

Hough, Jerry F. and Fainsod, Merle. *How the Soviet Union Is Governed.* rev. and enl. ed. Cambridge: Harvard University Press, 1979.

Ignatenko, I. M. and Mokhovikov, S. S., eds. *Kommunisticheskaia partiia Belorusii v tsifrakh 1918–1978.* Minsk: Belarus', 1978.

Iudin, I. N. *Sotsial'naia baza rosta KPSS.* Moscow: Izdatel'stvo politicheskoi literatury, 1973.

Iurchuk, V. I., ed. *Ocherki istorii kommunisticheskoi partii Ukrainy.* 4ed. Kiev: Izdatel'stvo politicheskoi literatury ukrainy, 1977.

Ivanov, V. I. et al., eds. *Nekotorye voprosy partiinogo i sovetskogo stroitel'stva.* Rostov-on-the-Don: Rostovskii-na-Donu Gos. Ped. Institut, 1969.

Kalinin, V. B., Nechipurenko, V. I., and Savel'ev, V. M., eds. *Kommunistichskaia partiia v Velikoi Otechestvennoi voine (iiun' 1941 g.–1945 g.).* Moscow: Izdatel'stvo politicheskoi literatury, 1970.

Kaplan, Cynthia S. "The Role of the Communist Party of the Soviet Union in the Implementation of Industrial and Agrarian Policy: Leningrad, 1946–1953." Unpublished Ph.D. dissertation, Columbia University, 1981.

————. "The Communist Party of the Soviet Union and Local Policy Implementation." *Journal of Politics,* 45 (February 1983): 2–27.

Karevskii, F. A. *Kolkhoznoe krest'ianstvo Kuibyshevskoi oblasti v otechestvennuiu voinu.* Kuibyshev: Kuibyshevskoe knzihnoe izdatel'stvo, 1970.

Khristoforov, N. V., ed. *Penzenskaia partiinaia organizatsiia v gody Velikoi Otechestvenoi voiny (1941–1945 gg.).* Saratov: Privolzhskoe knizhnoe izdatel'stvo, 1964.

Kniazev, S. P. et al., eds. *Ocherki istorii Leningradskoi organizatsii KPSS Chast' 2: Noiabr' 1917–1945.* Leningrad: Lenizdat, 1968.

Kolosev, A. and Zhukovin, U., eds. *Opyt Tselinskogo raikoma partii (Pis'ma o sel'skom raikome).* Astrakhan': Izdastel'stvo gazeta Volga, 1948.

Komkov, G. D. *Ideino-politicheskaia rabota KPSS v 1941–1945 gg.* Moscow: Izdatel'stvo Nauka, 1965.

KPSS v rezoliutsiiakh i resheniiakh s''ezdov, konferentsii i plenumov TsK. vol. 6: *1941–1954.* Moscow: Izdatel'stvo politicheskoi literatury, 1971.

"KPSS v tsifrakh." *Kommunist,* no. 15 (October 1967): 89–103.

"KPSS v tsifrakh." *Partiinaia zhizn',* no. 14 (July 1973): 9–26.

"KPSS v tsifrakh." *Partiinaia zhizn',* no. 21 (November 1977): 20–43.

Krasnov, A. V. *Bor'ba partii i rabochego klassa za vosstanovlenie i narodnogo khoziaistva SSSR (1943–1950 gg.).* Moscow: Mysl', 1978.

Krasnov, N. A. *Partiinye mobilizatsii na front v gody Velikoi Otechestvennoi voinu.* Moscow: Izdatel'stvo Moskovskogo Universiteta, 1978.

Kriulenko, I. M. et al., eds. *Rostovskaia oblastnaia organizatsiia KPSS v tsifrakh 1917–1975.* Rostov-on-the-Don: Rostovskoe knizhnoe izdatel'stvo, 1976.

Kurbatova, P. I. *Smolenskaia partiinaia organizatsiia v gody Velikoi Otechestvennoi voiny.* Smolensk: Smolenskoe knizhnoe izdatel'stvo, 1958.

Kutuzov, V. A. "Nekotorye voprosy partiinogo stroitel'stva v Leningradskoi organizatsii v pervye poslevoennye gody 1946–1948 gg.)." *Uchenye zapiski* Institut istorii partii Leningradskogo Obkoma KPSS, 1 Leningrad: Lenizdat, 1974.

Leningradskaia pravda.

Lewytzkyj, Borys. "Generations in Conflict." *Problems of Communism,* 16 (January 1967): 36–40.

Lieberman, Sanford R. "The Party Under Stress: The Experience of World War II." *Soviet Society and the Communist Party.* Edited by Karl W. Ryavec. Amherst: The University of Massachusetts Press, 1978.

Lysenko, N. A. *Podgotovka kadrov dlia sotsialisticheskogo sel'skogo khoziaistva 1929–1958 gg.* Moscow: Vysshaia shkola, 1975.

Miller, Robert. *One Hundred Thousand Tractors.* Cambridge: Harvard University Press, 1970.

Naumova, A. G. *Permskaia partiinaia organizatsiia gody Velikoi Otechestvennoi voiny (1941–1945 gg.).* Perm: Permskoe knizhnoe izdatel'stvo, 1960.

Partiinoe stroitel'stvo.

Partiinaia zhizn'.

Patolichev, N. S. *Ispytanie na zrelost'.* Moscow: Politizdat, 1977.

Petrov, Iu. P. *Partiinoe stroitel'stvo v sovetskoi armii i flote (1918–1961 gg.)* Moscow: Voennoe izdatel'stvo Ministerstva oborny SSSR, 1964.

Postovoi, E. S., ed. *Ocherki istorii Kommunisticheskoi partii Moldavii.* Kishinev: Partiinoe izdatel'stvo TsK KP Moldavii, 1964.

Resheniia partii i pravitel'stva po khoziaistvennym voprosam. Moscow: Izdatel'stvo politicheskoi literatury, 1967.

Rigby, T. H. *Communist Party Membership in the U.S.S.R. 1917–1967.* Princeton: Princeton University Press, 1968.

Rodionov, V. A. et al., eds. *Saratovskaia oblastnaia organizatsiia KPSS v tsifrakh 1917–1975.* Saratov: Privolzhskoe knizhoe izdatel'stvo, 1977.

Schapiro, Leonard. *Communist Party of the Soviet Union.* New York: Random House, 1959.

Sharaev, L. G., ed. *Ocherki Voroshilovgradskoi oblastnoi partiinoi organizatsii.* Kiev: Izdatel'stvo politicheskoi literatury ukrainy, 1979.

Shestakov, Z. V. et al., eds. *V boevykh riadakh leninskoi partii: Cheliabinskaia oblastnaia organizatsiia KPSS v tsifrakh 1917–1977.* Cheliabinsk: Iuzhno-ural'skoe knizhnoe izdatel'stvo, 1978.

Sheverdalkin, P. R., Zakharov, I. Z., and Likhomanov, M. I. *KPSS—vdokhnovitel' i organizator pobedy sovetskogo narod v Velikoi Otechestvennoi voine.* Moscow: Izdatel'stvo politicheskoi literatury, 1973.

Shitarev, G. I. et al., eds. *Moskovskaia gorodskaia i moskovskaia oblastnaia organizatsii KPSS v tsifrakh.* Moscow: Moskovskii rabochii, 1972.

Shivikov, L. V., ed. *Deiatel'nost' KPSS v pervye gody posle Velikoi Otechestvennoi voiny.* Moscow: Akademiia obshchestvennykh nauk pri TsK KPSS, 1978.

Shmarakov, N. I., ed. *Ocherki istorii Tul'skoi organizatsii KPSS.* Tula: Priokskoe knizhnoe izdatel'stvo Tula, 1967.

Shushkin, N. N. *Vo imia pobedy.* Petrozavodsk: Izdatel' Kareliia, 1970.

Shushkin, N. N. et al., eds. *Iz istorii partiinykh organizatsii severo-zapada RSFSR (1941–1945 gg.).* Petrozavodsk: Petrozavodskii Gos. Universitet, 1976.

Siniazhnikov, M. L., ed. *Ocherki istorii Kostromskoi organizatsii KPSS.* Yaroslavl': Verkhne-Volzhskoe knizhnoe izdatel'stvo, 1967.

Sladkov, A. F., ed. *Ocherki istorii Kaluzhskoi organizatsii KPSS.* Tula: Priokskoe knizhnoe izdatel'stvo, 1967.

Slepov, L. "Zadachi i soderzhanie kursa 'Partiinoe stroitel'stvo'." Lektsiia Vysshaia partiinaia shkola pri TsK KPRSS. Moscow: n.p., 1953.

————. *Mestnye partiinye organy.* Moscow: VPSh pri TsK KPSS, 1954.

Smirnov, V. A., ed. *Ocherki istorii Brianskoi organizatsii KPSS.* Tula: Priokskoe knizhnoe izdatel'stvo, 1968.

Smirnov, V. I., ed. *Ocherki istorii Kalininskoi organizatsii KPSS.* Moscow: Moskovskoi rabochii, 1971.

Smorodinskov, D. A., ed. *Ocherki istorii partiinoi organizatsii Tiumenskoi oblasti.* Sverdlovsk: Sredne-Ural'skoe knizhnoe izdatel'stvo, 1965.

Stremilov, V. V. "Leningradskaia partiinaia orgaizatsiia v period blokady goroda (1941–1943 gg.)." *Voprosy istorii KPSS,* no. 5 (1959): 101–21.

Stinchcombe, Arthur L. *Constructing Social Theories:* New York: Harcourt, Brace and World, 1968.

Sudarikov, N. "Berezhno otnosit'sia i kadram presedatelei." *Sotsialisticheskaia zakonnost',* no. 12 (December 1947): 4–6.

Surnichenko, S. I., ed. *Ocherki istorii Vladimirskoi organizatsii KPSS.* Yaroslavl': Verkhne-Volzhskoe knizhnoe izdatel'stvo, 1972.

Tiazhel'nikov, E. M., ed. *Ocherki istorii Cheliabinskoi oblastnoi partiinoi organizatsii.* Cheliabinsk: Iuzhno-ural'skoe knizhnoe izdatel'stvo, 1967.

Ul'ianov, L. N. *Trudovoi podvig rabochego klassa i krest'ianstvo Sibiri 1945–1953 gg.* Tomsk: Izdatel'stvo Tomskogo Universiteta, 1979.

Utenkov, A. Ia. *Bor'ba KPSS za vosstanovlenie narodnogo khoziaistva i dal'neishee razvitie sotsialisticheskogo obshchestva 1946–1955 gg.* Moscow: Izdatel'stvo vysshaia shkola, 1974.

Vasilenko, V. S. and Orekhov, E. P., eds. *Kommunisticheskaia partiia v period Velikoi Otechestvennoi voinu (iiun' 1941 goda–1945 god).* Moscow: Gospolitizdat, 1961.

Vasilenko, V. A. et al. *Istoriia Velikoi Otechestvennoi voiny Sovetskogo Soiuza 1941–1945.* Moscow: Voennoe izdatel'stvo Ministerstva oborony soiuza SSSR, 1965.

Vasil'ev, Iu. A. *Sibirskii arsenal 1941–1945*. Sverdlovsk: Sredne-Ural'skoe knizhnoe izdatel'stvo, 1965.

Volkov, I. M. "Kolkhoznaia derevniia v pervyi poslevoennyi god." *Voprosy istorii,* no. 1 (1966): 15–32.

———, ed. *Sovetskaia derevniia v pervye poslevoennye gody 1946–1950*. Moscow: Izdatel'stvo Nauka, 1978.

Volkov, P. M., ed. *Ocherki istorii Iaroslavskoi organizatsii KPSS*. Yaroslavl': Verkhne-Volzhskoe knizhnoe izdatel'stvo, 1967.

"Vse dlia fronta! Vse sily na razgrom vraga!" *Voprosy istorii KPSS,* no. 12 (1975): 82–98.

Vyltsan, M. A. *Ukreplenie material'no-tekhnicheskoi bazy kolkhoznogo stroia vo vtoroi piatiletke (1933–1937)*. Moscow: Izdatel'stvo Akademii Nauk SSSR, 1959.

———. *Sovetskaia derevnia nakanune Velikoi Otechestvennoi voiny*. Moscow: Politizdat, 1970.

———. *Zavershaiushchii etap sozdaniia kolkhoznogo stroia (1936–1937 gg.)*. Moscow: Izdatel'stvo Nauka, 1978.

Zakharov, F. P., et al., eds. *Kuibyshevskaia oblastnaia partiinaia organizatsiia v dokumentakh i tsifrakh (1902–1977 gg.)*. Kuibyshev: Kuibyshevskoe knizhnoe izdatelstvo, 1978.

Zaleski, Eugene. *Stalinist Planning for Economic Growth, 1933–1952*. Translated and edited by Marie-Christine MacAndrew and John H. Moore. Chapel Hill: The University of North Carolina Press, 1980.

Zelenin, I. E. *Obshchestvenno-politicheskaia zhizn' 1946–1958 gg. sovetskoi derevni*. Moscow: Izdatel'stvo nauka, 1978.

10

The Impact of World War II on Leningrad

EDWARD BUBIS
BLAIR A. RUBLE

The brutality and destruction unleashed by the Second World War were perhaps nowhere more intensely revealed than in Leningrad, the scene of the longest and most devastating siege of a major urban center in the history of modern warfare. To place the Leningrad Blockade in comparative perspective, more than ten times the number of people died in Leningrad between August 1941, and January 1944, than died in Hiroshima following the atomic blast of August 1945. By March 1943, the once vibrant city of 3.2 million souls had been reduced to a militarized encampment of just 639,000 inhabitants.[1] Moreover, German bombardment obliterated much of the city's physical plant. In addition to the loss of countless architectural and artistic treasures, the Germans destroyed 25 percent of Leningrad's capital stock, 16 percent of the city's housing stock, plus scores of miles of streets, sewer lines, and water lines.[2]

Beyond physical destruction and loss of life, Leningrad sustained far less tangible but perhaps ultimately more significant losses. Anthropologist Clifford Geertz, has written of the importance of charismatic active centers in the social order: the points at which a society's leading actors, ideas, and institutions come together.[3] Prerevolutionary St. Petersburg was such a center. However, as early as the 1890s, a national rail system, focused on Moscow and central Russia, began to diminish St. Petersburg's importance as a port of entry for Imperial Russia. Moreover, the city's peripheral location and lack of a large, wealthy, and populous hinterland further eroded the city's importance as an industrial center, at least in relation to Moscow. Postrevolutionary Leningrad continued to function as an active center in Soviet society despite a ruinous series of corrosive events: the transfer of the Soviet capital from the city to Moscow in 1918; the end of massive importation of industrial raw materials to be processed at ports of entry; the dispatch of the Academy of Sciences from Leningrad to Moscow in 1934; and the decimation in 1934 of the local political elite during the purges following the assassination of Leningrad Party First Secretary Sergei Kirov. After the Second World War, Moscow emerged as the sole charismatic active center remaining in the Soviet Union. Meanwhile, Leningrad rebuilt after the war so that, by the 1950s, prewar population levels had been achieved and economic production levels surpassed. Nonetheless, the city's once preeminent (and, after 1918, coequal) status in comparison to that of Moscow was lost, seemingly forever. In this final sense, then, the war's impact on Leningrad has probably been permanent and most certainly has been negative. To better understand how this situation developed, it is necessary to look beyond aggregate growth rates to examine the evolving composition of the Leningrad work force, political life, and economic and scientific bases.

The Transformation of the City's Work Force

Unfortunately, the available data are not sufficient to identify the social composition of the city's postwar population with any certainty. All one can do is try to make a reasonable and reasoned attempt to reconstruct what occurred on the basis of very scattered and incomplete data. In making such an assessment, it appears that the high level of population turnover that took place in Leningrad during the first half of the 1940s resulted in the replacement of one of the most educated and skilled urban populations in the Soviet Union by one that was relatively unskilled and undisciplined. Such characteristics were shared by the populations of other urban centers across the Soviet Union so that Leningrad came to resemble other typical Soviet provincial centers more than it resembled the country's major charismatic center, Moscow.

Of Leningrad's prewar metropolitan population of 3.2 million, nearly 1.4 million are not accounted for by official statistics on wartime population losses.[4] Such statistical lacunae probably result from the scores of more pressing concerns burdening the local wartime leadership rather than the problem of data collection. In addition, population shifts throughout the war were probably taking place too quickly to be recorded accurately. We know, for example, that between March 1943 and September 1945 the city's population doubled from 639,000 to over 1.2 million.[5] It appears unlikely that Leningraders, spread halfway to Vladivostok, would have been able to make the necessary hundred- and thousand-mile treks across a war-torn Soviet Union back to their native city in sufficient numbers to account for this increase. The characteristics of the new population suggest that much of the city's postwar population may have been drawn from rural areas rather than from among returning wartime evacuees.[6] If this is the case, Leningrad experienced a qualitative decline in its population in the sense that the new Leningraders were not well suited to the needs of the specialized industrial and scientific enterprises that had dominated the city's economy prior to the war. This qualitative decline occurred despite the quantitative recovery of prewar personnel and population reserves.

Leningrad was a traditionally male city, yet by April 1945, 76 percent of all Leningraders employed in industry were now female, a figure suggesting that women were the predominant sex in the city's population as a whole.[7] Postwar in-migration increased the city's male population, as might be expected in a period of demobilization. Still, the city remained predominately female throughout the postwar period at a rate slightly higher than those of the USSR and RSFSR general and urban populations as a whole.[8] This feminization of Leningrad can be attributed to several factors, not the least of which is the high participation levels and losses of Leningrad males at the front or in support positions both during the Winter War with Finland and the blockade. The process may also have been augmented by a significant in-migration from already female-dominated rural areas.

Local officials criticized the relatively undisciplined nature of the postwar Leningrad population during the first months of postblockade reconstruction.[9] This general social indiscipline, which apparently was pronounced in the city's industrial establishments, might be another symptom of extensive rural flight and in-migration to Leningrad. In December 1946, Petr Sergeevich Popkov, the wartime chairman of the Leningrad City Soviet, who had recently become first secretary of the Leningrad City and Regional Party Committees, reported to the Leningrad City Party Committee that labor turnover had soared to 58.6 percent in the city's factories, a situation that necessitated inordinately high levels of overtime work.[10]

Once again, the data are far from complete and one must infer more from the available sources than is perhaps advisable. Still, commentaries by local Leningrad political and economic elites point to behavior that could be expected of large numbers of demobilized soldiers, of rural in-migrants to the city's industrial plants, or both.[11] At a minimum, the image offered of the Leningrad proletariat during the period is not that of a highly skilled, long-employed labor elite. Rather, it suggests a work force consisting of fairly substantial numbers of low-skilled peasant workers, be they former soldiers or new migrants directly from the collective farm.

The immediate postwar period, then, was one of considerable instability and change in the city's population and work force. By the time of the 1959 census, the city's metropolitan population barely surpassed its prewar level of 3.2 million residents. Yet, these 3.2 million plus inhabitants were qualitatively different from the 3.2 million who had inhabited the city prior to the Second World War. Leningrad's population was now more rural and less skilled than before. Although other Soviet cities experienced similar postwar trends, the consequences for Leningrad proved far greater than elsewhere. The highly disciplined and technologically advanced workers of whom Leningrad politicians had been so proud in the past had been swamped by yet another wave of migrants from the countryside. These

Table 10.1   Membership in Leningrad City Party Organization, 1939–1954 (on January 1)

Date	Full Members	Candidate Members	Total Membership
1939	100,610	29,972	130,582
1940	114,591	36,737	151,328
1941	117,745	34,048	151,793
1942	61,842	12,386	74,228
1943	30,305	13,588	43,893
1944	35,363	14,280	49,643
1945	56,982	14,269	71,251
1946	95,217	16,452	111,669
1947	156,047	23,100	179,147
1948	176,741	22,677	199,418
1949	189,511	17,318	206,829
1950	196,664	13,915	210,579
1951	200,213	14,935	215,148
1952	204,071	16,658	220,729
1953	207,545	15,967	223,512
1954	219,965	8,696	228,661

Source: S. S. Dmitriev, et al., *Leningradskaia organizatsiia KPSS,* 70. See also B. Ruble, *The Russian Review,* 42, no. 3, (July 1983), 309.

changes were sufficiently large that they cannot be explained solely by the 632,253 civilian deaths cited in official Soviet publications. More people undoubtedly died during the blockade than Soviet statistical handbooks acknowledge. Moreover, a large percentage of the half-million evacuees probably never returned to live in Leningrad. The city may have survived the war, but not necessarily with its prewar population intact.

The Transformation of the City's Political Elite

Changes within the city's governing elite were, if anything, even more dramatic than those that were taking place within the population at large. During the first two years of the war, the membership of the Leningrad Party organization dropped by nearly 75 percent (See Table 10.1). This decline occurred at a time when the national Party membership increased, so that, by the end of World War II, only 2 percent of the All-Union Communist Party (Bolshevik) membership hailed from Leningrad, as opposed to some 10 percent when Kirov was assassinated in 1934 (See Table 10.2). Such developments eroded Leningrad's prewar political power base, a base that had helped to sustain the city as an active center in Soviet society throughout the 1920s and 1930s.

While the relative weight of Leningrad Party membership within the

Table 10.2   Leningrad Party Membership as a Percentage of National Party Membership, 1917–1971 (selected years)

Year	(On January 1) Percentage
1917 [On October 1]	16.6
1927	8.1
1934	10.3
1939	5.7
1941	3.9
1946	2.0
1952	3.3
1956	3.8
1966	3.3
1971	3.1

Source: S. S. Dmitriev et al., *Leningradskaia organizatsiia KPSS, v tsifrakh, 1917–1973 gg.* (Leningrad: Lenizdat, 1974), 70; N. A. Petrovich, et al., *Partiinoe stroitel'stvo*, 62. See also B. Ruble, *The Russian Review*, 42, no. 3 (July 1983), 310.

national Communist Party organization declined, the composition of the Leningrad Party itself also underwent considerable change. For example, 54,000 of the 153,531 Leningrad Party members on 1 July 1941, left for the front almost immediately following the outbreak of hostilities.[12] By January 1943, death rolls contained the names of 13,000 Party members, and Party membership plummeted to 43,893.[13] Between 1943 and 1945, 21,608 new members joined the city's Communist Party.[14] Moreover, many of the 368,416 recruits, who joined the Party on the Leningrad front during the war, remained in the city,[15] so that two-thirds of all the members of the Leningrad city Party organization in 1947 had not been in the Party when fighting broke out.[16]

The makeup of Party leadership councils was altered even more than that of Party membership at large. In September 1952, 663 of 759 delegates elected to the Eleventh Regional Party Conference had been elected to such a gathering for the first time, as had 91 of 99 alternate delegates.[17] Regional Party First Secretary V. M. Andrianov, who had been brought in from Sverdlovsk in 1949 to supervise a massive purge of the Leningrad Party, reported to that gathering that more than 2,000 Party leaders (in addition to another 1,500 state, trade union, and *Komsomol* officials) had advanced in rank during his brief tenure in office.[18] In October 1952, Andrianov told the Nineteenth Party Congress in Moscow that such advancement proved necessary as a result of the previous distortion of ideological work in Leningrad that had led to "toadyism and servility" in personnel practices.[19] One can assume, then, that the new incumbents had benefited from the involuntary departure of their predecessors.

Table 10.3 Composition of Leningrad City and District Soviets, 1939 and 1947 (percentage)

Category	1939	1947
Educational Background		
Higher education	41.0	54.5
Secondary education	30.0	25.2
Primary education	29.0	20.3
Age		
29 or younger	23.2	4.6
30–39	48.7	30.0
40–49	19.9	47.2
50 or older	8.2	18.2

Source: Z. V. Stepanov, ed., *Ocherki istorii Leningrada*, 38–39. See also B. Ruble, *The Russian Review*, 42, no. 3 (July 1983), 313.

Municipal government institutions proved no more stable than those of the Party. In May 1944, the Leningrad City Soviet convened for the first time since the war began. Less than one-third of the soviet's deputies attended as 708 of 1037 council members were either dead or still at the front.[20] When, in 1947, a new city soviet as well as fourteen new district soviets met for the first time, their deputies were, as a group, older and better educated than their prewar counterparts (See Table 10.3).

Uncertainty within local political institutions accelerated following the death of former Leningrad Party First Secretary, Andrei Zhdanov, in August 1948, as his major rivals, Giorgii Malenkov and Lavrenti Beria, set in motion a large scale purge of Zhdanov's associates and protégés in Leningrad and beyond. Before the end of March 1949, nearly every senior Leningrad Party official had been removed from his post, never to be seen again. By September 1952, more than one-quarter of all primary Communist party committees in Leningrad changed secretaries with perhaps as many as 2,000 other officials losing their jobs as well.[21] This purge of local political elites consumed a leadership cohort that had sustained the city's political power base throughout much of the 1920s and 1930s. Subsequent Leningrad leaders may have been present in the city during the late 1940s; for the most part, however, the Leningrad political elite of the 1960s and 1970s did not enter active political life until after these purges, known as the Leningrad Affair, had run their course.

The Leningrad Affair makes a sharp demarcation in the city's political history, one which completed a process of political decline begun with the transfer of the national capital to Moscow in 1918. The discontinuities in the Leningrad population and in the city's political life undermined the remaining vestiges of the city's heritage as an active center in Russian and Soviet cultural and political development. Throughout the 1940s and in large part because of the destruction of the war, Leningrad was coming to resemble other Soviet provincial centers more than it resembled Moscow.

This break with the prewar past becomes ever more evident as one examines changes in the Leningrad economy brought about by the war's destruction.

The Transformation of the City's Economic Base

If, in 1913, 12 percent of the country's gross industrial output was produced in Leningrad, only 10 percent was produced in the city in 1940 and merely 7 percent in 1960.[22] This relative decline occurred despite a steady and, at times, rapid absolute increase in the city's productive capacity (See Table 10.4). By 1969, for example, Leningrad industry would produce as much in one week as local industry had produced in the entire year of 1928.[23] This diminishing relative importance of the Leningrad economy on the national scene was accompanied by perhaps more pernicious phenomena as the once diverse Leningrad industrial complex became ever more specialized. Such specialization constrained opportunities for the spontaneous interaction of diverse social and economic forces, which many urbanists suggest make great cities great.[24] As a result, Leningrad ceased to function as an economic charismatic center and came increasingly to resemble other specialized Soviet provincial economic centers.

In 1945, then Regional Party First Secretary, Aleksei Kuznetsov, reported to the USSR Supreme Soviet that 75 percent of the city's industrial equipment had been evacuated or destroyed during the war.[25] At the same time, the city's gross industrial output in 1945 fell to just 32 percent of the 1940 levels.[26] Meanwhile, as discussed previously, the qualifications of local industrial workers declined sharply.[27] In certain key sectors, the reduction of productive capacity was enormous. In 1945, for example, Lenergo (the organization responsible for the city's power supply) was able to generate only 22.9 percent of its 1940 kilowatt capacity.[28] Remarkably, the city's overall industrial output managed to surpass prewar levels as early as 1950.[29] From the available data it now appears that this achievement was accomplished through the abandonment of the previous productive capacity in a variety of industrial sectors with an accompanying specialization in a more limited range of economic activity.

The policy of local economic specialization emerged during the Fourth Five-Year Plan period (1946–1950) as economic planners emphasized the city's shipbuilding and modern machine-building sectors at the expense of other formerly important local industries. On the positive side, Leningrad industry came to specialize in such technologically intensive industries as radio-electronics, radio-technics, optics, precision machine tools, and the like. Indeed, many of the city's oldest, largest, and most important industrial establishments such as the famous Kirov, Elektrosil and Metal factories underwent extensive modernization.[30] At the same time, some traditional Leningrad industries developed at a slower rate than they had previously in Leningrad and expanded at a slower rate than the same industry was then growing nationally (See Table 10.5). Gross output in light and food industries in Leningrad in 1940, for example, had been 9 times and 6.8

Table 10.4 Production of Selected Industrial Products, USSR and Leningrad, 1940, 1950, and 1955

Product	1940 USSR	1940 Leningrad	1950 USSR	1950 Leningrad	1955 USSR	1955 Leningrad	Leningrad % of USSR 1940	1950	1955
Hydroturbines, thousands of kwt	207.7	200.2	314.9	159.0	1491.9	839.0	96.4	50.5	56.2
Generators for hydroturbines, thousands of kwt	154.6	154.6	258.0	196.9	1413.0	889.0	100.0	76.3	62.9
Spinning frames for cotton, units	1109.0	520.0	1958.0	676.0	1990.0	506.0	46.9	34.5	25.4
Passenger cars, units	1051.0	315.0	912.0	221.0	1751.0	311.0	30.0	24.2	17.8
Cotton cloth, billions of meters	3954.0	129.0	3899.0	156.0	5904.0	234.0	3.3	4.0	4.0
Woolen cloth, billions of meters	119.7	5.3	155.2	7.3	251.0	11.6	4.4	4.7	4.6
Hosiery, millions of pairs	485.4	79.8	472.9	47.0	771.5	62.4	16.4	9.9	8.1
Knitted goods, millions of units	183.0	24.0	197.5	20.8	430.1	36.7	13.1	10.5	8.5
Leather footwear, millions of pairs	211.0	34.6	203.4	27.2	274.5	30.4	16.4	13.4	11.1
Rubber footwear, millions of pairs	69.7	39.9	110.4	50.1	131.1	64.1	57.2	45.4	48.9
Paper, thousands of tons	812.0	57.3	1193.0	73.0	1862.0	81.2	7.1	6.1	4.4
Confectionery goods, thousands of tons	790.0	91.3	993.0	85.1	1382.0	102.0	11.6	8.6	7.4
Soap (40 percent equivalent)	700.0	97.9	816.0	95.0	1075.0	108.6	10.0	11.6	10.1

Sources: *Narodnoe khoziaistvo SSSR (1956)*, 55–59; *Narodnoe khoziaistvo goroda Leningrada (1957)*, 22–27.

Table 10.5 Relative Increase in Productivity of Selected Branches, 1940, 1950, and 1960

Economic Branch	1940 (1913=1)		1950 (1913=1)		1960 (1913=1)	
	USSR	Leningrad	USSR	Leningrad	USSR	Leningrad
Gross output of industry	7.7	12.0	1.7	1.3	5.2	3.6
Chemical and petrochemical industry	17.5	7.4	2.0	0.9	7.7	3.1
Machine-construction industry	29.6	22.0	2.1	1.5	9.0	5.6
Light industry	4.7	9.0	1.1	1.0	2.8	2.2
Food industry	3.8	6.3	1.0	0.9	2.3	1.7

Sources: *Narodnoe khoziaistvo SSSR, Iubileinii statisticheskii ezhegodnik* (Moscow: Statistika, 1972),132–133; *Leningrad i Leningradskaia oblast' v tsifrakh. Statisticheskii sbornik* (Leningrad: Lenizdat, 1971), 23.

Table 10.6   Structure of Leningrad Industry in 1960 (percentage of total)

Branch	Output	Quantity of Workers	Capital Funds
Iron and steel industry	2.6	2.5	6.0
Non-ferrous metallurgy	1.2	0.6	0.8
Power plants	0.5	0.5	8.4
Metal-fabricating industries	35.1	49.8	56.3
Chemical industry	8.1	6.2	6.0
Wood-working and paper industry	3.1	4.0	2.7
Building-materials industry	1.6	2.0	3.5
Light industry	24.2	21.5	6.9
Food industry	18.4	5.5	5.5

Source: Ia. A. Lavrikov, E. V. Mazalov, *Leningradskaia promyshlennost' i ee rezervi* (1960), 15.

times above their 1913 levels while the analagous indices for the national light and food industries were only 4.7 times and 3.8 times respectively. In the postwar period the correlation between the rates in Leningrad light and food industries and in the national branches were reversed, so that by 1960 both Leningrad industries were at or below the national average rate of production increase. In the final analysis, the significance of both sectors within the economic structure of Leningrad diminished substantially (See Tables 10.6 and 10.7).[31]

The process of specialization occurred not only among industries but within individual economic sectors as well. In the crucial metalworking industry, Leningrad's production of electric-power equipment, metalworking, machine tools, and communication equipment expanded throughout the

Table 10.7   Output of Selected Leningrad Industries, 1956

Industry	1956 as Percentage of	
	1940	1950
All branches	259	203
Machine-construction industry	353	241
Power plants and supply	103	166
Chemical industry	231	240
Rubber industry	195	206
Wood-working and paper industry	194	180
Building-materials industry	575	257
Tailoring industry	164	180
Textile industry	191	184
Leather, footwear and fur industries	142	167
Food industry	141	160

Source: *Narodnoe khoziaistvo goroda Leningrada* (1957), 18.

Table 10.8   Investment in the National Economy, 1918–1960

Plan Period	USSR (billions of rubles)	Leningrad (billions of rubles)	Leningrad as Percentage of USSR
1918–August, 1928	4.4	0.1	2.3
First Five-Year Plan (September 1928–1932)	8.8	0.4	4.5
Second Five-Year Plan (1933–1937)	19.7	0.9	4.6
Third Five Year-Plan (1938–June, 1941)	20.4	0.6	2.9
War period (July 1941–1945)	20.5	0.4	2.0
Fourth Five-Year Plan (1946–1950)	47.4	1.2	2.5
Fifth Five-Year Plan (1951–1955)	89.8	1.8	2.0
Sixth Five-Year Plan (1956–1960)	168.0	3.2	1.9

Sources: *Narodnoe khoziaistvo SSSR za 60 let* (1972), 432; *Leningrad i Leningradskaia oblast' v tsifrakh* (1971), 63.

first 15 years after the war at a rate nearly two times faster than did the city's production of transportation machinery, hoisting and conveying machinery, and equipment for light industry.[32] Intersector and intrasector specialization combined to simplify the city's economic base and, in so doing, restricted its role in the national economy. This reduction in the scope of local economic activity appears to have been the result of a conscious policy decision, one which may have been beneficial in the short run immediately following the war as it facilitated the return to prewar aggregate production levels. Over the long run, however, the impact was profoundly negative for the overall health and vitality of the city. During the First and Second Five-Year Plans (1928–1937), Leningrad had received approximately 5 percent of all investment in the Soviet economy. During the postwar Fourth Five-Year Plan (1946–1950), the city's share of national economic investment was reduced to 2.5 percent despite obvious and critical needs for postwar reconstruction funds. Even the 2.5 percent investment level was not sustained during the 1950s as Leningrad's share of national eocnomic investment fell to 1.9 percent during the Sixth Five-Year Plan (1956–1960) (See Table 10.8). Such policies insured that Leningrad would no longer rival Moscow as an economic center, much as the evolving character of the Leningrad political elite discussed previously guaranteed that the northern capital would no longer challenge Moscow politically.

Leningrad—socially, politically, and economically—was coming to increasingly resemble other Soviet provincial centers while Moscow emerged as the single charismatic center in Soviet life.

The Transformation of the City's Scientific Base

Any discussion of Leningrad's loss of stature during the first half of the twentieth century would remain incomplete without mention of its lost primacy in science and education. On the eve of the First World War, St. Petersburg remained the unchallenged national academic center. Over the course of the next half century or so, the city's general academic stature eroded as Leningrad became an important, yet profoundly provincial, scientific axis. This relative decline occurred despite signs of aggregate growth. The number of scientific research organizations in Leningrad increased from 23 in 1914 to 141 in 1937.[33] Meanwhile, the national scientific and educational capacity was expanding at an even faster rate, so that, for example, Leningrad's educated population came to represent a shrinking percentage of the educated population of the Soviet Union as a whole (See Table 10.9). These trends, already apparent prior to the outbreak of World War Two, were accelerated during the postwar period.

The underlying causes of Leningrad's academic demise extend far beyond the impact of the war upon the city's scientific community. The most important single event in an extended process of deterioration most certainly remains the transfer of the USSR Academy of Sciences' headquarters to Moscow in 1934.[34] Even after that transfer, however, Leningrad remained the Soviet Union's most prominent educational and university research center (See Table 10.10). Moreover, Leningrad's loss of stature is attributable in part to the emergence of a genuinely national scientific and educational infrastructure for the first time in Russian (and Soviet) history.[35] In the final analysis, then, Leningrad's academic decline has been as much relative as absolute.

Such developments do not make the impact of the Second World War upon the city's scientific base negligible. The evacuation of educational and scientific research institutions during the blockade was more total than that of industry. Once the blockade was lifted, most academic establishments were reconstituted in Leningrad, although there is scattered evidence that the new institutions were not necessarily staffed by returning Leningrad scholars.[36] Indeed, it appears that once hostilities had ceased, many prominent and productive researchers either remained at their new institutions in the east or chose to move to the now dominant Moscow academic community (a process which has continued).

Had the diminution of Leningrad's scientific and educational capacity occurred in isolation, its impact upon the city's general well-being need not have been devastating. However, occurring as it did in concert with the other areas of decline discussed above, the reduction of the city's stature as an academic center only contributed to a larger process of disintegration. In this manner, the transformation of the city's scientific base resulting

Table 10.9 Numbers of Specialists with Higher and Technical Education in National Economy, 1913, 1940, and 1955 (without servicemen)

Years	Higher Education			Technical Education			Total		
	USSR (000s)	Lenin- grad (000s)	Leningrad as Percentage of USSR	USSR (000s)	Lenin- grad (000s)	Leningrad as Percentage of USSR	USSR (000s)	Lenin- grad (000s)	Leningrad as Percentage of USSR
1913	136	22	16.2	54	8	14.8	190	39	15.8
1940	908	75	8.3	1492	47	3.2	2400	122	5.1
1955	2184	114	5.2	2949	85	2.9	5133	199	3.9

Sources: *Leningrad za 50 let* (1967), 77; *Narodnoe khoziaistvo SSSR* (1956), 193.

Table 10.10   Research Assignments Made by RSFSR People's Commissariat of the Enlightenment, by Discipline and Location, 1935

| Discipline | Percentage | | | Number of Assignments |
	Moscow	Leningrad	Other	
Mathematics	35	38	27	244
Mechanics	35	53	12	98
Physics	26	37	37	308
Astronomy	42	43	15	209
Chemistry	29	37	34	326
Geography	36	46	18	80
Geology	0	20	80	54
Paleontology	0	65	35	23
Petrography	0	47	53	19
Mineralogy	0	63	37	16
Chrystography	0	100	0	5
Mineral sciences	41	23	36	70
Microbiology	80	15	5	97
Botany	19	14	67	184
Genetics	36	16	48	25
Zoology	38	32	30	241
Histology	43	43	14	37
Physiology	26	70	4	186
Anthropology	100	0	0	18
History	25	75	0	99
Linguistics	0	100	0	90
Psychology	62	38	0	64
Party history	0	100	0	46
Total	31	42	27	2539

Sources: Upravlenie universitetov i nauchno-issledovatel'skikh uchrezhdenii NKP RSFSR; *Svodnyi plan nauchnogo-issledovatel'skii rabot institutov i kafedr universitetov NKP RSFSR na 1935 g.,* in Blair A. Ruble, "The Expansion of Soviet Science," 542.

from the war, while far less dramatic than the other spheres of urban life examined here, nonetheless proved to be profoundly damaging to Leningrad's status among Soviet urban centers.

Conclusion

By the late 1950s, Leningrad appeared to have more than recovered from the impact of the Second World War. The city's population had finally surpassed its prewar level and the economic output rose far in excess of previous performance records. Yet, Leningrad's visible health obscured deeper, long-term, destructive patterns of urban development which had been either initiated or exacerbated by the city's harrowing experience during the war. Leningrad's vaunted work force had lost much of its historic competitive edge, created by formerly high skill levels in relation to other

Soviet industrial centers. Its previously powerful political machine had been crushed, only to be replaced by a far less potent local Party elite. The city's economic base had lost ground in relation to the rest of the Soviet economy while individual industrial sectors began to experience absolute decline in addition to the general pattern of comparative decrescendo. Finally, Leningrad's academic community relenquished national prominence to Moscow and now found itself in competition in specific disciplines with newer scientific centers developing in Novosibirsk and some of the larger republican capitals. In short, behind the restored neoclassical facades along the Nevskii, the Moika, and the Fontanka emerged an increasingly provincial urban center. The city had little but pretense to compete with against Moscow, which had, by then, emerged as the Soviet Union's sole charismatic center. Leningrad, for its part, became, more simply, second city.

The war and the immediate postwar period proved to be decisive for the pattern of decline just described. Despite the loss of many important functions to Moscow during the 1920s and 1930s, Leningrad had remained a direct competitor to the Soviet capital in numerous other spheres. Both physically and psychologically, the war destroyed much of the city. Perhaps even more important in the long run, the war's destruction provided an excuse for anti-Leningrad leaders in Moscow (who, after all, emerged as predominant in the wake of the Leningrad Affair) to justify the diminution of Leningrad economic and academic capacity. Leningrad's former preeminence could now be destroyed through simple inaction as opposed to requiring direct force. By not rebuilding secondary economic sectors, for example, central economic planners insured that Leningrad's economic base would diminish in national stature and significance. The end result has been that, to a considerable degree, Leningrad has never recovered from the impact of World War II.

Notes

1. Leon Goure, *The Siege of Leningrad: August, 1941–January, 1944* (New York: McGraw-Hill Book Company, 1964), 239.

2. V. A. Kamenskii, A. I. Naumov, *Leningrad. Gradostroitel'nyi problemy razvitiia* (Leningrad: Stroiizdat, 1977), 144; N. S. Aleshin et al., *Leningrad. Entsiklopedicheskii spravochnik* (Moscow: Bol'shaia Sovetskaia Entsiklopediia, 1957), 134; and E. Bubis, G. Popov, K. Sharligina, *Optimal'noe perspektivnoe planirovanie kapital'nogo remonta i rekonstruktsii zhilishnogo fonda* (Leningrad: Stroiizdat, 1980), 42.

3. Clifford Geertz, "Centers, Kings, Charisma: Reflections on the Symbolics of Power," in Joseph Ben-David, Terry Nichols Clark (eds.), *Culture and Its Creators* (Chicago: University of Chicago Press, 1977), 150–71, 309–14.

4. Official data identify a low population of 639,000 in March, 1943 as well as 554,000 evacuees and 632,253 civilian deaths. These figures account for approximately 1.8 million persons in a prewar population of 3.2 million. L. Goure, *The Siege of Leningrad,* 239; Harrison E. Salisbury, *The 900 Days: The Siege of Leningrad* (New York: Harper & Row, 1969), 513–18.

5. L. Goure, *Siege of Leningrad,* 239; "Iz letopisi sobytii," *Leningradskaia panorama,* 1982, No. 6:7.

204   Edward Bubis and Blair A. Ruble

6. V. A. Ezhov, "Izmeneniia v chislennosti i sostave rabochikh Leningrada v posle-voennyi period (1945–1950gg.)," *Vestnik Leningradskogo universiteta, seriia istorii, iazyka i literatury,* No. 2 (1966):15–21.

7. Ibid., 19.

8. G. M. Romanenkova, "Sotsial'no-ekonomicheskie posledstviia demograficheskogo razvitiia," in N. A. Tolokontsev, G. M. Romanenkova (eds.), *Demografiia i ekologiia krupnogo goroda* (Leningrad: Nauka, 1980), 54–55; TsSU SSSR, *Itogi vsesoiuznogo perepisi naseleniia 1970 goda* (Moscow: Statistika, 1972), Vol. 2:5–11, Tables 1–2.

9. See, for example, N. Shiktorov, "Ukrepim obshchestvennyi poriadok i bezopasnost' v Leningrade," *Leningradskaia pravda* (23 October 1945):2–3.

10. P. S. Popkovo "Rech' na plenume Leningradskogo gorkoma VKP (b). 28 dekabriia 1946 goda," *Leningradskaia pravda,* (1 January 1947):2–3.

11. V. A. Ezhov, "Izmeneniia v chislennosti i sostave rabochikh," *Vestnik Leningradskogo Universiteta seriia istorii, iazyka i literatury* no. 2 (1966), 15–21.

12. S. S. Dmitriev et al., *Leningradskaia organizatsiia KPSS v tsifrakh, 1917–1973 gg.* (Leningrad: Lenizdat, 1974), 39–45.

13. Ibid.

14. Ibid., 74–75.

15. S. P. Kniazev, "Kurs na vosstanovlenie posle sniatiia blokady (1944–1945 gg.)," in Institut istorii partii Leningradskogo obkoma KPSS—Filial Instituta Marksizma-Leninizma pri TsK KPSS, *Ocherki istorii Leningradskoi organizatsii KPSS, Chast' II: noiabr' 1917–1945gg.* (Leningrad: Lenizdat, 1968), 649.

16. S. S. Dmitriev, et al., *Leningradskaia organizatsiia KPSS,* 45–51.

17. N. A. Romanov, "Doklad predsedatelia mandatnoi komissii" *Leningradskaia pravda* (25 September 1952):3.

18. V. M. Andrianov, "Doklad sekretariia Leningradskogo oblastnogo komiteta VKP (b)" *Leningradskaia pravda,* (28 September 1952) 2–4. Frol' Kozlov repeated the two-thousand person figure in his report to the Nineteenth Party Congress the following month (F. R. Kozlov, "Rech'" *Leningradskaia pravda* [16 October 1952]:3).

19. V. M Andrianova, "Rech'" *Leningradskaia pravda* (9 October 1952):3–4.

20. A. R. Dzeniskevich, V. M. Koval'chuk, G. L. Sobolev, A. N. Tsamutali, V. A. Shishkin, *Nepokrennyi Leningrad,* 2nd ed. (Leningrad: Nauka, 1974), 455.

21. In September, 1952, City Party Committee Secretary A. I. Alekseev indicated to a city party conference that 1213 officials had been appointed in recent months to primary party posts. Later, Alekseev noted that there were 4230 such primary party organizations (A. I. Alekseev, "Doklad sekretariia Leningradskogo gorodskogo komiteta VKP (b)" *Leningradskaia pravda* (23 September 1952), 2–3). At the subsequent regional party conference, Regional Party First Secretary V. M. Andrianov refered to 2000 new officers having been appointed during his brief tenure in Leningrad, a figure repeated by Regional Party Second Secretary Frol' Kozlov at the Nineteenth Party Congress a month later ("Doklad tov. Andrianova, [28 September 1952] "Rech' tov. Kozlova," 16 October 1952).

22. Planovaia komissiia ispolkoma Lengorsoveta and Statisticheskoe upravlenie goroda Leningrada. *Leningradskia promyshlennost' za 50 let* (Leningrad: Lenizdat, 1967), 6; and other estimates calculated on the basis of Soviet data by Edward Bubis. Unfortunately, totally reliable economic data for Leningrad during and following the war is not available. Therefore, one must compare the relatively more reliable data for the 1930s and 1950s to determine how the Leningrad economy might have performed and developed throughout the decade of the 1940s.

23. N. B. Lebedeva et al., *Partiinaia organizatsiia i rabochie Leningrada* (Leningrad: Lenizdat, 1974), 44.

24. See, for example, Jane Jacobs, *The Economy of Cities* (New York: Vintage Books, 1970).

25. A. A. Kuznetsov, "XI sessiia Verkhovnogo soveta soizuza, l-ogo sozyva, preniia po dokladu o Gosudarstvennom biudzhete SSSR na 1945 god. Rech'" *Leningradskaia pravda* (28 June 1945), 2.

26. Ia. A. Lavrikov, E. Mazalov, *Leningradskaia promyshlennost' i ee reservy* (Leningrad: Lenizdat, 1960), 9.

27. *Leningrad. Entsiklopedicheskii spravochnik,* 134; *Leningradskaia promyshlennost' za 50 let,* 27.

28. *Leningradskaia promyshlennost' za 50 let,* 29.

29. *Leningrad, Entsiklopedicheskii spravochnik,* 135.

30. *Leningradskaia promyshlennost' za 50 let,* 29.

31. For a discussion of subsequent changes in the Leningrad economic structure, see Blair A. Ruble, "Romanov's Leningrad," *Problems of Communism* (November–December 1983), 36–48.

32. Statisticheskoe upravlenie goroda Leningrada *Narodnoe khoziaistvo goroda Leningrada. Statisticheskii sbornik* (Moscow: Gosstatizdat, 1957), 20.

33. I. Osipov. *Leningrad i Leningradskaia oblast' za XX let Sovetskoi vlasti* (Leningrad: Lenoblizdat, 1937), 37.

34. *Leningrad. Entsiklopedicheskii spravochnik,* 411–412.

35. Blair A. Ruble, "The Expansion of Soviet Science," *Knowledge: Creation, Diffusion, Utilization,* Vol. 2, No. 4 (June 1981):529–553.

36. Several regional educatonal and research institutions east of the Urals, for example, trace their origins to the evacuated academic institutions of the War period; Ibid.

References

Aleshin, N. S. et al. *Leningrad. Entsiklopedicheskii spravochnik.* Moscow: Bol'shaia Sovetskaia Entsiklopediia, 1957.

Alekseev, A. I. "Doklad sekretariia Leningradskogo gorodskogo komiteta VKP (b)." in *Leningradskaia pravda,* September 23, 1952, 2–3.

Andrianov, V. M. "Doklad sekretariia Leningradskogo oblastnogo komiteta VKP (b)." In *Leningradskaia pravda,* September 28, 1952a, 2–4.

————. "Rech'." In *Leningradskaia pravda,* October 9, 1952b, 3–4.

Ben-David, Joseph and Terry Nichols Clark (eds.) *Culture and Its Creators.* (Chicago: University of Chicago Press, 1977).

Bubis, E., G. Popov and K. Sharligina. *Optimal'noe perspektivnoe planirovanie kapital'nogo remonta i rekonstruktsii zhilishnogo fonda.* Leningrad: Stroiizdat, 1980.

Dmitriev et al. *Leningradskaia organizatsiia KPSS v tsifrukh, 1917–1973 gg.* Leningrad: Lenizdat, 1974.

Dzeniskevich, A. R., V. M. Koval'chuk, G. L. Sobolev, A. N. Tsamutali and V. A. Shishkin *Nepokrennyi Leningrad* (second edition). Leningrad: Nauka, 1974.

Ezhov, V. A. "Izmeneniia v chislennosti i sostave rabochikh Leningrada v poslevoennyi period (1945–1950 gg.)." No. 2. In *Vestnik Leningradskogo universiteta, seriia istorii, iazyka i literatury,* 1966, 15–21.

Goure, Leon. *The Siege of Leningrad: August 1941–January, 1944.* New York: McGraw-Hill Book Co., 1964.

Institut istorii partii Leningradskogo obkoma KPSS—Filian Instituta Marksizma-Leninizma pri TsK KPSS. *Ocherki istorii Leningradskoi orgranizatsii KPSS, Chast' II: noiabr' 1917–1945 gg.* Leningrad: Lenizdat, 1968.

"Iz letopisi sobytii." In *Leningradskaia panorama,* No. 6. 1982, 7.

Jacobs, Jane. *The Economy of Cities.* New York: Vintage Books, 1970.

Kamenskii, V. A. and A. I. Naumov. *Leningrad. Gradostroitel' nyi problemy razvitiia.* Leningrad: Stroiizdat, 1977.

Kozlov, F. R. "Rech'," In *Leningradskaia pravda,* 16 October 1952, 3.

Kuznetsov, A. A. "XI sessiia Verkhovnogo soveta soiuza, l-ogo sozyva, preniia po dokladu o Gosudarstvennom biudzhete SSSR na 1945 god. Rech." In *Leningradskaia pravda,* 28 June 1945, 2.

Lavrikov, Ia. A. and E. V. Mazalov. *Leningradskaia promyshlennost' i ee rezervi.* Leningrad: Lenizdat, 1960.

Lebedva, N. B. et al. *partiinia organizatsiia i rabochie Leningrada.* Leningrad: Lenizdat, 1974.

206   Edward Bubis and Blair A. Ruble

Petrovich, N. A. et al. *Partiinoe stroitel'stvo.* Moscow: Politizdat, 1976.
Planovaia komissiia ispolkoma Lengorsoveta and Statisticheskoe upravlenie goroda Leningrada. *Leningradskaia promyslennost' za 50 let.* Leningrad: Lenizdat, 1967.
Popkov, P. S. "Rech'." In *Leningradskaia pravda,* 1 January 1947, 2–3.
Romanov, N. A. "Doklad predsedatelia mandatnoi komissii." In *Leningradskaia pravda,* 25 September 1952, 3.
Ruble, Blair A. "The Expansion of Soviet Science," In *Knowledge: Creation, Diffusion, Utilization.* Vol. 2, No. 4. 1981, 529–553.
_____. "Romanov's Leningrad." In *Problems of Communism,* November-December 1983, 36–48.
Salisbury, Harrison E. *The 900 Days: The Siege of Leningrad.* New York: Harper & Row, 1969.
Shiktorov, N. "Ukrepim obshchestvennyi poriadok i bezopasnost' v Leningrade." In *Leningradskaia pravda,* 23 October, 1945, 2–3.
Statisticheskoe upravlenie goroda Leningrada. *Narodnoe khoziaistvo goroda Leningrada.* Moscow: Gosstatizdat, 1957.
_____. *Leningrad i Leningradskaia oblast' v tsifrakh. Statisticheskii sbornik.* Leningrad: Lenizdat, 1971.
Stepanov, Z. V., ed. *Ocherki istorii Leningrada.* Leningrad: Nauka, 1970.
Tolokontsev, N. A. and G. M. Romanenkova, eds. *Demografiia i ekologiia krupnogo goroda.* Leningrad: Nauka, 1980.
Tsentral'noe statisticheskoe upravleniia SSSR. *Narodnoe khoziaistvo SSSR. Statisticheskii sbornik.* Moscow: Gosstatizdat, 1956.
_____. *Itogi vsesoiuznogo perepisi naseleniia 1970 goda.* Moscow: Statistika, 1972a.
_____. *Narodnoe khoziaistvo SSSR za 60 let. Iubileinii statisticheskii sbornik.* Moscow: Statistika, 1972b.
Upravlenie universitetov i nauchno-issledovatel'skikh uchrezhdenii NKP RSFSR *Svodnyi plan nauchnogo-issledovatel'skii rabot institutov i kafedr universitetov.* Moscow: Narkompros RSFSR OGIZ UchPEDIGIZ, 1935.

11

Demographic Consequences of World War II on the Non-Russian Nationalities of the USSR

BARBARA A. ANDERSON
BRIAN D. SILVER

World War II is a spectacular event in Soviet demographic history. In the course of the war, over 20 million people are reported to have died. More than 25 million people were evacuated to the east and south. More than 22 million people found their territories annexed to the Soviet Union in the period just preceding, during or just after the war. At least 10 million children were not born during that time who otherwise would have been. Three million people emigrated or remained among those permanently displaced from the Soviet Union after the war. More than a million non-Russians were uprooted from their homelands and deported to Siberia and Central Asia because of their alleged collaboration with the German occupying army.

Demographers seldom focus attention on singular historical events such as wars, but tend rather to focus on long-term trends and patterns of behavior. The effects of famine, war, and natural disasters are viewed as major perturbations in otherwise "normal" patterns of fertility, mortality, and migration.[1] For example, after noting the deep troughs in the course of marital fertility in Russia resulting from the First World War, collectivization, and World War II, Coale, Anderson, and Harm write that:

> [The troughs] occurred during years for which primary demographic data are nonexistent or inaccessible and for which information on social and economic

conditions is also unsatisfactory. Moreover, even if a detailed analysis were possible, it would be a study of pathological instances of reduced fertility rather than of the normal conditions under which fertility falls.[2]

The authors then add the following, however:

There is the possibility, which we can only mention without judging its probability, that these prolonged traumata strongly influenced subsequent trends.

This chapter examines both the immediate impact and the long-term indirect consequences of World War II on a set of demographic changes and patterns among the non-Russian nationalities of the USSR. Effects on the Soviet population as a whole are reviewed as a background for examination of differential patterns and trends among non-Russian nationalities.

In 1941, the total population of the Soviet Union was 200 million. This number was not achieved again until 1956.[3] It is commonplace to note that some Soviet nationalities suffered such serious war-related losses that recovery of their pre-war population size took a long time; however, no quantitative estimates of the absolute or relative differences in population losses of Soviet nationalities due to World War II have been published.[4]

We do not estimate the direct losses to individual nationalities due to the war. Rather, we are interested in assessing some of the implications of the *differential* impact of the war on the non-Russian nationalities. Our main thesis is that the differential impact of the war is reflected in differential ratios of males to females, and that these differentials contribute to varying rates of interethnic marriage and to subsequent linguistic and ethnic russification.

We do not regard the war as the sole cause of the linguistic or ethnic russification of non-Russian nationalities. Many other factors have been shown to affect that process.[5] But the severe impact of the war on the sex ratios of many non-Russian nationalities appears to have accentuated and accelerated the process of russification.[6]

Overview of the Demographic Impact of the War on the Soviet Population

It is well known that the Soviet Union's turbulent history of famines, wars, and revolution has had a major impact on the age distribution of the population. Figures 11.1 and 11.2 show the age distribution of the Soviet population as a whole by sex by single year of age in 1959.[7] In a population with a tranquil history, the number of people by age typically declines monotonically. The Soviet age distribution exhibits three large troughs.

The trough for those in their teens in 1959 results from increased mortality

Figure 11.1
Number of Males in the Soviet Union by Single Year of Age, 0-48 in 1959,
as Estimated by Baldwin

Figure 11.2
Number of Females in the Soviet Union by Single Year of Age, 0-48 in
1959, as Estimated by Baldwin

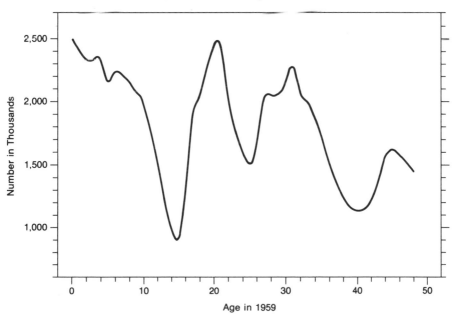

of the young and from births that did not occur during World War II. The number of births during the war was reduced due both to postponement of marriage and to reduced fertility among the married.[8]

The trough for those in their mid-twenties in 1959 results from reduced births and increased mortality of the young during the period of the collectivization of agriculture and the famine of 1932–1933.

The very large trough that reaches a low point for those age 40 in 1959 has two sources. This third trough includes the cohort born during World War I, the 1917 Revolution, and the Civil War. As in World War II, troubled times led to a temporary reduction in births and increased mortality of the very young. This resulted in a small birth cohort from that period. The third male trough is much larger than the third female trough because males in that cohort were young adults during World War II and, thus, were among the main war combat fatalities.

The male deficit was not caused solely by war. In normal populations, the male deficit increases monotonically with age, since males typically have somewhat worse mortality rates than females. Females usually become the majority after about age 20. However, singular events such as wars, which have a strong differential mortality effect on males and females, can lead to a sharp increase in the male deficit.

Figure 11.3 shows the increasing male deficit with age in the Soviet population in 1959. It shows the sex ratio by year of age for 1959—the number of males at a given age per 1,000 females at that age. It is apparent in Figure 11.3 that during World War II males had substantially higher mortality than females. Since the two more recent troughs resulted from the reduction of births and from mortality of the very young, it is reasonable that the occurrence of the first two troughs should not be linked to large differences in the number of people by sex. The third trough, however, is linked to a precipitous decline in the ratio of males to females.

The deficit of males who were young adults during World War II has had a serious effect on the marital status of women. For every age group between 20 and 69, the proportion of females currently married was lower in 1959 than in either 1939 or 1970.[9] This suggests that the large male losses from World War II had substantial effects on the marital status of women throughout a wide age range.

The proportion of women married at any given time is a combination of the proportion who have never married, the proportion widowed, and the proportion divorced. In the main, women age 40-49 in 1959 would have reached marriageable age during the 1930s and probably would have married and begun bearing children before World War II. Since the mean childbearing age is approximately 30, the children of these women, on average, would have been age 10–19 in 1959.[10]

A substantial portion of these women would have become war widows. Those who bore children before the war often would have become heads of single-parent households, since their chances of remarrying were limited

Figure 11.3

Sex Ratio (Males per 1,000 Females) in the Soviet Union by Single Year of
Age, 0-48 in 1959, Based on Baldwin's Estimates

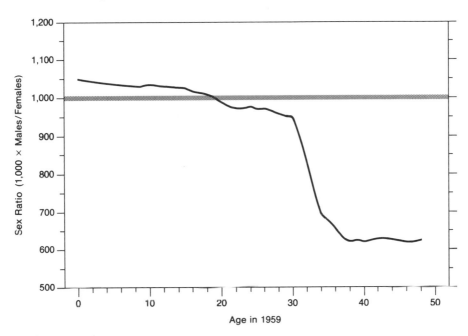

if they became widowed. We shall refer to this group as the *War Widow cohort.*

For the Soviet population as a whole, 58.3 percent of women age 40-49 in 1959 (the War Widow cohort) were married. Had the proportion of 40-49 year-olds who were married in 1959 approximated a more typical figure (based on the proportions for 1939 and 1970), between 70 and 75 percent would have been currently married.

Women age 30-39 in 1959 reached the mean age of marriage during or just after World War II. Their potential husbands would be those men in the cohort most depleted by the direct effects of World War II. We shall refer to this cohort of women as the *War Bride cohort.* The children of this cohort on average would have been age 0-9 in 1959.[11]

For the War Bride cohort, the main effect of the male deficit would be that many never married. In 1959, 75.5 percent of 30-39 year-old Soviet women were married. Had the proportion of 30-39 year-old women who were married as of 1959 more closely approximated the proportion of women who were married as of 1939 and 1970, between 80 and 85 percent would have been currently married.

Overview of Differences in the
Demographic Impact of the
War among Soviet Nationalities

In order to assess the relative impact of the war on different cohorts, data by age are needed. Data by age from the 1939 census (or as adjusted to 1940 by Notestein)[12] are available for the Soviet population as a whole as well as for many regions. But age data for 1939 *by nationality* are not available, and hence estimation of war losses based on direct comparisons of 1939 and 1959 age data for specific nationalities cannot be made.

We therefore rely on 1959 Soviet census data to examine retrospectively the effects of the war by age cohort, with primary emphasis on determining the *relative* war losses by nationality and on assessing some of the long-term consequences of the differences in war losses. We examine the differential impact of the war on the 34 non-Russian nationalities for which age data are available in the 1959 Soviet census.[13]

To facilitate comparisons in the first part of the data presentation, we aggregate the 34 non-Russian nationalities into 10 groupings, based on major differences in war experiences and in cultural and other background characteristics. The groupings are given in Table 11.1. Later in the analysis, the nationalities will be treated as separate cases rather than in groupings.

SEX RATIOS

We gauge the relative losses by nationality directly attributable to World War II by examining age-specific sex ratios (the number of males per 1,000 females in the age group). Sex ratios are a better indicator of the direct effect of World War II on a nationality than is the size in 1959 of the cohort who were young adults during World War II since this is the small cohort born during the Revolution, World War I, and the Civil War. Sex ratios are presented for the ten groupings and for the Russians in Table 11.2.

It is often noted that the Russians, Ukrainians, and Belorussians suffered especially severely in World War II.[14] Large male deficits (low sex ratios) within these Slavic nationalities among those born in 1909–1913 (age 30-34 in 1943) are therefore not surprising. Among the cohort of Russians age 20-24 in 1943, for example, there were only 605 males for every 1,000 females alive in 1959. In the same cohort of Ukrainians, there were 645 males for every 1,000 females; and among Belorussians, 678 males per 1,000 females.

It is more surprising that in this cohort the male deficit for the Tatar-Bashkir grouping is even greater than the deficit for the Ukrainians and Belorussians and that the deficit for the traditionally non-Moslem ASSR-level nationalities is greater than that of any of the three Slavic nationalities.

Table 11.1   Groupings of Thirty-Four Non-Russian Nationalities in the Analysis

Grouping (or Nationality)	Nationalities within Grouping	1959 Population (in Thousands)	Predominant Traditional Religion
Balts	Estonians	988.6	Lutheran
	Latvians	1,399.5	Lutheran
	Lithuanians	2,326.1	Roman Catholic
Ukrainians	Ukrainians	37,252.9	Orthodox/Uniate
Belorussians	Belorussians	7,913.5	Orthodox/Uniate
Moldavians	Moldavians	2,214.1	Orthodox
Armenian-	Armenians	2,786.9	Gregorian Chris.
Georgian	Georgians	2,692.0	Geo. Autoceph. (Orthodox)
Non-Moslem	Buryats	253.0	Orthodox/Buddhism
ASSR	Chuvash	1,469.8	Orthodox
	Karelians	167.3	Orthodox
	Komi	287.0	Orthodox
	Mari	504.2	Orthodox
	Mordvinians	1,285.1	Orthodox
	Ossetians	412.6	Orthodox/Islam
	Udmurts	624.8	Orthodox
Tatar-Bashkir	Tatars	4,967.7	Islam
	Bashkirs	989.0	Islam
Moslem SSR	Azerbaidzhanis	2,939.7	Islam
	Kazakhs	3,621.6	Islam
	Kirgiz	968.7	Islam
	Tadzhiks	1,380.3	Islam
	Turkmenians	1,001.6	Islam
	Uzbeks	6,015.4	Islam
Dagestanis	Avars	270.4	Islam
	Dargins	158.1	Islam
	Kabards[a]	203.6	Islam
	Kumyks	135.0	Islam
	Lezghians	233.1	Islam
Deported	Balkars	42.4	Islam
	Chechen	418.8	Islam
	Ingush	106.0	Islam
	Kalmyks	106.1	Buddhism

[a]Kabards are not generally considered a Dagestani ethnic group but are included with the Dagestanis because, except for the Dagestanis they are the only North Caucasus nationality in the analysis who were not deported during World War II.

Among the Tatars-Bashkirs, in the cohort age 20-24 in 1943, 618 males were still alive in 1959 for every 1,000 females. Among the non-Moslem ASSR-level nationalities, 572 males per 1000 females in the cohort age 20-24 in 1943 were alive in 1959. In the next older cohort (those who were age 25-29 in 1943), both the Tatars-Bashkirs and the non-Moslem ASSR-level nationalities had a larger male deficit in 1959 than did any of the three Slavic nationalities.

Table 11.2   **Sex Ratios in 1959, by Age and Grouping (number of males per 1000 females)**

Year of Birth:	1909– 1913	1914– 1918	1919– 1923	1924– 1928	1929– 1933	1934– 1938
Age in 1943:	30–34	25–29	20–24	15–19	10–14	5–9
Balts	698	702	720	781	948	928
Ukrainians	629	611	645	797	933	982
Belorussians	647	650	678	792	976	965
Moldavians	852	803	853	892	914	850
Armenians- Georgians	803	703	747	996	996	891
Non-Moslem ASSR	565	558	572	811	927	915
Tatars- Bashkirs	544	577	618	844	971	944
Moslem SSR	873	755	784	1093	1022	943
Dagestanis	760	632	745	1064	988	926
Deported	982	799	779	1034	1052	864
Russians	589	606	605	807	955	973
34 Non-Russian Groups	734	665	699	936	977	919

Even though most of the ASSR's were beyond the front during the war, an extremely high proportion of the males old enough for military service must have been drafted and died during the war.[15] V. I. Kozlov has noted the serious male deficit among the ASSR-level nationalities.[16] He attributes this deficit to the large war losses of these groups resulting from the fact that the groups were predominantly rural. Few men from the ASSR-level nationalities would have been deferred as a result of holding strategic civilian jobs. Although many industrial plants were evacuated to cities in the non-Russian areas of the Volga-Viatka region, these plants generally brought with them a nonindigenous skilled work force. These new industries provided some job opportunities in the lower-skilled occupations for the local populations, primarily for women and youths, but provided few jobs carrying deferments for adult males of the local nationalities.[17]

A high proportion of Moslem SSR-level group members also were rural, but the male war losses among these nationalities were apparently a much lower proportion of the young adult male population. It could be that the location of the ASSR's in European Russia led to men from the ASSR-level nationalities being sent to fight on the European front, whereas conscripts from the traditionally Moslem SSR-level nationalities generally served in less hazardous locations.

PROPORTIONS MARRIED

The differential demographic impact of the war by nationality is depicted also in Table 11.3, which shows the number of women married per 1000

Table 11.3   Number of Women Married per Thousand Women, by Age in 1959

Year of Birth:	1909– 1913	1914– 1918	1919– 1923	1924– 1928	1929– 1933	1934– 1938
Year Age 20:	1929– 1933	1934– 1938	1939– 1943	1944– 1948	1949– 1953	1954– 1958
Balts	638	674	722	725	657	366
Ukrainians	552	608	705	760	737	481
Belorussians	545	605	712	760	724	448
Moldavians	681	737	795	807	768	569
Armenians- Georgians	638	678	763	817	765	509
Non-Moslem ASSR	463	539	643	690	664	395
Tatars- Bashkirs	474	561	669	725	716	492
Moslem SSR	704	774	859	903	913	824
Dagestanis	604	681	765	826	808	637
Deported	609	674	782	828	821	630
Russians	532	614	720	776	761	482
34 Non-Russian Groups	581	648	739	784	763	553

women by age in 1959 for the ten nationality groupings. There is great variability in the proportion of women married, both among groupings and across the age categories. There is very little intergroup variability in the proportions of men married at any age.

Although there are substantial differences among Soviet nationalities in female age at first marriage,[18] the female mean age of marriage has been in the early 20s for most Soviet nationalities throughout the period considered.[19] Thus, those most susceptible to widowhood from World War II would be women born in 1909–1918 (the War Widow cohort), while those most likely to be affected by the war by having to defer marriage or never being able to marry would be those born in 1919–1928 (the War Bride cohort).

The proportions married among women born before 1929 are low for Ukrainians, Belorussians, Russians and, for most ages, Balts. However, the Tatars-Bashkirs, and even more so the non-Moslem ASSR-level nationalities, have especially low proportions married among the cohorts most severely affected by the war, reflecting the severe shortage of men belonging to those nationalities.

NATIVE LANGUAGE

Another concomitant of the war is a change in patterns of language preference. For successive cohorts of Ukrainians, Belorussians, and Moldavians born before the 1917 Revolution, for example, larger and larger proportions claimed Russian as their native language in 1959. In other words, the 1959 census data suggest progressively higher levels of linguistic russification among those who reached school age before the 1917 Revolution.

This trend was reversed immediately after the Revolution. The first few cohorts of Ukrainians, Belorussians, and Moldavians born after the Revolution had successively smaller proportions who claimed Russian as their native language. This apparent decline in linguistic russification may be related to the establishment of native-language schools in the postrevolutionary period in those parts of the Ukraine, Belorussia, and Moldavia that were inside the USSR in the interwar period.

For Ukrainian, Belorussian, and Moldavian children reaching school age during World War II (age 5-9 in 1943), however, there was a slight increase in the proportion who claimed Russian as their native language in 1959, followed by somewhat lower levels of linguistic russification among the postwar cohorts. Thus, for these western SSR-level nationalities, the increase in the proportion claiming Russian as native language associated with World War II was short term, affecting only those of primary school age at the height of the war.

A similar pattern of changing proportions for the cohorts reaching school age before the 1917 Revolution and claiming Russian as native language can be found among many other non-Russian nationalities. Like the Ukrainians, Belorussians, and Moldavians, the proportion linguistically russified among those born in 1934–1938 (age 5-9 in 1943) was higher in 1959 than among those born somewhat earlier, for the ASSR-level nationalities in the RSFSR. However, for these ASSR-level nationalities, unlike for the Ukrainians, Belorussians, and Moldavians, the increased linguistic russification of those aged 5-9 in 1943 marked only the beginning of a sharp upturn in linguistic russification for successive cohorts.

Figures 11.4 and 11.5 illustrate the patterns of change. They show the number per thousand population by age, sex, and rural-urban residence claiming Russian as their native language in 1959 for Ukrainians and Chuvash, respectively. The Chuvash case is representative of the experiences of other non-Moslem ASSR-level nationalities in the RSFSR.

For both Ukrainians and Chuvash, the cohort born in 1934–1938 shows a slightly higher proportion claiming Russian as their native language than the next older (preceding) cohort. For both the Ukrainians and the Chuvash, the main source of this increase was the linguistic russification of those living in rural areas in 1959, especially rural males. The further rise in linguistic russification for the later cohorts among the Chuvash, however, was due to the linguistic russification of Chuvash who lived in urban places in 1959.

We believe the war is also a watershed in ethnic russification for ASSR-level groups, such as the Chuvash. Although there is evidence that assimilation of these groups by Russians has occurred over a period of several centuries,[20] especially rapid rates of linguistic and ethnic assimilation have appeared among these nationalities in the postwar period.[21]

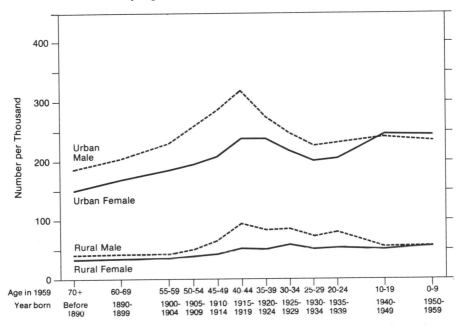

Figure 11.4
Number of Ukrainians per Thousand with Russian as Native Language in
1959 by Age, Sex, and Urban-Rural Residence

Figure 11.5
Number of Chuvash per Thousand with Russian as Native Language in
1959 by Age, Sex, and Urban-Rural Residence

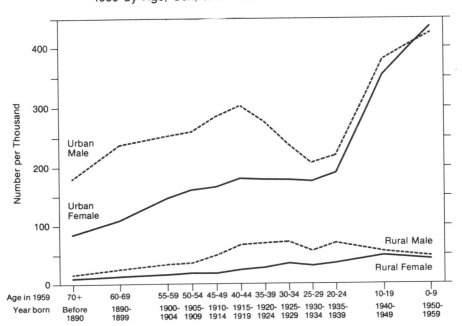

Table 11.4   Pearson Correlations between Sex Ratio and Proportion of Females Married by Age for 34 Non-Russian Nationalities, 1959

Proportion Females Married for Cohort Born in: / Sex Ratio for Cohort Born in:	1909–1913	1914–1918	1919–1923	1924–1928
1909–1913	.796	.754	.713	.683
1914–1918	.819	.767	.710	.617
1919–1923	.885	.840	.779	.731
1924–1928	.693	.721	.752	.824

Sex Ratios, Proportions of Women Married, and Interethnic Marriage

MALE DEFICITS AND THE PROPORTION OF WOMEN MARRIED

The differential effect of the war on the sex ratios among Soviet nationalities, as shown in Table 11.2, may be related to the chances of women to marry. Table 11.4 shows Pearson correlations between the sex ratio by age and the proportion of women reported as married in 1959 for several age groups for the 34 non-Russian nationalities. The strong positive correlations suggest a close link between the severity of the male shortage and the chances of women from different nationalities to marry. The correlations are strongest for the two 5-year age cohorts that were most directly affected by male participation in the war, those born between 1914 and 1918 and between 1919 and 1923. Statistical analysis (not shown here) of the impact of the shortage of men on the proportion of women married reveals that women who were in the age groups that suffered the heaviest male war losses also experienced greater difficulty in marrying (or marrying again) *relative to the supply of men in their age group* than did somewhat older or somewhat younger women.

MALE DEFICITS AND THE PROPORTION OF WOMEN IN INTERETHNIC MARRIAGES

A short supply of men of a given nationality depresses the proportion of females in the same nationality who marry. However, if females in the nationality are not totally unwilling to marry men from other nationalities, entering an interethnic marriage is another way to become married. Although all Soviet nationalities suffered some male deficit due to the war, we might expect to find that the more severe the deficit of males for a nationality, the greater the tendency of female members of that nationality who did marry to marry men of other nationalities.

Unfortunately, systematic data on interethnic marriage by age are not available for most Soviet nationalities. To develop an indicator of the relative extent of interethnic marriage among the non-Russian nationalities, we used 1959 census data on the size of the male and female age cohorts and on the proportions of males and females married by age to estimate the number of married men and women by age and by nationality.

Comparison of the estimated numbers of women and men who reported themselves in 1959 as married reveals that larger *numbers* of women than of men are married at all ages. Although part of this difference may be due to problems of misreporting of marriage information, among the non-Russian nationalities much of the surplus of married women is probably due to interethnic marriage.[22] The *relative* differences among nationalities in the reported numbers of married women and married men can be used to estimate the *relative* tendency of women of different nationalities to marry men of other nationalities.

An indicator of interethnic marriage should link females to males of the most appropriate age cohorts for marriage. Because of the problems of determining the most likely ages of potential spouses and because there is probably greater variability in age match-ups of spouses for those cohorts affected directly by the war, we use a cumulative measure of the extent of interethnic marriage. We estimate the relative extent of interethnic marriage among female nationality members who are a certain age *or older,* specifically, those who were age 30 or older and those who were age 40 or older in 1959.

The construction of the interethnic marriage indicator is described in Appendix A at the end of this chapter. The interethnic marriage indicator is based on two assumptions. First, it assumes that the tendency for married women in a nationality to be in interethnic marriages is strongly related to the tendency for both male and female group members to be in interethnic marriages. Second, it assumes that the tendency for married women in a nationality to be married to a man from any other nationality is strongly related to the tendency for married women in a nationality to be married to a Russian.

Table 11.5 shows the Pearson correlations between this intermarriage indicator and the sex ratios. These are generally strong and negative; when there is a severe male deficit, women tend to marry men from other nationalities. Simultaneously, based on data analyses not shown here, when there is a shortage of men of their nationality, women tend to marry less, but the proportion of women from nationalities with a severe male deficit who do marry is greater than it would have been if women were strictly ethnically endogamous. In other words, had women in nationalities with a severe male deficit been unwilling to enter interethnic marriages, the proportion of females married would be even lower.

Table 11.5   **Pearson Correlations between Sex Ratio and Estimated Proportion of Females Ethnically Intermarried by Age for 34 Non-Russian Nationalities, 1959**

Estimated Proportion Females Intermarried for Cohort Born in:	1909–1913	1914–1918	1919–1923	1924–1928
Sex Ratio for Cohort Born in:				
1909–1913	−.792	−.825	−.868	−.848
1914–1918	−.765	−.808	−.842	−.761
1919–1923	−.711	−.733	−.801	−.778
1924–1928	−.743	−.724	−.744	−.823

Hypothesized Factors Affecting Linguistic and Ethnic Russification

INTERETHNIC MARRIAGE

The most obvious way in which the large imbalance in the number of males and females in the population could have affected russification is through the effects of interethnic marriage on linguistic and ethnic russification of the non-Russian spouse and the linguistic and ethnic russification of the children of interethnic marriages.

Interethnic marriage sets the stage for the linguistic russification of the next generation. Linguistic russification would probably be more common among children of interethnic marriages than among children whose parents were both members of the same non-Russian nationality. In marriages between Russians and non-Russians, children typically become bilingual. Also, the children of interethnic marriages would be more likely to come to claim Russian as their native language than would the non-Russian spouses themselves.

Moreover, a high incidence of interethnic marriage could contribute to a decrease in the availability of schooling in the non-Russian nationality's traditional language. We know that in the postwar years, the decision to reduce the amount of native-language schooling for a given nationality has been partially based on the prevailing degree of bilingualism among non-Russian children.[23] To the extent that this is true, intermarriage would lead to a decreasing necessity for schooling in the group's non-Russian language, which, in turn, could lead to loss of facility in that language.

Interethnic marriage could be especially important in the process of ethnic assimilation in the USSR because of the workings of the internal passport system. Children whose parents are both of the same nationality are legally required to claim their parents' nationality as their own nationality on their internal passport. A child whose parents are of different nationalities can legally claim the nationality of either parent.[24]

This legal control on ethnic affiliations also could regulate the shift of subjective ethnic identifications. Even the supposedly completely subjective choice of nationality in the Soviet censuses could be strongly affected by the existence of an "official" nationality on the passport (and other official documents such as work records). The leading Soviet ethnic demographer, V. I. Kozlov,[25] claims that the choice of the passport nationality involves a crystallization or fixing of ethnic affiliation that makes subsequent change in ethnic self-identification highly improbable.[26]

Therefore, interethnic marriage is probably an important route through which changes in subjective ethnic attachment occur in the USSR. However, we do not expect that it is the only route, nor do we believe that if change in ethnic self-identification occurs at all, it always occurs through passport identification or even during adolescence. Although ethnic russification is most likely to occur during adolescence, a substantial amount of ethnic russification occurs after adolescence among groups, such as the Karelians and Mordvinians, that have high overall rates of ethnic russification[27].

MOBILITY ASPIRATIONS IN THE PRESENCE OF A MALE DEFICIT

As in other industrial societies, most jobs in the Soviet Union are highly sex-stratified.[28] If there were a shortage of males of the indigenous nationality, the positions in the group's titular area that were traditionally held by males could have been filled by male Russians more often than would have been true otherwise. This could have provided an incentive for young persons of the indigenous nationality with mobility aspirations to russify linguistically and ethnically. Furthermore, if many of these traditionally male jobs were filled by women of the indigenous nationality, the large proportion of Russians in these jobs also could have provided an incentive for women aspiring to these jobs to russify linguistically and ethnically.

More generally, as the urbanization and educational attainments of the non-Russian populations accelerated in the postwar period, the Russian numerical predominance in the urban populations of the autonomous republics could have combined with increased mobility aspirations of non-Russian youths to accelerate their linguistic and ethnic russification.

Although we lack data bearing directly on the question of aspirations and perceptions—the subjective dimension—we can establish enough central facts about the ethnic makeup of the labor force in the autonomous republics to make a plausible case for why the losses in World War II could have increased the incentives for non-Russians to assimilate.

In 1959, a large majority of the urban populations of all of the autonomous republics were Russians. In Karelia, for example, Karelians constituted only 6.5 percent of the urban population of the republic, whereas Russians were 72.5 percent. In the Komi ASSR, Komi comprised 26.4 percent of the urbanites, whereas Russians comprised 59.2 percent. In the Tatar ASSR, Tatars made up 29.4 percent of the urbanites, and Russians 61.1 percent. In the Chuvash Autonomous Republic, Chuvash made up 35.9 percent of the population, Russians 56.9 percent.

During the ensuing eleven years until the 1970 census, the titular nationalities generally increased their share of the urban population while the Russians decreased their share, but Russians continued to dominate the most highly skilled jobs in most sectors of the economy. In 1959 in the Karelian ASSR, for example, Russians constituted 75.4 percent of the engineers, whereas Karelians were only 2.8 percent. Seventy-three percent of the medical doctors were Russians, while only 1.0 percent were Karelians— only 11 of the 1,064 medical doctors in the republic were Karelians.[29] In the Komi ASSR in 1960, 24.5 percent of the specialists with higher educational degrees were Komi, whereas Russians comprised 59.3 percent of such specialists.[30]

In the Tatar ASSR in 1966, Tatars constituted 33.2 percent of all specialists with higher degrees working in the economy, while Russians constituted 57.1 percent.[31] In 1950 and 1953, Tatars amounted to about 40 percent of all "workers" and white-collar "employees" (*sluzhashchie*) in construction, about 30 percent of workers and employees in industry, and about 20 percent in transportation.[32] The Tatar proportion of workers and employees in construction, industry, and transportation increased substantially by 1963, but Tatars still represented much less than a majority of the workers and employees in those sectors of the economy.[33]

Of the ASSR-level nationalities, in the 1950s and 1960s, only the Chuvash comprised a majority of the specialists with higher education working in their titular republic. In the late 1950s, between 56 and 60 percent of such specialists were Chuvash, whereas between 35 and 39 percent were Russians.[34]

The plausibility of the argument that the imbalance between the number of males and females resulting from World War II accelerated the linguistic and ethnic russification of non-Russians does not depend on establishing precisely when the numerical dominance of Russians in the urban populations and the skilled labor force came about. Judging from available data in the 1926 Soviet census, this dominance has provided a context over an extended period of time within which adolescents completing secondary school, especially those living in or moving to urban areas, would find it desirable to reidentify as Russian linguistically and ethnically.

However the severe imbalance in the relative number of females and males among many of the ASSR-level nationalities, resulting from the war, could have further reduced the competitiveness of workers from the local nationalities and thereby further increased the incentives for youths of the local nationalities to assimilate. If the indigenous labor supply is sharply reduced in certain cohorts because of losses during World War II, managers would tend to recruit new workers from outside the republic, who typically would have a different ethnic and linguistic background than that of the local nationality.

The incentives for members of indigenous non-Russian nationalities to become russified and the focus on nonlocal labor recruitment also would have been reinforced by the decision in the late 1950s to shift the language of government administration in the autonomous republics (as well as in the autonomous provinces and national *okrugi*) from the local languages to Russian.[35] As a concomitant of this switch in language use, employment in state institutions, in which the members of the local nationalities had been much more heavily represented than in the skilled labor force of the industrial sectors of the urban economy, would become more attractive to Russians. At the same time, command of the Russian language would become a more important qualification for non-Russians who sought jobs in state institutions.

We use as an indicator of *Russian dominance of high-level jobs* in a group's titular area the number of specialists with higher education who were Russians divided by the number of specialists with higher education who were Russians or members of the titular nationality. Thus, the measure indicates the relative balance between Russians and the titular nationality among specialists with higher education. This measure is strongly related to the proportion of the urban population who are Russians. It is a reasonable indicator of the extent to which Russians dominate high-level jobs and, thus, whether non-Russian young people in a given region would be likely to perceive russification as important for social mobility.[36]

The overall presence of Russians also would make the relevance of russification to social mobility clearer. We use as the indicator of *contact with Russians* the relative mix of group members and Russians within the non-Russian group's titular area. Specifically, the indicator is the number of Russians in the group's titular area divided by the sum of the number of Russians and the number of group members in the titular area.[37]

OTHER FACTORS

We also expect the *general* social and demographic context within which non-Russians find themselves to be important for linguistic and ethnic russification. Earlier empirical work has shown traditional religion to be related to interethnic marriage[38] and linguistic russification,[39] and urbanization to be related to linguistic and ethnic russification.[40]

Urban Residence. Because urban populations of the non-Russian territories have much larger proportions of Russians in them than do rural populations, the more urban the non-Russian population, the more likely that non-Russians will marry Russians. Also, especially for the ASSR-level nationalities, native-language schooling is less available in urban than in rural areas. Furthermore, because desirable jobs that might often be held by Russians would typically be in urban areas, non-Russians in urban areas are likely to be in competition with Russians and to see the benefits of fluency in Russian and perhaps of redefining their linguistic and ethnic identities as Russian.

Even though urban residence is likely to affect interethnic marriage, linguistic russification, and ethnic russification, in the analysis we will not explicitly examine the effect of urban residence on ethnic processes. There was a great deal of rural-urban migration since World War II, and the characteristics of residents of urban areas in 1959 do not necessarily accurately reflect the characteristics of the urban population during World War II and in the immediate postwar period.

Traditional Religion. Traditional religion would be expected to affect the extent of interethnic marriage and linguistic and ethnic russification primarily because nationalities that are more akin to Russians in religion, in particular the traditionally Orthodox nationalities, will already have had considerable exposure to Russian culture and would not have a religious barrier to close contact and to assimilation. On the other hand, other factors being equal, Moslem nationalities would have a religious barrier to assimilation that might retard, though not completely prevent, interethnic marriage with Russians as well as linguistic and ethnic russification.

At the same time, we would not expect traditional religion to be equally important for intermarriage, linguistic russification, and ethnic russification. We expect traditional religion to affect interethnic marriage[41] and the shift to Russian as the native language among non-Russians, but once non-Russians have adopted Russian as their native language, further religious barriers to change in *ethnic* self-identification to Russian are unlikely to be important.[42]

In this analysis, traditional religion is indicated by a variable that assumes the value of one if the group is not traditionally Moslem and the value of zero if the group is traditionally Moslem.

Earlier Linguistic Russification. Even in 1926, *narodnosti* differed greatly in the proportion claiming Russian as their native language. Earlier levels of group linguistic russification could affect willingness to enter interethnic marriages as well as susceptibility to russification among those who became adults during and shortly after the war.

To take into account the possible effects of prior levels of linguistic russification on wartime and postwar rates of linguistic and ethnic russification, we use data from the 1959 census on the proportion linguistically russified among those who were age 60 or older—persons born before 1899. In general, we expect that the greater the extent of linguistic russification among those age 60 or older in 1959, the greater the extent of linguistic russification among those who were young adults during the war.

ADDITIONAL NOTE ON INDICATORS

The two youngest age groups for which data are reported from the 1959 census are those age 0-9 and those age 10-19. The mothers of most of those

Table 11.6   Estimated Number per Thousand Ethnically Russifying, 1959–1970, Among People Age 0–8 and 9–18 Years in 1959

Age in 1959:	0–8 Years	9–18 Years
Grouping:		
Balts	26	13
Ukrainians	19	20
Belorussians	8	22
Moldavians	3	56
Armenians-Georgians	0	57
Non-Moslem ASSR	72	207
Tatars-Bashkirs	18	154
Moslem SSR	0	86

Note: Assuming expectation of life at birth of 67.6 years for Balts, Ukrainians, Belorussians, Armenians, and Georgians; and of 62.8 years for other groups. Negative estimated reidentification represented as 0.

age 0-9 in 1959 would be those age 30-39 in 1959. The mothers of most of those age 10-19 in 1959 would be those age 40-49. Therefore, we will relate the characteristics of those age 30-39 in 1959 to the characteristics of those age 0-9 in 1959; we will relate the characteristics of those age 40-49 in 1959 to the characteristics of those age 10-19 in 1959.

Linguistic Russification. The linguistic russification of the generations who were young adults during the war will be indicated by the proportion claiming Russian as their native language in 1959 among those age 30-39 and those age 40-49 in 1959. The measures of linguistic russification are measures of the native language as of 1959. They are not direct measures of *change* in the native language.

The measure of *ethnic russification* is different. There is no census question asking people who claim to be members of a given nationality whether at some earlier time they claimed to be members of a different nationality. Our measure of ethnic russification is based on the estimated loss of members of a nationality in a particular cohort between the 1959 and 1970 censuses above and beyond what could be accounted for by mortality or emigration out of the area of enumeration.[43] Thus, the measure of ethnic russification is a measure of *change* in ethnic self-identification from non-Russian to Russian nationality between 1959 and 1970. It is not a measure of the proportion of those born into a nationality who still claimed that nationality in 1959 or 1970.

Table 11.6 shows the number per thousand persons age 0-8 in 1959 (age 11-19 in 1970) and the number per thousand age 9-18 in 1959 (age 20-29 in 1970) estimated to have changed their ethnic self-identification between 1959 and 1970. In most cases, the target nationality of the ethnic reidentifiers

Table 11.7a   Pearson Correlations Among Background and Ethnic Process Variables Used in Multivariate Analysis

A. War Bride Cohort

	Sex Ratio 30–39	Inter-married 30 or older	Linguistic Russification 30–39	Linguistic Russification 0–9	Ethnic Russification 0–8
Non-Moslem	−.518	.406	.338	.375	.446
Contact with Russians	−.100	.053	.024	.224	.616
Linguistic Russification 60 or older	−.524	.505	.972	.810	.674
Sex Ratio 30–39	1.000	−.857	−.660	−.761	−.767
Intermarried 30 or older	−.857	1.000	.606	.713	.751
Linguistic Russification 30–39	−.660	.606	1.000	.898	.793
Russian specialists	−.103	−.034	.059	.218	.604
Linguistic Russification 0–9	−.761	.713	.898	1.000	.906
Ethnic Russification 0–8	−.767	.751	.793	.906	1.000

was the Russians although this is not always true. For example, Bashkirs tend to reidentify as Tatars.

For this reason, in estimating the extent of linguistic and of ethnic russification, we create a *combined* Tatar-Bashkir case. The net numbers of Tatars and Bashkirs together who reidentify ethnically (as something other than Bashkirs *or* Tatars) are treated as part of a single case, and all the variables and indicators used to explain the extent of russification of the Tatars-Bashkirs are also based on a combination of Tatar and Bashkir data.

Table 11.6 shows very high estimated proportions ethnically russifying among the traditionally non-Moslem ASSR-level groups. Such high rates could not have been in place for long, or there would be no members of these nationalities left. We suspect that the heavily unbalanced sex ratio and the high proportions intermarrying resulting from World War II could well have triggered a high level of ethnic russification among these nationalities.

Table 11.7b   Pearson Correlations continued:

B. War Widow Cohort

	Sex Ratio 40–49	Inter-married 40 or older	Linguistic Russification 40–49	Linguistic Russification 10–19	Ethnic Russification 9–18
Non-Moslem	−.319	.399	.335	.340	.161
Contact with Russians	−.230	.126	−.014	.269	.667
Linguistic Russification 60 or older	−.457	.446	.987	.804	.350
Sex Ratio 40–49	1.000	−.834	−.527	−.681	−.689
Intermarried 40 or older	−.823	1.000	.485	.548	.390
Linguistic Russification 40–49	−.527	.485	1.000	.853	.410
Russian specialists	−.152	.013	.023	.257	.720
Linguistic Russification 10–19	−.681	.548	.853	1.000	.689
Ethnic Russification 9–18	−.689	.390	.410	.689	1.000

Preliminary Correlational Analysis

Table 11.7 shows the Pearson correlations between the variables of interest for the War Bride cohort (those age 30-39 in 1959) and those age 0-9 in 1959. Table 11.7 also shows the analogous information for the War Widow cohort (those age 40-49 in 1959) and those age 10-19 in 1959. All the correlations except those including an estimate of ethnic russification refer to the 34 non-Russian nationalities.[44] The correlations including an estimate of ethnic russification refer to 24 non-Russian groups.[45]

The correlations are generally consistent with the pattern proposed. The imbalance in the number of males and females brought on by World War II appears to be related to a variety of changes in ethnic processes—interethnic marriage and linguistic and ethnic russification.[46] For the War Bride cohort (in Panel A and Table 11.7), the severity of the male deficit was strongly related to the extent of interethnic marriage. In addition, the sex ratio was strongly negatively related to all the linguistic and ethnic russification variables. The greater the proportion of men relative to women in a given cohort, the lower the level of linguistic russification of persons in either that cohort or the younger cohorts, and the lower the rate of ethnic russification of the younger cohorts.

That the sex ratio has at least as strong a correlation with all the linguistic and ethnic russification variables as does the interethnic marriage variable suggests that the sex ratio affected russification through more paths than simply interethnic marriage. The strong relation of the sex ratio to both the russification variables and the interethnic marriage variable means that distinguishing the separate effects of interethnic marriage from other effects of the sex ratio will be difficult to detect.

All of the linguistic russification variables are strongly related to each other. Groups that had a high degree of linguistic russification among the older generation tend to continue to have a high degree of linguistic russification among later generations. All of the linguistic russification variables are also strongly related to ethnic russification.

The pattern of correlations for the War Widow cohort, shown in Panel B, is generally similar to that for the War Bride cohort. However, the relation between whether the group is traditionally Moslem and ethnic russification is weaker for those age 9-18 in 1959 than for those age 0-8 in 1959. The relations between linguistic russification and ethnic russification are also somewhat weaker for those in their teens in 1959 than for those who were younger.

Multivariate Analysis of Ethnic Intermarriage, Linguistic Russification, and Ethnic Russification

We now examine the results of multivariate analyses of the roles of the hypothesized factors in accounting for three ethnic processes: interethnic marriage, linguistic russification, and ethnic russification. The analysis examines the simultaneous effects of several variables as well as traces the direct and indirect effects of those variables.

Panel A of Figure 11.6 schematically presents the relations between the effects of World War II and the ethnic processes. The ethnic processes are arranged from top to bottom in the assumed temporal order in which they occur. On the right are contextual background variables. On the left is the sex ratio variable.

EXPECTED LINKAGES

A low sex ratio (i.e., a high male deficit) is expected to lead to greater interethnic marriage. Interethnic marriage in combination with linguistic russification of parents is expected to lead to linguistic russification of children. Linguistic russification of children is expected to lead to ethnic russification of children.

Figure 11.6
Results of Multiple Regression Analysis of Ethnic Process Variables

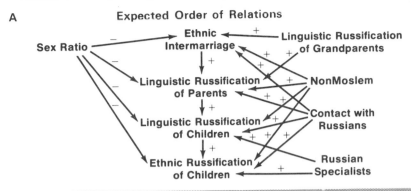

A   Expected Order of Relations

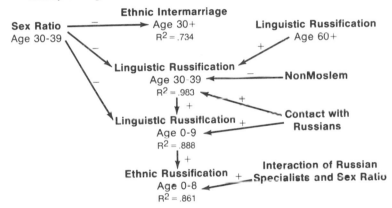

B   Multiple Regression Results for War Bride Cohort

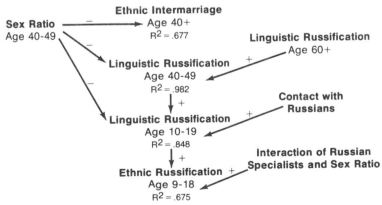

C   Multiple Regression Results for War Widow Cohort

The higher the proportion of high-skilled jobs in the area that are held by Russians the greater the expected linguistic and ethnic russification of children. In addition, the greater the degree of contact with Russians, the greater the expected interethnic marriage, linguistic russification, and ethnic russification. Finally, non-Moslems are expected to be more likely to intermarry and to russify linguistically and ethnically than are Moslems.

MAIN PROCEDURES

Because the statistical testing of all of these hypothesized linkages is very complex, we will not describe it step-by-step but instead only summarize the main statistical procedures and results.

We initially tested the model depicted in Figure 11.6 through separate multiple regressions, with each ethnic process variable in turn taken as the dependent variable. For each ethnic process variable, we tested for the effects of the sex ratio, the background variable indicating whether the nationality had a non-Moslem traditional religion, and the variable indicating the extent of contact with Russians. An interaction term between non-Moslem traditional religion and contact with Russians was considered, based in part on our previous research findings[47] and in part on the expectation that traditional religion would have a special joint effect with interethnic contact.

An interaction term between the sex ratio variable and the Russian specialist variable also was considered.[48] The basic idea behind this interaction term is that the effect of the Russian dominance of the skilled jobs in an area on the perception of the importance of russification for mobility by members of the indigenous nationality is greater when the male deficit within the indigenous nationality is greater.

At each stage we tested for the effects of the sex ratio variable, the interethnic marriage variable, and the immediately preceding linguistic russification variable. Thus, the sex ratio variable, interethnic marriage, and linguistic russification of parents were considered in the explanation of linguistic russification of children; the sex ratio variable, interethnic marriage, and linguistic russification of children were all considered in the explanation of ethnic russification of children.

A larger set of background variables was examined at an earlier stage in the analysis, including population size of the nationality, education of the parental generation, and official status of the nationality in the federal hierarchy. None of these other variables proved to make a significant contribution to the explanation of any of the ethnic process variables once the effects of the main theoretical variables were considered. For example, the size of the population of the nationality has no bearing on interethnic marriage once the effects of the sex ratio are considered; nor does it affect ethnic reidentification once the effects of interethnic contact and previous linguistic russification of children and adolescents is taken into account.

STATISTICAL RESULTS

Panels B and C of Figure 11.6 show the relationships that were found through the multiple regression analysis to provide the best explanation. Appendix B at the end of this chapter gives the actual regression equations. In contrast to Figure 11.6A, arrows between the variables are omitted from Figures 11.6B and 11.6C if the relationships between the variables proved not to be statistically significant once the effects of the other variables were taken into account. All of the relationships indicated by the arrows are statistically significant at the .05 level, with the sign ($+$ or $-$) on the arrow indicating whether the relation between the variables is positive or negative. The 34 non-Russian nationalities (33 cases) were included except for the analysis of ethnic reidentification, for which 24 non-Russian nationalities (23 cases) were included.

Given the high correlations shown in Table 11.7, as well as the small number of cases, several alternative patterns of relationships among the hypothesized variables would have been statistically significant. Hence, choice of the "best" model explaining ethnic processes depends in part on certain judgments about the logical and theoretical priority among the variables.[49]

In Figure 11.6, panels B and C, the proportion of the total variance explained in the interethnic marriage, linguistic russification of children, and ethnic russification of children (the R^2 value) is shown below each ethnic process variable. In every case, a substantial (and statistically significant) proportion of the variance was accounted for. We shall review the main results with respect to each ethnic process variable in turn.

Interethnic Marriage. For both the War Bride cohort and the War Widow cohort, the sex ratio was the factor most strongly related to interethnic marriage. The lower the sex ratio (the greater the male deficit), the larger the proportion of married women in the nationality with husbands from a different nationality. Furthermore, once the sex ratio was taken into account, no other variable could account for an additional statistically significant proportion of the variance in interethnic marriage.

This result runs counter to previous research and to a large body of evidence from the Soviet experience indicating that traditional religion strongly affects rates of interethnic marriage. It is likely that in more normal times traditional religion would have had a strong and independent effect, but at least for the cohorts in which the variation in the sex ratio across nationalities was large, the influence of the sex ratio was dominant and nullified the effects of other factors, including traditional religion, population size, and the extent of linguistic russification of the earlier generation (those age 60 or older in 1959).

Linguistic Russification of Those Who Were Young Adults During World War II. In accounting for the linguistic russification of those age 30-39 and those age 40-49 in 1959, the prior level of linguistic russification—the proportion claiming Russian as their native language among those age 60 or older in 1959—is by far the most important variable. The greater the proportion of the older generation that was linguistically russified, the greater the proportion of those age 30-39 or 40-49 who were linguistically russified in 1959. Thus, there is an extremely strong intergenerational continuity in the relative levels of linguistic russification of the non-Russian nationalities. As shown in Table 11.7, the correlation between the proportion claiming Russian as their native language among those age 60 or older and those age 40-49 in 1959 is .987; the correlation among those age 60 or older and those age 30-39 in 1959 is .972.

Despite the strength of these intergenerational links, the sex ratio is important in explaining the degree of linguistic russification of both the 30-39 and 40-49 year-olds. The greater the male deficit, the greater the linguistic russification of these adults, above and beyond what would be expected based on the linguistic russification of the oldest members of the same nationality. Thus, the unequal numbers of males and females *disrupted the normal continuity* between the linguistic russification of one generation and the next.

For the War Bride cohort, but not for the War Widow cohort, non-Russians were also more russified linguistically the higher their degree of geographic intermixing with Russians. Also, for the War Bride cohort, once linguistic russification of those age 60 or older, the sex ratio, and contact with Russians are taken into account, traditionally non-Moslem groups have somewhat lower linguistic russification among those age 30-39 in 1959 than traditionally Moslem groups.

Traditionally non-Moslem groups, however, had much greater contact with Russians, greater prior linguistic russification, and larger male deficits than traditionally Moslem groups. Thus, the negative coefficient for non-Moslem traditional religion does not imply that traditionally non-Moslem groups actually had lower levels of linguistic russification among young adults.

Table 11.7 shows that the Pearson correlation between the non-Moslem variable and linguistic russification of those age 30-39 in 1959 was positive and statistically significant: .338. The change of sign in the multiple regression for the non-Moslem variable suggests that the non-Moslem variable is acting as a correction factor.

The entire multiple regression analysis was replicated on the 23 cases used in the analysis of ethnic russification. When that was done, the results were substantially the same as those for the 33 cases. The only major exception was that the coefficient for the non-Moslem variable in the analysis of the linguistic russification of those age 30-39 in 1959 was not significantly different from zero. The Deported groups and the Dagestani groups were the Moslem groups included in the 33 cases but excluded from the 23 cases. Hence, the statistical significance of the non-Moslem variable for the 33 cases appears to be related to peculiarities of the Deported groups and the Dagestani groups.[50]

Linguistic Russification of Children. In accounting for the linguistic russification of the children of the War Widow and War Bride cohorts, the same factors are important. Linguistic russification of the parental generation is strongly positively related to linguistic russification of the children's generation. For both cohorts of children, the sex ratio and the degree of geographic intermixing with Russians have statistically significant independent effects on the extent of their linguistic russification. The greater the male deficit and the greater the contact with Russians, the greater the degree of linguistic russification of children, above and beyond what would be expected from the degree of linguistic russification in the parental generation. Thus, although the linguistic russification of the children reflects a high degree of *continuity* with that of the parental generations, the linguistic russification of children is also independently affected by the extent of the imbalance between the number of males and females in the parental generation.

Surprisingly, the extent of interethnic marriage among the parental generation does not appear to play a strong independent role in accounting for the linguistic russification of the children. This is surprising because the simple correlations between the interethnic marriage indicator and the measure of linguistic russification of the children are moderate to strong: the correlation between intermarriage of persons age 40-49 and linguistic russification of persons age 10-19 in 1959 is .55; the correlation between the same variables for the 30-39 year-olds is .71.

However, the results of the multivariate analysis may be explained by the fact that the sex ratio variable has an even stronger relationship with the linguistic russification of the children than does the interethnic marriage indicator. The correlations between the natural logarithm of the sex ratio of the parental generations and the linguistic russification of the children's generations is -0.68 for the children age 10-19 in 1959 and -0.71 for the children age 0-9. The dominant effect of the sex imbalance on the linguistic russification of the children's generation overshadows and statistically overwhelms the effect of interethnic marriage. While interethnic marriage *may* play an intermediate role in accounting for linguistic russification, the impact of the sex imbalance in the parental generation is so great that it masks any effect of interethnic marriage.

At the same time, recall that the linguistic russification of the parental generation is strongly related to the linguistic russification of the children's generation and that the parent's linguistic russification was also itself significantly affected by the sex imbalance in that generation. Hence, the continuity in the linguistic russification of the War Widow and War Bride cohorts and their children is itself partly a product of the sex imbalance resulting from the war.

Ethnic Russification. The same factors that are most important for linguistic russification are important for ethnic russification: previous linguistic russification, the sex ratio, and interethnic mixing. However, the form in which these factors operate for ethnic russification differs somewhat from their form for linguistic russification.

The measure of the extent to which Russians dominated the jobs held by specialists with higher education works better than the measure of overall interethnic contact. The relationship between ethnic russification, the sex ratio, and Russian dominance of specialist jobs is best expressed statistically as an interaction effect. The greater the male deficit in the parental generation, the more strongly Russian dominance of specialist jobs is related to ethnic russification of children.

Thus, the impact of the war on the sex ratios, combined with the Russian dominance of the specialist jobs in the non-Russian republics—especially in the ASSR's—appears to have had a serious effect on subsequent ethnic russification of non-Russian youths. The extent of linguistic russification of the parental generation and the extent of linguistic russification of the children's generation both are due in part to the sex imbalance in the parental generation. As a result, the amount of the ethnic russification of the children that may be attributed directly and indirectly to the sex imbalance of the parental generation is even more substantial than that indicated in the direct effect of the interaction term on ethnic russification.

Conclusion

The severe sex imbalance among some nationalities as a result of World War II appears to have marked the beginning of a major increase in russification. The shortage of males led to increased interethnic marriage and also to substantially higher linguistic russification. Linguistic russification further facilitated the ethnic russification of the next generation.

Contact between the non-Russian nationalities and Russians was important in this process. For linguistic russification, the extent of geographic intermixing in the non-Russian nationality's titular area between non-Russians and Russians was important. For ethnic russification, the extent to which high-level jobs in the group's titular area were dominated by Russians was more important than general interethnic contact.

The negligible role of traditional religion in accounting for linguistic russification runs counter to our earlier research findings. Although in those analyses, too, the majority of the variance in linguistic russification could be attributed to demographic factors such as interethnic contact and urbanization, Moslems were far less likely to shift their native language to Russian than were non-Moslems in comparable demographic contexts. There are several possible reasons for the differing results between the present analysis and earlier ones.

One reason could be that the earlier analyses included a larger number of cases (54 versus 33). A second reason could be that some of the factors taken into account in the current analysis may already indirectly reflect the religious dimension. For example, previous levels of linguistic russification partly reflect the fact that the titular nationalities of the autonomous republics that were most russified linguistically in the prerevolutionary period were those that had been converted to the Russian Orthodox religion.

Third, at each step in this analysis, we took linguistic russification of an earlier cohort into account. Traditional religion of the group could explain general *differences* among groups in the tendency to russify linguistically yet not explain *changes* in the tendency to russify linguistically.

The finding that traditional religion does not play an independent role in *ethnic* russification, on the other hand, is consistent with earlier research. Once linguistic russification is taken into account, traditional religion does not play an independent role.

Of the variables considered, two proved to be keys to every ethnic process: prior linguistic russification and the sex ratio. The high correlation of linguistic russification across the generations reminds us that this process is prolonged and has a high degree of continuity over time.[51]

In contrast to linguistic russification, sex ratios are volatile and are susceptible to sudden disturbances associated with calamitous historical events. Moreover, if the short-term disturbances in the sex ratios are large enough, they can have both short-term and long-term effects. Working in combination with other aspects of the demographic context of the autonomous republics, the sex imbalance brought on by the war appears to have accelerated russification of many of the non-Russian nationalities, particularly the titular nationalities of the autonomous republics in the RSFSR. When one considers also the effects of forced deportation and exile on the vitality of several entire nationalities[52], World War II may be characterized as a turning point in the demographic history of most of the autonomous republic nationalities[53]. It may well be that for the autonomous republic nationalities as a whole, the immediate losses during the war, however large they were, were less significant for the groups' long-term survival than the accelerated russification that followed and was substantially induced by the war.

Notes

1. By some accounts, the USSR's loss of military and civilian population during World War II, the birth deficit during the war, and the lower postwar birthrates resulting from the deficit of males, led to a total loss of over 50 million people by 1959 compared to the expected population at that time. See V. V. Pokshishevskii, *Geografiia naseleniia SSSR: ekonomiko-geograficheskie ocherki* (Moscow: Prosveshchenie, 1971), 34; and Robert A. Lewis and Richard H. Rowland, *Population Redistribution in the USSR: Its Impact on Society, 1897–1977* (New York: Praeger, 1979), 103.

2. Ansley J. Coale, Barbara A. Anderson, Erna Harm, *Human Fertility in Russia Since the Nineteenth Century* (Princeton: Princeton University Press, 1979), 17.

3. Lewis and Rowland, *Population Redistribution,* 104.

4. V. I. Kozlov, *Natsional'nosti SSSR (Etnodemograficheskii obzor),* Second Edition (Moscow: Finansy i statistika, 1982), 290.

5. For a discussion of some other factors related to linguistic and ethnic russification, see Barbara A. Anderson and Brian D. Silver, "Changes in Linguistic Identification in the USSR, 1959–1979," Presented at the Annual Meeting of the Population Association

of America, San Diego, April 1982; Brian D. Silver, "Social Mobilization and the Russification of Soviet Nationalities," *American Political Science Review,* Vol. 68 (March 1974): 45–66; and Barbara A. Anderson, "Some Factors Related to Ethnic Reidentification in the Russian Republic," in Jeremy R. Azrael, ed., *Soviet Nationality Policies and Practices* (New York: Praeger, 1978), 309–33.

6. We use the term russification to denote a change in subjective identification from non-Russian to Russian. We use the term *linguistic* russification to refer to change from non-Russian to Russian *native language* as measured by responses to the census question on "native language" (*rodnoi iazyk*). We use the term *ethnic* russification to refer to change from non-Russian to Russian self-identification as measured by responses to the census question on "nationality" (*natsional'nost'*). For discussion of the measurement of language and nationality in recent Soviet censuses, see Brian D. Silver, "The Language and Ethnic Dimensions in Russian and Soviet Censuses," in Ralph S. Clem, ed., *Research Guide to the Russian and Soviet Censuses,* forthcoming.

7. Godfrey Baldwin, *Estimates and Projections of the Population of the U.S.S.R., by Age and Sex: 1950 to 2000,* U.S. Department of Commerce, Bureau of Economic Analysis, International Population Reports, Series P-91, No. 23 (Washington, D.C.: Government Printing Office, 1973).

8. Coale, Anderson, Harm, *Human Fertility in Russia,* 17.

9. G.A. Slesarev, *Demograficheskie protsessy i sotsial'naia struktura sotsialisticheskogo obshchestva* (Moscow: Nauka, 1978), 60.

10. Some of the children of women age 40-49 in 1959 would be age 0-9 or age 20-29. However, the vast majority of those age 0-9 would have had younger mothers, and most of those age 20-29 would have had older mothers. Thus, those age 10-19 in 1959 comprise the group the majority of whose mothers would be age 40-49 in 1959.

11. Some of their children also would have been age 10-19 in 1959.

12. Frank W. Notestein, et al., *The Future Population of Europe and the Soviet Union: Population Projections, 1940-1970* (Geneva: League of Nations, 1944).

13. The 1959 Soviet census presented age data by nationality only for the union republic-level nationalities within the Soviet Union as a whole and for the ASSR-level nationalities whose titular areas were within the RSFSR. The data for union republic-level nationalities refer to the nationality's population within the Soviet Union as a whole. The data for ASSR-level nationalities refer to the nationality's population within the RSFSR. U.S.S.R., Ts.S.U., *Itogi vsesoiuznoi perepisi naseleniia 1959 goda* (Moscow: Gosstatizdat, 1962–1963).

14. See, for example, A. A. Isupov, *Natsional'nyi sostav naseleniia SSSR (Po itogam perepisi 1959 g.)* (Moscow: Statistika, 1964, 24; A. L. Perkovskii and S. I. Pirozhkov, "Ukrainskaia Sovetskaia Sotsialisticheskaia Respublika," in T. V. Riabushkin, ed., *Naselenie soiuznykh respublik* (Moscow: Statistika, 1977), 66–81; A. A. Rakov, Ia. Z. Rubin, A. N. Peshkova, "Belorusskaia Sovetskaia Sotsialisticheskaia Respublika," in Riabushkin, *Naselenie soiuznykh respublik,* 82-100.

15. Sex-selective ethnic assimilation could account for some of the male deficit for some nationalities. It seems implausible, however, that sex-selective assimilation could account for a high proportion of such a large male deficit.

16. V. I. Kozlov, *Natsional'nosti SSSR (Etnodemograficheskii obzor).* (Moscow: Statistika, 1975), 172-3.

17. I. S. Gurvich, "K voprosu o vliianii Velikoi Otechestvennoi Voiny 1941–1945 gg. na khod etnicheskikh protsessov v SSSR," *Sovetskaia etnografiia,* 1976, no. 1:39–48; and Sh. M. Munchaev, "Evakuatsiia naseleniia v gody Velikoi Otechestvennoi Voiny," *Istoriia SSSR,* 1975, no. 3:133–141.

18. V. I. Kozlov, *Dinamika chislennosti narodov* (Moscow: Nauka, 1969), 122.

19. Coale, Anderson, Harm, *Human Fertility in Russia.*

20. See, for example, T. I. Kozlova, *Etnografiia narodov povolzh'ia* (Moscow: Izdatel'stvo Moskovskogo universiteta, 1964), 25–27.

21. Barbara A. Anderson and Brian D. Silver, "Estimating Russification of Ethnic Identity among Non-Russians in the USSR," *Demography,* Vol. 20 (November 1983): 461-489.

22. Widows often report to census-takers that they are married. Men living apart from their wives often report that they are not married, while their wives report themselves as married. For details with respect to the 1959 Soviet census, see Barbara A. Anderson, "Family and Fertility in Russian and Soviet Censuses," in Ralph S. Clem, ed., *Research Guide to the Russian and Soviet Censuses,* forthcoming.

23. Brian D. Silver, "The Status of National Minority Languages in Soviet Education: An Assessment of Recent Changes," *Soviet Studies,* Vol. 26 (January, 1974): 28–40.

24. Victor Zaslavsky and Yuri Luryi, "The Passport System in the USSR and Changes in Soviet Society," *Soviet Union,* Vol. 6 (1979): 137–53.

25. Kozlov, *Dinamika chislennosti,* 298, and Kozlov, *Natsional'nosti SSSR* (1975) 230–231.

26. For a similar argument, see Victor Zaslavsky, *The Neo-Stalinist State: Class, Ethnicity, and Consensus in Soviet Society* (Armonk, N.Y.: M. E. Sharpe, 1982), 92–94.

27. Anderson and Silver, "Estimating Russification."

28. Michael Paul Sacks, *Work and Equality in Soviet Society: The Division of Labor by Age, Gender, and Nationality* (New York: Praeger, 1982).

29. Ts.S.U. RSFSR, Stat. upr. Karel'skoi ASSR, *40 let Karel'skoi ASSR: statisticheskii sbornik* (Petrozavodsk: Gosstatizdat, 1960), 71.

30. Ia. N. Beznosikov, *Kul'turnaia revoliutsiia v Komi ASSR* (Moscow: Nauka, 1968), 212.

31. Ts.S.U. RSFSR, Stat. upr. Tatarskoi ASSR, *Dostizheniia Tatarskoi ASSR k 50-letiiu sovetskoi vlasti: statisticheskii sbornik* (Kazan': Statistika, 1967), 90.

32. Ts.S.U. SSSR, Stat. upr. Tatarskoi ASSR: *Narodnoe khoziaistvo Tatarskoi ASSR: statisticheskii sbornik* (Kazan':Tatknigoizdat, 1957), 162.

33. *Dostizheniia Tatarskoi ASSR k 50-letiiu,* 87.

34. See, for example, Ts.S.U. RSFSR, St. upr. Chuvashskoi ASSR, *Chuvashiia za 40 let v tsifrakh* (Cheboksary: Chuvashskoe gosizdat, 1960), 138; and Ts.S.U. RSFSR, St. upr. Chuvashskoi ASSR, *Sovetskaia Chuvashiia za 45 let: statisticheskii sbornik* (Cheboksary: Chuvashknigoizdat, 1966), 126.

35. Iu. D. Desheriev and I. F. Protchenko, *Razvitie iazykov narodov SSSR v sovetskuiu epokhu* (Moscow: Nauka, 1968), 122.

36. For the union republics, the data are for the year 1960 and are derived from Ts.S.U., *Vysshee obrazovanie v SSSR: statisticheskii sbornik* (Moscow: Gosstatizdat, 1961), 70–71.

The data for the autonomous republics come mainly from statistical yearbooks for those republics and refer either to 1960 or to the year nearest to 1960 for which information was published: Ts.S.U. RSFSR, Stat. upr. Bashkirskoi ASSR *Bashkiria za 50 let: statisticheskii sbornik* (Ufa: Statistika, 1969), 89–90 (for the year 1960); Ts.S.U. RSFSR, Stat. upr. Buriatskoi ASSR, *Buriatskaia ASSR za 50 let* (Ulan-Ude: 1967), 64 (for the year 1966); *Chuvashiia za 40 let v tsifrakh* 138 (for 1959); *40 let Karel'skoi ASSR,* 71 (for 1959); Beznosikov, *Kul'turnaia revoliutsiia v Komi ASSR,* 212 (for 1960); Ts.S.U. RSFSR, Stat. upr. Mariiskaia ASSR, *Mariiskaia ASSR za 50 let: statisticheskii sbornik* (Ioshkar-Ola: Mariiskoe knizhnoe izdatel'stvo, 1970), 87 (for 1968); Ts.S.U. RSFSR, Stat. upr. Mordovskoi ASSR, *Mordovskaia ASSR za gody Sovetskoi vlasti (v tsifrakh): statisticheskii sbornik* (Saransk, 1967), 138 (for 1960); *Dostizheniia Tatarskoi ASSR k 50-letiiu,* 90 (for 1966); Ts.S.U. RSFSR, Stat. upr. Yakutskoi ASSR, *Yakutiia za 50 let v tsifrakh* (Yakutsk: Statistika, 1967), 109 (for 1966). For the Bashkir ASSR, the numbers of Bashkir and Tatar specialists are combined before the measure is derived.

For three autonomous republics (Dagestan, North Ossetia, and Udmurtia) no data on specialists by nationality have been published. To estimate the number of specialists of the titular nationality of those autonomous republics in 1960, we prorated the number of specialists with higher education among those nationalities working *in the RSFSR as a whole in 1960* according to the proportion of the *urban population* of that nationality living in the RSFSR in 1959 that resided inside the nationality's titular republic. The total number of specialists by nationality in 1960 was taken from *Vysshee obrazovanie,* 70. The number of *Russian* specialists with higher education working in these ASSR's in 1960 was estimated by first taking the total number of specialists working in the ASSR in 1960 (from Ts.S.U. RSFSR, *Narodnoe khoziaistvo RSFSR v 1960 godu: statisticheskii ezhegodnik* (Moscow: Gosstatizdat, 1961), 404–406), subtracting the estimated number of specialists who belonged to the titular nationality, and then multiplying the remainder by the proportion Russian among the part of the urban population of the ASSR in 1959 that was not of the titular nationality.

37. This variable gives similar results to the proportion of Russians in the titular area's population or the proportion of group members in the titular area's population, but the results are somewhat stronger than for the alternative indicators of contact.

38. Brian D. Silver, "Ethnic Intermarriage and Ethnic Consciousness Among Soviet Nationalities," *Soviet Studies,* Vol. 30 (January, 1978), 107–16.

39. Silver, "Social Mobilization," and Brian D. Silver, "Language Policy and the Linguistic Russification of Soviet Nationalities," in Jeremy R. Azrael, ed., *Soviet Nationality Policies and Practices* (New York: Praeger, 1978), 250–306.

40. Anderson, "Some Factors."

41. Silver, "Ethnic Intermarriage and Ethnic Consciousness."

42. Anderson, "Some Factors."

43. Anderson and Silver, "Estimating Russification," explains the estimation of ethnic russification in detail.

44. Tatars and Bashkirs are treated as a single nationality in this and subsequent tables. Thus, for the analysis of linguistic russification there are 34 groups, but 33 separate cases.

45. Again, since the Tatars and Bashkirs are combined into a single case, there are 24 groups in the analysis of ethnic reidentification but 23 cases.

46. The correlations with the natural logarithm of the sex ratio are shown. The natural logarithm is used because the difference between no male deficit and a small male deficit is less important than the difference between a moderate male deficit and a large male deficit. The correlations with the (unlogged) sex ratio were similar but generally weaker.

47. Anderson and Silver, "Changes in Linguistic Identification," and Brian D. Silver, "Language Policy and the Linguistic Russification."

48. This term was the product of the Russian specialists and the inverse of the sex ratio variable. Recall that the sex ratio variable is the natural logarithm of the sex ratio.

49. This is in keeping with standard procedure in multivariate analyses of this kind. See Ronald J. Wonnacott and Thomas H. Wonnacott, *Econometrics* (New York: Wiley), 65–66.

50. Among the Deported groups and among the Dagestani groups, the boundaries are not always stable or clearly defined. See Anderson, "Some Factors," and Ronald Wixman, *Language Aspects of Ethnic Patterns and Processes in the North Caucasus* (Chicago: University of Chicago, Department of Geography, Research Paper No. 191, 1980).

51. It is important to bear in mind that high intergenerational correlations in linguistic russification do not necessarily imply great stability in the actual *levels* of linguistic russification.

52. See Robert Conquest, *The Nation Killers* (London: Macmillan, 1970); and Aleksandr M. Nekrich, *The Punished Peoples* (New York: Norton, 1978).

53. Because the Deported nationalities had not completely returned from exile at the time of the 1959 census, we cannot make reliable estimates of their rates of ethnic russification between 1959 and 1970.

54. V. I. Perevedentsev, *270 Millionov* (Moscow: Finansy i statistika, 1982), 21.

Appendix A
Measurement of Interethnic Marriage

It is not easy to obtain a good measure of the extent of intermarriage by nationality, if by "measure" one means an estimate of the actual number of women of a given nationality within a given age group who marry men from other nationalities. Developing a measure is difficult because the exact target age group of potential husbands for women of a given age is not well defined and varies across nationalities.

During the postwar period, for the Soviet population as a whole, on the average, husbands have been two to three years older than their wives.[54] However, this average age difference varies across nationalities, with higher average age gaps for traditionally Moslem than for traditionally non-Moslem nationalities. Also, when males are in short supply, women tend to marry men from a greater age range than is normally true. Consequently, a precise estimate of the number of women in interethnic unions cannot be obtained readily from a comparison of the number of males and the number of females in a nationality reported as married within the same age range or within any well-defined age range.

Therefore, we do not attempt to develop a *measure* of interethnic marriage but instead use an *indicator* of the relative extent of interethnic marriage among nationalities, a variable that reflects the relative differences in intermarriage across groups.

The intermarriage indicator is developed for women age 30 or older, as well as for women age 40 or older in 1959. We have developed intermarriage indicators by comparing the number of married women a given age or older with the number of men that age or older, even though we know that many men will be married to women younger than the cutoff age. A cumulated measure is less sensitive to the problem of matching of ages of spouses than would be an intermarriage indicator that defined the ages of potential spouses more narrowly.

The intermarriage indicator used for those age 30 and above, for example, is the number of female nationality members age 30 or older married minus the number of male nationality members age 30 or older married in 1959 per 1000 married female nationality members age 30 or older. The indicator registers the tendency of those married female nationality members to be married to men from other nationalities. It is not affected by the sex ratio as such.

People have commonly viewed the sex ratio (male deficit) as affecting the chances of women to marry. If there were only 50 percent as many males eligible for marriage as females among, say, the Chuvash, then if the proportion married of Chuvash women was only half as large as the proportion married of Chuvash men, the *number* of married Chuvash men and of married Chuvash women would be identical. Therefore, the inter-marriage indicator is an indicator of the *net* tendency of female group members to marry exogamously.

Two additional features of the measures should be mentioned. First, the intermarriage indicator does not take into account the proportion of *men* of a given nationality who marry women of another nationality. It therefore does not reflect what proportion of the total number of group members—men as well as women—have spouses of a different nationality than their own. Second, the intermarriage indicator reflects the differences in the proportions of married women who are married to men of another nationality but does not identify the nationality of the men in these interethnic marriages. Many ethnically mixed marriages do not involve Russian men. Therefore, the indicator of interethnic marriage may not completely reflect the relative differences in the extent of intermarriage between non-Russian women and Russian men.

Appendix B
Multiple Regression Equations

Table 11.1B Multiple Regression Equation for War Bride Cohort

	Dependent Variable			
	Inter-married 30 plus	Linguistic Russi-fication 30–39	Linguistic Russi-fication 0–9	Ethnic Russi-fication 0–8
Independent Variables				
Sex Ratio 30–39 p value	−.857 (.000)	−.229 (.000)	−.271 (.003)	
Linguistic Russification 60 plus p value		.877 (.000)		
Non-Moslem p value		−.068 (.028)		
Contact with Russians p value		.065 (.016)	.179 (.008)	
Linguistic Russification 30–39 p value			.715 (.000)	
Sex Ratio–Russian Specialists Interaction p value				.233 (.026)
Linguistic Russification 0–9 p value				.788 (.000)
R^2	.734	.983	.888	.861
F ratio	85.569	397.468	77.015	61.789
p value	(.000)	(.000)	(.000)	(.000)
N of cases	33	33	33	23

Table 11.2B Multiple Regression Equation for War Widow Cohort

	Dependent Variable			
	Inter-married 40 plus	Linguistic Russification 40–49	Linguistic Russification 10–19	Ethnic Russification 9–18
Independent Variables				
Sex Ratio 40–49 p value	−.823 (.000)	−.097 (.001)	−.247 (.010)	
Linguistic Russification 60 plus p value		.943 (.000)		
Contact with Russians p value			.222 (.006)	
Linguistic Russification 40–49 p value			.727 (.000)	
Sex Ratio-Russian Specialists Interaction p value				.536 (.002)
Linguistic Russification 10–19 p value				.394 (.018)
R^2	.677	.982	.848	.675
F ratio	65.104	819.288	53.859	20.783
p value	(.000)	(.000)	(.000)	(.000)
N of cases	33	33	33	23

Beta coefficients and p values are shown, as well as the R^2 value for the overall equation, the F value for the overall equation, and the p value for the overall equation. All coefficients and all overall equations are significant at the .05 level.

12

World War II in Soviet Literature

DEMING BROWN

World War II has been an obsessive theme of Soviet literature for more than four decades. Any Russian work that pretends to deal with the essentials of the twentieth century must somehow cope with it. For example, although the narrative of Pasternak's *Doctor Zhivago* ends with the year 1929, the book is nevertheless equipped with a postscript in which several important characters meet at the front in World War II. A recent excellent novel *Live and Remember* (*Zhivi i Pomni*)[1] by Valentin Rasputin, a man from a much younger generation than that of Pasternak, features a military deserter from that same front. Every year dozens of lesser works of fiction about the war, as well as memoirs and films, continue to be produced for a Soviet audience that never seems to tire of such material.

From the moment when Hitler's armies attacked the USSR until the defeat of the Germans four years later, the efforts of the Soviet writing community were almost completely devoted to the war. Although many writers were exempt from military service as such, and although some older writers were evacuated eastward at the war's gravest stages, nearly a thousand of them joined the armed forces as combatants or military correspondents, and 417 of them were killed.[2]

The writers' full commitment to the war effort, although encouraged by Soviet authorities, was essentially voluntary and spontaneous. In the first months after Hitler's attack, they became journalists, producing reportage, sketches, and pamphlets. Poets read their verses to enthusiastic audiences at the front. Within a year, stories and plays were being written. Konstantin Simonov's novel of Stalingrad, *Days and Nights* (*Dni i Nochi*)[3] began appearing serially in 1943, and other war novels soon followed.[4] A great amount of wartime writing was little more than reportage, and much of it tended to rely purely on sentiment and patriotic fervor for its effects. Under these circumstances, poetry fared somewhat better than prose. Generally speaking, the highest achievement of wartime writing was in the lyrics of such poets as Anna Akhmatova, Margarita Aliger, and Pavel Antokolsky.

A great amount of wartime writing was strongly hortatory, urging Russians to endure and inciting them to smash the enemy. The most effective pamphleteer in this respect, among Soviet army personnel and the civilian population as well, was Ilya Ehrenburg, who observed that "our writers have helped [the people] to see the enemy. Hatred is the moral justification of war. We hate the Germans not only because they kill defenseless people. We hate the Germans because we must kill them."[5] Indeed, many writers concentrated on inciting fellow Russians to take the most violent revenge on the Germans, as did Simonov in a poem entitled "Kill Him!" (*"Ubei Ego!"*), which closes with these lines:

> *So kill at least one of them!*
> *As soon as you can,*
> *Each one you see,*
> *Kill him! Kill him! Kill!*[6]

Wartime censorship required that writers largely avoid mentioning short-comings in the Soviet military effort, as well as elements of defeatism that were known to exist in the early months of the conflict. For example, a chapter of Simonov's *Days and Nights,* depicting some soldiers as indifferent about the cause and suspicious of their leaders, was excised by the authorities.[7] Nevertheless, wartime writing was less programmed and more candid, both in tone and in substance, than that of the immediate prewar years.

As it became less stereotyped, less pompously Party-minded and official, Soviet writing grew more intimate and personal. Focusing on the rank and file—the peasant, the worker, the clerk—as they endured ordeals with courage and dignity, literature emphasized the strengths of simple Russians. The most memorable of these is probably Vasilii Tyorkin, the soldier-protagonist of Alexander Tvardovsky's long poem.[8] Vasia Tyorkin is a genuine folk hero, not larger than life, yet endowed with the most engaging and admirable qualities of his people—ingenuity and staunchness in the presence of danger, good humor, robust wit and love of fun, generosity, and a sense of patriotic duty. Tvardovsky presents Vasia with sympathy and affectionate humor and, without sentimental proclamations about his heroism, manages to suggest that the war was won not by the country's political apparatus and leadership but by the people.

In featuring ordinary Russians, writers expressed pride in the folk for their staunchness and moral toughness and tended to deemphasize the role of the Soviet state. The defense of Russia against the Nazis meant, of course, a defense of human decency in general. But the Nazi policy of exterminating Russian culture also brought about a defiant determination to affirm the Russian national character and to revive and preserve Russian cultural values and traditions. Thus Anna Akhmatova, who had every reason to loathe the Soviet government and indeed did so, could publish the following lines in *Pravda* in March 1942:

It is you, Russian tongue, we must save, and we swear
We will give you unstained to the sons of our sons:
You shall live on our lips, and we promise you—never
A prison shall know you, but you shall be free
Forever.[9]

Wartime literature was also burdened with grief. Pavel Antokolsky's "Son" (1943) is a long poem in memory of his only son, who had been killed in action the year before. It describes the boy, who will remain "forever an eighteen-year-old," tells how and why he died, commemorates the generation that perished in the war, and presents the personal tragedy of a father as a symbol of the tragedy of an entire nation.[10] The most famous wartime work by Margarita Aliger is "Zoya" (1942), a long narrative poem about the schoolgirl, Zoya Kosmodemyanskaya, who became a partisan and was captured, tortured, and hanged by the Germans.[11] But even sadder is Aliger's poem, "Music," a requiem for her husband, a young composer killed at the front in the first months of the war.[12] Perhaps the most accurate reflection of the emotional complexity of Russian wartime experience is Olga Berggolts' "February Diary" (1942), a portrait of Leningrad under blockade—miserable, freezing, and starving, but proud and defiant:

In mire, in gloom, in hunger, in sorrow,
Where death, like a shade, dragged along at our heels,
We were so happy,
Breathed such wild freedom,
That our grandchildren would have envied us.[13]

Years later, in 1956, Julia Neiman suggested the reason for this seemingly inappropriate wartime elation: the war had permitted Russians simply to be themselves. In a poem entitled "1941," Neiman wrote:

Bright as a torch it flamed, that shining year!
Like crumbling plaster, subterfuge flaked off,
And causes were laid bare, effects revealed;
And through the blackout and the camouflage
We saw our comrades' faces—undisguised.
The dubious yardsticks that we measured by—
Forms, questionnaires, long service, rank and age—
Were cast aside and now we measured true:
Our yardsticks in that year were valor, faith.[14]

During the war itself, ideological considerations of literature and indocrination in correct attitudes toward service to the state were subordinated to compassionate, proud depiction of suffering, courage, and endurance. In this sense the war provided a tonic to the literary community, which responded to its modest taste of creative freedom with enthusiasm. Political controls were always present, however, and the Party never ceased to regard literature as its own instrument. As the war progressed and victory became more evident, official manipulation of literature increased. Ehrenburg's vicious anti-German satire, for example, was now curtailed, since it was no longer needed. Likewise, writers were officially discouraged from dwelling on human loss and grief; postwar reconstruction would demand more optimistic literature, composed in a major key.

In the postwar years the Soviet government encouraged the literary community to continue to write about the war. Two of the best war novels— Vera Panova's *The Train*[15] and Victor Nekrasov's *Front-Line Stalingrad*[16]— appeared within a year of its close. *The Train,* a deceptively simple narrative about the routine life of a hospital train, is notable for the absence of heroics, preaching, or obvious propaganda. Alternating between episodes on the train and flashbacks to show the character's prewar, civilian existence, it portrays ordinary people as they love, relate to their families, suffer, and show courage or cowardice. Nekrasov's novel tells, in a calm, everyday first-person manner, of the strengthening of morale that led to the stiffening of resistance against Hitler's forces. The narrative is so free of large generalizations and lofty rhetoric that the novel was criticized for being insufficiently ideological. Nevertheless, it won a Stalin prize in 1947.

Panova and Nekrasov were exceptional, however, for shortly after the war, literature concerning it became, in response to official pressure, intensely political and chauvinistic. The function of war fiction became one of demonstrating the role of the Communist party leadership and ideology in mobilizing for victory, of showing the indispensability of Stalin's leadership, and of proving that the heroic exploits that won the war could only have been accomplished by the especially endowed New Soviet Man. Moreover, it was Soviet patriotism, coming from Communist belief, and not feelings of Russian national identity and love of Russian soil, that provided the will to win against the Germans. A notorious example of the way in which writing about the war was subjected to political discipline is Alexander Fadeyev's novel, *The Young Guard.* Originally issued in 1945, it was found to have neglected the Party's purportedly leading role in organizing underground resistance against the German occupiers. The novel was withdrawn from circulation, Fadeyev rewrote it thoroughly, and the politically sanitized version appeared in 1951.[17]

The writing that began to appear after the Twentieth Party Congress in 1956, however, reasserted, and even expanded upon, the humane quality of literature written during the war. All of this was especially true of writers and poets of the "war generation," those who had been in their teens and early twenties when they served as soldiers and junior officers. Experience at the front had largely shaped their personalities, and they all shared a mixture of bitter memories and nostalgia. By 1956 there had been a number of developments to give their writing its own particular characteristics. Over a decade had passed since the war's end, and the distance enabled them to understand better what they had experienced and witnessed—not only self-sacrifice and bravery but also cowardice and betrayal.

There was increased emphasis on the individual human experience and its significance: the moral problems involved in command decisions; the effects on the human psyche of the fear and sight of death and the loss of comrades; the nature of a sense of duty, of loneliness, of self-reliance, and of bravery. The Party's role was deemphasized in favor of that of the ordinary citizen-soldier as a person relying on himself and his comrades, and not on political leadership. Although some writers continued to paint broad, epic canvases of the war, many others wrote "one-hero" books, examining closely the mentality and psychology of a lone soldier or partisan. Writing became somewhat less heroic than before, often dwelling on the sheer ghastliness of war and its senseless, nightmarish qualities.

The tendency to concentrate on the ugliness of military action and its effects on the individual has led conservative Soviet critics to argue that in certain instances the reader's attention is directed away from the positive goals and heroic nature of the Soviet war effort. Most often cited in this respect is Bulat Okudzhava's *Good Luck, Schoolboy!* (*Bud' Zdorov, Shkoliar*), whose hero is a green recruit of eighteen in his first combat experience— alone, forlorn and afraid, and willing to admit it. (This short novel, which appeared in an obscure almanac in 1961, has never been republished in the Soviet Union.)[18] Okudzhava, together with such gifted writers as Baklanov and Bykov, has been accused of "Remarquism"—painting war in such dismal colors that the work is an implicit argument against the institution of war itself. An attitude of absolute pacifism, which finds no distinction between just and unjust wars, is of course antithetical to official Soviet ideology. Critics have also speculated on the resemblance of these writers to other Western writers of the "lost generation" of World War I. These Soviet writers' emphasis on the blood, filth, violence, cruelty of the battlefield, and the gloom that emanates from their works, does suggest at times the kind of despair expressed by such writers as Remarque and Hemingway. In defending these writers against such ideological accusations, sympathetic critics point out that their fiction does not present the war as something senseless; it is a just war of defense, shown to be motivated by legitimate hatred of the enemy.[19]

Perhaps the most interesting measure of controls over war literature is the changing image of Stalin in its pages. During the war itself, and especially after 1943, when Soviet forces went on the offensive, literature emphasized his role in Russian military successes. In the Khrushchev years, however, through the novels of Simonov,[20] Grigorii Baklanov,[21] Vasilii Bykov,[22] and others, a different wartime Stalin emerged—a bungler whose military unpreparedness and mass purges of army officers had paved the way for the initial, rapid German advances deep into Russia. His failure to heed advice, his cruelty, rigidity, suspicion, and his penchant for ostentatious military successes were shown to have crippled the war effort by causing needless sacrifices of human life and resources. But in the late 1960s and 1970s a positive Stalin reappeared. Bondarev's *Hot Snow* (*Gorjachii Sneg*),[23] a novel of the Battle of Stalingrad, shows him as a wise and decisive leader, and a chauvinistic novel by Ivan Stadnyuk, entitled *War* (*Voina*),[24] portrays him in reverential colors.

In view of the obvious importance of ideological controls and ideological controversies over Soviet literature about the war, one should at least speculate about the influence of the Communist Party on such literature. Clearly a large proportion of those who wrote prominently about the war were Party members. From a list of 36 such writers, I have been able to identify 23 as members: 7 of these had joined the party before World War II, 14 joined during the war, and 2 joined after its close. (From a larger list of 114 writers—which includes many who did not feature the war in their writing—I have been able to identify 41 as party members. Of these, 11 had joined before the war, 21 joined during the war, and 9 joined after its close.) As these figures illustrate, the large-scale recruitment into the party during the war[25] included a large proportion of those individuals who were then, or subsequently became, professional writers.[26]

A general comparison of war literature written by Party members, with literature on the same topic by non-Party writers, discloses, in my opinion, no difference. The same degree of patriotism is present in the works of either group. Attitudes toward Stalin and his role in the war seem to have no relationship to an author's Party affiliation. Most importantly, among the Party members themselves there is obviously a broad spectrum of attitudes toward the war. Thus, both Simonov, the severe critic of Stalin's wartime behavior, and Stadnyuk, whose works laud Stalin's role, were Party members. Bondarev, who stresses his Russian soldiers' consciousness of duty to the fatherland, was a Party member, but so also was Okudzhava, whose soldiers seem preoccupied with other concerns. Party discipline no doubt affected attitudes and themes in the war writing of Party members at various times in a loose and general way. The fundamental fact, however, is that literature about war by both Party and non-Party writers was subject to the same overall controls. Both groups wrote as members of the same community.

Many stories and novels written by the war generation employ a time span that enables them to embrace both the war and the ensuing period up to the death of Stalin (or thereabouts). Such works usually draw a contrast between front-line morality, where individual honesty, loyalty, and cooperation among comrades are indispensable, and where the single purpose of destroying a monolithic enemy brings about a pragmatic knowledge of right and wrong, and a complex and corrupt peacetime scene, where falsity and moral compromise are a prominent feature of life. Bondarev's *Silence* (*Tishina*)[27] is one such novel. Similar in this respect is Nekrasov's *Home Town* (*V Rodnom Gorode*),[28] whose hero faces the psychological and moral problems of learning how to live as a civilian, of overcoming the tremendous hold that front-line values and associations have over him, and of enduring his disillusionment in a postwar world that still contains much evil.

Often literary works that are ostensibly about the war examine ethical problems that transcend the war and are in fact timeless. The works of Bykov, Baklanov, Nekrasov, and Bondarev are frequently concerned with moral explorations and questions of ends and means of the kind that are not likely to be confronted directly in Soviet literature about contemporary society. The war is thus a device for raising issues that might be considered taboo in other contexts. In Solzhenitsyn's story "An Incident at Krechetovka Station,"[29] for example, Lieutenant Zotov, a young Soviet officer, turns in to the authorities a man who *may* be a spy for the Germans. Whether the man is guilty or not, he is virtually certain to be disposed of as one. In performing a military duty, Zotov may have destroyed an innocent man; the thought will torment him for life.

Nearly all of the works I have mentioned were published in the Soviet Union[30] and thus give a censored representation of the war. A contrast to these is the novel of Vasily Grossman, *Life and Fate* (*Zhizn' i sud'ba*), published abroad in 1980.[31] A prominent writer of fiction and wartime correspondent, Grossman achieved great popular success with one of his first war novels, *The People are Immortal* (*Narod bessmerten*)[32] in 1942, and with the first volume of a large, panoramic novel of the war, *For the Just Cause* (*Za pravoe delo*)[33] in 1952. *Life and Fate,* the intended second volume of this novel, was completed in 1960. The manuscript was seized by the KGB in 1961.

It is plain to see why *Life and Fate* could not be published in the USSR. Centering on the Battle of Stalingrad, it portrays not only the stubborn heroism of Soviet troops and officers but also the efforts of political commissars to extract political gain from the battlefield operations at the expense of military efficiency and through waste of human lives. The novel often digresses from the military front to depict civilian life, to show the lingering effects of the terror of 1937–1938 on wartime morale, and to argue that the patriotic fervor of Russians in defense of their motherland was closely linked to feelings of Great Russian chauvinism and a concomitant scorn of the non-Russian Soviet populace. Anti-Semitism, within both the governmental hierarchy and the population at large, is prominently displayed. In addition, the novel depicts not only Hitler's death camps and gas chambers but also Stalin's wartime concentration camps. There is a clear suggestion that in some respects the situations of Jews under Hitler and Stalin were similar. Moreover, the novel argues that much of the Soviet governmental repression which is associated with the postwar years had actually begun during the war itself.

In a brief presentation such as this one, there is not room to consider every important aspect of the impact of World War II on Soviet literature. I have not mentioned, for example, other treatments of the holocaust, much of which took place on Soviet soil. I have only lightly touched upon the theme of postwar reconstruction and rehabilitation, which was extremely prominent in the immediate postwar years. Nor have I considered the concern of Soviet writers about the era of nuclear armament which World War II inaugurated. The official Soviet isolationism and anti-Western campaign that came as a kind of perverse reaction against the wartime coalition had a profound impact on Soviet culture that has not been discussed here. The war also produced a large number of less tangible results which are very important but difficult to measure. Among these are lingering feelings of pride that come from the knowledge that the Russians were victors in a war of national defense against an external aggressor, and the complex, no doubt contradictory, mixture of attitudes resulting from the Soviet Union's new status as one of the two superpowers and master of Eastern Europe. Writers, of course, are acutely aware of these matters, but, under the conditions of Soviet censorship, they express their awareness in literature so subtly and unsystematically that it is difficult to define. Finally, one must say that, because literature in the Soviet Union nearly always represents a direct reaction to public events, the impact of World War II on that literature was total. It is impossible to imagine what Soviet literature would have been like had that war not taken place.[34]

Notes

1. Valentin Rasputin, *Live and Remember* (New York: Macmillan Publishing Company, 1978). Prose works that have been translated will be cited in the English language edition only.

2. *Kratkaia literaturnaia entsiklopediia,* 1972, 7:111.

3. Konstantin Simonov, *Days and Nights* (New York: Simon and Schuster, 1945).

4. Even before this time, Stalin had personally promoted the creation of literature to propagandize his views of how to conduct the war. Accounts of the use of Alexander Korneichuk's play, *The Front,* which was published in *Pravda* (August 24–27, 1942) for this purpose, can be found in Alexander Werth, *Russia at War: 1941–1945* (London: Barrie and Rockliff, 1964), pp. 423–26 and Vera S. Dunham, *In Stalin's Time: Middleclass Values in Soviet Fiction* (Cambridge, Cambridge University Press, 1976), 5–7.

5. Quoted in Joshua Kunitz, *Russian Literature since the Revolution* (New York: Boni and Gaer, 1948), 783.

6. Constantine Mikhailovich Simonov, "Kill Him," Vladimir Markov and Merrill Sparks, eds., *Modern Russian Poetry* (Indianapolis, Ind.: The Bobbs-Merrill Company, 1967), 761.

7. L. Lazarev, "Eto stalo istoriei," *Novy Mir,* 1967, no. 6: 243.

8. Aleksandr Tvardovskii, "Vasili Terkin," *Stikhotvoreniia. Poemy* (Moskva: Khoduzhestvennaia Literatura, 1971), 309–465.

9. Anna Akhmatova, "Muzhestvo," *Beg vremeni* (Moskva-Leningrad: Sovetskii Pisatel', 1965), 340.

10. Pavel Antokol'skii, "Syn," *Antologiia russkoi sovetskoi poezii: 1917–1957* (Moskva: Gosizdat, 1957), 1:427.

11. Margarita Aliger, "Zoia," *Stikhotvoreniia i poemy v dvukh tomakh* (Moskva: Khudozhestvennaia Literatura, 1970), 1:148–93.

12. Aliger, "Muzyka," Ibid., 140–143.

13. Ol'ga Berggol'ts, "Fevral'skii dnevnik," *Vernost'* (Leningrad: Sovetskii Pisatel', 1970), 78.

14. Juliia Neiman, "1941," *Literaturnaia Moskva, 1956. Sbornik vtoroi* (Moskva: Gosizdat, 1956), 296. Translated by Walter N. Vickery in Patricia Blake and Max Hayward, eds., *Dissonant Voices in Soviet Literature* (New York: Pantheon Books, 1962), 156.

15. Vera Panova, *The Train* (New York: A. A. Knopf, 1949).

16. Victor Nekrasov, *Front-Line Stalingrad* (London: Harvill Press, 1962).

17. *Kratkaia literaturnaia entsiklopediia,* (1972), 7:878.

18. Bulat Okudzhava, "Bud' zdorov, shkoliar," *Tarusskie Stranitsy* (Kaluga: Kaluzhskoe Knizhnoe Izdatel'stvo, 1961), 50–75.

19. L. Lazarev, "Pamiat'," *Voprosy Literatury,* 1965, 5:75.

20. Konstantin Simonov, *The Living and the Dead* (Garden City, New York: Doubleday and Company, 1962); *Soldatami ne rozhdaiutsia* (Moskva: Sovetskii Pisatel', 1964).

21. Grigorii Baklanov, *Tri povesti* (Moskva: Gosizdat, 1963); *Iul' 41 Goda* (Moskva: Sovetskii Pisatel', 1965).

22. Vasily Bykov, *The Third Flare* (Moscow: Foreign Languages Publishing House, no date); Vasil Bykov, *Alpine Ballad* (Moscow: Progress Publishers, 1966); Vasily Bykov, *The Ordeal* (New York: E. P. Dutton and Co., 1972); Vasil' Bykov, *Voennye povesti* (Moskva: Voenizdat, 1966); Vasil' Bykov, *Frontovye stranitsy* (Minsk: Belarus', 1966).

23. Jurii Bondarev, *Goriachii sneg* (Moskva: Voennoe Izdatel'stvo Ministerstav Oborony SSSR, 1974).

24. Ivan Stadniuk, *Voina,* (Moskva: Sovremennik, 1977); 1 and 2. (Moskva: Voennoe Izdatel'stvo Ministerstva Oborny SSSR, 1980), vol. 3.

25. See T. H. Rigby, *Communist Party Membership in the USSR: 1917–1967* (Princeton: Princeton University Press, 1968), 271–72 and the essay by Cynthia Kaplan in chapter 9 of this book.

26. These figures are based on a perusal of biographical entries in *Kratkaia literaturnaia entsiklopediia,* 8 vols., Moskva, 1962–1975. They do not pretend to be exhaustive. Nor can they be absolutely accurate: biographical entries in the encyclopedia indicate only the status of the individual vis-à-vis the party *at the time when the entry was printed.*

27. Yuri Bondaryev, *Silence* (Boston: Houghton Mifflin Company, 1966).

28. Viktor Nekrasov, "V rodnom gorode," *Izbrannye proizvedeniia* (Moskva: Gosizdat, 1962), 248–470.

29. Alexander Solzhenitsyn, "An Incident at Krechetovka Station," *Stories and Prose Poems* (New York: Farrar, Straus, and Giroux), 167–240.

30. The exception is Pasternak's *Doctor Zhivago.*

31. Vasilii Grossman, *Zhizn' i sud'ba* (Lausanne, Suisse, 1980).

32. Vasilii Grossman, "Narod bessmerten," *Povesti. Rasskazy. Ocherki* (Moskva: Voenizdat, 1958), 104–251.

33. Vasilii Grossman, *Za pravoe delo* (Moskva: Voenizdat, 1955).

34. A portion of the material in the present article originally appeared in Deming Brown, *Soviet Russian Literature Since Stalin* (Cambridge: Cambridge University Press, 1978).

13

Debates About the Postwar World

JERRY F. HOUGH

May and June 1943 were tense months for Joseph Stalin. The great battle of Kursk was approaching, and, with real nervousness, Stalin had accepted the advice of his top generals to wait for a German attack and then to counterattack. The General Staff had warned that the attack would come in the May 10–12 period, then in the May 19–26 period, but nothing had happened.[1] (The attack finally came on July 5 and was decisively repelled in the second half of the month.) At the same time Roosevelt and Churchill held a meeting on May 10 to which neither Stalin nor any of his representatives was invited. Stalin is reported to have been very suspicious; then on June 4 he was informed that there would be no second front in Europe in 1943. As a sign of his extreme irritation, he recalled his pro-Western ambassadors, Ivan Maisky and Maxim Litvinov, from London and Washington, respectively.[2]

With the Soviet victory in Kursk, Stalin's mood noticeably lightened. He was confident enough to begin celebrating victories with artillery salutes accompanied by firework bursts, and his thoughts clearly began turning to the nature of the postwar world.[3] On August 21 the Central Committee and Council of People's Commissars issued a decision on economic reconstruction; its receiving four pages in *Pravda* was more significant than its contents.[4] On September 4 a commission on the armistice was created with Klement Voroshilov as chairman, one on peace agreements under Litvinov, and another under Maisky on reparations.[5] By the end of 1943 Stalin was consulting his ministers about postwar currency reform and the trade network that should be established with the end of rationing.[6]

Within five years, much had changed. The Grand Alliance had given way to intense cold war, and the East European countries were being subjected to full Communization on the Soviet model. The tightest control had been clamped on intellectual life and particularly on any direct or indirect contact with Western intellectual life. The trend toward greater privatization in agriculture had ended, and the kolkhozy for the first time in a decade were put under the leadership of outsiders who were selected for their ability to impose discipline.[7] The primacy of heavy industry had been reaffirmed.

Yet, this process was a relatively slow one. Hints of the new developments can be found, especially in retrospect, from 1943 onward, but in many respects the situation still had elements of ambiguity for several years after the war. One American specialist on the Soviet Union has recently described the period 1945–1947 as one of détente, in comparison with the entente of World War II and the Cold War of 1948–1953.[8] Another believes that the death of Zhdanov in 1948 (or really his defeat several months before his death) was necessary to usher in full repression at home.[9]

Westerners have had many explanations for the rather gradual and sometimes ambivalent movement toward cold war and the reinstitution of rigid controls. The interpretation that came to be dominant in the United States in the 1950s was that Stalin was in control, that he knew the direction in which he wanted to move, but that he did so slowly in order to minimize potential opposition at home and abroad. In recent years, a number of American historians have implied that Stalin was genuinely undecided or at least committed to an intermediate position, and that American policy pushed him toward a policy of cold war. An earlier view was that Stalin hoped for a continuation of the Grand Alliance, but that he faced serious opposition from within the Politburo, perhaps from Malenkov and Beria,[10] perhaps from Tito and Zhdanov,[11] perhaps from unspecified hard-liners.[12]

We probably will never be certain about Stalin's pattern of thinking. The memoirs that Viacheslav Molotov, Stalin's closest confidant in these years, is said to have written may be illuminating. Georgii Malenkov and Lazar Kaganovich, key figures in these days, are apparently still alive and may have written something, and there may even be a hidden manuscript by the late Anastas Mikoyan, who wrote excellent memoirs on the 1920s. Nevertheless, Stalin was an extremely devious man, and it is far from clear that he revealed his true thoughts to anyone.

To an extent that is often not appreciated, however, the ambivalence in public posture in the early years gave middle-level officials and scholars the possibility of advancing different views about the contemporary situation and about the policy that should be followed in the postwar period. These debates are fascinating to follow, both because they indicate our need to avoid a simplistic view of the Soviet political process, even in Stalin's totalitarian system, and because they illuminate the complexity of the issues that Stalin was facing.

The Two Programs

It is not difficult to document that many people in the Soviet Union hoped for, spoke out for, and even expected a very different postwar world than actually emerged. Many of the sharpest ideological themes had been muted during the war. (Even in his first speech after the German attack, Stalin had included the old Russian greeting "Brothers and Sisters" in his opening salutation, rather than "Comrades" alone.)[13] The United States and Great Britain were described as peaceloving rather than imperialist, and contacts with foreigners were somewhat relaxed. The fact that the country held together in the face of the military disasters in the summers of 1941 and 1942 indicated a high level of support for the regime and suggested a possibility of lower levels of repression. The fact that the industrialization program of the 1930s had created enough of an economic base to defeat Hitler suggested that resources could now be diverted from heavy industry to consumer-related reconstruction.

Many thought that these developments presaged a permanent change in the postwar period. The writer Ilya Ehrenburg has testified not only to his feelings, but to those of others, as well:

> I firmly believed that after victory everything would suddenly change. . . . When I recall conversations at the front and at the rear, when I re-read letters, it is clear that everybody expected that once victory had been won, people would know real happiness. We realized, of course, that the country had been devastated, impoverished, that we would have to work hard, and we did not have fantasies about mountains of gold. But we believed that victory would bring justice, that human dignity would triumph.[14]

It was one thing to hope that the postwar period would be better. It was another to define what the postwar period should be. Those who had benefitted from some policy adopted in the 1930s were naturally loathe to abandon it. Those who wanted a postwar world that was different from that of the prewar tried to find ways to advocate or legitimate it—or to argue against the hard-line trends that were emerging.

Both in the 1940s and at the present time, the most severe censorship is imposed on the presentation of a comprehensive and integrated program. Lawyers then and now can argue about the legal code; specialists on the West could and can use various techniques to suggest a foreign policy posture; economists can talk about the economy, and philosophers can advance different interpretations of Marxism-Leninism in a policy-relevant manner. What is difficult is for someone to combine these arguments. What is difficult is to argue, for example, that a particular economic reform is needed and that this in turn requires a change in the relationship to Western governments, to Western ideas, or to Communist deviation in Western and Eastern Europe.

In the mid-1940s, probably the clearest expression of two major comprehensive policies (probably *the* two major competing programs) appears in a pair of two-part articles published almost simultaneously in *Pravda* in April 1945. One was written by Andrei Vyshinsky, the first deputy commissar of foreign affairs, and the other by Petr Pospelov, the chief editor of *Pravda.*

For an American accustomed to thinking of Vyshinsky as the prosecutor in the show trials of the 1930s, as the agent for the imposition of Communist rule in Rumania in February 1945, and as the man who condemned the United States in the vilest terms in the United Nations in the postwar period, it will come as a surprise that it was Vyshinsky who appealed for a major moderation in policy.[15] It was Pospelov, the man to be chosen in 1955 to examine the materials on Stalin's crimes,[16] who presented the hard-line position.

Vyshinsky's article was entitled "Lenin—the Great Organizer of the Soviet State,"[17] and in it he repeatedly emphasized the stability of the Soviet state and system, the degree of popular support for it.

> In the decisive days of the second world war, the Soviet state rose to the occasion, again and again confirming the invincibility of the Soviet system, its vitality and its great creative capabilities. The Soviet system . . . showed a level of stability and unshakeability that is explainable only by the fact that the powerful roots of its historical being have sunk deep into the soil of the Soviet land. . . . Now when the war is coming to an end, when all the tests of the first months and years are far in the past . . . it is not difficult to be convinced by the real strength of the Soviet state.

The point of such statements—and they were repeated throughout the article—seemed to be that political change was possible in the postwar period. Vyshinsky insisted on the need for one-party rule (but only briefly), and he acknowledged that the state, including "the organs of repression," would not wither away in the transition from socialism to communism so long as there was capitalist encirclement. Nevertheless, he did repeatedly mention the transition from socialism to communism as a possibility, and any reader knew that communism was to be less repressive than socialism. He emphasized "the Stalinist teaching . . . about the inevitability of changes in the primary functions of the proletariat state, depending on changing historical conditions," and he asserted that "in the process of growth and development of the socialist state, its forms, its methods of activity, and its functions change."

Indeed, in complaining about "the underevaluation of the Soviet state and its role," Vyshinsky seemed to imply that it could have a bigger role vis-à-vis the party, and, as shall be discussed, this implication seemed confirmed when Pospelov's answering article put enormous emphasis on the party. Vyshinsky seemed to make the same point in emphasizing the "abundance of remarkable people" in the Soviet Union and the importance of initiative, innovation, and "the use of the many forms of people's creativity in the interests of socialism."

There were two specific areas in which Vyshinsky emphasized the need for a responsive policy. First, he called the question of the peasantry "one of the most important of any revolution, particularly the proletarian revolution." He called the union with the peasants the basis of Soviet power. He quoted Lenin on the danger of exploiting the middle peasantry and the need "to take into account the peculiar conditions of life of the peasantry, to learn from the peasants the methods of transition to the best system, and *not to dare to command them (ne smet' komandovat').*"[18] Vyshinsky emphasized the importance of doing "everything possible to help the peasants to live better" and cited a Lenin statement that "the middle peasantry will be on our side in the Communist society only when we secure the best economic conditions for its life."

Second, Vyshinsky gave great attention to the nationality question. He strongly damned nationalism and chauvinism, the latter word in the Soviet Union always referring to Great Russian nationalism. He demanded full equality for all nationalities and quoted Stalin on the need to maintain contact with the masses in the outlying districts (*okraina*). Specifically, he insisted that "all Soviet organs in the outlying districts—the courts, the administrative system, the economic organs, etc.—be staffed as much as possible out of local people."

Although Vyshinsky implied that the stability of the system permitted rule with a lighter hand, he suggested even more strongly that stability rested on popular support.

Comrade Stalin said that soviet power 'is not power which is isolated from the people. On the contrary, it is a unique kind of power which came out of the Russian masses and is near and dear for them.' . . . Comrade Stalin indicated that this explains the great, unprecedented force and resiliency which Soviet power usually manifests in the critical minutes of its life. It is necessary to evaluate this peculiarity of Soviet power exceptionally highly, since it is precisely in this indisputable quality of it that the key to explaining its force and vitality lies.

Vyshinsky was the number two official in the foreign ministry, but he did not discuss foreign policy directly. However, his assertions about the need for one-party rule, for moderation in the policy toward the peasants, and for the reliance upon local personnel in the outlying districts almost surely embodied his program for Eastern Europe as well as the Soviet Union. He quoted a Lenin statement about the transition to socialism that "the concrete conditions and forms of this transition inevitably are and should be different depending on the conditions under which the movement directed at the creation of socialism begins," and this surely meant that the Soviet model should not be imposed on Eastern Europe exactly.

Vyshinsky said much less that seemed relevant to relations with the West, but one sentence in his discussion of the formation of the Soviet federation had a very contemporary ring: "Comrade Stalin warned against the danger of an attack on us from the outside, against the danger of economic isolation for our federation, and also against the danger of an organized diplomatic boycott." In the context of the rest of his program, Vyshinsky certainly seemed to be saying that a moderate policy in Eastern Europe was necessary to avoid these foreign policy dangers as well.

The opposing program was presented by Petr Pospelov in two articles in *Pravda,* the first of which ran in the issue that carried Vyshinsky's second article.[19] If Vyshinsky wrote about the state, then Pospelov wrote about the Party, and his Party was not one that made compromises or concessions. It was a "heroic party," which was characterized by its "ideological implacability its organized nature, and its iron discipline." It was a party of "advanced ideas," which "became a great mobilizing and organizing force in the struggle against the forces of society which are becoming obsolete." The words *mobilize, organize,* and *transforming* occurred again and again.

Like Vyshinsky, Pospelov wrote at length about the strength of worker and peasant support for the regime during the war. For him, however, the source of this support was not the ties of the Party to the masses, but its ability to inspire them. The Party won its authority with the aforementioned ideological implacability; it gained support in the Civil War by its struggle against "foreign invaders" and "the bourgeois-landlord counterrevolution"; it inspired "millions" with "Stalin's theory of the possibility of victory of socialism in one country."

Although Vyshinsky had referred to new forms of rule, to greater initiative for the masses, and apparently even for a relaxation of the collective farm system, Pospelov left no doubt about his attitudes toward such ideas. He again and again attacked "socialist-democratic parties of the West" that "sunk into the bog of opportunism" and represented "Marxism in words" alone. Pospelov's article did not use any words such as *medium peasantry* but talked about the "collective farm peasantry" and its "fervent patriotism." He did mention the equality of the peoples of the Soviet Union, but he alluded to the "drawing together" (*sblizhenie*) of peoples rather than the danger of chauvinism. He emphasized "the noble Soviet patriotism, in which the national traditions of people are connected in a harmonious manner with the general vital interests of all the toilers of the Soviet Union."

Vyshinsky had spoken of socialist competition in a context that suggested reliance on voluntary cooperation in the economy and perhaps even greater use of market mechanisms, but Pospelov dragged in a quotation from Stalin about socialist competition with a very different thrust: "It would be foolish to think that our working class, which made three revolutions, will go for labor enthusiasm and a shock work movement in order to manure the soil for capitalism. . . . Take away from it confidence in the possibility of building socialism and you destroy any basis for competition."

Pospelov's emphasis was upon "the paramount advantages of a planned, socialist system of economy." "No other state would have been able in such a short period of time to reconstruct the whole economy on a military basis, achieve a 'great resettlement' of factories to the East from regions temporarily occupied by the enemy, and quickly provide its army with such a quantity of excellent-quality armaments, which were necessary to the decisive victories over Hitler's Germany." Similarly, in talking about the past, Pospelov asserted that there was "no other path of quick economic restoration of the country besides the power of the Soviets and socialist transformation," and it was clear that he was also talking about the future.

Pospelov too said little about foreign policy directly, but the thrust of his argument was obviously that Eastern Europe should follow the Soviet model. His rather ugly attacks on socialist democratic parties certainly suggested that there was no third path between classical Soviet socialism and classical capitalism nor any more moderate path to socialism, a position, as shall be seen, contrary to that being advanced by men such as Eugen Varga.

The sharp criticism of the socialist democratic parties may also have been a way of suggesting that there were no moderate forces in the West who might reduce governmental hostility to the Soviet Union. At a minimum, Pospelov's fervent support for Stalin's theory of socialism in one country conveyed precisely the opposite message of Vyshinsky's warning about economic isolation or diplomatic boycott. He ended his article with a Stalin statement about Soviet war aims that left little doubt about his own priorities: "The enslaved peoples who fell under the yoke of the German aggressors look upon us as their liberators. A great liberating mission fell to our lot. Be worthy of this mission. The war which you are fighting is a liberation war, a just war." Pospelov's last sentence ended with the prediction that "the ideas of Lenin and Stalin . . . show the path . . . to the happiness and friendship of the liberated peoples." He surely was talking about liberation from capitalism as well as the Germans.

Intellectual Freedom

The packages of views represented by the Vyshinsky and Pospelov articles were, in a sense, the most normal "liberal" and "conservative" ones. However, a number of the issues in the packages were, in fact, divisible from each other, and sometimes they were combined in different ways. The controversies about the role of Andrei Zhdanov reflect, I suspect, this divisibility. He seems to have been a relative moderate on questions of intellectual freedom, but a hard-liner on questions of communization of Europe and the diversity of roads to socialism.[20] Nikita Khrushchev seems to have favored increased payments to the peasants but to have opposed any movement toward privatization in agriculture, even toward small work links.[21] One of the leading ideologists, Petr Fedoseev, combined strong support for a maintenance of good relations with the United States (this will be discussed later) and a denunciation of chauvinism with an equally strong support for a centralized planning system ("private property divides society," he said).[22] In addition, of course, politics is seldom a matter of black-and-white views, but a spectrum of confused and imprecise ideas, with many people inclined to think that "the truth lies somewhere in between."

Of the specific issues that were involved in the competing programs for the postwar period, the one that was dearest to the hearts of the Soviet intelligentsia was the degree of individual freedom to be permitted after the war. If the interpretation of the origin of the Cold War presented by George Kennan and Adam Ulam (that Stalin feared good relations with the West lest they undercut the rationale for terror and open the Soviet Union to dangerous ideas)[23] is correct, then this question was also the crucial one for Stalin.

The argument that the postwar period should feature greater freedom and toleration could be made in a variety of simple or complex ways. A few of the more daring intellectuals even tried to advocate a relaxation of terror in a fairly direct manner. The head of the Institute of Law (and a subordinate of Stalin's in the People's Commissariat of Nationalities in the 1920s) wrote a rather favorable assessment of Franklin Roosevelt, especially praising him for making an advance in the definition of freedom, including, naturally, "freedom from fear."[24] In a famous case, a leading historian described the reasons for the abolition of the *oprichina,* Ivan the Terrible's equivalent to the secret police, in terms that all leading intellectuals knew were supposed to have contemporary meaning:

> When the tsar despaired of the dedication of the most prominent *oprichina* leaders to him and understood that the parallel existence of two courts—the old state and the *oprichina*—served no purpose, then their further existence became an unproductive expenditure of funds. Two events ended the tsar's doubts on this question: on August 16th he received news of the brilliant victory of the Zemstvo commanders over the khan, Devlet, and then the news of the death of his chief enemy, the Polish king, Zygmunt.[25]

In literature, an Alexander Tvardovsky could also be extremely direct: "Many of us, believing in the organizational principle, want to try 'to organize a miracle' in the realm of art. In my opinion, this is a hopeless attack. The chief thing is not to plan any obligatory outlook for us, but . . . to create an atmosphere favorable for the manufacture of miracles."[26] At other times the point could be made more indirectly. The film-maker Sergei Eisenstadt utilized Stalin's well-known admiration for Ivan the Terrible to make a movie about that tsar that showed the *oprichniki* as a "gang of degenerates, like the American Ku-Klux-Klan," to quote a later Central Committee criticism of it.[27] A long discussion about the validity of the views of a prerevolutionary scholar, Alexander Veselovsky, on literary influences and literary criticism had both direct and indirect implications about literary freedom.[28]

In the legal realm, the criminologists continued a discussion of legal code that had begun in the late 1930s and had been interrupted by the war. A number of proposals were made, including the renunciation of the principle of analogy, which would provide the citizen with greater legal protection.[29] The head of the theory of state and law department of the Central Committee's Academy of Social Sciences, Mikhail Strogovich, wrote a textbook on criminal procedure that went so far as to assert that Russia had adopted (and, no doubt, should continue to adopt) the most progressive experience of the West.[30]

In history and philosophy, a scholar could easily advocate freer criticism and self-criticism, but those specific words were as much a tool of the witch-hunters as the liberals. Nevertheless, in the early postwar years, some progressive scholars were very forthright in expressing this view, even in sessions called to denounce orthodox views. At one such session held in June 1947, M. D. Kammari asserted, "Comrade Stalin teaches us that it is wrong either to improve history or to make it worse, either to embellish it or blacken it. It is necessary to describe it as it is, with all its contradictions, with its progressive and reactionary sides and the struggle between them."[31] At the same time, M. M. Rozental' declared, "[Philosophical] science cannot be cowardly. Its task is not to repeat truth, but to develop it in accordance with new conditions. . . . One factor which retards our work . . . [is] a fear of discussion."[32]

The subtle way to speak out for freer expression of unorthodox ideas was to suggest the legitimacy of moderate ideas in the past, either because radical figures of the past had been tolerant of them or because radical views had evolved from more moderate ideas. This technique had already been used in the 1920s and was the immediate cause for Stalin's suppression of the historians in 1931. The debate that angered Stalin most was one about the nature of the German Social Democrats before World War I and Lenin's relationship to them.[33] In one article in particular, A. G. Slutsky argued that Lenin had often had a mixed view of German Social Democratic leaders such as Bebel and Kautsky until they spoke out against the creation of the Bolsheviks in 1912. In Slutsky's words, "Lenin believed that arguments among the so-called 'left' were not of primary importance since he in essence considered that the disputing sides both came out of Marxism."[34] Slutsky also quoted Luxemburg and Bebel on the value of bourgeois democracy because it increased the freedom of revolutionaries to work against the capitalist system.[35]

Stalin undoubtedly saw this line of argument as an attack on his refusal to cooperate with the German Social Democrats against Hitler (and was right in so seeing it), and in 1931 he severely condemned Slutsky as a "slanderer" and a "falsifier" who was accusing Lenin of "centrism" and "opportunism."[36] In 1934, however, when Stalin was moving toward a Popular Front policy himself, he co-authored a directive about history textbooks that partially reversed his 1931 letter. The directive criticized historians who neglected "the role and influence of Western European bourgeois-revolutionary and proletarian-socialist movements in Russia" and who forgot that "the Russian revolutionaries considered themselves pupils and successors of the well-known figures of bourgeois-revolutionary and Marxist thought in the West."[37]

In the postwar period those who tried to promote a more tolerant attitude toward unorthodox ideas continued to emphasize the themes that Stalin had raised in 1934. The head of the Propaganda Administration of the Central Committee wrote, or at least signed, a history of Western European philosophy that, although critical, treated the Western philosophical tradition with respect and described Marxism as emerging out of it.[38] Indeed, a critic charged that "Comrade Aleksandrov finds only the positive, only the progressive aspects in each philosophical tendency and in each individual question developed by this or that philosopher."[39]

Stalin's 1931 letter made it difficult to discuss Lenin's cooperation with more moderate figures, but the same point could be made in discussions of the nineteenth-century revolutionary movement. Chernyshevsky and Dobroliubov, the most radical of the pre-Marxist revolutionaries, received the highest praise, but if a scholar emphasized that they sometimes cooperated with less radical figures, that implied the legitimacy of such cooperation in general. Similarly, a scholar could write about these revolutionaries in a way that emphasized their attacks on the xenophobic nationalism of the conservative Slavophils.[40]

Obviously these views in favor of greater intellectual freedom and greater tolerance of unorthodox ideas were not the only ones to appear in the press. For every Tvardovsky who warned against attempts "to organize a miracle," there were others who asserted that "the coming generation wants to be real fighters for the fatherland [and] seeks a book which would show it the path,"[41] who "warned writers against spiritual, ideological, and literary demobilization, given the contemporary international situation."[42] Although everyone in the 1947 discussion of the Aleksandrov book had to criticize it (Stalin had already done so), there were those who *deeply* meant it: "Marxist philosophy by its very essence is revolutionary and critical. . . . In the book of Comrade Aleksandrov, we do not feel this spirit of militant Bolshevik dedication in science; the book "does not adhere to Lenin's principle of partyness in philosophy [and is] a distortion of the whole history of philosophy"; the book does not use "the language of a Marxist. . . . The decisive peculiarity of the philosophy of Marxism-Leninism is that it is a revolutionary weapon."[43]

Just as there were subtle ways to advocate toleration of alien ideas, so the same techniques could be used to advocate the opposite. With the reaffirmation of the Western roots of Marxism-Leninism suggesting a more open attitude to Western ideas, so the denial of these roots had a very different implication.[44] One could emphasize that Leninism came primarily out of the Russian revolutionary movement, that men such as Chernyshevsky developed the materialistic base of Leninism more than men such as Feuerbach. And, of course, if assertions that Chernyshevsky cooperated with moderates meant that cooperation with nonradicals was possible in the contemporary world, then an emphasis on Chernyshevsky's "principled" rebuff of the moderates had the opposite meaning.

It should not be assumed that disagreement with the ideas of men such as Aleksandrov necessarily implied a determination to suppress them. To a considerable extent, even the hard-liners in the Moscow intellectual community were reluctant to take this step. When Stalin demanded that the Institute of Philosophy hold a meeting to discuss Aleksandrov's book in early 1947, the session was not critical enough, and a second one was convened, with provincial scholars invited. The latter were generally less restrained. Even a man such a Mitin was accused of being too protective of those with the "wrong" ideas.[45]

Nevertheless, an insistence on "partyness" and on "Marxism-Leninism as a revolutionary weapon," at a minimum, gave an excuse for others to repress. In 1947, the most radical of the philosophers, Vonifatii Kedrov, could still be appointed chief editor of the new philosophy journal,[46] and, as will be discussed shortly, Eugen Varga could still express his ideas on the peaceful roads to socialism. At the end of 1947 and increasingly in 1948, however, the situation became increasingly grim for those with unorthodox ideas.

The Economy

Another subject that provoked intense debate at the end of the war was the economy. Or, rather, one should say that the economy provided the framework for a wide variety of conflicts. Each region pushed for higher priority in the funding of postwar reconstruction and economic development,[47] and a broader debate raged on the priority to give the reconstruction of European Russia in comparison with the continued expansion of the more eastern regions;[48] each ministry pushed for more money for the sphere of activity that it supervised;[49] ministries fought over bureaucratic turf (for example, officials of the Ministry of Trade and the Consumers' Coops became involved in a dispute over whether the latter should develop commission stores in the cities);[50] crackpots (or innovators, depending upon one's point of view) followed Lysenko's example in fighting for ideas that had significant investment consequences.[51] A question such as whether the Ukraine should plant winter or spring wheat and what system of crop rotation it should use involved not only agronomists but even Politburo members.[52]

The severe competition for funds among regions and among ministries obviously created headaches for the planners, but the major difficulties centered on the broader priority questions. Those who wanted an emphasis on consumption and social justice often wrote of agriculture. Vyshinsky's fervent appeal for a better life for the peasants has already been noted, and this theme was expressed in a number of articles published in these years. The light industry and trade administrators, and also the Ministry of Finances, were pushing the production of consumer goods.[53] The position that proved to be the winning one emphasized the need to maintain the priority of heavy industry.

Because of these regional and bureaucratic disputes, the various economic issues could not coalesce into neat packages. For example, as will be discussed shortly, the trade officials naturally seemed to be part of the group pushing for more resources for the consumer sector, but they had little interest in the expansion of private trade. When the minister of trade of the time later wrote that only a centralized trade network could have saved the country in the famine of 1946,[54] it is extremely likely that he was taking a position that he also made at the time. Similarly, the Ministry of Agriculture had every reason to appeal for more funds for agriculture, but also for the preservation of the collective farm system.

Sufficient work has not been done on the major economic debates to permit them to be described confidently and fully, and this is a subject on which fruitful work is clearly possible. During the early part of the war, Gosplan was "the working apparatus" of Nikolai Voznesenskii, the chief economic decision maker of the time, and it was completely absorbed in month-to-month planning and even day-to-day checking on production output.[55] Only in mid-1943 did it begin to prepare a long-range plan for the first time and to face the questions that it raised.[56] Clearly major problems emerged, for little has been reported, and a draft prepared in August 1944 must have been rejected.[57]

The most interesting—and to a considerable extent the most unclear— position focused on the dangers of inflation. Russia and Germany had both had runaway inflation after World War I, and the problem of excess purchasing power was clearly going to be a serious one after the war, especially when rationing was abolished.[58] One way to soak up excess purchasing power was to increase the production of consumer goods, and this solution was pushed not only by the light industry administrators and trade officials, but also by the Ministry of Finances, which was most directly concerned with the monetary problem.[59]

A second obvious solution to a problem of excess purchasing power is to raise prices, and this question was fought out on the issue of so-called commercial stores, in which goods could be purchased without a rationing card, but at prices well above those in the normal stores. (Certain types of shoes and woolen cloth were, for example, sold at 12 and 14½ times the normal price.)[60] The establishment of commercial stores was discussed at a conference in January 1944, and the first twenty food stores were opened in April. By the beginning of 1946 there were commercial food stores in 130 cities and commercial industrial goods stores in forty. In 1946 they provided 24 percent of the total trade turnover by money indicators, although of course, not by volume of physical goods.[61]

These stores aroused controversy from the beginning. The Minister of Finance, A. Zverev, proposed opening them in all cities immediately, whereas the food and light industry ministers thought that it was necessary to go more slowly.[62] The central issue came to a head in 1946: As rationing was to be abolished and a single price level was to be established in all stores, should it be essentially at a market equilibrium level (that is, very high, as in the commission stores) or at the subsidized rates of the state stores? On 16 September it was decided to set prices at an intermediate level, but this, of course, meant that those fighting for market prices had lost.[63] In 1949, a leading construction minister returned to the fray with an analogous proposal to build cooperative housing at high prices, but his idea was apparently rejected in a summary fashion.[64]

The question of prices and inflation means that the postwar economic debates may have been much more complex than is sometimes assumed in the Western literature. The participants in the discussions about the law of cost and about the nature of money that were a prominent feature of the literature beginning in 1943[65] must have included people who were suggesting that the market have a bigger role in determining prices. Some were, no doubt, pushing for a widening of the private network as well as state commercial stores. In agriculture, the system of small link work teams, which had become very widespread during the war,[66] received continued strong support (including that of the Central Committee secretary for agriculture, Andrei Andreev). Some of these supporters must have had in mind a de facto return to family farming within a formal collective farm framework. Nevertheless, until the history of these economic debates is written, caution is advised. An appeal for more rational prices could simply refer to the need for some change in the prices set by the planning organs for the state enterprises and have nothing to do with any thoroughgoing decentralization on the basis of market mechanisms.

Thus, the position of the top Soviet planner, Nikolai Voznesenskii, may well have been misunderstood in the Western literature. In 1930 at the Sixteenth Party congress, Stalin had said that income always grows faster than production under socialism.[67] Voznesenskii was the first Soviet economist who directly expressed his disagreement with this in print. In his major book, *The War Economy of the USSR in the Period of the Fatherland War,* he warned against the dangers of inflation if income were greater and asserted that "the price of a commodity in the socialist society of the USSR is based on its cost or the expenses of production."[68] He insisted that there were economic laws of socialism, specifically "laws of production and distribution," that must be taken into account, and he said that the plan must use the "law of cost" which is "the most elementary of these laws."[69]

As a result, there has been some tendency to see Voznesenskii as the leader of the progressive forces against unspecified conservatives, as a man who was trying to introduce "capitalist devices" and was probably killed in a 1950 purge because of these views.[70] It is, in fact, highly unlikely that Voznesenskii favored decentralization or market mechanisms. In the literature he comes across as a man of "unusually strong will," who repeatedly pushed for long-range planning and who was attracted to grandiose plans demanding central direction, such as the redirection of rivers from the Arctic to the south.[71] Indeed, despite his calls for more scientific planning, the criticisms of him and Gosplan in this period are for "voluntarism."[72] In the debates about governmental intervention in the economy in the West (to be discussed in the next section), Voznesenskii himself took a very conservative position, essentially ridiculing the idea that this had anything to do with planning.[73]

Although Voznesenskii was clearly concerned with the problems of inflation and of price rationalization (including the subsidized prices in heavy industry), it is possible that the really controversial aspect of his position related to agriculture. The leading Soviet historian on price formation was later to estimate that requisition prices in the 1930s were set at only 10 to 15 percent of the costs of production. Of course, this estimate depended on the price assigned peasant labor, but the historian was surely right in his general point: "Recognition of the action of the law of cost . . . would have required the conclusion that requisition prices should be raised. . . . For the readers of this work [of Voznesenskii's] the question arose at once about the need to change requisition prices." The historian was also right that "in conditions of a sharp deviation of requisition prices for agriculture from their cost and an excessively low level of prices on heavy industry products," Voznesenskii's words "were a fairly daring statement."[74]

This is not the place for an elaborate discussion of Politburo alignments. Rather the analysis of Voznesenskii has merely been a tentative effort to remind the reader of the likely complexity of the economic debates of the time and the need for caution in our conclusions. The struggle for price reforms and the commercial stores was not always a struggle for the market and the consumer. In many cases, the supporters of the former were simply seeking to rationalize and strengthen central planning. In many cases, they were trying to end shortages and excessive purchasing power by setting high prices, rather than by a mass increase in the production of goods for the consumer.

For this reason, the economic debates were also debates on social policy. Khrushchev, as Stalin correctly chided him,[75] really was a *narodnik* (populist) who was pushing for a change in income distribution in favor of the peasant, but opposing the private sector. Many of those favoring rationalization and price increases were, in practice, supporting the interests of the managerial and professional urban population against those of lower income, who in immediate terms at least were favored by a policy of subsidization of consumer prices. These debates, no doubt, were also related to those on whether to emphasize class origins in admission to college and the Party see Fitzpatrick (chapter 8) and Kaplan (chapter 9), but such speculation goes well beyond the level of our present knowledge.

Eastern Europe and Different Roads to Socialism

The question of economic policy inside the Soviet Union was also closely related to policy in Eastern Europe. If the Soviet Union were going to change its economic system, then that change would have an impact on what to impose on Eastern Europe. More important in terms of real political choices, if Eastern Europe were to be permitted a significant degree of autonomy and variation in its development, this latitude would legitimate pressure for change inside the Soviet Union. If Eastern Europe were to follow the objective "laws of socialism" as manifested in the Soviet experience, then it would be hard to argue that the Soviet Union should or could deviate from these laws itself.

By all indications, a wide variety of options was considered for Eastern Europe. One may have been incorporation of these countries into the Soviet Union. The Soviet money issued in 1937 depicted a state seal with eleven ears on the sheaves: one to represent each of the union republics. By the beginning of the war, the number of republics had increased to sixteen, but despite frequent suggestions, Stalin refused to change the money until 1948. During the war, Molotov "said that there is no sense in doing so, for only after the war will it be finally clear how many union republics there will be."[76] Since Molotov could scarcely admit in public that republics might be lost, an increase in their number through the incorporation of Eastern European countries must have been a live option.

By contrast, some of the leading figures in the foreign policy establishment were pushing very hard for a moderate policy in Eastern Europe. Although it is still impossible to be absolutely certain, one seemed to be the Finnish communist Otto Kuusinen. Writing under the pseudonym N. Baltiisky, he was speaking optimistically about the British trade unions as late as November 1946,[77] but in an article in June 1945 he seemed to be making an even more radical point within the framework of a defense of the patriotism of foreign communists:

> In all history there has not been a single patriotic movement which had as its goal the encroachment on the equality and freedom of other nations. All important patriotic movements of the XVIII and XIX centuries were directed at liberating their own countries from alien dependence or at repelling an alien attack—for example, the North American war for independence of 1775 and 1783, the revolutionary wars of the French people from 1792 to 1794, the national-liberation struggle of the Greeks (1821–29), the Poles (1830, 1846, 1863), and a series of other peoples.
>
> It is understandable that the readiness to struggle for the freedom of one's own nation is one thing, but the readiness to struggle for the suppression of another nation is something completely different. The first is patriotism. The second is not. For example, dominion over colonies, the preservation of privileges which allows the metropolis to oppress and exploit colonial nations can in no way honestly be motivated by patriotic considerations.
>
> . . . The most important Russian democratic publicists of the last century felt this particulary sharply and they strongly emphasized this important side of patriotic ideology.[78]

The assertions about the unpatriotic nature of the dominance of others were supposedly directed at European colonial powers and at the criticism of foreign communists who supported the liberation of the colonies of their countries. Nevertheless, the remarkable reference to the national-liberation struggle of the Poles in 1830, 1846, and 1863 against Russian dominance must have rung an enormous bell with an audience accustomed to Aesopian discourse on sensitive subjects. A foreign audience would not find the reference to the Russian publicists very meaningful, but a Russian would, no doubt, know that the two whom Kuusinen quoted (Belinsky and Dob-roliubov) had opposed the tsarist repression of the Polish rebellions.

The question of one-party domination of most of the Eastern European countries may have been decided fairly early, but the character of those regimes, especially in the short term, remained controversial. The new regimes were called "people's democracies" to suggest that they were not identical with the Soviet Union, but the content of that phrase was the subject of intense dispute.[79] In countries such as Hungary, an intense political struggle raged over questions such as collectivization. Those who wanted the Eastern European countries to follow the Soviet model found it easy to talk about the universal character of the laws of socialism and the glories of the Soviet model as Pospelov had done. Their opponents could, like Vyshinsky, refer to historical peculiarities.

The most important debate about Eastern Europe was that which emerged around the work of Eugen Varga, the director of the Institute of the World Economy and World Politics and a regular consultant to Stalin for two decades. In late 1946 he published a major book, *Changes in the Economics of Capitalism as a Result of World War II,* which summarized his views, but the book was soon subjected to devastating criticism. Although he was never arrested, his institute was abolished. He was forced to recant, and he virtually ceased to be published for the rest of Stalin's life.[80]

Some Westerners have believed that Varga was punished for excessive optimism about the economic future of capitalism—for predicting a long-term postponement of a new depression—but this perception is not accurate. Although Varga suggested that capitalism would not experience a full-scale depression for ten years, this prediction assumed that Europe was so devastated that it would require a decade to reach prewar levels of production. (In actuality, it was to take only three to five years.) That is, Varga was predicting a major depression after about the same interval as between 1917 and 1929, but without the real boom of the 1920s.[81] He explicitly compared the coming postwar cycle to that of 1929–1937 (which included the abortive boom of 1933–1937), rather than to that of 1921–1929, and as a critic correctly pointed out, "comrade Varga indicates by this that there will be a repeat of a depression of a special kind."[82] In addition, Varga predicted an interim moderate depression in the United States in two or three years. This scenario might be and sometimes was, criticized, but it scarcely was an unforgivable heresy. When Varga was forced to write an abject ten-page recantation in 1949, he did not even mention this question,[83] and a year earlier he had had to acknowledge that the interim American depression had not occurred as soon as he had predicted.[84]

The heart of Varga's "error" actually lay in his analysis of the Western political systems. Adopting a phrase first used by Lenin, "state-monopoly catpialism," Varga argued that the state had become an increasingly important actor in Western economic life. It had a "decisive role" in the wartime economy and even afterward did not return to prewar levels.[85] Moreover, Varga asserted that "the question of "planning" . . . will again become urgent in two or three years when the regular crisis of overproduction occurs."[86]

The real problem with Varga's analysis came in his treatment of the determinants of government action. In the orthodox view, the state was completely subordinate to the "monopolies" and to them alone.[87] By contrast, Varga asserted that the Western government, although ultimately controlled by "the financial oligarchy,"[88] sometimes defended the interests of the capitalist class as a whole, instead of the immediate, narrow interests of the monopolistic bosses. Since the basic interest of the capitalist class as a whole was preservation of the capitalist system, and since this goal sometimes required policies (for instance, price control in wartime) that were against the immediate profit interests of the "monopolies," governmental policy could not reflect the latter.

In practice, Varga treated the government and societal political forces as having a considerable independence in immediate terms. For example, he explained the end of price control in the United States by strictly political factors: the death of President Roosevelt and the election of a Republican Congress in 1946.[89] In response to criticism, he expressed scorn at the idea that "now in 1947 the working class and the Labor Party has no influence on the policy of England, that the financial oligarchy makes all the policy."[90] He asserted that the worker "lays claim to a much more significant role in making decisions on all political questions and will fight for the achievement of this role.[91]

More important, Varga was suggesting that the influence of the masses on the bourgeois state could become so great that it could serve as a vehicle for the transformation of capitalism and the peaceful transition to socialism. To say that the bourgeois state was subordinate to the monopolies alone meant that it could not be used to achieve any worker goals, let alone evolution to solution. It implied that there was no medium ground between a full bourgeois and a full socialist system. Varga, however, treated the Eastern European countries as being part of the capitalist world but as having "economies of a new type," as being "democracies of a new type."[92] This, to repeat, was in September 1946. In March 1947, in an article entitled "Democracies of New Type," he acknowledged that the Eastern European countries were "not capitalist states in the usual sense of the word" but still asserted that they were "something completely new in the history of mankind."[93] As a critic noted, this still implied that their path of development, being completely new, would not be identical to Soviet socialism.[94]

This analysis of Eastern Europe further implied that capitalism in Western Europe could take on radically different, and much more progressive, forms than it had in the past. Indeed, in his March 1947 article, Varga specifically asserted that "bourgeois nationalization . . . means progress in the direction of democracy of a new type."[95] In the concluding predictions in his book, Varga had made much the same point in more general terms: "The chief focus of the political struggle between the two basic classes of capitalist society, the bourgeoisie and the proletariat, will be the question of the greater or lesser participation in the administration of the state."[96]

This view of the bourgeois state was perilously close to the argument of the so-called revisionists of the turn of the century whom Lenin had so vehemently repudiated, identical to it, in the view of many of Varga's critics. His discussion of Eastern Europe was surely an Aesopian way of suggesting that the communization of that region not be carried through to its conclusion, perhaps in order to strengthen the "democratic forces" in Western foreign policy, perhaps to make a gradual transformation of Western Europe more likely because less threatening, perhaps to save his native Hungary from the worst aspects of Stalinism.

Even after the March 1947 conference that severely criticized his book, Varga stubbornly held to his views for some time. In October 1947, after the "two camp" doctrine was enunciated at the time of the formation of the Cominform, he expressed his opinion with even greater sharpness:

> Bourgeois Europe . . . itself has now recognized that the capitalist social order needs basic reform, that it is impossible to get by without such measures as nationalization of the important branches of production, state control over the economy, "planning" of the economy. . . .
>
> Today thirty years after the victory of the Great October Revolution, *the struggle in Europe is becoming in its historical development more and more a struggle for the tempos and forms of transition from capitalism to socialism.* Although the Russian way, the Soviet system, is undoubtedly the best and the fastest method for transition from capitalism to socialism, historical development, as Lenin had predicted, shows that other ways are also available for the achievement of this goal.[97]

This persistence, this "non-party relationship to criticism," this petition of "a clearly revisionist thesis," as Konstantin Ostroviianov, the director of the Institute of Economics and a relative moderate, expressed it,[98] was the last straw. A number of other scholars of his institute had been publishing somewhat similar views,[99] and at the end of 1947 the entire institute was abolished.

Foreign Policy

The debate on foreign policy in general was, of course, closely associated with that on Eastern Europe and roads to socialism. As shall be discussed, the same arguments about the bourgeois state that had implications about the possibility of a peaceful evolution to socialism also had implications about the driving forces of Western foreign policy and the threat that the West posed. More basically, however, the central question in the debates on Soviet relations with the West was whether moderation in Soviet policy in Eastern Europe would produce sufficient benefits.

For this reason, the debates on relations with the West had a number of aspects. To some extent, of course, the issue could be the depth of the moral obligation that the Soviet Union had to fulfill a "liberating" role in

Eastern Europe, as Pospelov had emphasized. The natural counter to this argument was that a heavy hand in Eastern Europe would frighten the West and undercut a strong trend toward an evolution to socialism in Western Europe. Thus, it is at least a possibility that Varga was exaggerating his optimism about such evolution to support his foreign policy argument.

A second aspect to the foreign policy debate centered on economic questions. Clearly the Soviet Union had a major need for aid and trade in its economic reconstruction, and the question was whether it could receive it from the West at acceptable political cost. It was easy enough to say that the Soviet economy needed reconstruction, and some linked this question to foreign policy; Vyshinsky's indirect warning against economic boycott has already been mentioned. In 1944, an article in *Bol'shevik* linked cooperation with the West with the battle to prevent runaway inflation. The author supported Soviet entry into the International Monetary Fund, as well as efforts to achieve stability of foreign currencies and normal foreign trade after the war. "The USSR is interested in such postwar collaboration, for this collaboration will permit us to accelerate and facilitate the process of the reconstruction of our economy."[100]

Pospelov's previously cited fervent support for socialism in one country represented not only a proud assertion that the Soviet Union could go alone, but surely also the demand that it not accept any foreign restrictions. Mikhail Iovchuk, a Central Committee official who was the most vigorous supporter of a Russocentric view (many years later an acquaintance called him a "Black Hundreder"), took the same position by praising Russia for deciding "not to dogmatically borrow the achievements of Western European civilization, not to assimilate them 'in the manner of India,' but to create a more advanced social structure which better answered the interests of the masses than Western European civilization." Iovchuk asserted that Chernyshevsky "had spoken out against attempts of aliens (*chuzhezemtsy*) to turn Russia completely into a colony of some European state,"[101] and one suspects that the "aliens" he currently had in mind were Jews such as Varga.

The major aspect of the debate on foreign policy centered on the question of whether cooperation with the West was possible on acceptable grounds. In private and even several times in print, the former foreign minister, Maxim Litvinov, now in the shadows, proposed a more limited security policy that might permit a more durable relationship with the West:

The crux of the matter was not the desirability of an empire (that was now taken for granted) but rather the ways and means of its possible integration into an international order compatible with the Western notions. To Litvinov, Anglo-American support of any settlement his government would wish to enforce in east central Europe was indispensable for Russia's true security. Keenly aware of the depth of Western sympathy for his country's security needs, he was also convinced that such support could be obtained if only the limits of those needs were stated sensibly and clearly enough."[102]

As Litvinov himself told Americans from 1943 on, the tendency toward isolation, suspicion, and parochialism within the Soviet leadership was very strong.[103] To a considerable extent, it was a suspicion of Western ideas and their possible impact upon Soviet society. It was a suspicion that a collaborative relationship with the West would permit the infusion of Western ideas and a weakening of the dictatorship and of national unity (that is, separatist movements in the republics). Hence the debates about Western ideas that have already been discussed were, to a great extent, also debates about foreign policy.

The question of the Western threat also had a purely military–foreign policy side to it as well. The debate about the nature of the bourgeois state that was analyzed in the previous section clearly referred to the Western threat in addition to the possiblity of a peaceful transition to socialism. Those who were emphasizing the subordination of the state to the monopolies scarcely had a benign view of the "monopolies." Rather such theorists accepted Lenin's theory of imperialism, in particular, his theory that economic factors drove the capitalist countries to war with each other.

During 1945 the conservatives were increasingly open in suggesting that World War II was not the result of an attack by the "fascists" against the "peace-loving" nations (the wartime line), but of the capitalist system itself. In May, for example, a major-general, B. Antropov, launched a severe attack on Clausewitz's dictum that "war is state policy continued by other means" (a dictum that Lenin had repeated).

> According to Clausewitz, policy is built on the desires and opinions of the sovereign. . . . [These propositions] are a clear expression of an idealistic interpretation of the concepts of the state and politics. . . . Lenin emphasized that politics and economics are indistinguishable from each other, that politics is the concentrated economics. The roots of politics must be sought, he emphasized, in the economic position of the classes which head the state.[104]

The fervent support of Lenin's analysis of the economic roots of foreign policy was obviously meant to remind the readers of the rest of the analysis, and "the sovereign" whose desires and opinions did not cause World War II was, of course, Hitler.

Others tried to present a more nuanced picture. The answer to Antropov, published in a long-delayed "August" issue of *Bol'shevik,* which was signed to press on October 9, was written by the new chief editor of *Bol'shevik,* Petr Fedoseev. Fedoseev criticized those who thought that "international relations develops completely independent of classes," but he pointedly quoted Lenin (Clausewitz was not mentioned) to the effect that war is a continuation of policy by other means. However, Fedoseev distinguished between World War I and World War II: In World War I, the war was a continuation of the capitalists' policy of plundering colonies, but in World War II, the issue of colonies was not involved, and Germany was seeking world domination.[105]

Fedoseev began his article with a strong attack on fascist ideologists who prepared the world for World War II by "proposing the theory that war is an eternal and unavoidable phenomenon." He ended the article with the contention that "Leninism does not consider war inevitable, even in present conditions. War can be averted if the peace-loving nations act in concord." He wrote as if he thought that this was possible. His assertion that the "bourgeois use of dictatorship and war led Germany into a blind alley" suggested that the bourgeoisie of other countries would not follow the same path; his assertion that "the goals pursued in the war determine the policy of these states after the war" seemed reassuring about American aims; his praise of Soviet foreign policy for being "flexible, far-seeing, and effective" was, if not a prediction, at least intended as advice.[106]

Yet another technique used to deemphasize the Western threat was to assert that there were divisions ("contradictions") among them that the Soviet Union could exploit. Varga himself often wrote about American-British rivalry,[107] but this theme was stressed even more by his associate, I. Lemin. Every other nation is "a potential ally or a potential enemy," Lemin wrote, and he reassured his audience that "England by no means intends to surrender without a battle" in its struggle with the United States.[108]

Another way to try to suggest a less threatening West and, simultaneously, to undercut the logic of Lenin's analysis in *Imperialism* was to present the image of the bourgeois state that has already been discussed in the last section. Varga himself was arguing that Lenin's analysis of the inevitability of war between capitalist countries had become outmoded by the rise of the United States and the Soviet Union to super power status after World War II,[109] but he was also making the same point when he argued that a multiplicity of forces determined the actions of the Western state. Indeed, in his book, which was signed to press in late September 1946, after the start of the Zhdanovschina, he explicitly stated that "the democratic forces in all countries" were so strong a potential impact on governmental policy that "the relationship of the capitalist countries to the Soviet Union will not be the same as it was in the prewar period."[110]

Of course, these points in turn were subject to attack. The previously discussed assertions that the Western governments were completely subordinated to the monopolies had nearly as pessimistic an implication for foreign policy as for peaceful evolution of the West to socialism. When the new governments such as India were described as tools of the monopolistic bourgeoisie and the landlords, as they were by those dubious of collaboration,[111] this characterization had the same implications. In addition, those who wanted to say that the Soviet Union could not take advantage of "capitalist contradictions" spoke of class solidarity among the bourgeoisie and the domination of the United States over what came to be known as the imperialist "camp," a camp that included countries such as India that called themselves neutral.

The argument about a Western threat could be a two-edged sword. If the West was really a major military threat in the short run, then Soviet expansionism was as dangerous as collaboration with the West was impossible. As a consequence, it is possible to read some warnings about the danger of war as a call for Soviet caution in Eastern Europe. It was possible to read a warning by Georgii Malenkov that "it is wrong to underevaluate one's own forces" or one can "fall into panic and intimidate one's self" as a call for an aggressive foreign policy,[112] but such interpretations are highly doubtful.

Surely Stalin did worry about the possible reaction of the West to events in East Europe, and the gradual nature of the Soviet takeover may well have reflected this caution. Nevertheless, it is most unclear that this was reflected in the public debate. Those who were talking about a Western threat were saying that it was inherent to capitalism, and such an argument gave little support for a Soviet policy of self-denial in Eastern Europe. The clear-cut hard-liner on the Politburo, Lazar Kaganovich, who warned of continuing capitalist encirclement, found it natural to warn against "complacency and self-satisfaction," to call for "increased Bol'shevik vigilance," and to call upon the regime "to consolidate our victory," the latter almost surely a reference to Eastern Europe.[113] The Malenkov-type assertion, especially when coupled with an attack on those who base their analysis on ideological citations, was almost surely meant to be a justification for détente, rather than the opposite.

Conclusion

For the average American, it has probably been quite interesting to read that the Soviet press, even under Stalin, contained a far wider range of views of key policy questions than is usually assumed, but the major question remains, do the debates mean that the course of history in the second half of the 1940s might have been radically different than it was? Might Eastern Europe have been only "Finlandized" rather than have the Soviet model imposed on it? Might the Cold War have been avoided?

The first answer to these questions is that we really cannot be certain. The second is that the answer is probably far more complex than is usually assumed. Most of the discussion of the Cold War has been very vague in defining the term *cold war*. Any informed speculation about how the postwar period might or might not have evolved differently must rest on a precise definition of different options at different times. It must focus not just on American and Soviet foreign policy acts, but also on other events such as the unexpected famine of 1946.[114]

Certainly any thought about an Eastern Europe that was as independent as Finland was to be should not focus primarily on possible mistakes by President Truman in the spring and summer of 1945. When medals were awarded to scholars of the Academy of Sciences on the 220th anniversary of the Academy in June 1945, Eugen Varga was not included among the top 131 medal winners as his status almost dictated, but in the next group of 375.[115] Even at that early date his position in the debates was not fully respectable.

The Litvinov warnings from 1943 testify to the depths of Stalin's suspicions. The disinclination of the Polish government in exile in London to be "Finlandized" and the broken Western promises about a Second Front in 1942 and 1943 were certain to raise the gravest doubts in a person such as Stalin. Roosevelt's selection of Harry Truman as his vice presidential candidate in 1944 was even worse. When Germany had invaded the Soviet Union in June 1941, Truman had told *The New York Times* that "if we see that Germany is winning, we ought to help Russia, and if Russia is winning we ought to help Germany and that way let them kill as many as possible."[116] It may be that a Stalin would have found something to suspect, regardless of what the West did.

It is more problematical whether communist rule in Eastern Europe could have had a less severe character and whether some of the harshness of Soviet-American relations, including the Korean War, could have been avoided. There is not the slightest evidence to challenge the conventional view of the 1950s and 1960s about "Stalin's unrestricted autocratic command of Soviet foreign policy in these years,"[117] not the slightest evidence that critics of the emerging policy were thinking of the possibility of defeating and removing Stalin. However, since Stalin sharply curtailed the debates in 1948–1949 as the policy line was firmly established, it is possible that his previous willingness to have different lines presented meant that he had not fully made up his mind.

If I read it correctly (which I may well not have), Zhdanov's position was that the United States could impose its system in Western Europe and the Soviet Union could impose its in Eastern Europe, but that an effort should be made to maintain reasonable Soviet-American relations.[118] On the day after the beginning of the conference to denounce Varga's book in 1947, Stalin had a month-old interview with Harold Stassen published in *Pravda*.[119] In the interview he repeatedly emphasized the possibility of Soviet-American cooperation (*sotrudnichestvo*), not just coexistence. Since he stated that "if both sides begin to abuse each other with names such as monopolists or totalitarians, then there will not turn out to be cooperation," and since Varga was being denounced for not calling the United States a monopolist-dominated regime, Stalin may have been subtly writing off the possibility of cooperation. However, he may well have been willing to exchange trade for a correct Soviet-American relationship if the West were willing.

Yet, if Zhdanov and Stalin had such hopes, they were being naive. Quiet Western acceptance of the communization of East Europe, particularly of Poland, whose invasion had led to the declaration of war against Germany in 1939, was an action that democratically elected governments of the United States and Great Britain were scarcely going to be able to take. By the same token, it is difficult to imagine a democratic United States in this time being able to prepare for decisive military action to moderate Soviet behavior in Eastern Europe, a policy that probably had a better chance of success than an attempt at reassurance.[120]

In 1945–1946, the United States and the Soviet Union were each new to the role of super power, and they had had no time to adjust to nuclear weapons. President Truman was quite inexperienced, and Stalin was a man with a most awful side to his personality. Today, forty years after the end of World War II, military equality has been achieved, nuclear weapons have become old-hat, and Soviet ideology has mellowed. The same Soviet debates that raged in 1944–1946 continue today, with the same interconnections among foreign policy, relationship to Western ideas, and economic policy. Yet, after forty years the Soviet Union and the United States still have not found a way to conduct their rivalry in a measured way, and those Americans who talk most about promoting human rights and liberty in the Soviet Union and Eastern Europe follow a foreign policy that undercuts—one might almost say, destroys—those fighting for liberalization within the Soviet Union. Instead of criticizing our inexperienced predecessors, it would be more fruitful for us to survey the subsequent experience and reflect more about the difficult tasks of today.

Notes

1. S. M. Shtemenko, *General'nyi shtab v gody voiny, Kniga pervaia* (Moscow: Voenizdat, 1981), 210–40, esp. 224–28.

2. I. M. Maisky, *Vospominaniia Sovetskogo diplomata, 1925–45 gg.* (Moscow: Nauka, 1971), 676–77.

3. See the discussion in Shtemenko, *General'nyi shtab v gody voiny,* 446–49. The salutes also had a significance for others. Ilya Ehrenburg recalls that "from that day in August when the stars of the first salvo rocketed into the Moscow sky, I began to look about me carefully and to reflect about the kind of world it would be after victory." Ilya Ehrenburg, *The War 1941–45* (London: MacGibbon & Kee, 1964), 119.

4. *Pravda,* 22 August 1943, 1–4.

5. Maisky, *Vospominaniia Sovetskogo diplomata,* 699. V. Kardashov, *Voroshilov* (Moscow: Molodaia gvardiia, 1976), 331. *Istoriia Kommunisticheskoi partii Sovetskogo Soiuza* (Moscow: Politizdat, 1970), vol. 5, book 1, 549, 674.

6. A. G. Zverev, *Zapiski ministra* (Moscow: Politizdat, 1973), 231, and D. V. Pavlov, *Stoikost'* (Moscow: Politizdat, 1979), 194–95.

7. For the new kolkhoz chairmen, see Jerry F. Hough, "The Changing Nature of the Kolkhoz Chairman," in James R. Millar, ed., *The Soviet Rural Community* (Urbana, IL: University of Illinois Press, 1971), 103–120.

8. William Taubman, *Stalin's American Policy: From Entente to Détente to Cold War* (New York: W. W. Norton & Company, 1982), 5–6.

9. Werner G. Hahn, *Postwar Soviet Politics: The Fall of Zhdanov and the Defeat of Moderation 1946–1953* (Ithaca, NY: Cornell University Press, 1982), 9–13.

10. George F. Kennan, "Excerpts from a Draft Letter Written at Some Time During the First Months of 1945," *Slavic Review,* XXVII, 3 (September, 1968), 481–984.

11. Franz Borkenau, *European Communism* (New York: Harper, 1953).

12. See, for example, Edward R. Stettinius, Jr., *Roosevelt and the Russians: The Yalta Conference* (Garden City, NY: Doubleday, 1949), 309–11. This view is generally supported in William O. McCagg, Jr., *Stalin Embattled, 1943–1948* (Detroit: Wayne State University Press, 1978), esp. 94–95, 143–46, and 258–59.

13. The speech is found in I. V. Stalin, *Sochineniia*, edited by Robert McNeal (Stanford: The Hoover Institution on War, Revolution, and Peace, 1967) vol II, 1.

14. Ehrenburg, *The War 1941–45,* 124.

15. Robert Sharlet has recently noted, however, that behind the scenes Vyshinsky seemed to be a leading force for the regularization of the legal system.

16. Roy A. Medvedev and Zhores A. Medvedev, *Khrushchev: The Years in Power* (New York: Columbia University Press, 1976), 67–68.

17. *Pravda,* 21 April 1945, 3, and 22 April 1945, 4. The quotations from Vyshinsky that follow are from these two issues.

18. This phrase was only one of two in dark print in Vyshinsky's two-piece article, and it was also in dark print in the original Lenin text.

19. *Pravda,* 22 April 1945, 3, and 23 April 1945, 3.

20. Werner Hahn notes the difference between Zhdanov's position on culture and science compared with economics, but does not draw the conclusion that the economics debate was really a foreign policy one. *Postwar Soviet Politics,* 88.

21. Stalin, *Stalin Embattled,* 359–60, note 23.

22. P. Fedoseev, "Marksizm-leninizm ob istokakh i kharaktere voin," *Bol'shevik,* no. 16 (August 1945):39, 41–43.

23. X, "The Sources of Soviet Conduct," *Foreign Affairs* 25, no. 4 (July 1947):510. Kennan said that the Soviet stress on an outside menace is founded "in the necessity of explaining away the maintenance of dictatorial authority at home." A similar interpretation is found in Adam Ulam, *Expansion and Coexistence* (New York: Frederick A. Praeger, Publishers, 1968), 400–03.

24. I. P. Trainin, "O demokratii," *Sovetskoe gosudarstvo i pravo,* no. 1 (1946):19.

25. S. Veselovsky, "Uchrezhdenie Oprichnogo dvora v 1565 g. i otmena ego v 1572 g.," *Voprosy istorii,* no. 1 (1946):99.

26. *Literaturnaia gazeta,* 22 May 1945, 1.

27. *Bol'shevik,* no. 16 (August 1946):52. For a discussion of the general question, see Leo Yaresh, "Ivan the Terrible and the *Oprichnina*," in Cyril Black, ed., *Rewriting Russian History: Soviet Interpretations of Russia's Past,* (New York: Frederick A. Praeger, Publishers, 1956), 216–32.

28. Robert M. Hankin, "Postwar Soviet Ideology and Literary Scholarship," in Ernest J. Simmons, ed., *Through the Glass of Soviet Literature* (New York: Columbia University Press, 1953), 266–79.

29. Peter H. Solomon, Jr., *Soviet Criminologists and Criminal Policy: Specialists in Policy-Making* (New York: Columbia University Press, 1978), 21–22 and 26–27. The discussion is scattered through the issues of the journal *Sotsialisticheskaia zakonnost'* of 1946 and 1947.

30. M. S. Strogovich, *Ugolovnyi protsess* (Moscow: Iuridicheskoe izdatel'stvo, 1946). For a selection of the most controversial statements in this book, see *Sovetskoe gosudarstvo i pravo,* no. 6, (1948):73–86, and no. 4 (1949):43–44.

31. *Voprosy filosofii,* no. 1 (1947):16.

32. *Ibid.,* 90.

33. For a short description of the debate, see George M. Enteen, *The Soviet Scholar-Bureaucrat: M. N. Pokrovskii and the Society of Marxist Historians* (University Park, Penn.: Pennsylvania State University Press, 1978), 145–50. Also see V. A. Dunaevsky, "Bol'sheviki i germanskie levye na mezhdunarodnoi arene (nekotorye aspekty temy v osveschenii sovetskoi istoriografii kontsa 20-kh-nachala 30-kh godov," in S. D. Skazkin, ed., *Evropa v novoe i noveishee vremia* (Moscow: Nauka, 1966), 491–513.

34. A. Slutsky, "Bol'sheviki o germanskoi s-d v period ee predvoennogo krizisa," *Proletarskaia revoliutsiia,* no. 6 (June 1930):38–72. The quotation is from 60.

35. *Ibid.,* 42, 59–60.

36. I. V. Stalin, "O nekotorykh voprosakh istorii bol'shevizma," in I. V. Stalin, *Sochineniia* (Moscow: Gospolitizdat, 1951), XIII, 84–102.

37. I. Stalin, A. Zhdanov, and S. Kirov, "Zamechaniia po povodu konspekta uchebnika po istorii SSSR," in *K izucheniiu istorii* (Moscow: Gospolitizdat, 1938), 23. The directive was written on 8 August 1934.

38. G. F. Aleksandrov, *Istoriia zapadnoevropeiskoi filosofii*, 2d ed. (Moscow: Izdatel'stvo AN SSSR, 1946). In the Soviet Union it is often more important who signs something—that is, takes responsibility for it—than writes it. Several of the exchanges in the stenographic report of the conference that criticized the book suggested that Aleksandrov had relied very heavily on the prominent scholars in the Institute of Philosophy. *Voprosy filosofii*, no. 1 (1947):158, 163, 223–34, 269.

39. M. B. Mitin, in *Voprosy filosofii*, no. 1 (1947):124. For a series of quotations from the Aleksandrov book that outraged conservatives, see *Ibid.*, 6–12, 32–33, 124–26, 281–84. See the discussion in Percy E. Corbett, "The Aleksandrov Story," *World Politics*, vol. 1, no. 2, 161–74.

40. Z. V. Smirnova, *Ibid.*, 111.

41. O. Mishakova (a secretary of the Central Committee of the Komsomol), in *Literaturnaia gazeta*, 22 May 1945, 1.

42. Vsevolod Vishnevsky, *Ibid.*, 26 May 1945, 1.

43. M. V. Emdin, M. B. Mitin, and P. F. Iudin, in *Voprosy filosofii*, no. 1 (1947):10, 124, 280.

44. The conflict over the relationship of the Soviet Union to Western ideas had many paradoxical elements. In particular, Marx and Engels were not Russians, and the greatest Western influence on Russia had been Marxism. To the extent that the opponents of Western influences were simply hostile to foreigners (including what they perceived to be an alien Jewish element in Russia), they had to be aware that, as one Soviet citizen later expressed it in a private conversation, Marx was "nobody but a German Jew." The official movement toward a Russocentric view began with a March 1944 Central Committee decision that attacked a relatively favorable treatment of Hegel, for to deemphasize Hegel was to deemphasize the Western tradition out of which Marx came and to deemphasize Marx himself. Two of the most militant Marxists, Mark Mitin and Pavel Iudin, were demoted at this time, the latter after fighting particularly hard for an emphasis of the European Marxist origins of Marxism-Leninism. (See P. Iudin, "Georgii Valentinovich Plekhanov," *Bol'shevik*, no. 10 (May 1943):17, and the discussion in *Voprosy filosofii*, no. 1 (1947):456.) It would be fascinating to understand the politics of the evolution of this theme during the war. It is possible that many who began pushing a Russian-centered interpretation thought that they were fighting a radical, revolutionary policy in favor of a moderate one and then discovered that their line was coopted by the virulent xenophobes.

45. *Voprosy filosofii*, no. 1 (1947):362.

46. See the discussion in Hahn, *Postwar Soviet Politics*, 70–78, esp. 74.

47. McCagg, *Stalin Embattled, 1943–1948*, 89–90, and Timothy Dunmore, *The Stalinist Command Economy* (New York: St. Martins Press, 1980), 89–90. The stenographic reports of Supreme Soviet sessions are a good source for specific requests.

48. Dunmore, *The Stalinist Command Economy*, 42–45, 54–57.

49. *Ibid.*, 99–100, 109–14. For a discussion of the ministerial struggles over the spoils in occupied Germany, see Vladimir Rudolph in Robert Slusser, ed., *Soviet Economic Policy in Postwar Germany* (Ann Arbor: Research Program on the USSR, 1953), 20–22, 31–35.

50. A. V. Liubimov, *Torgovlia i snabzhenie v gody velikoi otechestvennoi voiny* (Moscow: Ekonomiki, 1968), 209–210.

51. The Lysenko question was not simply one of ideological rigidity but had major implications for the amount of money that should be spent on agriculture. David Jorawsky is probably correct in suggesting that Stalin supported Lysenko in significant part because his theories implied that higher agricultural productivity could be achieved without expensive fertilizer.

52. Sidney I. Ploss, *Conflict and Decision-Making in Soviet Russia* (Princeton, N.J.: Princeton University Press, 1965), 34–36.

53. Zverev, *Zapiski ministra*, 229.

54. Liubimov, *Torgovlia i snabshenie v gody velikoi otechestvennoi voiny*, 201.

55. A. Zelenovsky, "Iz opyta raboty Gosplana SSSR v gody velikoi otechestvennoi voiny," *Plannovoe khoziaistvo*, no. 5 (1975):61.

56. F. Kotov, "Velikie pobedy i progress ekonomiki," *Ibid.*, no. 5 (1980):15.

57. Eugene Zaleski, *Stalinist Planning for Economic Growth* (Chapel Hill, N.C.: University of North Carolina Press, 1980), 296–97.

58. In 1945, the amount of goods available for each ruble in circulation was three times less than in 1940. G. M. Sorokin, "Ekonomiia i planirovanie v pervye gody tretei piatiletki i v gody velikoi otechestvennoi voiny (1938–1945)," in *Shagi piatiletok: razvitie ekonomiki SSSR* (Moscow: Ekonomiki, 1968), 159.

59. Zverev, *Zapiski ministra,* 227–30.

60. Pavlov, *Stoikost',* 197.

61. This paragraph is based on *Ibid.,* 194–201.

62. Pavlov, *Stoikost',* 195.

63. *Ibid.,* 201.

64. S. Z. Ginzburg, *O proshlom—dla budushchego* (Moscow: Politizdat, 1983), 299–300.

65. M. I. Sabluk, *Razvitie marksistskoi teorii deneg v sotsialisticheskom obshchestve* (Kiev: Vishcha shkola, 1982), 127–32.

66. Iu. V. Arutiunian, *Sovetskoe krest'ianstvo v gody velikoi otechestvennoi voiny,* 2d ed. (Moscow: Nauka, 1970), 84–85.

67. See the discussion in D. K. Trifonov and L. D. Shirokopad, eds., *Istoriia politicheskoi ekonomii sotsializma,* 2d ed. (Leningrad: Izdatel'stvo Leningradskogo universiteta, 1983), 510.

68. N. A. Voznesenskii, *Voennaia ekonomii SSSR v period Otechestvennoi voiny* (Moscow: Gospolitizdat, 1948), 139, 145–48. See the discussion in Trifonov and Shirokopad, *Istoriia politicheskoi economii sotsializma,* 279–85, 510–14.

69. Voznesenskii, *Voennaia ekonomii SSSR,* 145.

70. Gerald Segal, "Automation, Cybernetics and Party Control," *Problems of Communism,* 15, no. 2 (March–April 1966):5.

71. V. Kolotov, "Predsedatel' Gosplana," *Literaturnaia gazeta,* 30 November 1963, 2; Kolotov, *Nikolai Alekseevich Voznesensky,* 327–32.

72. Ia. E. Chadaev, *Ekonomika SSSR v period velikoi otechestvennoi voiny (1941–1945 gg.)* (Moscow: Mysl', 1965), 93.

73. Voznesenskii said that it was "sheer nonsense" to speak of a stronger governmental role in the West attributing the idea to "some theoreticians who consider themselves Marxists." Voznesenskii, *Voennaia ekonomika SSSR,* 30–32 and 183–85. See the discussion in Hahn, *Postwar Soviet Politics,* 87–89.

74. A. N. Malafeev, *Proshloe i nastoiashche teorii tovarnogo proizvodstva pri sotsializma* (Moscow: Politizdat, 1975), 115–16. Peter Wiles discusses the differences between Voznesensky and Stalin on the law of value and ridicules Stalin as an abstract ideologist. However, if the issue was agriculture, then the Stalin 1952 attack makes sense, for he was in the process of rejecting greater expenditures for agriculture at that time. P. J. D. Wiles, *The Political Economy of Communism* (Cambridge, Mass.: Harvard University Press, 1962), 104–6.

75. N. Khrushchev, "Za tesnuiu sviazi literatury i iskusstva s zhizn'iu naroda," *Kommunist,* no. 12 (August 1957):13.

76. Zverev, *Zapiski ministra,* 216. The question was also related to that of a Balkan federation. See Elliot R. Goodman, *The Soviet Design for a World State* (New York: Columbia University Press, 1966), 326–38.

77. N. Baltiisky, "K itogam Braitonskogo kongressa britanskikh tred-unionov," *Novoe vremia,* no. 21 (November 1, 1946):7–9.

78. N. Baltiisky, "O patriotisme," *Ibid.,* no. 1 (June 1945):5.

79. See H. Gordon Skilling, "People's Democracy in Soviet Theory," *Soviet Studies* 3, no. 1 (July 1951):16–33; no. 2 (October 1951):131–49. Also see Zbigniew K. Brzezinski, *The Soviet Bloc* (Cambridge, Mass.: Harvard University Press, 1960), 25–32 and 45–58.

80. For a bibliography of Varga's works (including the postwar years), see E. S. Varga, *Kapitalizm posle vtoroi mirovoi voiny* (Moscow: Nauka, 1974), 521–54.

81. E. Varga, *Izmeneniia v ekonomike kapitalizma v itoge vtoroi mirovoi voiny* (Moscow: Gospolitizdat, 1946), 269.

82. "Diskussiia po knige E. Varga 'Izmeneniia v ekonomike kapitalizma v itoge vtoroi mirovoi voiny', 7, 14, 21 maia 1947 g., Stenograficheskii otchet," *Mirovoe khoziaistvo i mirovaia politika,* no. 11 (November 1947 suppl.):19.

83. E. Varga, "Protiv reformistskogo napravleniia v rabotakh po imperializmu," *Voprosy ekonomiki,* no. 3 (1949):79–88.

84. *Ibid.,* no. 9 (1948):56.

85. Varga, *Izmeneniia v ekonomike kapitalizma,* 32, 318.

86. *Ibid.,* 68.

87. For a description of the orthodox position, see Richard Nordahl, "Stalinist Ideology: The Case of the Stalinist Interpretation of Monopoly Capitalist Politics," *Soviet Studies* 26, no. 2 (April 1974):243–47.

88. "Diskussiia po knige E. Varga," 50.

89. *Ibid.,* 2.

90. *Ibid.,* 61.

91. Varga, *Izmeneniia v ekonomike kapitalizma,* 38.

92. *Ibid.,* 303.

93. E. Varga, "Demokratiia novogo tipa," *Mirovoe khoziaistvo i mirovaia politika,* no. 3 (1947):3.

94. Comment of E. S. Lazutkin, *Voprosy ekonomiki,* no. 9 (1948):104–5.

95. Varga, "Demokratiia novogo tipa," 3.

96. Varga, *Izmeneniia v ekonomike kapitalizma,* 318.

97. E. Varga, "Sotsializm i kapitalizm za tridtsat' let," *Mirovoe khoziaistvo i mirovaia politika,* no. 10 (1947):4–5.

98. *Voprosy ekonomiki,* no. 1 (1948):88; no. 8 (1948):71, 98–99.

99. In the words of Ostroviianov, "the mistakes of Comrade Varga in significant degree are typical of many works of the former Institute of World Economy and World Politics." *Ibid.,* no. 1 (1948):87. For the best—if highly colored—description of the institute, see *Ibid.,* no. 8 (1948):88–92. Other major scholars of the institute who were severely criticized were—in the usual order of criticism, from worst to bad—I. Trakhtenberg, L. Eventsov, M. Bokshitsky, V. Lan, A. Shpirt, I. Lemin, and S. Vishnev.

100. Z. Atlas, "Mirovaia valiutnaia problema," *Bol'shevik,* no. 15 (August 1944):40.

101. M. Iovchuk, "Klassiki russkoi filosofii XIX veka," *Bol'shevik,* no. 12 (June 1944):26.

102. Vojtech Mastny, *Russia's Road to the Cold War* (New York: Columbia University Press, 1979), 223–24. For Litvinov's public advocacy under the pseudonym of N. Malinin, see *Ibid.,* 219, 231–32.

103. For a collection and analysis of these statements, see Vojtech Mastny, "The Cassandra in the Foreign Commissariat: Maxim Litvinov and the Cold War," *Foreign Affairs,* 54, no. 2 (January 1976):366–76.

104. B. Antropov, "O Klauzetse i ego uchenii o voine," *Bol'shevik,* no. 10 (May 1945):39.

105. Fedoseev, "Marksizm-leninizm ob istokakh i kharaktere voin," 32, 52–54.

106. *Ibid.,* 32, 45, 46, 51, 57.

107. Varga chose this theme for an article that he was invited to contribute to the American journal *Foreign Affairs* in 1947. E. Varga, "Anglo-American Rivalry and Partnership," 25, no. 4 (July 1947):583–92. While speaking of the alliance between the "reactionary" forces of Truman and Bevin, he pointed to the forces pushing in the other direction. Varga's article was printed immediately after George Kennan's famous "X" article (556–82) and in retrospect gives a very paradoxical quality to Kennan's article. Kennan was writing about "the" Soviet way of looking at the world, at least among members of the older generation, but the editors chose as a representative of Soviet thinking an older man who did not have such views and who, even in the *Foreign Affairs* article, was implicitly criticizing them.

108. Quoted in Alfred J. Rieber, *Stalin and the French Communist Party, 1941–1947* (New York: Columbia University Press, 1962), 257–58. Rieber juxtaposes the positions of Lemin and Varga, but their differences on foreign policy were relatively minor. For a fuller discussion of Lemin and his position, see Franklyn J. C. Griffiths, *Images, Politics,*

and Learning in Soviet Behaviour Toward the United States (Ph.D. dissertation, Columbia University, 1973), 374–78.

109. For a later retrospective discussion of the issues, see E. Varga, *Ocherki po problemam politekonomii kapitalizma* (Moscow: Politizdat, 1964), 78–88. For a discussion in 1948, see "O nedostakhakh i zadachakh nauchno-issledovatel'skoi raboty v oblasti ekonomiki," *Voprosy ekonomiki,* no. 9 (1948):55. Both for pro-détente and anti-détente forces there was a tension between the argument about the inevitability of war among capitalist states and the existence of contradictions among them. To say that war was inevitable created both a sense of threat and a sense that the contradictions were big enough to call for a flexible Soviet foreign policy. Most were "inconsistent" (the Stalinists said war was inevitable, but the United States dominated the capitalist world; the pro-détente forces reversed the arguments), but Lemin spoke out, with qualifications, for Lenin's doctrine on war and criticized Varga on tactical grounds ("harmful from a political point of view") for repudiating it.

110. Varga, *Izmeneniia v ekonomike kapitalizma,* 319.

111. E. Zhukov, "Obostrenie krizisa kolonial'noi sistemy," *Bol'shevik,* no. 23 (December 1947):54.

112. *Pravda,* 8 February 1946, 2.

113. *Ibid.,* 8 February 1946, 4.

114. In early 1946 everything looked normal with the harvest. By May–June, the situation had become "alarming." Pavlov, *Stoikost',* 198.

115. *Pravda,* 11 June 1945, 1–2; 13 June 1945, 1. As an added offense to Varga, the list of the 375 medal holders was divided precisely at the point in the alphabet where his name appeared so that he appeared in the list on 13 June, rather than 11 June.

116. *New York Times,* 24 June 1941, 7.

117. Robert C. Tucker, *The Soviet Political Mind* (New York: Frederick A. Praeger, 1963), 158.

118. *Pravda,* 3 February 1946, 3.

119. *Pravda,* 8 May 1947, 1.

120. Vojtech Mastny is right to remind us that the wave of revisionist literature criticizing the United States for causing the cold war by being too hard-line was preceded by criticism of the United States for causing the problems by being too accommodating. McCagg reports the evidence that Stalin seemed afraid of the West (*Stalin Embattled,* 14), and one should not reject offhand the possibility that a credible hard-line stance might have caused some moderation in his policy.

14

Conclusion: Impact and Aftermath of World War II

No society in modern times has absorbed a blow of the severity of Operation Barbarossa and survived as a political, economic, and social entity. The Soviet experience in World War II and its impact upon postwar Soviet society have scarcely been charted by Western students of Soviet society. As a consequence, the war and the immediate postwar periods are the least understood of the years since 1917.

There are three critical questions about World War II and its impact, which the essays contained in this volume go some way toward answering. First, how large was the impact of World War II on the Soviet system? Second, how did the Soviet Union survive the impact? And third, what permanent changes did the war impose upon the structure and functioning of the main institutions of Soviet society?

The Impact of the War Upon the Soviet Union

The economic cost of World War II to the Soviet people has now been estimated, using several different conceptual approaches. Susan Linz's estimates (Chapter 2) of material losses range from four to ten years effort by the labor force available in 1940 or 1945. If the loss of manpower is included, the economic cost of World War II is more than doubled. Put differently, the economic cost of the war was equal to, and possibly even somewhat greater than, the total wealth created during the industrialization drive of the 1930s.

It would be interesting to know how Soviet war costs stack up against the costs of the war to the other major participants. There can be little doubt that Soviet war costs were greater than the costs experienced by any other country in the war, both in total and on a per capita basis. Unlike the other major participants in the war, the Soviet Union lost territory, population and capital stock at the very beginning of the war and was obliged to fight a prolonged war with diminished capacity. Moreover, the Soviet economy was fully employed at the outset of war and could not fall back upon excess capacity.

Perhaps the various estimates that Susan Linz and I have developed[1] will inspire others to attempt to estimate war costs for the other participants. The costs to Britain and to Germany would doubtless be the most interesting to estimate for comparative purposes. Judging by the length of the war effort and by the degree of war mobilization, my best guess is that Great Britain would come out second to the USSR in per capita war costs in any such comparison.

Of course, economic cost represents only a portion of the total human costs of war. The human costs of war must, for example, include certain costs that are essentially infinite, such as the loss of one's own life or death and injury to loved ones. They also have to register costs imposed by interrupted and broken careers, family separation, incarceration, and mental and physical stress. Soviet official sources report a total of 20 million lives lost in the war, about half of whom were military personnel. Total casualties have never been quoted officially. I have estimated them elsewhere at approximately 30 million—which is about 15 percent of the 1940 population.[2] Even this large number would not include war-related physical consequences, such as those caused by chronic malnutrition. All of these considerations suggest that the cost of World War II was exceptionally pervasive, as well as differentially heavy, for the Soviet population. Few families could have avoided loss of a close family member. Fewer still could have avoided severe physical or mental distress. It is no surprise that the memory of World War II remains active for a large proportion of the contemporary Soviet population and that it is still a dominant literary theme.

How the Soviet Union Survived the War

How did the Soviet Union survive so costly and ferocious a war? Where did the resources come from to win the war? At the aggregate level the answer is straightforward. As the tables and analysis show in Chapter 2, the population as a whole both increased its work effort and reduced its claims on current output during the war years. Allocation priorities shifted sharply in favor of military uses at the expense of investment, consumption, and nonmilitary administrative expenses (in that order).

This radical reallocation of resources was financed, in the proper sense of the word, primarily through new taxes (particularly the "war tax" on personal incomes) and by means of extraordinary deficit financing by the State budget. Special donations from individuals and collective farms provided a small but significant source of funds. Moreover, budgetary funds were centralized to finance an increased share of total spending by the central government.[3]

World War II caused drastic changes in resource allocation patterns. The railway system played a key and largely successful role in effecting the physical reallocation of resources. As Holland Hunter put it in Chapter 3: "Instead of contributing to a collapse of the regime, as Russian railroads had done in World War I, Soviet railroads in World War II provided sturdy links which held the whole country together." The principal reason for success appears to have been the organizational framework, discipline, and experience that were developed in response to the transportation crises generated by various phases of the industrialization drive of the 1930s.

Sanford Lieberman suggests in Chapter 4 an even more general conclusion with respect to the system of administration that developed under Stalin in prewar years: "The Stalinist system, even at the height of the crisis of war, still appears to have been viable. Indeed, . . . it is doubtful whether the country would have been able to survive had a different system been in effect." The implication is, then, that the experimentation and institution-building of the 1930s produced a system with features that made it unusually adaptable to wartime demands. The State Defense Committee (GKO) was superimposed upon the existing administrative structure as a small, highly-centralized, decision-making unit. Together with the "plenipotentiary system," which facilitated quick and decisive changes in priorities in specific sectors of the war effort, the GKO increased the degree of central control in all areas. As Lieberman points out, these changes were not inventions of wartime, but innovations based upon historically successful responses to crises in the Bolshevik past. An increased degree of personalization of power and of accountability for its exercise during the war were consistent with the general administrative philosophy developed in the 1930s, and these principles remain the hallmark of Soviet administrative practice today. The specific administrative structure, specifically the GKO, that was created during the war, however, was dissolved subsequently. No new permanent administrative structure emerged from the war experience.

The high degree of central control which the GKO-plenipotentiary system provided obviously facilitated resource reallocation as well as troop concentration and strategic planning. The evacuation of industry represented just a part of the general mobilization and concentration of capital and labor upon wartime tasks. It illustrates particularly well the way the system could be brought to bear upon a specific but complex task that had to be accomplished promptly. The evacuation of industry from territory threatened by German troops was paralleled by the evacuation of peasants and their animals. If this was less successful than the evacuation of industry it was because, as Alec Nove points out in Chapter 5, they were low on the priority list. They had to walk, and they queued to pass through bottlenecks.

An even more massive reallocation of resources was involved in the movement of able-bodied males out of rural areas and in the requisition of trucks, tractors, draft animals, and equipment belonging to collective farms. The rural agricultural sector was literally plundered of resources that might be of use in the war effort. Thus, the pattern of forced resource extraction witnessed during both War Communism and the First Five-Year Plan was repeated in support of the war effort. This time, however, it included depletion of the agricultural capital stock. It was successful according to Alec Nove (Chapter 5) because the peasants' "patriotism overrode their hatred of the system. . . ."

Central planning and enterprise management during the war have not yet received much attention anywhere. Soviet sources suggest that the prewar system remained intact in general structure.[4] The materials balancing system, centralized allocation of scarce materials, overcommitment target setting, labor controls, and "micromanagement" by ministries apparently continued to characterize the process. What changed were the priorities themselves and the degree of neglect of low priority demand. Enterprises producing low priority products and services operated fitfully, if at all, as materials became available. Many simply shut down. Although it seems to be true that the prewar structure of the Soviet economy lent itself to rapid conversion to war economy status, the changes in priorities, in demand patterns, and in the extent of labor mobilization indicate unambiguously that the prewar economy was *not* a "war economy."

The State Defense Committee succeeded in the establishment and maintenance of the new priorities required by a successful military defense of the Soviet Union. From a strategic standpoint, the low point in economic and military capacity occurred some time in mid-1942. By summer's end in 1942, the Soviet economy had been put on a full war footing, and economic indices began to turn up. Grain yields and output continued to decline through 1943, however, making that year in all likelihood the most miserable for the population as a whole.

It is clear that the majority of the Soviet population accepted the sacrifices imposed upon it by World War II, and the minority was coerced to go along. Patriotism was a major factor by all accounts. Stalin's willingness to strike a bargain with the church for support during the war doubtless afforded another source of popular support. In an important sense, World War II validated both the economic and administrative structures that had been created by the Bolsheviks during the 1930s and the party itself. They had been tested under the most extreme conditions imaginable and proved out.

Short-Term Consequences of the War

In the years after 1945 prewar statistical patterns began to reassert themselves in many areas. The high priority accorded postwar reconstruction delayed a "return to normalcy," but something very much like "High Stalinism" had been reestablished by the time of Stalin's death early in 1953. From the vantage point of thirty years later, it is possible to separate out the temporary and the long-term consequences of the war.

Several potentially important changes induced by the war proved to be only temporary. The primacy of capital investment and growth was reestablished. Wartime militarization of the labor force faded slowly but surely. The increased centralization of all operations was relaxed gradually too, as may be seen, for example, from budgetary data.[5] The sharp increase in the ratio of direct to indirect taxes as sources of budgetary revenue (which occurred as a result of the war tax on personal income and the decline in turnover tax revenue) was reversed after the war, returning to the normal shallow U-shaped curve that most developing countries exhibit. Resort to deficit financing was sharply diminished in the postwar period, as the Ministry of Finance returned to the practice of extreme financial conservatism. Direct (coupon) rationing was also phased out in favor of a return to queuing, to special distributions, and all the other manifestations of chronic commodity deficits.

Money wages, prices, and other pecuniary and financial institutions were bypassed or diminished during the height of the war effort. Direct physical allocation was generally preferred because it permitted better control over priorities and because it operated without the lags money flows generally entail. The same phenomenon had been observed both during War Communism and the industrialization drive of the early 1930s. Depecuniarization during World War II did not, however, reflect an ideological preference, as had been the case in the earlier periods. On the contrary, care was taken to minimize adverse effects upon the various incentive and accounting systems. Books were kept, saving was encouraged, taxes were utilized rationally. Money, prices, money wages, the budget and the banking system regained significant instrumental roles after the war, and they have continued to grow more important as control and allocation mechanisms ever since.

Censorship of statistical data and secretiveness about problems, accidents and other matters regarded as either strategic or potentially embarrassing had become quite extensive prior to the war. The outbreak of war led to a policy of total blackout, a policy that continued unabated afterwards until well after Stalin died. Although still extensive, censorship has been gradually modified since that time, but with typical policy zig-zags. The information base available today is better than at any time since the end of the 1920s.[6]

As Sheila Fitzpatrick indicated in Chapter 8, a "return to normalcy" was delayed in the Soviet Union until after Stalin's death. The immense cost of World War II provided part of the reason for the delay. Continued sacrifice was required to reconstruct the damage wrought by the war and to lay an economic base that could support the new postwar military prominence of the USSR in world affairs. Large segments of the population had also been "contaminated" either through voluntary or involuntary contact with the outside world. Thus the continued need for "vigilance" and "discipline." Stalin's death in March 1953 is probably the best date to mark the close of postwar reconstruction of the Stalinist system.

Long-Term Consequences of the War

World War II accelerated certain structural changes that were already underway prior to its outbreak. The evacuation of industry from the west and wartime construction in the east was consistent with plans to shift the center of industrial gravity eastward. The policy was in fact interrupted in the immediate postwar years as the Soviet Union absorbed reparations evacuated from occupied Axis countries and concentrated on reconstruction of territory in European Russia that had been occupied and fought over during the hostilities.

Wartime policy toward agriculture and rural life accelerated the flow of able-bodied, skilled workers to urban occupations. Postwar policy failed to rectify the damage done to the sector during the war, and agriculture fell steadily farther behind the other sectors in most respects. By the end of postwar recovery, Soviet agriculture had at best regained 1940 per capita production levels, but it had become relatively more backward both technically and in the quality of life. World War II and the rigors of postwar reconstruction contributed to, but did not originate the sector's problems. The war did, however, make a solution more difficult because of the male deficit that was caused by differential exposure of peasant males to combat and the reluctance of survivors to return to the village.

The postwar relative decline of Leningrad was also prefigured in prewar policy. The war only accelerated the process by which Moscow gained economic and political ascendency. As Ruble and Bubis have shown in Chapter 9, Leningrad has become one of several important provincial cities rather than the "second city" of prewar years. This would seem to be a characteristic outcome in highly centralized politico-economic systems and assignable only in part to the impact of war.

The most dramatic change that the war brought about for Soviet leadership externally was in the USSR's strategic position in world affairs. The Soviet Union had not been regarded as a military power of the first rank prior to World War II. Insofar as it was regarded as a threat, it was an ideological threat. The fear was that workers, and especially the unemployed among them, would see in Bolshevik Russia a preferred alternative to capitalism. At the end of the war, the Soviet Union disposed of the most powerful ground forces in the world, and it occupied by reason of victory in battle the better part of what is called Eastern Europe today. For Western leaders, it was as though Ghengis Khan had returned and was once again poised in the east at the head of hordes of ideologically saturated barbarians.

As Robert Slusser has shown (Chapter 7), the very weight and rapidity of Soviet troop movements in 1944 caused British postwar planners to anticipate the division of Europe. There might very well have been nothing left for the other Allies to claim. The question at the close of hostilities in Europe was not whether the Soviet Union and the United States would divide the world up between themselves, for that had already occurred de facto. The question was whether they would ever withdraw from the territories they occupied. The answer seems to be in the negative.

Thus, the Soviet Union emerged from World War II as a major international presence, but it was a presence based upon a very slender economic base, especially by comparison with the United States. Despite the fact that it was 20 percent smaller than it had been in 1941, the Soviet economy had become the second largest economy in the world. Germany and Japan were defeated and occupied. The economy of Great Britain had been badly damaged by both the length and the intensity of her share of the war effort against the Axis powers. Thus the Soviet Union had become a superpower essentially by default, and there was an order of magnitude difference between the two superpowers. The United States economy had more than doubled in size during the war, and the Soviet economy at best was a quarter its size. The "two camps" outcome of the high-level Soviet debates about the postwar world, that Jerry Hough has explored in Chapter 13, had significant implications, therefore, for the quality of life of the Soviet population.

Given conflict between the two superpowers, the economic size differential between them put an extremely heavy burden upon the Soviet economy and the population. Unlike prewar industrialization, postwar reconstruction had to be conducted along with a relatively heavy burden of defense spending. This is important in explaining why "the return to normalcy" took so long.

Reparations extracted from former Axis powers were obviously important in reducing the cost of the reconstruction effort. The experience in evacuation of industry early in the war may have come in handy in planning and executing evacuation of industrial plant and equipment as reparations. Given the long-term economic interdependency that has been enforced for members of the Soviet bloc in Eastern Europe, however, this was a form of borrowing from Peter to pay Paul.

Although agricultural production had not yet regained the 1940 level, postwar reconstruction was pronounced complete in 1950. International responsibilities and the cost of maintaining a competitive military estab- lishment in the chilly climate of the 1950s meant a slower recovery of individual living standards than was the case in Europe or Japan.

The demographic impact of the war was probably the most dramatic internal consequence of the war. There were two aspects of the demographic impact. First, males were at greater risk of death during the war than females, and the impact skewed the sex distribution of the population correspondingly. Together with the earlier differential demographic impact of the First World War, the revolutions of 1917, the civil war, and the purges, there was a 20 million deficit of males at the end of the war.

Barbara Anderson and Brian Silver have explored the rather subtle link between the male deficit and linguistic russification (Chapter 11), thanks to the existence of data on this topic. This is truly the tip of a fascinating iceberg, for the impact of the male deficit upon a large range of other sociological, demographic and economic variables must have been large and significant for many types of behavior that we have no data to test. We simply do not know, for example, how and to what degree the male deficit caused changes in attitudes toward marriage, divorce, household responsibilities, and other familial relations.

The second dimension of the demographic impact of the war was generational. The differential loss of males of draft age during the war created a gap in the leadership cohort whose members are approximately between the ages of 57 and 67 today. It has contributed, therefore, to the geriatric character of the highest governing bodies in the Soviet Union today. Similarly, the baby boom following World War II created a bulge with the same kinds of adverse long-run implications for economic growth and income distribution that are being observed in the United States today. It will be decades before the echoes of these demographic anomolies fade away altogether.

The long-run impact of the war upon the party apparatus has been explored carefully by Cynthia Kaplan (Chapter 9). As she shows, the war interrupted a trend toward a more indirect style of party leadership, a trend that was resumed in the postwar period. The widespread use of the plenipotentiary system of central intervention continued, however, to characterize management of agricultural production, which reflected the low level of membership in rural areas and the poor quality of local agricultural management. It may be apt to note that this tendency toward differential party policy culminated in an unsuccessful attempt by Khrushchev to bifurcate the party apparatus completely along urban-rural lines. The main impact of the war upon the party, however, was the massive influx of new members during the war. The purges had already thinned party ranks of long-term experienced members. Thus the party was almost completely renewed by the end of the war, and it had presumably acquired some of the luster that surrounded returning war veterans.

Generally speaking, the war proved the workability and the reliability of political and economic institutions. The new generation of party members that had occupied positions in the various nonmilitary as well as military institutions during the war was doubtless persuaded by the headiness of success in war of the efficacy of the Soviet system. If the 1930s was the period during which Soviet institutions were created, the war was the time of their testing. The postwar years were, by contrast, years of conservatism, not experimentation. It was a period during which the prewar system was reestablished in most of its particulars. Only the death of Stalin in 1953 appears to have foreclosed reestablishment also of the periodic purge.

The generation of party members that survived World War II is still, for all practical purposes, in charge. It seems reasonable to speculate that the conservatism of contemporary Soviet domestic policy reflects not merely the conservatism that comes normally with advancing age, but also the conviction of men and women who survived the most devastating land invasion in modern history that the principal political and economic institutions of the Soviet Union are still more workable and reliable in the long run than any available alternative. One persisting effect of World War II has been, therefore, the gradual petrification of the system.

Notes

1. In addition to Susan Linz's calculations in Chapter 1, see also James R. Millar and Susan J. Linz, "The Cost of World War II to the Soviet People," *Journal of Economic History* 38, no. 4 (December 1978):959–62.

2. *The ABCs of Soviet Socialism* (Urbana: The University of Illinois Press, 1981).

3. For an extended treatment see my "Financing the Soviet Effort in World War II, *Soviet Studies* 32, no. 1 (January 1980), pp. 106–23.

4. See, for example, *Istoriia Velikoi Otechestvennoi voiny Sovetskogo Soiuza 1941–1945 gg.* (Moscow, 1961), t.6, and G. S. Kravchenko, *Ekonomika SSSR v gody Velikoi Otechestvennoi voiny* (Moscow, 1970).

5. For supporting data see "Financing the Soviet Effort in World War II," and James R. Millar and Donna Bahry, "Financing Development and Tax Structure Change in the USSR," *Canadian Slavonic Papers* 21, no. 2 (June 1979):165–74.

6. The current period is one of retrenchment with respect to economic and demographic data. The Khrushchev years may have been a "golden age."

Index

Contributors

BARBARA A. ANDERSON is a professor of sociology and research scientist of the Population Studies Center at the University of Michigan—Ann Arbor. She is a co-author of *Human Fertility in Russia Since the Nineteenth Century,* and author of *Internal Migration During Modernization in Late Nineteenth Century Russia* and of numerous articles on population and on Soviet ethnic and demographic processes.

DEMING BROWN, professor of Russian literature at the University of Michigan, is the author of *Soviet Russian Literature Since Stalin, Soviet Attitudes Toward American Writing,* and numerous articles on Russian literature of the nineteenth and twentieth centuries.

EDWARD BUBIS is a visiting scholar at the Center for International Studies at the Massachusetts Institute of Technology. Prior to emigrating from the Soviet Union in 1982, he served as an associate professor of urban planning and operations research of the Leningrad Engineering-Economics Institute and as a consultant of the Leningrad City Housing and Urban Development Authorities. He is the author of several books, including *Economics of Urban Planning* and *Optimal Programming in Urban Planning and Municipal Services Economics.*

SHEILA FITZPATRICK is a professor of history at the University of Texas at Austin. Her most recent books are *Education and Social Mobility in the Soviet Union, 1921–1934* and *The Russian Revolution.* She is currently working on a book on the social history of the Stalin period.

WILLIAM C. FLETCHER, Director of Soviet and East European studies and professor of religious studies at the University of Kansas, is an authority on religion in the USSR, with ten books and numerous major articles to his credit.

JERRY F. HOUGH, professor of political science at Duke University and staff member of the Brookings Institution, is the author of *The Soviet Prefects, The Soviet Union and Social Science Theory, How the Soviet Union Is Governed, Soviet Leadership in Transition, The Polish Crisis: American Policy Options,* and the forthcoming *The Struggle for the Third World: Soviet Debates and American Options.*

HOLLAND HUNTER, professor of economics at Haverford College, has tested prewar Soviet planning with an economywide model and surveyed current Soviet economic problems. For his recent analysis of Soviet transport developments, see the Hunter-Kaple paper in Part 1 of U.S. Congress Joint Economic Committee *Soviet Economy in the 1980s.*

CYNTHIA S. KAPLAN, assistant professor of political science at the University of Chicago, has presented papers and published on the behavior of local party organizations in the USSR. She is completing a book on the Communist Party of the Soviet Union and agriculture and is currently engaged in research on the transformation of the Soviet countryside.

WASSILY LEONTIEF, 1973 Nobel laureate, is Director of the Institute for Economic Analysis at New York University and author of several books, including *The Structure of the American Economy 1919–1929, Input-Output Economics,* and *The Future of the World Economy.*

SANFORD R. LIEBERMAN is an associate professor of political science at the University of Massachusetts at Boston. He is also an associate of the Russian Research Center of Harvard University and has been a visiting professor of political science at Harvard. His research interests center on Soviet domestic affairs during World War II.

SUSAN J. LINZ, visiting assistant professor of economics at the University of California at Irvine, has authored and co-authored several works relating to the impact of World War II on the Soviet economy. Her current research focuses on microeconomic decision-making in contemporary Soviet economy.

ALEC NOVE is a professor emeritus of economics at the University of Glasgow. His books include *The Soviet Economic System, Was Stalin Really Necessary? Economic History of the USSR, Political Economy and Soviet Socialism,* and most recently, *The Economics of Feasible Socialism.*

JAMES R. MILLAR, professor of economics at the University of Illinois at Urbana—Champaign and recently editor of the *Slavic Review,* is the author of *ABCs of Soviet Socialism* and numerous articles in Slavic and economic journals.

BLAIR A. RUBLE, Assistant Director of the National Council for Soviet and East European Research, is the author of *Soviet Trade Unions, Their Development in the 1970s* and co-editor of several works, including *Industrial Labor in the USSR.* He has published numerous articles and reviews and is currently working on a monograph examining local politics and planning in Leningrad.

BRIAN D. SILVER is professor of political science at Michigan State University. He has published numerous articles on Soviet nationality affairs and Soviet population and is co-editor of *Soviet Asian Ethnic Frontiers.*

ROBERT M. SLUSSER, professor emeritus of history at Michigan State University, is editor of *Soviet Economic Policy in Postwar Germany* and author of *The Berlin Crisis of 1961.*